Jutta Vesper
Diplom-Dolmetscherin AIIC
Haffstrasse 12
5300 Bonn 3

parat

G. Korzak

Dictionary of Fracture Mechanics
English/German

Wörterbuch Bruchmechanik
Deutsch/Englisch

© VCH Verlagsgesellschaft mbH, D-6940 Weinheim (Bundesrepublik Deutschland), 1989

Vertrieb:

VCH Verlagsgesellschaft, Postfach 10 11 61, D-6940 Weinheim (Bundesrepublik Deutschland)

Schweiz: VCH Verlags-AG, Postfach, CH-4020 Basel (Schweiz)

Großbritannien und Irland: VCH Publishers (UK) Ltd., 8 Wellington Court, Wellington Street, Cambridge CB1 1HW (Großbritannien)

USA und Canada: VCH Publishers, Suite 909, 220 East 23rd Street, New York, NY 10010-4606 (USA)

ISBN 3-527-27891-5 (VCH Verlagsgesellschaft mbH)   ISSN 0930-6862
ISBN 0-89573-896-1 (VCH Publishers)

parat

Günter Korzak

Dictionary of Fracture Mechanics

English/German
German/English

Wörterbuch Bruchmechanik

Deutsch/Englisch

Dipl.-Ing. Günter Korzak
c/o VCH, Lektorat NW
P.O.B. 10 11 61
D-6940 Weinheim

> Das vorliegende Werk wurde sorgfältig erarbeitet. Dennoch übernehmen Autoren, Herausgeber und Verlag für die Richtigkeit von Angaben, Hinweisen und Ratschlägen sowie für eventuelle Druckfehler keine Haftung.

1. Auflage 1989

Published jointly by
VCH Verlagsgesellschaft, Weinheim (Federal Republic of Germany)
VCH Publishers, New York, NY (USA)

Lektorat: Dr. Hans-Dieter Junge
Herstellerische Betreuung: Dipl.-Wirt.-Ing. (FH) Bernd Riedel

Library of Congress Card No.: 89-38756
British Library Cataloguing in Publication Data
Korzak, Günter
   Dictionary of fracture mechanics
   1. Materials. Fracture. Mechanics
   I. Title II. Series
   620,1'126
   ISBN 3-527-27891-5

CIP-Titelaufnahme der Deutschen Bibliothek
Korzak, Günter:
Dictionary of fracture mechanics: English/German; German/English = Wörterbuch
Bruchmechanik / Günter Korzak. – 1. Aufl. – Weinheim; New York, NY: VCH, 1989
  (Parat)
  ISBN 3-527-27891-5 (Weinheim)
  ISBN 0-89573-896-1 (New York)
NE: HST

© VCH Verlagsgesellschaft mbH, D-6940 Weinheim (Federal Republic of Germany), 1989

Gedruckt auf säurefreiem Papier

Alle Rechte, insbesondere die der Übersetzung in andere Sprachen, vorbehalten. Kein Teil dieses Buches darf ohne schriftliche Genehmigung des Verlages in irgendeiner Form – durch Photokopie, Mikroverfilmung oder irgendein anderes Verfahren – reproduziert oder in eine von Maschinen, insbesondere von Datenverarbeitungsmaschinen, verwendbare Sprache übertragen oder übersetzt werden. Die Wiedergabe von Warenbezeichnungen, Handelsnamen oder sonstigen Kennzeichen in diesem Buch berechtigt nicht zu der Annahme, daß diese von jedermann frei benutzt werden dürfen. Vielmehr kann es sich auch dann um eingetragene Warenzeichen oder sonstige gesetzlich geschützte Kennzeichen handeln, wenn sie nicht eigens als solche markiert sind.
All rights reserved (including those of translation into other languages). No part of this book may be reproduced in any form – by photoprinting, microfilm, or any other means – nor transmitted or translated into a machine language without written permission from the publishers. Registered names, trademarks, etc. used in this book, even when not specifically marked as such, are not to be considered unprotected by law.
Druck: betz-druck gmbh, D-6100 Darmstadt 12. Bindung: Georg Kränkl, D-6148 Heppenheim.
Printed in the Federal Republic of Germany.

Instructions for use

All entries are alphabetically ordered and, if appropriate, combined with groups of related words. Groups of word combinations are thought to be useful for the understanding of linguistic laws. Annotations in italics may be helpful in relating the entry to a special technical scope. Within the entries the source-language terms are bold-faced.

In the German alphabet the mutated vowels ä, ö and ü are ordered as ae, oe and ue; ß is ordered as ss.

Benutzungshinweise

Im Taschenwörterbuch sind die Eintragungen in alphabetisch geordneten Wortnestern zusammengestellt, wobei Wert darauf gelegt ist, möglichst unterschiedliche Kombinationen des Nestwortes aufzunehmen, um die Bildungsgesetze der Wortkombinationen sichtbar werden zu lassen. Angaben in Kursivschrift helfen bei der Zuordnung des Begriffes zu einem speziellen Anwendungsfall oder zu einem bestimmten technischen Bereich. Innerhalb der Wortstellen sind die Eintragungen in der Ausgangssprache hervorgehoben.

Im Alphabet sind die Buchstaben ä, ö und ü wie ae, oe und ue eingeordnet; ß ist wie ss behandelt.

Preface

Advanced technology requires more and more specialized technicians, engineers, students and scientists. This Dictionary is thought to facilitate the jump to the scientific-technical language of fracture mechanics. Furthermore, it should be a helpful tool for the translator who deals with specialized literature.

This Dictionary summarizes the most important and frequently used terms in the field of fracture mechanics (modes of fracture, concepts and criteria of fracture mechanics, cracks and crack growth, test methods, specimens . . .). Some general terms are also included which have a special meaning in the scope of this book.

Publisher and author hope the Dictionary may fulfil its purpose, namely, to be an effective tool with minimum expense for every user.

Günter Korzak

Vorwort

Die moderne Technik fordert eine immer stärkere Spezialisierung für Techniker, Ingenieure, Studenten und Wissenschaftler. Dieses Taschenwörterbuch soll den Übergang zur Fachsprache der Bruchmechanik erleichtern. Es soll aber auch dem Übersetzer bei der Übersetzung von Fachliteratur helfen.

Das Taschenwörterbuch enthält wichtige und oft gebrauchte Begriffe der Bruchmechanik (Bruchtypen, Konzepte und Kriterien der Bruchmechanik, Risse und Rißwachstum, Prüfverfahren, Prüfkörper . . .). Aufgenommen wurden ebenfalls allgemeine Begriffe mit speziellem Begriffsinhalt. Ein Taschenwörterbuch kann kein großes Fachwörterbuch ersetzen; in vielen Fällen jedoch wird es dieses ergänzen.

Autor und Verlag wünschen, daß dieses Buch seinen Zweck erfüllen möge, nämlich jedem Benutzer bei minimalem Aufwand eine maximale Hilfe zu sein.

Günter Korzak

English – German
Englisch – Deutsch

A → argon
abrasion {wear} Abrieb *m*
abrasive abrasiv
  abrasive wear abrasiver Verschleiß *m*
absolute absolut
  absolute crack size absolute Rißgröße *f*
  absolute resistance to fracture absoluter Bruchwiderstand *m*
  absolute test absolute Prüfung *f*
accelerate/to beschleunigen
accelerated ag[e]ing test beschleunigte Alterungsprüfung *f*
accelerated crack propagation beschleunigte Rißausbreitung *f*
acceleration Beschleunigung *f*
  crack acceleration Rißbeschleunigung *f*
  fatigue crack acceleration Ermüdungsrißbeschleunigung *f*
accuracy {e.g. **failure analysis**} Genauigkeit *f* {z.B. Schadensanalyse}
  precision, accuracy {of the apparatus} Meßgenauigkeit *f* {eines Gerätes}
acid brittle steel beizspröder Stahl *m*
acid-proof steel säurebeständiger Stahl *m*, säurefester Stahl *m*
acoustic akustisch, Schall-
  acoustic emission Schallemission *f*
  acoustic emission analysis Schallemissionsanalyse *f*, SEA
  acoustic emission inspection Schallemissionsprüfung *f*
action of load Lastangriff *m*
activation Aktivierung *f*, Aktivieren *n*
  activation energy Aktivierungsenergie *f*
adhesive adhäsiv
  adhesive wear adhäsiver Verschleiß *m*
adsorp/to adsorbieren
adsorption Adsorption *f*
  adsorption-induced embrittlement adsorptionsinduzierte Versprödung *f*
AES → electron spectroscopy
after-shrinkage Nachschwindung *f*
Ag → silver

age-hardenable alloy alterungsfähige Legierung *f*
age/to altern
ag[e]ing Alterung *f*
  ag[e]ing test Alterungsprüfung *f*
  accelerated ag[e]ing test beschleunigte Alterungsprüfung *f*
  heat ag[e]ing Wärmealterung *f*, thermische Alterung *f*
  method for ag[e]ing Alterungsmethode *f*, Alterungsverfahren *n*
  resistance to ag[e]ing Alterungsbeständigkeit *f*
  strain ag[e]ing Verzerrungsalterung *f*
air Luft *f*
  air temperature Lufttemperatur *f*
Al → aluminium
align/to ausrichten
alignment Ausrichtung *f*, Ausrichten *n*
alligatoring "Krokodilhaut" *f* {Metalloberfläche}
alloy Legierung *f*
  alloy steel Legierungsstahl *m*, legierter Stahl *m*
  age-hardenable alloy alterungsfähige Legierung *f*
  alumin[i]um alloy Aluminiumlegierung *f*
  alumin[i]um-copper alloy Aluminium-Kupfer-Legierung *f*
  alumin[i]um-copper-silicon alloy Aluminium-Kupfer-Silizium-Legierung *f*
  alumin[i]um-lithium alloy Aluminium-Lithium-Legierung *f*
  alumin[i]um-magnesium-silicon alloy Aluminium-Magnesium-Silizium-Legierung *f*
  alumin[i]um-zinc-magnesium alloy Aluminium-Zink-Magnesium-Legierung *f*
  arc-welded alloy steel lichtbogengeschweißter legierter Stahl *m*
  arc-welded alumin[i]um alloy lichtbogengeschweißte Aluminiumlegierung *f*
  arc-welded titanium alloy lichtbogengeschweißte Titanlegierung *f*

alloying

arc-welded heat-resistant alloy lichtbogengeschweißte hitzebeständige Legierung *f*
austenitic alloy austenitische Legierung *f*
bronze alloy Sonderbronze *f*
cast alumin[i]um alloy Aluminium-Guß-Legierung *f*
cobalt alloy Cobalt-Legierung *f*
cobalt-chromium alloy Cobalt-Chrom-Legierung *f*
cobalt-chromium-molybdenum alloy Cobalt-Chrom-Molybdän-Legierung *f*
copper alloy Kupferlegierung *f*
copper-bismuth alloy Kupfer-Wismut-Legierung *f*
copper-nickel alloy Kupfer-Nickel-Legierung *f*
copper-zinc alloy Kupfer-Zink-Legierung *f*
corrosion-resistant alloy korrosionsbeständige Legierung *f*
ferritic iron-alumin[i]um alloy ferritische Eisen-Aluminium-Legierung *f*
gold palladium alloy Gold-Palladium-Legierung *f*
heat-resistant wrought alloy warmfeste Knetlegierung *f*
high-strength alumin[i]um alloy hochfeste Aluminiumlegierung *f*
high-temperature alloy hochwarmfeste Legierung *f*
iron alloy Eisenlegierung *f*
iron-alumin[i]um alloy Eisen-Aluminium-Legierung *f*
iron-chromium alloy Eisen-Chrom-Legierung *f*
iron-chromium-alumin[i]um alloy Eisen-Chrom-Aluminium-Legierung *f*
lead alloy Bleilegierung *f*
light alloy Leichtmetallegierung *f*
low-melting alloy niedrigschmelzende Legierung *f*
magnesium alloy Magnesiumlegierung *f*
nickel alloy Nickellegierung *f*
nickel-copper alloy Nickel-Kupfer-Legierung *f*
nickel-molybdenum-vanadium alloy Nickel-Molybdän-Vanadium-Legierung *f*
niobium alloy Niobiumlegierung *f*
platinum-carbon alloy Platin-Kohlenstoff-Legierung *f*
platinum-rhodium alloy Platin-Rhodium-Legierung *f*
plutonium-gallium alloy Plutonium-Gallium-Legierung *f*
tin alloy Zinnlegierung *f*
titanium alloy Titanlegierung *f*
tungsten alloy Wolframlegierung *f*
vanadium-niobium alloy Vanadium-Niob-Legierung *f*
weldable alloy schweißbare Legierung *f*
wrought alloy Knetlegierung *f*
wrought alumin[i]um alloy Aluminium-Knetlegierung *f*
zinc alloy Zinklegierung *f*
alloying Zulegieren *n*, Legieren *n*
alloying addition Legierungszusatz *m*
alloying element Legierungselement *n*
alternating wechselnd, Wechsel-
alternating bending Wechselbiegebeanspruchung *f*
alternating load Wechsellast *f*
alternating loading Wechselbeanspruchung *f*
aluminium (GB), aluminum (US), Al Aluminium *n*, Al
alumin[i]um alloy Aluminiumlegierung *f*
alumin[i]um bronze Aluminiumbronze *f*
alumin[i]um-copper alloy Aluminium-Kupfer-Legierung *f*
alumin[i]um-copper-silicon alloy Aluminium-Kupfer-Silizium-Legierung *f*
alumin[i]um-lithium alloy Aluminium-Lithium-Legierung *f*

alumin[i]um-magnesium-silicon alloy Aluminium-Magnesium-Silizium-Legierung *f*
alumin[i]um-zinc-magnesium alloy Aluminium-Zink-Magnesium-Legierung *f*
arc-welded alumin[i]um alloy lichtbogengeschweißte Aluminiumlegierung *f*
cast alumin[i]um alloy Aluminium-Guß-Legierung *f*
high-strength alumin[i]um alloy hochfeste Aluminiumlegierung *f*
wrought alumin[i]um alloy Aluminium-Knetlegierung *f*
aluminum → aluminium
ambient temperature Umgebungstemperatur *f*
amorphous {material} amorph {Werkstoff}
amplitude Amplitude *f*
  constant amplitude konstante Amplitude *f*
  constant amplitude cyclic loading zyklische Beanspruchung *f* mit konstanter Amplitude
  constant load amplitude konstante Lastamplitude *f*
  load amplitude Lastamplitude *f*
  loading amplitude Beanspruchungsamplitude *f*
  stress amplitude Spannungsamplitude *f*
analysis Analyse *f*
  analysis of brittle fracture Sprödbruchanalyse *f*
  analysis of crack shape Rißformanalyse *f*
  analysis of deformation Verformungsanalyse *f*
  analysis of strain Dehnungsanalyse *f*
  acoustic emission analysis Schallemissionsanalyse *f*, SEA
  crack analysis Rißanalyse *f*
  crack-arrest safety analysis Rißarrestsicherheitsanalyse *f*
  crack growth analysis Rißwachstumsanalyse *f*
  differential thermal analysis <abb.:DTA> Differentialthermoanalyse *f*, DTA
  dynamic stress analysis dynamische Spannungsanalyse *f*
  elastic-plastic analysis elastisch-plastische Analyse *f*
  elastic-plastic analysis of fracture elastisch-plastische Bruchanalyse *f*
  elastic stress analysis elastische Spannungsanalyse *f*
  electron spectroscopy for chemical analysis <abb.: ESCA> Elektronenspektroskopie *f* für die chemische Analyse
  failure analysis Schadens(fall)analyse *f*; Fehleranalyse *f* {Bruch}
  fractographic analysis fraktrographische Analyse *f*
  fracture analysis Bruchanalyse *f*
  fracture analysis diagram <abb.: FAD> Bruchanalysendiagramm *n*
  fracture surface analysis Bruchflächen-Analyse *f*, Analyse *f* von Bruchflächen
  instability analysis Instabilitätsanalyse *f*
  loading analysis Beanspruchungsanalyse *f*
  safety analysis Sicherheitsanalyse *f*
  service failure analysis Betriebsschadensanalyse *f*
  static stress analysis statische Spannungsanalyse *f*
  stress analysis, analysis of stress[es] Spannungsanalyse *f*
  thermal analysis thermische Analyse *f*
  thermogravimetric analysis <abb.: TGA> thermogravimetrische Analyse *f*, TGA
  three-dimensional elastic stress analysis dreidimensionale elastische Spannungsanalyse *f*
  three-dimensional stress analysis dreidimensionale Spannungsanalyse *f*
analyze/to analysieren
angle Winkel *m*

angular

angle of crack extension Rißausbreitungswinkel *m*
angle of crack growth Rißwachstumswinkel *m*
angle of failure Bruchwinkel *m*
crack angle Rißausbreitungswinkel *m*, Rißwinkel *m*
theoretical angle of crack extension <syn: theoretical crack angle> theoretischer Rißausbreitungswinkel *m*
angular wink[e]lig, winkelförmig, Winkel-
angular dependence Winkelabhängigkeit *f*
angular function Winkelfunktion *f*
anisotropic anisotrop
anisotropic ductile material anisotroper duktiler Werkstoff *m*
anisotropic elastic body anisotroper elastischer Körper *m*
anisotropic elasticity anisotrope Elastizität *f*
anisotropic material anisotroper Werkstoff *m*
anisotropic medium anisotropes Medium *n*
anisotropic yield anisotropes Fließen *n*
anisotropy Anisotropie *f*
anisotropy of materials Werkstoffanisotropie *f*
induced anisotropy induzierte Anisotropie *f*
inherent anisotropy natürliche Anisotropie *f*
strain-induced anisotropy dehnungsinduzierte Anisotropie *f*
structure anisotropy Gefügeanisotropie *f*
annealing twin {metals} Glühzwilling *m* {Metalle}
anode Anode *f*
anomaly {structure} Anomalie *f* {Gefüge}
antimony, Sb Antimon *n*, Sb
apparatus Apparat *m*, Gerät *n*; (i.e.s.) Prüfgerät *n*, Prüfvorrichtung *f*

automatic Vicat softening point apparatus automatisches Prüfgerät *n* zur Bestimmung der Vicat-Erweichungstemperatur
basic apparatus Grundgerät *n*
drop-weight test apparatus Prüfeinrichtung *f* für den Fallgewichtsversuch, Prüfeinrichtung *f* für den DWT-Versuch
falling weight impact strength apparatus Kugelfallprüfmaschine *f* {zur Bestimmung der Schlagzähigkeit}
flammability apparatus Entflammbarkeits-Prüfgerät *n*
linear expansion apparatus Gerät *n* zur Bestimmung der linearen Ausdehnung
test apparatus Prüfeinrichtung *f*, Prüfgerät *n*
thermal conductivity test apparatus Wärmeleitfähigkeits-Prüfgerät *n*
three-point bending test apparatus Dreipunkt-Biegevorrichtung *f*
Vicat apparatus {determination of softening point} Vicat-Prüfgerät *n* {zur Bestimmung der Vicat-Erweichungstemperatur}
Vicat softening point apparatus Gerät *n* zur Bestimmung der Vicat-Erweichungstemperatur *f*
appearance Aussehen *n*; Erscheinungsbild *n* {Oberflächen}
fracture appearance Bruchaussehen *n*, Bruchbild *n*; Brucherscheinung *f*
fracture appearance transition temperature <abb.: FATT> Brucherscheinungsübergangstemperatur *f*, FATT
macroscopic fracture appearance makroskopische Brucherscheinung *f*; makroskopisches Bruchbild *n*
type of fracture appearance Brucherscheinungsform *f*
applicable anwendbar

applicability {e.g. of results} Übertragbarkeit *f*, Anwendbarkeit *f* {z.B. von Ergebnissen}
applicability {of concepts, criteria} Anwendbarkeit *f* {von Konzepten, Kriterien}
apply/to anwenden
approximate/to {mathematics} nähern {Mathematik}
approximation {mathematics} Näherung *f* {Mathematik}
approximation solution Näherungs-lösung *f*
arc Bogen *m* <geometrisch>
arc welding Lichtbogenschweißen *n*
arc-welded alloy steel lichtbogengeschweißter legierter Stahl *m*
arc-welded alumin[i]um alloy lichtbogengeschweißte Aluminiumlegierung *f*
arc-welded low-carbon steel lichtbogengeschweißter kohlenstoffarmer Stahl *m*
arc-welded stainless steel lichtbogengeschweißter nichtrostender Stahl *m*
arc-welded titanium alloy lichtbogengeschweißte Titanlegierung *f*
arc-welded titanium lichtbogengeschweißtes Titan *n*
arc-welded hardenable carbon steel lichtbogengeschweißter härtbarer Kohlenstoffstahl *m*
arc-welded heat-resistant alloy lichtbogengeschweißte hitzebeständige Legierung *f*
circular arc crack kreisbogenförmiger Riß *m*
standard arc-shaped (tension) specimen Standard-C-Form-Zugprobe *f*
area Gebiet *n*, Bereich *m*, Umfeld *n*
area around the crack tip Rißspitzenumfeld *n*
area around the crack tip Rißspitzenbereich *m*
area of crack front Rißfrontbereich *f*
area of crack growth Rißwachstumsumfeld *n*, RW-Feld *n*

cracked area rißbehafteter Bereich *m*
cross-sectional area Querschnittsfläche *f*
fracture area Bruchzone *f*
reduction in area Querschnittsabnahme, Querschnittsverringerung *f*
specimen area Probenbereich *m*, Probenfläche *f*
argon, A Argon *n*, A
array Feld *n*
crack array Rißfeld *n*
dislocation array Versetzungskonfiguration *f*
arrest {cracks} Arrest *m*, Stoppen *n*, Anhalten *n* {Risse}
arrest behavio[u]r {cracks} Arrestverhalten *n* {Risse}
arrest-crack arretierter Riß *m*
arrest-crack length Arrestrißlänge *f*
arrest lines *pl* Rastlinien *fpl* {Bruchfläche}
arrest strip Rißstoppstreifen *m*
arrest toughness {cracks} Arrestzähigkeit *f* {Risse}
arrest zone {in materials: crack arrest} Arrestzone *f* {in Werkstoffen: Rißarrest}
concept of dynamic crack arrest dynamisches Rißarrest-Konzept *n*
concept of static crack arrest statisches Rißarrest-Konzept *n*
crack arrest Rißarrest *m*, Rißarretierung *f*, Rißauffang *m*, Rißstillstand *m*, Rißstopp *m*
arrest/to {a crack} stoppen {einen Riß}
arrested crack aufgefangener Riß *m*
arrested microcrack aufgefangener Mikroriß *m*
arresting {cracks} Arretieren *n*, Stoppen *n*, Anhalten *n* {Risse}
arresting crack arretierender Riß *m*
arresting of cracks Arretierung *f*, Stillstand *m* von Rissen
crack arresting Rißarrestprozeß *m*
arsenic, As Arsen *n*, As
artificial crack künstlicher Riß *m*
As → arsenic

assembly

assembly Montage *f*; Aufbau, Anordnung *f*
  test assembly Prüfaufbau *m*, Prüfanordnung *f*
  test specimen assembly Prüfkörperanordnung *f*
assess/to beurteilen
assessment Beurteilung *f*
  assessment of fracture Bruchbeurteilung *f*
  failure assessment Versagensbeurteilung *f*
  fracture-mechanical assessment bruchmechanische Beurteilung *f*
asymmetric asymmetrisch, unsymmetrisch
asymmetry Asymmetrie *f*, Unsymmetrie *f*
atmosphere {corrosion} Atmosphäre {Korrosion}
  industrial atmosphere {corrosion} Industrieatmosphäre *f* {Korrosion}
  marine atmosphere {corrosion} Meeresatmosphäre *f*, Seeatmosphäre *f* {Korrosion}
  rural atmosphere {corrosion} Landatmosphäre *f* {Korrosion}
attack {materials} Angriff *m* {Werkstoff}
  deposit attack Korrosion *f* unter Ablagerungen {z.B. Karosserieteile von Kraftfahrzeugen}
  impingement attack {corrosion: turbulent flow of liquid} Angriff *m* durch Flüssigkeitsschlag {Korrosion: turbulente Flüssigkeitsströmungen}
attack/to {materials} angreifen {Werkstoff}
Auger electron spectroscopy <abb.: AES> Auger-Elektronenspektroskopie *f*, AES
austenite Austenite *m*
austenitic austenitisch
  austenitic alloy austenitische Legierung *f*
  austenitic manganese steel austenitischer Manganstahl *m*
  austenitic stainless steel austenitischer nichtrostender Stahl *m*
  austenitic steel austenitischer Stahl *m*
automatic automatisch, selbsttätig
  automatic indication automatische Anzeige *f*
  automatic Vicat softening point apparatus automatisches Prüfgerät *n* zur Bestimmung der Vicat-Erweichungstemperatur
average {mathematics} Mittel *n*, Mittelwert *m* {Mathematik}; Durchschnitt *m*
average... durchschnittlich, Durchschnitts-, Mittel-
  average burning rate mittlere Verbrennungsgeschwindigkeit *f*
  average coefficient of linear thermal expansion mittlerer linearer Wärmeausdehnungskoeffizient *m*
  expansion mittlerer linearer Wärmeausdehnungskoeffizient *m*
  average crack length mittlere Rißlänge *f*
  average load Mittellast *f*
  average stress intensity mittlere Spannungsintensität
axial axial
  axial shrinkage axiale Schwindung *f*
  axial strain axiale Dehnung *f*, Dehnung *f* in axialer Richtung
  axial stress Axialspannung *f*
axially loaded axial beansprucht
axis Achse *f*
  axis of symmetry Symmetrieachse *f*
  crack axis Rißachse *f*
  major axis {ellipse} Hauptachse *f* {Ellipse}
  minor axis {ellipse} Nebenachse *f* {Ellipse}

B

B → **boron**
babbitt metal Babbitt-Metall *n*
bainitic {structure} bainitisch {Gefüge}
  bainitic structure bainitisches Mikrogefüge *n*

balge Beule *f*
band {e.g. on fracture surface} Band *n* {z.B. auf Bruchflächen}
  deformation band Deformationsband *n*
  shear band Scherband *n*
  slip band Gleitband *n*
  twin band Zwillingsband *n*
banded structure {metals} Zeilengefüge *n* {Metalle}
bar {specimen} Stab *m* {Probe}
  circumferencially cracked round bar specimen Rundstab *m* mit konzentrischem Außenriß
  circumferencially notched round bar specimen Rundprobe *f* mit Umdrehungskerbe
  circumferential-notched bar Rundstab *m* mit Umlaufkerbe
  concentric round bar konzentrischer Rundstab *m*
  notched bar gekerbter Stab *m*, Kerbstab *m*
  short bar specimen Kurzstabprobe *f*
  smooth tensile bar glatter Zugstab *m*
  tensile bar runde Zugprobe *f*, Zugstab *m*
  tensile bar dimensions Zugstababmessungen *fpl*
  test bar Probestab *m*, Prüfstab *m*
  type of test bar Probestabform *f*
Barenblatt theory {crack extension} Barenblatt-Theorie *f* {Rißerweiterung}
barium, Ba Barium *n*, Ba
base-metal Grundmetall *n*
basic apparatus Grundgerät *n*
basic equation Grundgleichung *f*
basis 1. Basis *f*, Grundlage *f*; 2. Hauptbestandteil *m*
basis material Grundwerkstoff *m*
bath Bad *n*
  bath temperature {conditioning of the specimen} Badtemperatur *f* {Temperieren von Proben}
  cooling bath Kühlbad *n*
  temperature bath Temperierbad *n*

Bauschinger effect Bauschinger-Effekt *m*
Be → **beryllium**
beach marks *pl* Rastlinien *fpl* {Bruchfläche}
beam Balken *m*
  double-cantilever beam < abb.: DCB > **specimen** < syn.: specimen > Doppelbalken[biege]probe *f*, DCB-Probe *f*
  tapered double-cantilever beam specimen < syn.: TDCB specimen > konische Doppelbalken[biege]probe *f*, keilförmige Doppelbalkenbiegeprobe *f*, TDCB-Probe *f*
bearing measurement Messung *f* der Tragfähigkeit
bearing strength Tragfähigkeit *f*
behavio[u]r {materials} Verhalten *n* {Werkstoffe}
  behavio[u]r at fracture Bruchverhalten *n*
  arrest behavio[u]r {cracks} Arrestverhalten *n* {Risse}
  brittle behavio[u]r sprödes Verhalten *n*
  brittle erosion behavio[u]r sprödes Erosionsverhalten *n*
  brittle fracture behavio[u]r Sprödbruchverhalten *n*, sprödes Bruchverhalten *n*
  crack behavio[u]r Rißverhalten *n*
  crack closure behavio[u]r Rißschließverhalten *n*
  crack-propagation behavio[u]r Rißausbreitungsverhalten *n*
  crack-tip behavio[u]r Rißspitzenverhalten *n*
  crack toughness behavio[u]r Rißzähigkeitsverhalten *n*
  creep behavio[u]r Kriechverhalten *n*
  cyclic stress-strain behavio[u]r zyklisches Spannungs-Dehnungs-Verhalten *n*
  deformation behavio[u]r Verformungsverhalten *n*
  degradation behavio[u]r Abbauverhalten *n*

ductile behavio[u]r zähes Verhalten *n*
ductile behavio[u]r duktiles Verhalten *n*
ductile fracture behavio[u]r zähes Bruchverhalten *n*
dynamic crack behavio[u]r dynamisches Rißverhalten *n*
elastic material behavio[u]r elastisches Werkstoffverhalten *n*
elastic-plastic behavio[u]r elastisch-plastisches Verhalten *n*
elastic-plastic material behavio[u]r elastisch-plastisches Werkstoffverhalten *n*
elastic-plastic stress-strain behavio[u]r elastisch-plastisches Spannungs-Dehnungs-Verhalten *n*
elasto-plastic fracture behavio[u]r elasto-plastisches Bruchverhalten *n*
fatigue behavio[u]r Ermüdungsverhalten *n*
fracture behavio[u]r Bruchverhalten *n*
fracture-mechanical behavio[u]r bruchmechanisches Verhalten *n*
hardening behavio[u]r Verfestigungsverhalten *n*
inelastic behavio[u]r unelastisches Verhalten *n*
leak-before-break behavio[u]r Leck-vor-Bruch-Verhalten *n*
linear-elastic behavio[u]r linearelastisches Verhalten *n*
linear-elastic fracture behavio[u]r linear-elastisches Bruchverhalten *n*
material behavio[u]r Werkstoffverhalten *n*
mechanical behavio[u]r mechanisches Verhalten *n*
microscopic fracture behavio[u]r mikroskopisches Bruchverhalten *n*
perfectly plastic behavio[u]r vollplastisches Verhalten *n*
plastic behavio[u]r plastisches Verhalten *n*
stress-strain behavio[u]r Spannungs-Dehnungs-Verhalten *n*

surface-crack behavio[u]r Oberflächenrißverhalten *n*
temperature behavio[u]r {of plastics} Temperaturverhalten *n* {von Kunststoffen}
time-dependent fracture behavio[u]r zeitabhängiges Bruchverhalten *n*
toughness behavio[u]r Zähigkeitsverhalten *n*
transition behavio[u]r Übergangsverhalten *n*
transition-temperature behavio[u]r Übergangstemperaturverhalten *n*
bend/to {specimens} biegen {Proben}
bending Biegung *f*, Biegebeanspruchung *f*
bending fatigue Dauerbiegebeanspruchung *f*
bending fatigue test Dauerbiegeprüfung *f*
bending length {bending test} Biegelänge *f* {Biegeprüfung}
bending load Biegebeanspruchung *f*, Biegelast *f*
bending measurement Messung *f* unter Biegebeanspruchung
bending modulus Biegemodul *m*
bending moment Biegemoment *n*
bending properties Biegeeigenschaften *fpl*, Eigenschaften *fpl* bei Biegebeanspruchung
bending strength Biegefestigkeit *f*
bending stress Biegespannung *f*
bending stress distribution Biegespannungsverteilung *f*
bending stress-intensity factor Biegespannungsintensitätsfaktor *m*
bending test Biegeversuch *m*, Biegeprüfung *f*
alternating bending Wechselbiegebeanspruchung *f*
bending modulus, modulus of bending Biegemodul *m*
coefficient of bending strength Biegefestigkeit[sbeiwert] *f[m]*
fatigue bending test Dauerbiegeversuch *m*

four-point bending Vier-Punkt-Biegung f
four-point bending technique Vierpunkt-Biegeprüfung f
four-point bending test Vierpunkt-Biegeprüfung f, Vierpunkt-Biegeversuch m
four-point bending test apparatus Vierpunkt-Biegevorrichtung f
fracture by bending Biegebruch m
pure bending reine Biegung f
rupture modulus in bending Bruchmodul m bei Biegebeanspruchung
three-point bending Dreipunkt-Biegung f
three-point bending technique Dreipunkt-Biegeprüfung f
three-point bending test Dreipunkt-Biegeprüfung f, Dreipunkt-Biegeversuch m
three-point bending test apparatus Dreipunkt-Biegevorrichtung f
unidirectional bending einseitige Biegung f
bend Biege-
bend specimen Biegeprobe f
bend test fixture Spannvorrichtung f für den Biegeversuch
beryllium, Be Beryllium n, Be
Bi → **bismuth**
biaxial zweiachsig
biaxial compression zweiachsige Druckbeanspruchung f
biaxial fatigue zweiachsige Ermüdung f
biaxial stress zweiachsige Spannung f
biaxial stress state zweiachsiger Spannungszustand m
biaxial tensile stress field zweiachsiges Zugspannungsfeld n
biaxial tension zweiachsiger Zug m
biaxiality Zweiachsigkeit f
bifurcate, to {cracks} [sich] verzweigen {Risse}
bifurcation {cracks} Verzweigung f, Verzweigen n {Risse}

crack bifurcation Rißverzweigungsvorgang m
bimaterial specimen aus zwei Werkstoffen bestehende Probe f
bismuth, Bi Wismut n, Bismut n, Bi
blank experiment Blindversuch m
blister {defect} Blase f {Fehler}
blue brittleness {steel} Blausprödigkeit f {Stahl}
blunt {crack} stumpf {Riß}
blunt crack abgestumpfter Riß m, abgerundeter Riß m, stumpfer Riß m
blunt crack tip abgestumpfte Rißspitze f
blunt fatigue crack abgestumpfter Ermüdungsriß m
blunt notch abgestumpfte Kerbe f, abgestumpfter Kerb m
blunt/to abstumpfen
blunting {cracks} Abstumpfung f, Abstumpfen n, Abrundung f {Risse}
blunting line {cracks} Rißabstumpfungsgerade f, Wölbungsgerade f {Risse}
crack blunting Rißabstumpfung f
crack tip blunting Abstumpfung f (Abstumpfen n) der Rißspitze
body Körper m
body-centered cubic kubisch-raumzentriert {Metall}
anisotropic elastic body anisotroper elastischer Körper m
elastic body elastischer Körper m
elastic-plastic body elastisch-plastischer Körper m
homogeneous body homogener Körper m
infinite body unendlicher Körper m
linear-elastic body linear-elastischer Körper m
loaded body beanspruchter (belasteter) Körper m
notched body gekerbter Körper m
rigid body starrer Körper m
solid body fester Körper m
three-dimensional body dreidimensionaler Körper m
unloaded body unbelasteter Körper m, nicht beanspruchter Körper m

boiler Kessel *m*
  boiler steel Kesselstahl *m*
border of crack propagation Rißausbreitungsgrenze *f*
boron, B Bor *n*, B
boundary Grenze *f*
  boundary conditions Grenzbedingungen *fpl*, Randbedingungen *fpl*
  boundary loading Grenz[flächen]belastung *f*, Randbelastung *f*
  boundary stress Randspannung *f*
  boundary value Randwert *m*
  boundary value method {dropweight test} Grenzwertverfahren *n* {Fallgewichtsprüfung}
  boundary-value problem Grenzwertproblem *n*, Randwertproblem *n*
  boundary value test {maximum notch sharpness and loading rate} Grenzwertprüfung *f* {größtmögliche Kerbschärfe und Belastungsgeschwindigkeit}
  elastic boundary-value problem elastisches Grenzwertproblem *n*
  elastic-plastic boundary value problem elastisch-plastisches Randwertproblem *n*
  grain boundary Korngrenze *f*
  phase boundary Phasengrenze *f*
  segregation in grain boundary Korngrenzenausscheidung *f*
  small-angle grain boundary Kleinwinkelkorngrenze *f*
  subgrain boundary Subkorngrenze *f*
  three-dimensional boundary-value problem dreidimensionales Grenzwertproblem *n*
  tilt boundary {crystal} Kippgrenze *f* {Kristall}
  twist boundary {crystal} Verschränkungs[korn]grenze *f* {Kristall}
Br → bromine
branch/to {cracks} [sich] verzweigen {Risse}
branched {cracks} verzweigt {Risse}
  branched crack verzweigter Riß *m*, Mehrfachriß *m*

branching {cracks} Verzweigung *f*, Verzweigen *n* {Risse}
  branching velocity Verzweigungsgeschwindigkeit *f*
  crack branching Rißverzweigung *f*
  microscopic crack branching mikroskopische Rißverzweigung *f*
branching crack Nebenriß *m*
brass Messing *n*
break Bruch *m*
break/to brechen
breaking Brechen *n*, Bruch *m*
  breaking stress Zerreißspannung *f*
  breaking through Durchbrechen *n*
  condition of breaking Bruchbedingung *f*
  breaking stress Bruchspannung *f*
Brinell hardness number < abb.: HB > Brinellhärte *f*
Brinell hardness test {indentation test} Brinellhärteprüfung *f* {Eindringprüfung}
brittle spröd[e]
  brittle behavio[u]r {of materials} sprödes Verhalten *n* {von Werkstoffen}
  brittle cleavage fracture spröder Spaltbruch *m*
  brittle crack propagation spröde Rißausbreitung *f*
  brittle-ductile transition Spröd[e]-Zäh-Übergang *m*, Übergang *m* "spröd[e]-zäh"
  brittle erosion behavio[u]r sprödes Erosionsverhalten *n*
  brittle fatigue fracture spröder Schwingungsbruch *m*
  brittle fracture Sprödbruch *m*
  brittle fracture behavio[u]r Sprödbruchverhalten *n*, sprödes Bruchverhalten *n*
  brittle fracture safety Sprödbruchsicherung *f*
  brittle fracture surface Sprödbruchfläche *f*
  brittle fracture test Sprödbruchprüfung *f*
  brittle fracture theory Sprödbruchtheorie *f*

brittle inclusion spröder Einschluß *m*
brittle material spröder Werkstoff *m*
brittle overload fracture spröder Gewaltbruch *m*
brittle point Versprödungstemperatur *f*, Sprödigkeitstemperatur *f*
brittle state spröder Zustand *m*
acid brittle steel beizspröder Stahl *m*
analysis of brittle fracture Sprödbruchanalyse *f*
concept of brittle fracture Sprödbruchkonzept *n*
concept of brittle fracture theory Konzept *n* der Sprödbruchtheorie
criterion of brittle fracture Sprödbruchkriterium *n*
elastic brittle fracture elastischer Sprödbruch *m*
ideal brittle material ideal-spröder Werkstoff *m*
intercrystalline brittle fracture interkristalliner Sprödbruch *m*
low-energy brittle fracture energiearmer Sprödbruch *m*
resistance to brittle fracture Sprödbruchwiderstand *m*
tendency to brittle fracture Sprödbruchneigung *f*
theory of brittle fracture Sprödbruchtheorie *f*
zone of brittle fracture Sprödbruchbereich *m*
brittleness {materials} Sprödigkeit *f* {Werkstoffe}
brittleness temperature Versprödungstemperatur *f*, Sprödigkeitstemperatur *f*; Kältebruchtemperatur *f*
brittleness temperature by impact Kältebruchtemperatur *f* bei Schlagbeanspruchung
brittleness temperature test Kältebruchtemperaturprüfung *f*
brittleness test Prüfung *f* der Sprödigkeit, Sprödigkeitsprüfung *f*
blue brittleness {steel} Blausprödigkeit *f* {Stahl}
hot brittleness Warmbrüchigkeit *f*
notch brittleness Kerbsprödigkeit *f*
low-temperature brittleness Kältebrüchigkeit *f*, Brüchigkeit *f* bei tiefen Temperaturen
temper brittleness Anlaßsprödigkeit *f*
broken {specimen} gebrochen {Probe}
bromine, Br Brom *n*, Br
bronze Bronze *f*
alumin[i]um bronze Aluminiumbronze *f*
bronze alloy Sonderbronze *f*
tin bronze Zinnbronze *f*
buckle {casting defect} Schülpe *f* {Gußfehler}
buckle {sheet} wellig {Blech}
buckle/to [aus]knicken {eines langen Stabes}; ausbeulen {Probe}
buckling [Aus]knicken *n* {eines langen Stabes}; Ausbeulen *n* {Probe}
buckling strength Knickfestigkeit *f*
criterion for buckling Knickkriterium *n*
bulk modulus {of elasticity} Kompressionsmodul *m*
burn/to brennen
burning Brennen *n*, Verbrennen *n*, Verbrennung *f*
burning rate Verbrennungsgeschwindigkeit *f*
burning test Brennbarkeitsprüfung *f*
burning time {the period in seconds that the specimen burns after removal of the ignition source} Brenndauer *f*
average burning rate mittlere Verbrennungsgeschwindigkeit *f*
burning rate Verbrennungsgeschwindigkeit *f*
surface burning characteristics Brandverhalten *n* der Oberfläche
burst {defect} Ausbruch *m* {Fehler}
burst/to bersten
bursting Bersten *n*
bursting pressure Berstdruck *m*
burst test Berstversuch *m*

C

C
C → carbon
C → compact...
Ca → calcium
caesium, Cs Cäsium *n*, Cs
Cb → columbium
C specimen Kompaktprobe *f*, C-Probe *f*
cadmium, Cd Kadmium *n*, Cadmium *n*, Cd
calcium, Ca Kalzium *n*, Calcium *n*, Ca
calculate/to berechnen
calculated berechnet; theoretisch
  calculated fracture stress theoretische Bruchspannung *f*
calculation Berechnung *f*
  calculation of service life Lebensdauerberechnung *f*
  crack-propagation calculation Rißausbreitungsberechnung *f*
calibrate/to eichen, Kalibrieren
calibration Eichen *n*, Eichung *f*, Kalibrieren *n*, Kalibrierung *f*
  calibration curve Eichkurve *f*
carbon, C Kohlenstoff *m*, C
carbon-molybdenum steel Kohlenstoff-Molybdän-Stahl *m*
carry/to {a specimen} tragen {eine Probe}
Cartesian coordinate system kartesisches Koordinatensystem *n*
Cartesian coordinates *pl* kartesische Koordinaten *fpl*
case {loading} Fall *m* {Beanspruchung}
  loading case Beanspruchungsfall *m*
  special case Spezialfall *m*
cast alumin[i]um alloy Aluminium-Guß-Legierung *f*
casting Guß *m*, Gießen *n*
  casting defect Gußfehler *m*
  iron casting Eisenguß *m*
  steel casting Stahlguß *m*
catastrophic katastrophenartig
  catastrophic crack extension katastrophenartige Rißerweiterung *f*
  catastrophic failure katastrophenartiger Bruch *m*
  catastrophic wear katastrophenartiger Verschleiß *m*
cathode Kat[h]ode *f*
cause {e.g. of fracture} Ursache *f* {z.B. eines Bruch[e]s}
  cause of failure Schadensursache *f*
  cause of fracture Bruchursache *f*
cause/to {e.g. a fracture or failure} verursachen {z.B. einen Bruch}
caustic Laugen-
  caustic cracking {stress-corrosion cracking} Laugenrissigkeit *f* {Spannungsrißkorrosion}
  caustic embrittlement Laugenrissigkeit *f* {Spannungsrißkorrosion}
cavitation Kavitation *f* {Bildung von Hohlräumen an Korngrenzen}
  cavitation damage Kavitationsschädigung *f*, Schädigung *f* durch Kavitation
  cavitation erosion Kavitationserosion *f*
cavity Hohlraum *m*
  grain-boundary cavity {crystal} Korngrenzenhohlraum *m*, Hohlraum *m* an Korngrenzen {Kristall}
  shrinkage cavity {defect} Lunker *m* {Fehler}
CCT → center-cracked tensile ...
Cd → cadmium
cellular zellig, porig
  cellular plastics Schaumkunststoff *m*
  cellular specimen zellige (porige) Probe *f*
cement/to {thin steel plates to each end of a specimen} einlassen {z.B. ein Stahlplättchen in eine Probe}
center {US}, centre {GB} Mitte *f*; Mittelpunkt *m*
  center crack Mittelriß *m*, Mittenriß *m*
  center-cracked flat specimen Flachprobe *f* mit Mittelriß

center-cracked flat tensile specimen Flachzugprobe *f* mit Mittelriß
center-cracked specimen {tensile specimen} Probe *f* mit Mittelriß {Zugprobe}
center-cracked tensile <abb.: CCT> **specimen** <syn.: specimen> Zugprobe *f* mit Mittelriß, mittig angerissene Zugprobe *f*
center-cracked tension specimen Mittelrißprobe *f*, CCT-Probe *f* {Zugprobe}
center line shrinkage Mittellinienlunkerung *f*
center-notched specimen Probe *f* mit Mittelkerb
center-notched tensile specimen in der Mitte gekerbte Zugprobe *f*
center of specimen Probenmitte *f*, Probenmittelpunkt *m*
central zentral, mittig, in der Mitte, mittlerer, Mittel-
central crack Zentralriß *m*
central specimen mittlere Probe *f* {von mehreren nebeneinander angeordneten Proben}
unloaded central crack lastfreier Zentralriß *m*
centrally notched specimen Probe *f* mit Mittelkerb
centre → center...
ceramic keramisch
ceramic material keramischer Werkstoff *m*
cesium, Cs Cäsium *n*, Cs
chamber Kammer *f*
  chamber temperature Kammertemperatur *f*
  cold chamber Kältekammer *f*
  heating chamber Wärmekammer *f*
  low-temperature working chamber Tieftemperaturprüfraum *m*
change Änderung *f*, Veränderung *f*
  change in crack length Rißlängenänderung *f*, Rißzuwachs *m*
  dimensional change Maßänderung *f*
  geometry change Geometrieänderung *f*

  volume change Volumenänderung *f*
  weight change Masseänderung *f*
characteristic Merkmal *n*, Kennzeichen *n*, Charakteristik *f*; charakteristisch
  characteristic of fracture Bruchmerkmal *n*
  crack-propagation characteristic Rißausbreitungscharakteristik *f*
  growth characteristic Wachstumscharakteristik *f*
  macroscopic characteristic of fracture makroskopisches Bruchmerkmal *n*
  microscopic characteristic of fracture mikroskopisches Bruchmerkmal *n*
characteristics Kennlinien *fpl*; Verhalten *n*
  fracture characteristics Bruchkennlinien *fpl*
  loading characteristics *pl* Belastungskennlinien *fpl*
  resistance-temperature characteristics Widerstand-Temperatur-Kennlinien *fpl*
  surface burning characteristics Brandverhalten *n* der Oberfläche
characterization Charakterisierung *f*, Kennzeichnung *f*
  characterization of loading Beanspruchungscharakterisierung *f*
Charpy (impact) test Charpy-Pendelschlagversuch *m*, Pendelschlagversuch *m* nach Charpy
Charpy impact resistance Charpy-Schlagfestigkeit *f*, Schlagfestigkeit *f* nach Charpy
Charpy machine Charpy-Prüfmaschine *f*
Charpy specimen {with notch} Charpy-Probe *f* {mit Kerb}
Charpy test {notch sensitivity} Charpy-Versuch *m* {Kerbempfindlichkeit}
  instrumented Charpy test instrumentierter Charpy-Versuch *m*
check Riß *m*

chemical chemisch
  chemical resistant steel chemikalienbeständiger Stahl m
Chevron
  Chevron crack starter notch Chevron-Rißstarterkerbe f
  Chevron notch Chevron-Kerbe f {Kerbe in Proben}
  Chevron notch specimen Probe f mit Chevron-Kerbe
chisel steel Meißelstahl m
chlorine, Cl Chlor m, Cl
chromium, Cr Chrom n, Cr
chromium-nickel-molybdenum steel Chrom-Nickel-Molybdän-Stahl m
circular kreisförmig, kreisrund, Kreis-
  circular arc crack kreisbogenförmiger Riß m
  circular crack kreisförmiger Riß m, Kreisriß m
  circular-crack initiation Kreisrißbildung f
  circular equivalent crack kreisrunder Ersatzriß m
  circular external crack kreisförmiger Außenriß m
  circular hole kreisrunde Bohrung f
  circular internal crack kreisförmiger Innenriß m
  circular notch runder Kerb m
circumference Umfang m, Peripherie f
circumferential peripher, Umfangs-
  circumferential corrosion-fatigue crack peripherer Ermüdungsriß m {Korrosion}
  circumferential crack Umfangsriß m
  circumferential notch Umfangskerb m
  circumferential notch {of a round test specimen} Umlaufkerbe f {einer Rundprobe}
  circumferential-notched bar Rundstab m mit Umlaufkerbe
  circumferential stress Umfangsspannung f
  normalized circumferential stress normierte Umfangsspannung f
  circumferentially cracked round bar specimen Rundstab m mit konzentrischem Außenriß
  circumferentially notched round bar specimen Rundprobe f mit Umdrehungskerbe
Cl → chlorine
clamp/to {a specimen} einspannen, festspannen, festklemmen {eine Probe}
  clamped {specimen} eingespannt, festgespannt {Probe}
  clamped specimen eingespannte Probe f
  clamping {specimen} Einspannen n, Festspannen n, Festklemmen n {Probe}
  clamping device Einspannvorrichtung f
  clamping pressure {for a specimen} Einspanndruck m, Spanndruck m {Proben}
clamshell marks pl Rastlinien fpl {Bruchfläche}
cleavability Spaltbarkeit f
cleavable spaltbar, spaltfähig
cleavage Spaltung f, Spalten n
  cleavage crack Spaltriß m
  cleavage failure Spaltbruch m
  cleavage facets Spaltbruchfacetten fpl
  cleavage fracture Spaltbruch m
  cleavage fracture condition Spaltbruchbedingung f
  cleavage fracture criterion Spaltbruchkriterium n
  cleavage fracture formation Spaltbruchbildung f
  cleavage fracture strength Spaltbruchfestigkeit f

cleavage fracture stress Spaltbruchspannung f
cleavage fracture surface Spaltbruchfläche f
cleavage fracture zone Spaltbruchbereich m
cleavage fracture Spaltbruch m
cleavage plane Spalt[bruch]ebene f
cleavage pre-crack Spaltanriß m
cleavage step {cleavage fracture} Spaltstufe f {Spaltbruch}
cleavage stress Spaltspannung f
  brittle cleavage fracture spröder Spaltbruch m
  intercrystalline cleavage fracture interkristalliner Spaltbruch m
  preferred cleavage plane bevorzugte Spaltebene f
  transcrystalline cleavage fracture transkristalliner Spaltbruch m
cleave/to spalten, aufspalten
climatic Klima-
  climatic testing Klimaprüfung f
closure Schließen n, Schließung f {Riß}
  crack closure Rißschließen n, Rißschließung f
  crack closure behavio[u]r Rißschließverhalten f
  fatigue crack closure Schließen n des Ermüdungsrisses
CLWL → crack-line-wedge-loaded
Co → cobalt
coalesce/to {voids, cracks} zusammenwachsen, sich vereinigen {Hohlräume, Risse}
coalescence {of voids, cracks} Zusammenwachsen n, Vereinigung f {von Hohlräumen, Rissen}
  crack coalescence Rißvereinigung f, Zusammenwachsen n von Rissen
  void coalescence Hohlraumvereinigung f, Hohlraumzusammenschluß m
coating Beschichtung f {Ergebnis}; Beschichten n {Vorgang}
  metal coating Metallbeschichtung f
  surface coating Oberflächenbeschichtung f

cobalt alloy Cobalt-Legierung f
cobalt, Co Kobalt n, Cobalt n, Co
cobalt-chromium alloy Cobalt-Chrom-Legierung f
cobalt-chromium-molybdenum alloy Cobalt-Chrom-Molybdän-Legierung f
COD <**crack opening displacement**> COD Rißöffnungsverschiebung f, COD
  COD concept {linear-elastic fracture mechanics} COD-Konzept n {Fließbruchmechanik}
  COD criterion Rißöffnungsverschiebungskriterium n, COD-Kriterium n
  COD design curve COD-Auslegungskurve f, COD-Konstruktionskurve f
  critical COD kritische Rißöffnungsverschiebung f
  load COD diagram Belastung-COD-Diagramm n
coefficient Koeffizient m, Beiwert m
  coefficient of bending strength Biegefestigkeit[sbeiwert] $f[m]$
  coefficient of cubic expansion kubischer Ausdehnungskoeffizient m
  coefficient of cubical expansion kubischer Ausdehnungskoeffizient m
  coefficient of cubical thermal expansion kubischer Wärmeausdehnungskoeffizient m
  coefficient of expansion Ausdehnungskoeffizient m
  coefficient of linear expansion linearer Ausdehnungskoeffizient m
  coefficient of linear thermal expansion linearer Wärmeausdehnungskoeffizient m
  average coefficient of linear thermal expansion mittlerer linearer Wärmeausdehnungskoeffizient m
cohesion Kohäsion f
  cohesion strength Kohäsionsfestigkeit f
  cohesion zone Kohäsionszone f
  modulus of cohesion Kohäsionsmodul m

cohesive kohäsiv, Kohäsions-
cohesive force Kohäsionskraft *f*
cold kalt; Kälte-
  cold bend strength Kältebiegefestigkeit *f*
  cold bend temperature Kältebiegetemperatur *f*
  cold bend test Kaltbiegeversuch *m*, Kältebiegeversuch *m*
  cold-brittle steel kaltspröder Stahl *m*, kaltbrüchiger Stahl *m*
  cold chamber Kältekammer *f*
  cold crack Kaltriß *m*
  cold deformation Kaltverformung *f*
  cold resistance Kältebeständigkeit *f*
  cold shot Kaltguß *m*
  cold shut {casting defect} Kaltschweißstelle *f* {Gußfehler}
collinear kollinear
  collinear crack kollinearer Riß *m*
  collinear cracks *pl* Rißserie *f*
collocation Kollokation *f*
columbium, Cb, niobium, Nb Niob *n*, Nb
columnar structure stengeliges Gefüge *n*
combustability Brennbarkeit *f*
combustible brennbar
compact < abb.: C > kompakt, Kompakt
  compact specimen < abb.: CS > Kompakt-Probe *f*, C-Probe *f*
  compact tension specimen Kompakt-Zug-Probe *f*, CT-Probe *f*
  compact tension < abb.: CT > **specimen** CT-Probe *f*, Kompakt-Zug-Probe *f*
  disk-shaped compact [tensile] < abb.: DCT > **specimen** scheibenförmige Kompaktzugprobe *f*, DCT-Probe *f*
  round compact tension < abb.: RCT > **specimen** Rund-Kompakt-Zugprobe *f*, RCT-Probe *f*
  standard compact tension < abb.: CT > **specimen** Standard-Kompakt-Zugprobe *f*
  standard disk-shaped compact (tension) specimen Standard-Rundscheiben-Zugprobe *f*
  wedge-loaded compact test specimen keilbelastete Kompakt-Probe *f*
comparability {of test results} Vergleichbarkeit *f* {von Prüfergebnissen}
comparative vergleichend, Vergleichs-
  comparative test, comparison test Vergleichsprüfung *f*
compare/to vergleichen
comparison Vergleich *m*
  comparison measurement Vergleichsmessung *f*
  comparison method Vergleichsmethode *f*
  comparison test Vergleichsprüfung *f*
compatibility Kompatibilität *f*
  compatibility conditions Kompatibilitätsbedingungen *fpl*
compatible kompatibel
complete vollständig, völlig; durchgehend {Bruch}
  complete fracture Durchbrechen *n*
complex komplex
  complex stress komplexe Spannung *f*
  complex stress function komplexe Spannungsfunktion *f*
compliance Nachgiebigkeit *f*
  compliance measurement Nachgiebigkeitsmessung *f*
  compliance method {method of crack length measurement} Compliance-Methode *f* {Rißlängenmeßmethode}
  elastic compliance elastische Nachgiebigkeit *f*
  normalized compliance normierte Nachgiebigkeit *f*
  theoretical compliance theoretische Nachgiebigkeit *f*
component Bauteil *n*; Komponente *f* {Mathematik}

component geometry Bauteilgeometrie *f*
component of displacement Verschiebungskomponente *f*
component strength Bauteilfestigkeit *f*
load component Lastkomponente *f* {z.B. eine Spannung}
local stress component lokale Spannungskomponente *f*
normal component of stress Normalspannungskomponente *f*
normal stress component Normalspannungskomponente *f*
shear component Schub-Komponente *f*
shear stress component Schubspannungskomponente *f*
strain component Dehnungskomponente *f*
stress component Spannungskomponente *f*
tangential stress component Tangentialspannungskomponente *f*
testing of component Bauteilprüfung *f*
thickness of component Bauteildicke *f*
width of component Bauteilbreite f
composite <syn.: composite material> Verbundwerkstoff *m*
fiber-reinforced composite faserverstärkter Werkstoff *m*
composition {materials} Zusammensetzung *f* {Werkstoffe}
compression Druck *m*; Druckbeanspruchung *f*
compression chucks {for tensile machine} Spannbacken *mpl* {Zugprüfmaschine}
compression modulus Kompressionsmodul *m*
compression specimen Probe *f* für den Druckversuch
compression test Druckversuch *m*
compression testing machine Druckprüfmaschine *f*

biaxial compression zweiachsige Druckbeanspruchung *f*
hydrostatic compression hydrostatische Druckbeanspruchung *f*
plain strain compression ebene (zweiachsige) Druckbeanspruchung *f*
plain strain compression test ebene (zweiachsige) Druckfestigkeitsprüfung *f*
positive compression positive Druckbeanspruchung *f*
uniaxial compression einachsiger Druck *m*
uniaxial compression loading einachsige Druckbelastung *f*
compressive... {force, loading} Druck- {Kraft, Belastung}
compressive deformation Druckverformung *f*, Deformation *f* infolge Druckbeanspruchung
compressive load Drucklast *f*
compressive residual stress Druckeigenspannung *f*
compressive residual stress curve Druckeigenspannungsverlauf *m*
compressive residual stress field Druckeigenspannungsfeld *n*
compressive strength Druckfestigkeit *f*
compressive stress Druckspannung *f*
compressive testing Druckprüfung *f*
external compressive load äußere Druckbelastung *f*
internal compressive load innere Druckbelastung *f*
maximum compressive strength maximale Druckfestigkeit *f*
computation Berechnung *f*
computer Computer *m*, Rechner *m*
  computer simulation Computer-Modellierung *f*
concave konkav, hohl
concavity {of failure locus} Konkavität *f*, Hohlwölbung *f* {Bruchstelle}
concentrated konzentriert; in einem Punkt angreifend {Kraft}

concentration

concentrated force punktförmig angreifende Kraft f
concentration Konzentration f
elastic stress concentration elastische Spannungskonzentration f
load concentration Lastkonzentration f
load concentration factor Lastkonzentrationsfaktor m
plastic strain concentration factor plastischer Dehnungskonzentrationsfaktor m
shear stress concentration Schubspannungskonzentration f
strain concentration Dehnungskonzentration f, Verzerrungskonzentration f
strain concentration factor Dehnungskonzentrationsfaktor m
stress concentration Spannungskonzentration f
stress concentration factor Spannungskonzentrationsfaktor f
theoretical stress concentration factor theoretischer Spannungskonzentrationsfaktor m
concentric konzentrisch, mittig
concentric round bar konzentrischer Rundstab m
concept Konzept n
concept of brittle fracture Sprödbruchkonzept n
concept of brittle fracture theory Konzept n der Sprödbruchtheorie
concept of dynamic crack arrest dynamisches Rißarrest-Konzept n
concept of elastic-plastic fracture mechanics Fließbruchmechanik-Konzept n
concept of fracture Bruchkonzept n
concept of fracture mechanics Konzept n der Bruchmechanik, Bruchmechanik-Konzept n
concept of limiting temperature {determination of toughness} Grenztemperatur-Konzept n {Zähigkeitsnachweis}
concept of linear-elastic fracture mechanics Konzept n der linear-elastischen Bruchmechanik
concept of static crack arrest statisches Rißarrestkonzept n
concept of stress intensity Spannungsintensitätskonzept n
concept of transition temperature {brittle fracture behavio[u]r} Übergangstemperaturkonzept n {Sprödbruchverhalten}
COD concept {linear-elastic fracture mechanics} COD-Konzept n {Fließbruchmechanik}
crack-arrest concept Rißarrestkonzept n
crack initiation concept Rißinitiierungskonzept n
energy concept {concept of fracture mechanics} Energie-Konzept n {Konzept der Bruchmechanik}
fracture concept Bruchkonzept n
fracture mechanics concept Bruchmechanik-Konzept n, Konzept n der Bruchmechanik
J integral concept {linear-elastic fracture mechanics} J-Integral-Konzept n {Fließbruchmechanik}
LEFM concept {LEFM linear-elastic fracture mechanics} LEBM-Konzept n {LEBM linear-elastische Bruchmechanik}
R curve concept {R crack resistance} R-Kurven-Konzept n {R Rißwiderstand}
safety concept Sicherheitskonzept n
conchoidal fracture Muschelbruch m
concrete Beton m
condition Bedingung f
condition of breaking Bruchbedingung f
condition of crack growth Rißwachstumsbedingung f
cleavage fracture condition Spaltbruchbedingung f
crack growth condition Rißwachstumsbedingung f

crack initiation condition Rißinitiierungsbedingung *f*
fatigue condition Ermüdungsbedingung *f*
fracture condition Bruchbedingung *f*
leak-before-break condition Leck-vor-Bruch-Bedingung *f*
material condition Werkstoffzustand *m*, Werkstoffbeschaffenheit *f*
stress condition Spannungsbedingung *f*
conditions *pl* Bedingungen *fpl*, Verhältnisse *npl*
boundary conditions Grenzbedingungen *fpl*, Randbedingungen *fpl*
compatibility conditions Kompatibilitätsbedingungen *fpl*
crack-arrest conditions Rißauffangbedingungen *fpl*
crack-propagation conditions Rißausbreitungsbedingungen *fpl*
creep conditions Kriechbedingungen *fpl*
failure conditions Versagenbedingungen *fpl*
grip conditions {specimen} Einspannbedingungen *fpl* {Probe}
loading conditions Beanspruchungsbedingungen *fpl*, Beanspruchungsverhältnisse *npl*, Belastungsbedingungen *fpl*, Lastbedingungen *fpl*
physical conditions {of the test} physikalische Bedingungen *fpl* {einer Prüfung}
service conditions Betriebsbedingungen *fpl*
steady state conditions stationäre Bedingungen *fpl*
test conditions {e.g. temperature, pressur, loading rate} Prüfbedingungen *fpl* {z.B Temperatur, Druck, Belastungsgeschwindigkeit}
yield conditions Fließbedingungen *fpl*
conductivity Leitfähigkeit *f*
  conductivity measurement Leitfähigkeitsmessung *f*
  thermal conductivity Wärmeleitfähigkeit *f*, Wärmeleitvermögen *n*
  thermal conductivity measurement Wärmeleitfähigkeitsmessung *f*
  thermal conductivity test apparatus Wärmeleitfähigkeits-Prüfgerät *n*
configuration Konfiguration *f*
  crack configuration Rißkonfiguration *f*
  crack-tip configuration Rißspitzenkonfiguration *f*
  load configuration Belastungskonfiguration *f*
  notch configuration Kerbkonfiguration *f*
  specimen configuration Probenkonfiguration *f*
  starter crack configuration Anfangsrißkonfiguration *f*
conical kegelförmig, konisch
constant konstant, gleichbleiben, Konstante *f*
  constant amplitude konstante Amplitude *f*
  constant amplitude cyclic loading zyklische Beanspruchung *f* mit konstanter Amplitude
  constant deformation konstante Verformung *f*
  constant force konstante Kraft *f*
  constant load konstante Last *f*
  constant load amplitude konstante Lastamplitude *f*
  constant-rate-of-loading instrument Prüfmaschine *f* mit konstanter Belastungsgeschwindigkeit
  constant stress konstante Spannung *f*
  constant stress level konstantes Spannungsniveau *n*
  crack-propagation constant Rißausbreitungskonstante *f*
  dynamic constant dynamische Konstante *f*
  fracture constant Bruchkonstante *f*
  geometry dependent constant geometrieabhängige Konstante *f*

constrain/to 22

material constant Werkstoffkonstante *f*
specific heat at constant pressure spezifische Wärme *f* bei konstantem Druck
specific heat at constant volume spezifische Wärme *f* bei konstantem Volumen
constrain/to {e.g. strain} behindern {z.B. Dehnung}
constraint {e.g. strain constraint} Behinderung *f* {z.B. Dehnungsbehinderung}
constraint factor Behinderungsfaktor *m*
deformation constraint Deformationsbehinderung *f*, Verformungsbehinderung *f*
elastic constraint elastische Behinderung *f*
plastic strain constraint plastische Dehnungsbehinderung *f*
strain constraint Dehnungsbehinderung *f*
yield constraint Fließbehinderung *f*
construct/to konstruieren, entwerfen
construction Konstruktion *f*, Bauwerk *n*
   material of construction Konstruktionswerkstoff *m*
constructional Konstruktions-
constructional material Konstruktionswerkstoff *m*
contamination {surface} Verunreinigung *f* {Oberfläche}
continuous kontinuierlich, ununterbrochen
continuum Kontinuum *n*
   continuum mechanics Kontinuummechanik *f*
   continuum theory Kontinuumstheorie *f*
   linear-elastic continuum linear-elastisches Kontinuum *n*
   three-dimensional continuum dreidimensionales Kontinuum *n*
contour {crack} Kontur *f*, Profil *n* {Riß}
   crack contour Rißkontur *f*
   crack-tip contour Rißspitzenkontur *f*
contract/to {crack tip} schrumpfen, sich zusammenziehen {Rißspitze}
contraction {crack tip} Kontraktion *f*, Schrumpfung *f* {Rißspitze}
control Einhaltung *f*; Kontrolle *f*; Prüfung *f*; Steuerung *f*
   fracture control Einhaltung *f* vorgeschriebenen Bruchverhaltens
   fracture control plan Bruchkontrollplan *m*, Bruchüberwachungsplan *m*
   load control Belastungskontrolle *f*
   production control Produktionskontrolle *f*, Produktionsüberwachung *f*
   quality control Qualitätskontrolle *f*, Qualitätsüberwachung *f*
   quality control test Qualitätsprüfung *f*
   visual control Sichtprüfung *f*
control/to kontrollieren, überwachen; steuern
convex konvex, gewölbt
convexity {of failure locus} Konvexität *f*, Wölbung *f* {Bruchstelle}
cool/to {specimens} kühlen, abkühlen {Proben}
cooler unit Kühlereinheit *f*
cooling {specimens} Kühlen *n*, Abkühlen *n* {Proben}
cooling bath Kühlbad *n*
cooling rate Abkühlungsgeschwindigkeit *f*
coordinates *pl* Koordinaten *fpl*
   Cartesian coordinates *pl* kartesische Koordinaten *fpl*
   cylindrial coordinates *pl* Zylinderkoordinaten *fpl*
   polar coordinates *pl* Polarkoordinaten *fpl*
copper, Cu Kupfer *n*, Cu
   high-purity copper hochreines Kupfer *n*
copper alloy Kupferlegierung *f*

copper-bismuth alloy Kupfer-Wismut-Legierung *f*
copper-nickel alloy Kupfer-Nickel-Legierung *f*
copper-zinc alloy Kupfer-Zink-Legierung *f*
corner crack Eckriß *m*
correct/to korrigieren, ausgleichen
correction Korrektur, Ausgleich *m*
  correction function Korrekturfunktion *f*
  normalized correction function normierte Korrekturfunktion *f*
  plasticity correction {crack length} Plastizitätskorrektur *f* {Rißlänge}
corrective factor Korrekturfaktor *m*
correlate/to korrelieren, in Wechselbeziehung stehen
correlation Korrelation *f*, Wechselbeziehung *f*
  correlation parameter Korrelationsparameter *m*
corrode/to korrodieren
corroded korrodiert
  corroded surface korrodierte Oberfläche *f*
corrosion Korrosion *f*
  corrosion failure Ausfall *m* durch Korrosion
  corrosion fatigue <abb.: CF> Schwingrißkorrosion *f*, Korrosionsermüdung *f*
  corrosion fatigue crack Korrosionsermüdungsriß *m*
  corrosion fatigue crack growth Korrosionsermüdungsrißwachstum *n*
  corrosion fatigue cracking Schwingungsrißkorrosion *f*
  corrosion-fatigue failure Ausfall *m* durch Korrosionsermüdung
  corrosion product Korrosionsprodukt *n*
  corrosion resistance Korrosionsbeständigkeit *f*
  corrosion-resistant alloy korrosionsbeständige Legierung *f*
  corrosion-resistant steel korrosionsbeständiger Stahl *m*
  circumferential corrosion-fatigue crack peripherer Ermüdungsriß *m* {Korrosion}
  crevice corrosion Spaltkorrosion *f*
  deposit corrosion Korrosion *f* unter Ablagerungen {z.B. Karosserieteile von Kraftfahrzeugen}
  electrolytic corrosion elektrolytische Korrosion *f*
  fretting corrosion Reibkorrosion *f*
  galvanic corrosion galvanische Korrosion *f*, Kontaktkorrosion *f*
  general corrosion Flächenkorrosion *f*
  grain-boundary corrosion Korngrenzenkorrosion *f*, interkristalline Korrosion *f*
  graphitic corrosion graphitische Korrosion *f*
  intercrystalline corrosion Korngrenzenkorrosion *f*, interkristalline Korrosion *f*
  interdendritic corrosion {alloy castings} Korrosion *f* zwischen Dendriten {Gußlegierungen}
  intergranular corrosion Korngrenzenkorrosion *f*, interkristalline Korrosion *f*
  poultice corrosion Korrosion *f* unter Ablagerungen {z.B. Karosserieteile von Kraftfahrzeugen}
  selective corrosion selektive Korrosion *f*
  stray-current corrosion Streustromkorrosion *f*
  stress corrosion cracking <abb.: SCC> Spannungsrißkorrosion *f*, SRK, Spannungskorrosionsrißbildung *f*
  stress corrosion failure Spannungskorrosionsbruch *m*
  stress corrosion threshold Spannungskorrosionsschwellwert *m*
corrosive korrosiv
  corrosive wear korrosiver Verschleiß *m*
Cr → chromium
crack Riß *m*

crack

crack arrest Rißarretierung *f*, Rißauffang *m*, Rißarrest *m*
crack-arrest concept Rißarrestkonzept *n*
crack-arrest conditions Rißauffangbedingungen *fpl*
crack-arrest experiment Rißarrestexperiment *n*
crack-arrest force Rißauffangkraft *f*
crack-arrest marks *pl* Rißarreststreifen *mpl*
crack-arrest parameter Rißarrestparameter *m*
crack-arrest process Rißarrestvorgang *m*, Rißarrestprozeß *m*
crack-arrest safety analysis Rißarrestsicherheitsanalyse *f*
crack-arrest specimen Rißarrestprobe *f*
crack-arrest temperature Rißauffangtemperatur *f*
crack-arrest temperature curve Rißauffangtemperatur-Kurve *f*
crack-arrest test Rißauffangversuch *m*
crack-arrest toughness Rißauffangzähigkeit *f*, Rißarrestzähigkeit *f*
crack-arrest zone Rißarrestzone *f*
crack-closure energy Energie *f* des Rißschließens
crack-driving force Rißausbreitungskraft *f*
crack-free rißfrei
crack-growth criterion Rißwachstumskriterium *n*
crack-initiation temperature Rißeinleitungstemperatur *f*
crack-initiation toughness Rißeinleitungszähigkeit *f*
crack-like rißartig, rißähnlich
crack-line-wedge-loaded <abb.: CLWL> <syn.: specimen> CLWL-Probe *f*
crack at the inner surface Riß *m* auf der Innenfläche
crack at the outer surface Riß *m* auf der Außenfläche

crack growth rate Rißwachstumsrate *f* Rißwachstumsgeschwindigkeit *f*
crack growth resistance Rißausbreitungswiderstand *m*
crack growth stage Rißwachstumsstadium *n*
crack growth velocity Rißwachstumsgeschwindigkeit *f*
crack fissure Rißspalt *m*
crack increment Rißinkrement *n*
crack initiation Rißinitiierung *f*, Rißauslösung *f*, Rißeinleitung *f*
crack initiation concept Rißinitiierungskonzept *n*
crack initiation condition Rißinitiierungsbedingung *f*
crack initiation process Rißinitiierungsprozeß *m*
crack initiation stress-intensity factor Rißinitiierungs-Spannungsintensitätsfaktor *m*
crack initiation toughness Rißinitiierungszähigkeit *f*
crack instability Rißinstabilität *f*
crack length Rißlänge *f*
crack ligament Rißligament *f*
crack line Rißlinie *f*
crack line loading Belastung *f* quer zur Rißlänge
crack location Rißanordnung *f*
crack model Rißmodell *n*
crack nucleation Rißkeimbildung *f*
crack nucleus Rißkeim *m*
crack opening Rißöffnung *f*
crack opening displacement <abb.: COD> Rißöffnungsverschiebung *f*, COD
crack opening displacement criterion <abb.: COD> Rißöffnungsverschiebungskriterium *n*, COD-Kriterium *n*
crack opening factor Rißöffnungsfaktor *m*
crack opening measurement Rißöffnungsmessung *f*
crack opening modus Rißöffnungsart *f*, Rißöffnungsmodus *m*
crack orientation Rißorientierung *f*
crack origin Rißursprung *m*

crack path Rißlaufweg m, Rißpfad m
crack pattern Rißmuster n
crack periphery Randgebiet n des Risses, Rißumgebung f
crack plane Rißebene f
crack plane orientation Orientierung f der Rißebene
crack problem Rißproblem n
crack profile Rißprofil n
crack propagating Rißfortschreiten n
crack propagation Rißausbreitung f, Rißentwicklung f, Rißfortschritt m
crack-propagation behavio[u]r Rißausbreitungsverhalten n
crack-propagation calculation Rißausbreitungsberechnung f
crack-propagation characteristic Rißausbreitungscharakteristik f
crack-propagation conditions pl Rißausbreitungsbedingungen fpl
crack-propagation constant Rißausbreitungskonstante f
crack-propagation curve Rißausbreitungskurve f
crack-propagation data Rißausbreitungsdaten fpl
crack-propagation direction Rißausbreitungsrichtung f, RAR
crack-propagation displacement Rißfortschrittsverschiebung f
crack-propagation energy Rißausbreitungsenergie f
crack-propagation mechanism Rißausbreitungsmechanismus m
crack-propagation mode Rißausbreitungsart f
crack-propagation model Rißausbreitungsmodell n
crack-propagation pattern Rißausbreitungsschema n
crack-propagation problem Rißausbreitungsproblem n
crack-propagation process Rißausbreitungsvorgang m
crack-propagation rate Rißfortschrittsrate f
crack propagation resistance Rißausbreitungswiderstand m

crack-propagation study Rißausbreitungsuntersuchung f
crack-propagation test Rißausbreitungsversuch m
crack-propagation theory Rißausbreitungstheorie f
crack-propagation time Rißausbreitungszeit f
crack region Rißbereich m
crack resistance Rißwiderstand m, R
crack resistance curve, R-curve Rißwiderstandskurve f, R-Kurve f
crack section Rißquerschnitt m
crack shape Rißform f
crack size Rißgröße f, Rißabmessungen fpl
crack slit Rißspalt m
crack speed Rißgeschwindigkeit f
crack stability Rißstabilität f
crack start Rißstart m
crack starter Rißstarter m {Ausgangsstelle des Bruch[e]s}
crack starter notch Rißstarterkerbe f
crack surface Riß[ober]fläche f
crack surface displacement Rißflächenverschiebung f
crack system Rißsystem n, Rißgruppe f
crack tip Rißspitze f
crack-tip behavio[u]r Rißspitzenverhalten n
crack tip blunting Abstumpfung f (Abstumpfen n) der Rißspitze
crack-tip configuration Rißspitzenkonfiguration f
crack-tip contour Rißspitzenkontur f
crack-tip deformation Rißspitzenverformung f
crack-tip displacement Rißspitzenverschiebung f
crack-tip element Rißspitzenelement n
crack-tip extension Rißspitzenaufweitung f
crack-tip field Rißspitzenfeld n
crack-tip geometry Rißspitzengeometrie f

crack

crack-tip opening Rißspitzenöffnung *f*
crack tip opening displacement <abb.: CTOD> Rißspitzenöffnungsverschiebung *f*, CTOD
crack-tip plane strain ebene Dehnung *f* an der Rißspitze
crack-tip profile Rißspitzenprofil *n*
crack-tip region Rißspitzenbereich *m*
crack-tip shape Form *f* der Rißspitze, Rißspitzenform *f*
crack-tip singularity Rißspitzensingularität *f*
crack-tip stress Spannung *f* an der Rißspitze
crack-tip stress distribution Spannungsverteilung *f* an der Rißspitze
crack-tip stress-intensity factor Spannungsintensitätsfaktor *m* an der Rißspitze
crack-tip temperature Rißspitzentemperatur *f*
crack-tip velocity Rißspitzengeschwindigkeit *f*
crack-tip zone Rißspitzenzone *f*
crack toughness Rißzähigkeit *f*
crack toughness behavio[u]r Rißzähigkeitsverhalten *n*
crack toughness measurement Rißzähigkeitsmessung *f*
crack toughness test Rißzähigkeitsversuch *m*
crack toughness value Rißzähigkeitswert *m*
crack type Rißart *f*
crack velocity Rißgeschwindigkeit *f*
crack-velocity ga[u]ge Dehnungsmeßstreifen *m* für die Rißgeschwindigkeitsmessung *f*
crack width Rißbreite *f*
absolute crack size absolute Rißgröße *f*
accelerated crack propagation beschleunigte Rißausbreitung *f*
analysis of crack shape Rißformanalyse *f*
area around the crack tip Rißspitzenumfeld *n*

arrested crack arretierter Riß *m*, aufgefangener Riß *m*
average crack length mittlere Rißlänge *f*
blunt crack tip abgestumpfte Rißspitze *f*
border of crack propagation Rißausbreitungsgrenze *f*
branched crack verzweigter Riß *m*
branched crack problem Rißverzweigungsproblem *n*
brittle crack propagation spröde Rißausbreitung *f*
center crack Mittenriß *m*
change in crack length Rißlängenänderung *f*, Rißzuwachs *m*
Chevron crack starter notch Chevron-Rißstarterkerbe *f*
creep crack propagation Kriechrißausbreitung *f*
critical crack length kritische Rißlänge *f*
critical crack opening displacement kritische Rißöffnungsverschiebung *f*
critical crack size kritische Rißgröße *f*
critical crack tip opening kritische Rißspitzenöffnung *f*
cryogenic crack propagation test Tieftemperaturrißausbreitungsversuch *m*
current crack length aktuelle Rißlänge *f*
dependence from the crack length Rißlängenabhängigkeit *f*
determination of crack resistance curve Kurvenbestimmung *f* {Rißwiderstand}
determination of the crack length Rißlängenbestimmung *f*
distance from crack tip Abstand *m* von der Rißspitze
dominant crack Hauptriß *m*
double-edge crack {specimens} beidseitiger Riß *m* {Proben}
ductile crack propagation duktile Rißausbreitung *f*

Dugdale crack model Dugdale-Rißmodell *n*
dynamic crack initiation dynamische Rißeinleitung *f*
dynamic crack problem dynamisches Rißproblem *n*
dynamic crack propagation dynamische Rißausbreitung *f*
dynamic crack resistance curve dynamische Rißwiderstandskurve *f*
effective crack length effektive Rißlänge *f*, wirksame Rißlänge *f*
effective crack size effektive Rißgröße *f*
elastic crack problem elastisches Rißproblem *n*
elastic crack propagation elastische Rißausbreitung *f*
elastic-plastic crack problem elastisch-plastisches Rißproblem *n*
elasto-plastic crack problem elasto-plastisches Rißproblem *n*
equivalent crack length äquivalente Rißlänge *f*
fatigue crack length Ermüdungsrißlänge *f*
fatigue crack prediction Ermüdungsrißvorhersage *f*
fatigue crack production Ermüdungsrißerzeugung *f*
fatigue crack propagation test Ermüdungsrißausbreitungsversuch *m*
fatigue crack propagation <abb.: FCP> Ermüdungsrißausbreitung *f*
fatigue crack surface Ermüdungsrißfläche *f*
fatigue crack test Ermüdungsrißversuch *m*
fatigue crack threshold Ermüdungsrißschwellwert *m*
fatigue crack transition Ermüdungsrißübergang *m*
fictitious crack length fiktive Rißlänge *f*
fictitious crack tip fiktive Rißspitze *f*
final crack length Endrißlänge *f*
forked crack verzweigter Riß *m*
hairline crack Haarriß *m*

hardening crack Härteriß *m*
hot crack Warmriß *m*
hot tear Warmriß *m*
initial crack Ausgangsriß *m*
initial crack length Ausgangsrißlänge *f*
intercrystalline crack propagation interkristalline Rißausbreitung *f*
interface crack {material A/material B} Grenzflächenriß *m* {Werkstoff A/Werkstoff B}
local crack propagation lokale Rißausbreitung *f*
local crack resistance lokaler Rißwiderstand *m*, örtlicher Rißwiderstand *m*
location of crack initiation Rißeinleitungsort *m*
macroscopic direction of crack propagation makroskopische Rißausbreitungsrichtung *f*
main crack Hauptriß *m*
maximum crack resistance maximaler Rißwiderstand *m*
maximum crack velocity maximale Rißgeschwindigkeit *f*
measurement of crack length Rißlängenmessung *f*
measurement of crack propagation Rißausbreitungsmessung *f*
measurement of crack speed Rißgeschwindigkeitsmessung *f*
microductile crack propagation mikroduktile Rißausbreitung *f*
minimum crack speed {for branching} Mindestrißgeschwindigkeit *f* {für die Verzweigung}
mode of crack loading Rißbeanspruchungsart *f*
near crack tip in der Nähe der Rißspitze, rißspitzennah
neighbo[u]rhood of crack tip, crack tip vicinity Rißspitzenumgebung *f*
non-propagating crack ruhender Riß *m*
non-propagating crack tip ruhende Rißspitze *f*

crack

non-steady crack propagation instationäre Rißausbreitung *f*
nonlinear crack problem nichtlineares Rißproblem *n*
nucleation of cracks Rißkeimbildung *f*
optical measurement of crack length optische Rißlängenmessung *f*
orthotropic crack system orthotropes Rißsystem *n*
overall crack rate Gesamtrißgeschwindigkeit *f*
oxidation of the crack surface Rißflächenoxidation *f*
physical crack length physikalische Rißlänge *f*
plane crack problem ebenes Rißproblem *n*
plane elastic crack problem ebenes elastisches Rißproblem *n*
plastic crack propagation plastische Rißausbreitung *f*
quasi-static crack velocity quasistatische Rißgeschwindigkeit *f*
quasi-static crack initiation quasistatische Rißeinleitung *f*
quenching crack Härteriß *m*
radius of the crack tip Rißspitzenradius *m*
range of crack length Rißlängenbereich *m*
rapid crack propagation schnelle Rißausbreitung *f*
rate of fatigue crack propagation Ermüdungsrißausbreitungsgeschwindigkeit *f*
region of crack propagation Rißausbreitungsbereich *m*
relative crack length relative Rißlänge *f*
relative crack size relative Rißgröße *f*, relative Rißabmessungen *fpl*
secondary crack Nebenriß *m*
shape of crack tip Rißspitzenform *f*, Form *f* der Rißspitze
shatter crack Haarriß *m*
slip-band crack propagation Gleitbandrißausbreitung *f*

solidification shrinkage crack Warmriß *m*
stable crack propagation stabile Rißausbreitung *f*
stage of crack propagation Rißausbreitungsstadium *n*
starter crack Ausgangsriß *m*
starter crack length Ausgangsrißlänge *f*
stationary crack ruhender Riß *m*
steady-state crack propagation stationäre Rißausbreitung *f*
stopped crack aufgefangener Riß *m*, gestoppter Riß *m*
stress-free crack surface spannungsfreie Riß[ober]fläche *f*
subcritical crack growth < abb.: SCC > unterkritisches Rißwachstum *n*
subcritical crack propagation unterkritische (vorkritische) Rißausbreitung *f*
surface crack opening displacement < abb.: SCOD > Oberflächen-Rißöffnungs-Verschiebung *f*
symmetrically loaded crack system symmetrisch belastetes Rißsystem *n*
terminal crack velocity Endgeschwindigkeit *f* des Risses
three-dimensional crack problem dreidimensionales (räumliches) Rißproblem *n*
three-dimensional crack system dreidimensionales Rißsystem *n*
through-thickness crack specimen Probe *f* mit durchgehendem Riß
thumbnail crack {bend specimen} Daumennagel-Riß *m* {Biegeprobe}
total crack length Gesamtrißlänge
transcrystalline crack propagation transkristalline Rißausbreitung *f*
two-dimensional crack problem zweidimensionales (ebenes) Rißproblem *n*
two-dimensional crack system zweidimensionales Rißsystem *n*
unstable crack initiation instabile Rißauslösung *f*

unstable crack propagation instabile Rißausbreitung *f*
velocity of crack propagation Rißausbreitungsgeschwindigkeit *f*
criterion for crack-driving force Rißausbreitungskraft-Kriterium *n*
crystallographic crack-propagation model kristallographisches Rißausbreitungsmodell *n*
dynamic crack-propagation theory Theorie *f* der dynamischen Rißausbreitung
effective crack-intensity effektive Spannungsintensität *f*
elastic crack-tip extension elastische Rißspitzenaufweitung *f*
plastic crack-tip extension plastische Rißspitzenaufweitung *f*
vertical crack-front curvature vertikale Rißfrontkrümmung *f*
crack/to reißen, rissig werden
cracked gerissen, angerissen, rißbehaftet
cracked area rißbehafteter Bereich *m*
cracked plate gerissene Platte *f*
cracked strip Streifen *m* mit Riß
circumferentially cracked round bar specimen Rundstab *m* mit konzentrischem Außenriß
double-edge cracked tensile specimen zweiseitig angerissene Zugprobe *f*
single-edge cracked eyebar {type of specimen} einseitig angerissener Augenstab *m* {Probenform}
single-edge cracked flat tensile specimen Flachzugprobe *f* mit einseitigem Randriß
single-edge cracked strip Streifen *m* mit einseitigem Randriß
single-edge cracked tensile specimen einseitig angerissene Zugprobe *f*, Zugprobe *f* mit Einzelrandriß *m*
cracking Rißbildung *f*, Rißverlauf *m*
cracking mechanism Mechanismus *m* der Rißbildung

caustic cracking {stress-corrosion cracking} Laugenrissigkeit *f* {Spannungsrißkorrosion}
corrosion fatigue cracking Schwingungsrißkorrosion *f*
creep cracking Kriechrißbildung *f*
criterion of cracking Kriterium *n* für die Rißbildung
delayed cracking verzögerte Rißbildung *f*
environmental cracking Rißbildung *f* durch Umgebungseinflüsse
fatigue cracking Ermüdungsrißbildung *f*
hydrogen cracking wasserstoffinduzierte Rißbildung *f*
hydrogen-induced cracking <abb.: HIC> wasserstoffinduzierte Rißbildung *f*
hydrogen-induced delayed cracking wasserstoffinduzierte verzögerte Rißbildung *f*
intercrystalline cracking, intergranular cracking interkristalline Rißbildung *f*
intergranular stress-corrosion cracking interkristalline Spannungsrißkorrosion *f*
seasoning cracking {brass: corrosion + internal stress} Spannungsrißkorrosion *f* {Messing: Korrosion + innere Spannung}
secondary cracking sekundäre Rißbildung *f*, Bildung *f* von Nebenrissen
stepwise cracking stufenweise Rißbildung *f*
stress corrosion cracking <abb.: SCC> Spannungskorrosionsrißbildung *f*, Spannungsrißkorrosion *f*, SRK
surface cracking {of the specimen} Rißbildung *f* auf der Oberfläche {von Proben}
tendency to cracking Riß[bildungs]neigung *f*
transcrystalline cracking, transgranular cracking transkristalline Rißbildung *f*
cracks *pl* Risse *mpl*
collinear cracks Rißserie *f*

detection of cracks Rißnachweis *m*
equally spaced cracks *pl* gleichmäßig angeordnete Risse *mpl*
formation of cracks Rißbildung *f*
production of cracks {in specimens} Rißeinbringung *f*, Rißerzeugung *f* {in Proben}
craze Fließband *n*
creep {materials} Kriechen *n*, Fließen *n* {Werkstoffe}; Zeitstand-
creep behavio[u]r Kriechverhalten *n*
creep conditions Kriechbedingungen *fpl*
creep crack Kriechriß *m*
creep crack growth Kriechrißwachstum *n*
creep crack propagation Kriechrißausbreitung *f*
creep cracking Kriechrißbildung *f*
creep curve Kriechkurve *f*
creep fracture Kriechbruch *m*
creep limit Kriechgrenze *f*
creep rate Kriechgeschwindigkeit *f*
creep resistance Zeitstandfestigkeit *f*
creep rupture Kriechbruch *m*, Zeitstandbruch *m*
creeprupture strength Kriechbruchfestigkeit, Zeitstandversuch *m*
creeprupture test Zeitstandversuch *m*
creep strain Kriechdehnung *f*
creep strength Kriechfestigkeit *f*
creep temperature Kriechtemperatur *f*
creep test Kriechversuch *m*
creep zone Kriechbereich *m*, Kriechzone *f*
intergranular creep rupture intergranularer Kriechbruch *m*
primary creep primäres Kriechen *n*
steady-state creep < syn.: secondary creep > stationäres Kriechen *n*
transgranular creep rupture transkristalliner Kriechbruch *m*
transient creep Übergangskriechen *n*

creep/to {materials} kriechen, fließen {Werkstoffe}
crevice {defect} Spalt *m*
crevice corrosion Spaltkorrosion *f*
criteria *pl* Kriterien *mpl*
 design criteria Entwurfskriterien *npl*
 yield criteria Fließkriterien *npl*
criterion, criteria *pl* Kriterium *n*, Kriterien *npl*
criterion for buckling Knickkriterium *n*
criterion for crack-driving force Rißausbreitungskraft-Kriterium *n*
criterion for crack extension force Rißausbreitungskraft-Kriterium *n*
criterion for damage Schädigungskriterium *n*
criterion for deformation Deformationskriterium *n*
criterion for fracture Bruchkriterium *n*
criterion for fracture mechanics bruchmechanisches Kriterium *n*
criterion for fracture propagation Bruchausbreitungskriterium *n*
criterion for fracture safety Bruchsicherheitskriterium *n*
criterion for strain Dehnungskriterium *n*
criterion of brittle fracture Sprödbruchkriterium *n*
criterion of crack extension Rißerweiterungskriterium *n*
criterion of cracking Kriterium *n* für die Rißbildung
criterion of normal stresses Normalspannungskriterium *n*
cleavage fracture criterion Spaltbruchkriterium *n*
crack criterion Rißkriterium *n*
crack-growth criterion Rißwachstumskriterium *n*
crack opening displacement criterion < abb.: COD > **criterion** Rißöffnungsverschiebungskriterium *n*, COD-Kriterium *n*

displacement criterion Verschiebungskriterium n
distortion energy criterion Verzerrungsenergiekriterium n
elastic-plastic fracture criterion elastisch-plastisches Bruchkriterium n
energy criterion Energiekriterium n
failure criterion Versagenskriterium n
fracture criterion Bruchkriterium n
fracture mechanics criterion bruchmechanisches Kriterium n
fracture safety criterion Bruchsicherheitskriterium n
Griffith-Orowan-Irwin criterion {crack propagation} Griffith-Orowan-Irwin-Kriterium n {Rißausbreitung}
leak-before-break criterion Leck-vor-Bruch-Kriterium n
linear elastic fracture criterion linear-elastisches Bruchkriterium n
macroscopic criterion makroskopisches Kriterium n
macroscopic fracture criterion makroskopisches Bruchkriterium n
microscopic criterion mikroskopisches Kriterium n
microscopic fracture criterion mikroskopisches Bruchkriterium n
principal normal stress criterion Hauptnormalspannungskriterium n
stability criterion {Griffith crack} Stabilitätskriterium n {Griffith-Riß}
stress criterion Spannungskriterium n
tensile stress criterion Zugspannungskriterium n
Tresca's criterion Fließkriterium n nach Tresca, Tresca-Fließkriterium n
Tresca's yield criterion Fließkriterium n nach Tresca, Tresca-Fließkriterium n
von Mises' criterion Fließkriterium n nach von Mises, von Mises-Fließkriterium n
von Mises' yield criterion Fließkriterium n nach von Mises, von Mises-Fließkriterium n
critical kritisch
critical COD kritische Rißöffnungsverschiebung f
critical crack depth kritische Rißtiefe f
critical crack dimensions kritische Rißabmessungen fpl
critical crack length kritische Rißlänge f
critical crack opening displacement kritische Rißöffnungsverschiebung f
critical crack size kritische Rißgröße f
critical crack tip opening kritische Rißspitzenöffnung f
critical defect size kritische Fehlergröße f
critical energy release rate kritische Energiefreisetzungsrate f
critical J integral kritisches J-Integral n
critical load kritische Last f
critical pre-crack size kritische Anrißgröße f
critical size {of a crack} kritische Größe f {eines Risses}
critical specific fracture energy kritische spezifische Bruchenergie f
critical strain kritische Dehnung f
critical stress kritische Spannung f
critical stress-intensity factor kritischer Spannungsintensitätsfaktor m
critical stress of fracture kritische Bruchspannung f
critical temperatur kritische Temperatur f
critical tensile stress kritische Zugspannung f
critical velocity kritische Geschwindigkeit f
cross direction Querrichtung f
cross-breaking strength Knickfestigkeit f

cross-breaking (strength) test Knickfestigkeitsprüfung f
cross-section, section Querschnitt m
cross-sectional area Querschnittsfläche f
cross-section of the crack Rißquerschnitt m
cross slip {crystal} Quergleitung f {Kristall}
nominal cross-section of the crack Rißnennquerschnitt m
rectangular cross-section rechteckiger Querschnitt m
reduction in cross-section Querschnittsreduzierung f, Querschnittsverringerung f
specimen cross-section Probenquerschnitt m
crush test Stauchprobe f
crush/to stauchen, zerdrücken, zerquetschen; zerkleinern
crushing Stauchung f, Stauchen n
crushing failure Bruch m durch Stauchung
cryogenic Tieftemperatur-, Kälte-
cryogenic crack propagation test Tieftemperaturrißausbreitungsversuch m
cryogenic temperatures Temperaturen fpl im Bereich der Temperatur des flüssigen Stickstoffs
cryogenic test Tieftemperaturversuch m
crystal Kristall m
  crystal lattice Kristallgitter n
  crystal structure Kristallstruktur f
  imperfection of crystal Kristallbaufehler m
  single crystal Einkristall m
crystalline kristallin
  crystalline fracture kristalliner Bruch m, Trennbruch m
  plane of crystalline fracture Trennbruchebene f
crystallinity Kristallinität f
crystallographic kristallographisch

crystallographic crack-propagation model kristallographisches Rißausbreitungsmodell n
crystallographic plane Kristallebene f
Cs → caesium
CS → compact specimen
CT → compact tension...
CTOD → crack tip opening displacement
cubic kubisch, räumlich
  body-centered cubic kubisch-raumzentriert {Metall}
  coefficient of cubic expansion kubischer Ausdehnungskoeffizient m
  face-centered cubic kubisch-flächenzentriert {Metall}
cubical kubisch, räumlich
  coefficient of cubical expansion kubischer Ausdehnungskoeffizient m
  coefficient of cubical thermal expansion kubischer Wärmeausdehnungskoeffizient m
cumulative crack Zerrüttungsriß m
cumulative fracture kumulativer Bruch m, Zerrüttungsbruch m
cup fracture Becherbruch m
cup-cone fracture Kalotten-Tassen-Bruch m, Teller-Tassen-Bruch m
current aktuell, laufend
  current crack extension aktuelle Rißerweiterung f
  current crack length aktuelle Rißlänge f
  current stress state aktueller Spannungszustand m
curvature Krümmung f, Wölbung f
  crack front curvature Rißfrontkrümmung f, Krümmung f der Rißfront
  notch root radius of curvature Kerbgrund-Krümmungsradius m
  radius of curvature {at the end of a crack} Krümmungsradius m {Rißende}
  vertical crack-front curvature vertikale Rißfrontkrümmung f

curve Kurve *f*, Verlauf *m*, {Diagramme, Kennlinien}
  calibration curve Eichkurve *f*
  CAT curve Rißauffang-Temperatur-Kurve *f*
  COD design curve COD-Auslegungskurve *f*, COD-Konstruktionskurve *f*
  compressive residual stress curve Druckeigenspannungsverlauf *m*
  crack-arrest temperature curve Rißauffang-Temperatur-Kurve *f*
  crack growth curve Rißwachstumskurve *f*
  crack-propagation curve Rißausbreitungskurve *f*
  crack resistance curve, < syn.: R-curve Rißwiderstandskurve *f*, R-Kurve *f*
  creep curve Kriechkurve *f*
  determination of crack resistance curve R-Kurvenbestimmung *f* {R Rißwiderstand}
  dynamic crack resistance curve dynamische Rißwiderstandskurve *f*
  fatigue curve Ermüdungskurve *f*
  fracture curve {diagram} Bruchverlauf *m* {Diagramm}
  fracture resistance curve Bruchwiderstandskurve *f*
  hardening curve Verfestigungskurve *f*
  J integral design curve J-Integral-Auslegungskurve *f*
  load-deformation curve Last-Verformungs-Kurve *f*
  load-displacement curve Lastverschiebungskurve *f*
  load-extension curve Kraftverlängerungskurve *f*
  loading curve Beanspruchungsverlauf *m*
  non-linear load-displacement curve nichtlineare Lastverschiebungskurve *f*
  notch impact toughness-temperature curve Kerbschlagzähigkeits-Temperatur-Kurve *f*, Kerbschlagzähigkeits-Temperaturverlauf *m*
  R curve concept {R crack resistance} R-Kurven-Konzept *n* {R Rißwiderstand}
  R curve {R crack resistance} R-Kurve *f* {R Rißwiderstand}
  reference curve Referenzkurve *f*
  regression curve Regressionskurve *f*
  residual stress curve Eigenspannungsverlauf *m*
  S-N curve < syn.: S-N diagram > {S stress, N number of cycles to failure}, **Wöhler curve** Wöhler-Kurve *f*, Dauerfestigkeitskurve *f*
  stress-strain curve Spannungs-Dehnungs-Kurve *f*
  yield stress curve Fließspannungskurve *f*
curved gekrümmt
  curved crack gekrümmter Riß *m*
  curved crack front gekrümmte Rißfront *f*
cycle Zyklus *m*; Lastspiel *n*
  load cycle Lastwechsel *m*, Lastzyklus *m*, Lastspiel *n*
  loading cycle Beanspruchungswechsel *m*
  stress cycle Lastspiel *n*
cycles *pl* Zyklen *mpl*; Lastspiele *npl*
  load cycles *pl* Lastwechsel *mpl*, Lastspiele *npl*
  load cycles at fracture Bruchlastspielzahl *f*
  number of load cycles Lastwechselfrequenz *f*, Lastspielfrequenz *f*
cyclic zyklisch
  cyclic J integral zyklisches J-Integral *n*
  cyclic load Wechsellast *f*
  cyclic loading zyklische Beanspruchung *f*, zyklische Belastung *f*.
  cyclic plastic deformation zyklische plastische Verformung *f*

cyclic stress intensity zyklische Spannungsintensität f
cyclic stress-intensity factor zyklischer Spannungsintensitätsfaktor m {Rißwachstum bei schwingender Beanspruchung}
cyclic stress-strain behavio[u]r zyklisches Spannungs-Dehnungs-Verhalten n
constant amplitude cyclic loading zyklische Beanspruchung f mit konstanter Amplitude
effective cyclic stress-intensity effektive zyklische Spannungsintensität f
cylinder Zylinder m
  isotropic cylinder isotroper Zylinder m
  thick-walled cylinder dickwandiger Zylinder m
cylindrical zylindrisch
  cylindrical coordinates pl Zylinderkoordinaten fpl
  cylindrical pore zylindrische Pore f

D

damage Schädigung f, Schaden m
  damage of materials Werkstoffschädigung f
  damage process Schädigungsprozeß m
  criterion for damage Schädigungskriterium n
  hydrogen damage {embrittlement, cracking, blistering} Wasserstoffschädigung f, Schädigung f durch Wasserstoff {Versprödung, Rißbildung, Blasenbildung}
  permanent damage bleibende Schädigung f, dauerhafte Schädigung f
  radiation damage {materials} Strahlenschaden m {Werkstoffe}
damage/to schädigen
damaging Schädigung f
  damaging energy Schädigungsarbeit f
  damaging force Schädigungskraft f

data Daten fpl, Angaben fpl
  crack-propagation data Rißausbreitungsdaten pl
  fracture propagation data Bruchausbreitungsangaben fpl
  impact strength data Schlagfestigkeitsangaben fpl
  materials data Werkstoffdaten fpl
  test data Prüfergebnisse npl
DCB → double-cantilever beam
DCT → disk-shaped compact tensile (tension)...
decohesion Dekohäsion f; Trennung f
decompose/to zersetzen
decomposition Zersetzung f
  decomposition temperature Zersetzungstemperatur f
decrease/to verringern, vermindern, absenken {Belastung, Last}
decreasing of f load Lastabfall m, Lastabsenkung f
deep tief, tiefliegend
  deep crack tiefer Riß m, Tiefenriß m
  deep crack growth Tiefenrißwachstum n
deep-draw/to {metals} tiefziehen {Metalle}
deep-drawing {metals} Tiefziehen n {Metalle}
defect {in materials} Fehler m {in Werkstoffen}
  defect surface fehlerhafte Oberfläche f
  casting defect Gußfehler m
  critical defect size kritische Fehlergröße f
  edge defect Kantenfehler m
  elliptical defect ellipsenförmiger Fehler m, elliptischer Fehler m
  isolated defect Einzelfehler m
  material defect Werkstofffehler m
  single defect Einzelfehler m
  surface defect, surface flaw Oberflächendefekt m
defect-free fehlerfrei
deflection Durchbiegung f

heat deflection temperature Formbeständigkeit f in der Wärme
temperature of deflection under load Formbeständigkeit f in der Wärme
deform/to verformen, deformieren
deformability Verformbarkeit f, Verformungsfähigkeit f
deformable verformbar
  permanent deformation bleibende Verformung f
deformation Deformation f, Formänderung f, Verformung f
  deformation band Deformationsband n
  deformation behavio[u]r Verformungsverhalten n
  deformation constraint Deformationsbehinderung f, Verformungsbehinderung f
  deformation field Verformungsfeld n
  deformation force Verformungskraft f
  deformation gradient Verformungsgradient m
  deformation of specimen Probenverformung f
  deformation properties pl Verformungseigenschaften fpl
  deformation rate Deformationsgeschwindigkeit f, Verformungsgeschwindigkeit f
  deformation resistance Verformungswiderstand m
  deformation state Verformungszustand m
  deformation tensor Verformungstensor m
  deformation testing machine Verformungs-Prüfmaschine f, Maschine f zur Prüfung der Verformung
  deformation under heat Formbeständigkeit f in der Wärme
  deformation zone {crack} Verformungsgebiet n {Riß}
  analysis of deformation Verformungsanalyse f
  cold deformation Kaltverformung f
  compressive deformation Druckverformung f, Deformation f infolge Druckbeanspruchung
  constant deformation konstante Verformung f
  crack-tip deformation Rißspitzenverformung f
  criterion for deformation Deformationskriterium n
  cyclic plastic deformation zyklische plastische Verformung f
  degree of deformation Verformungsgrad m
  direction of deformation Verformungsrichtung f
  elastic deformation elastische Verformung f
  elastic deformation energy elastische Verformungsenergie f
  elastic energy of deformation elastische Formänderungsenergie f
  elastic-plastic deformation elastisch-plastische Verformung f
  energy of deformation Verformungsenergie f
  energy of plastic deformation plastische Verformungsenergie f
  factor of deformation energy density {fracture criterion} Verformungsenergiedichtefaktor m {Bruchkriterium}
  finite deformation endliche Verformung f
  hinge-type deformation scharnierförmige Verformung f
  homogeneous deformation homogene Verformung f
  incompressible deformation inkompressible Deformation f
  inelastic deformation unelastische Verformung f
  infinitesimal deformation infinitesimale Verformung f
  inhomogeneous deformation inhomogene Verformung f
  linear-elastic deformation linear-elastische Verformung f

degradation

linear elastic deformation field linear-elastisches Verformungsfeld *n*
low-pressure deformation tester Niederdruck-Verformungsprüfgerät *n*
plane deformation state ebener Verformungszustand *m*
plastic deformation plastische Deformation *f*, plastische Verformung *f*
resistance to deformation Verformungswiderstand *m*
rigid-body deformation Starrkörperverformung *f*
slip deformation Gleitdeformation *f*
state of plane deformation ebener Verformungszustand *m*
static deformation statische Verformung *f*
stress deformation field Spannungsverformungsfeld *n*
tensile deformation Zugverformung *f*
theory of deformation Deformationstheorie *f*
three-dimensional deformation dreidimensionale Verformung *f*
time-dependent deformation zeitabhängige Verformung *f*
two-dimensional deformation ebene Verformung *f*, zweidimensionale Verformung *f*
two-dimensional deformation field zweidimensionales Verformungsfeld *n*
two-dimensional linear-elastic deformation field zweidimensionales linear-elastisches Verformungsfeld *n*
wedge-type deformation keilförmige Verformung *f*
degradation {materials: surface} Abbau *m*, Zersetzung *f* {Metalle: Oberflächen}
degradation behavio[u]r Abbauverhalten *n*
mechanical degradation mechanischer Abbau *m*

degrade/to {metals: surface} abbauen, zersetzen {Metalle: Oberflächen}
degree Grad *m*
degree of deformation Verformungsgrad *m*
degree of flammability Entflammbarkeitsgrad *m*
degree of homogeneity Homogenitätsgrad *m*
delamination Delamination *f*, Ablösung *f*
delamination fracture Delaminationsbruch *m*
delay {crack propagation} Verzögerung *f* {Rißausbreitung}
crack growth delay Rißwachstumsverzögerung *f*
fatigue crack delay Ermüdungsrißverzögerung *f*
delay/to {crack propagation} verzögern {Rißausbreitung}
delayed cracking verzögerte Rißbildung *f*
delayed fracture verzögerter Bruch *m*
hydrogen-induced delayed cracking wasserstoffinduzierte verzögerte Rißbildung *f*
dendrite {crystal} Dendrit *m* {Kristall}
denickelification {corrosion} Entnickelung *f* {Korrosion}
density Dichte *f*
dislocation density Versetzungsdichte *f*
factor of deformation energy density {fracture criterion} Verformungsenergiedichtefaktor *m* {Bruchkriterium}
strain-energy density Dehnungsenergiedichte *f*
strain energy density Verzerrungsenergiedichte *f*
dependence Abhängigkeit *f*
dependence from the crack length Rißlängenabhängigkeit *f*

angular dependence Winkelabhängigkeit *f*
pressure dependence Druckabhängigkeit *f*
temperature dependence {of properties} Temperaturabhängigkeit *f* {von Eigenschaften}
depletion {alloy} Verarmung *f* {Legierung}
deposit Ablagerung *f*
  deposit attack Korrosion *f* unter Ablagerungen {z.B. Karosserieteile von Kraftfahrzeugen}
  deposit corrosion Korrosion *f* unter Ablagerungen {z.B. Karosserieteile von Kraftfahrzeugen}
depth Tiefe *f*
  crack depth, depth of crack Rißtiefe *f*
  critical crack depth kritische Rißtiefe *f*
  detectable crack depth nachweisbare Rißtiefe *f*
  determination of crack depth Rißtiefenbestimmung *f*
  effective depth of crack effektive Rißtiefe *f*
  initial depth {surface crack} Anfangstiefe *f* {Oberflächenriß}
  measurement of crack depth Rißtiefenmessung *f*
  notch depth Kerbtiefe *f*
  relative crack depth relative Rißtiefe *f*
  specimen depth Probentiefe *f*
design Entwurf *m*, Konstruktion *f*
  design criteria *pl* Entwurfskriterien *npl*, Konstruktionskriterien *npl*
  COD design curve COD-Auslegungskurve *f*, COD-Konstruktionskurve *f*
  J integral design curve J-Integral-Auslegungskurve *f*
  specimen design Probenform *f*
design/to {structure} auslegen {Konstruktion}, entwerfen
destroy/to zerstören

destruction Zerstörung *f*
destructive zerstörend
detect/to {e.g. cracks in materials} nachweisen {z.B. Risse in Werkstoffen}
detectability Nachweisbarkeit *f*
detectable nachweisbar
  detectable crack nachweisbarer Riß *m*
  detectable crack depth nachweisbare Rißtiefe *f*
detection Nachweis *m*
  detection of cracks Rißnachweis *m*
  detection {e.g. of cracks in materials} Nachweis *m* {z.B. von Rissen in Werkstoffen}
  stress detection Spannungsnachweis *m*
determination Bestimmung *f*
  determination of crack depth Rißtiefenbestimmung *f*
  determination of crack resistance curve R-Kurvenbestimmung *f*
  determination of service life Lebensdauerermittlung *f*
  determination of the crack length Rißlängenbestimmung *f*
  experimental determination experimentelle Bestimmung *f*
  soft point determination Erweichungspunktbestimmung *f*, Bestimmung *f* des Erweichungspunktes
determining Bestimmung *f*, Bestimmen *n*
  non-steady state method of determining instationäres Bestimmungsverfahren *n*
deviate/to abweichen
deviation Abweichung *f*
  crack deviation Rißumlenkung *f*
  standard deviation Standardabweichung *f*
  stress deviation Spannungsumlagerung *f*
device Gerät *n*, Vorrichtung *f*
  clamping device Einspannvorrichtung *f*

dezincification 38

fastening device Befestigungselement *n*
dezincification {corrosion} Entzinkung *f* {Korrosion}
diagram Diagramm *n*, Schaubild *n*
　fracture analysis diagram <abb.: FAD> Bruchanalysendiagramm *n*
　fracture safety diagram Bruchsicherheits-Diagramm *n*
　load COD diagram Belastung-COD-Diagramm *n*
　load-deformation diagram Last-Verformungs-Diagramm *n*
　S-N curve <syn.: S-N diagram {S stress, N number of cycles to failure}>, <syn.: Wöhler curve> Wöhler-Kurve *f*, Dauerfestigkeitskurve *f*
　stress-crack extension diagram Spannungsrißaufweitungsdiagramm *n*, Spannungsrißaufweitungskurve *f*
　stress-strain diagram Spannungs-Dehnungs-Diagramm *n*
diameter Durchmesser *m*
　diameter of dimples Grübchendurchmesser *m*
　inside diameter {of the specimen} Innendurchmesser *m* {von Proben}
　outside diameter {of the specimen} Außendurchmesser *m* {von Proben}
　void diameter Porendurchmesser *m*
differential calorimetry Differentialkalorimetrie *f*
differential thermal analysis <abb.: DTA> Differentialthermoanalyse *f*, DTA
diffuse/to diffundieren
diffusion Diffusion *f*
　diffusion rate, diffusion velocity Diffusionsgeschwindigkeit *f*
dilatation {of materials} Ausdehnung *f* {von Werkstoffen}
dilate/to {materials} ausdehnen {Werkstoffe}

dilatometer {for determination of thermal expansion} Dilatometer *n* {zur Bestimmung der thermischen Ausdehnung}
dilatometry {determination of thermal expansion} Dilatometrie *f* {Bestimmung der thermischen Ausdehnung}
dimension Dimension *f*
dimension/to dimensionieren
dimonsional dimensional; Maß-
　dimensional change Maßänderung *f*
　dimensional stability test Formstabilitätsprüfung *f*, Prüfung *f* der Formstabilität
dimensioning Dimensionierung *f*
dimensionless dimensionslos
　dimensionless plastic zone dimensionslose plastische Zone *f*
　dimensionless stress dimensionslose Spannung *f*
　dimensionless stress intensity factor dimensionsloser Spannungsintensitätsfaktor *m*
dimensions *pl* Abmessungen *fpl*
　critical crack dimensions *pl* kritische Rißabmessungen *fpl*
　initial dimensions *pl* Anfangsabmessungen *fpl*
　minimum dimensions {specimens} Mindestabmessungen *fpl* {Proben}
　notch dimensions *pl* Kerbabmessungen *fpl*
　specimen dimensions *pl* Probenabmessungen *fpl*
　tensile bar dimensions *pl* Zugstababmessungen *fpl*
dimple {fracture surface} Grübchen *n* {Bruchfläche}
　dimple fracture, dimple rupture Grübchenbruch *m*
　dimple size Grübchengröße *f*
　intergranular dimple fracture intergranularer Grübchenbruch *m*
　oval dimple {dimple rupture} ovales Grübchen *n* {Grübchenbruch}
dimples *pl* Grübchen *npl*

diameter of dimples Grübchendurchmesser *m*
elongated dimples *pl* {dimple fracture} langgestreckte Grübchen *npl*, längliche Grübchen *npl* {Grübchenbruch}
shallow dimples *pl* {fracture surface} muldenförmige Grübchen *npl* {Bruchfläche}
shape of dimples {dimple rupture} Grübchenform *f*, Gestalt *f* der Grübchen {Grübchenbruch}
direct direkt
direct measurement direkte Messung *f*
direction Richtung *f*
direction of crack extension Rißausbreitungsrichtung *f*, RAR
direction of crack growth Rißwachstumsrichtung *f*
direction of deformation Verformungsrichtung *f*
direction of fracture Bruchrichtung *f*
direction of loading Beanspruchungsrichtung *f*, Lastrichtung *f*
crack direction Rißrichtung *f*
crack-propagation direction Rißausbreitungsrichtung *f*, RAR
cross direction Querrichtung *f*
fracture propagation direction Bruchausbreitungsrichtung *f*
loading direction Belastungssituation *f*, Lastrichtung *f*
longitudinal direction Längsrichtung *f*
macroscopic direction of crack propagation makroskopische Rißausbreitungsrichtung *f*
macroscopic direction of fracture propagation makroskopische Bruchausbreitungsrichtung *f*
principal loading direction Hauptbelastungsrichtung *f*
transverse direction Querrichtung *f*
disc {GB}, **disk** {US} Scheibe *f*
discontinuity Diskontinuität *f*, Unstetigkeit *f*

discontinuous diskontinuierlich, unterbrochen
disk {US}, **disc** {GB} Scheibe *f*
disk-shaped compact tensile (tension) <abb.: DCT>... scheibenförmige Kompaktzug-, DCT-
disk-shaped compact [tensile] specimen, DCT specimen scheibenförmige Kompaktzugprobe *f*, DCT-Probe *f*
disk-shaped tensile specimen Rundscheiben-Zugprobe *f*
standard disk-shaped compact (tension) specimen Standard-Rundscheiben-Zugprobe *f*
dislocation Versetzung *f*
dislocation array Versetzungskonfiguration *f*
dislocation barrier Versetzungshindernis *n*
dislocation density Versetzungsdichte *f*
dislocation distribution Versetzungsverteilung *f*
dislocation line Versetzungslinie *f*
dislocation loop Versetzungsring *m*
dislocation model Versetzungsmodell *n*
dislocation node Versetzungsknoten *m*
dislocation row Versetzungsreihe *f*
dislocation structure {e.g. at crack tip} Versetzungsstruktur *f* {z.B. an der Rißspitze}
dislocation theory Versetzungstheorie *f*
dislocation velocity Versetzungsgeschwindigkeit *f*
edge dislocation Stufenversetzung *f*
locked dislocation blockierte Versetzung *f*
patterns of dislocation Versetzungsanordnung *f*
screw dislocation Schraubenversetzung *f*
dislocations *pl* Versetzungen *fpl*
movement of dislocations Versetzungsbewegung *f*

displacement

multiplication of dislocations Versetzungsvervielfältigung *f*
pile-up of dislocations Versetzungsaufstauung *f*
displacement Verschiebung *f*
displacement criterion Verschiebungskriterium *n*
displacement field Verschiebungsfeld *n*
displacement function Verschiebungsfunktion *f*
displacement gradient Verschiebungsgradient *m*
displacement measurement Verschiebungsmessung *f*
displacement vector Verschiebungsvektor *m*
component of displacement Verschiebungskomponente *f*
crack flank displacement Rißflankenverschiebung *f*
crack front displacement Rißfrontverlagerung *f*
crack opening displacement <abb.: COD> Rißöffnungsverschiebung *f*, COD
crack opening displacement <abb.: COD> **criterion** Rißöffnungsverschiebungskriterium *n*, COD-Kriterium *n*
crack-propagation displacement Rißfortschrittsverschiebung *f*
crack surface displacement Rißflächenverschiebung *f*
crack-tip displacement Rißspitzenverschiebung *f*
crack tip opening displacement <abb.: CTOD> Rißspitzenöffnungsverschiebung *f*, CTOD
critical crack opening displacement kritische Rißöffnungsverschiebung *f*
local displacement lokale Verschiebung *f*
rigid-body displacement Starrkörperverschiebung *f*
surface crack opening displacement <abb.: SCOD> Oberflächen-Rißöffnungs-Verschiebung *f*

transverse displacement Verschiebung *f* in Längsrichtung, transversale Verschiebung *f*
dissipation {e.g. of energy} Verlust *m* {z.B. Energie}, Freisetzung *f*
energy dissipation Energieverlust *m*
distance Abstand *m*
distance along the crack Abstand *m* in Rißrichtung
distance between the clamps Einspannweite *f* {von Proben}
distance from crack tip Abstand *m* von der Rißspitze
distortion Verzerrung *f*
distortion energy criterion Verzerrungsenergiekriterium *n*
heat distortion point <syn.: **heat distortion temperature**> Formbeständigkeit *f* in der Wärme
distribution Verteilung *f*
bending stress distribution Biegespannungsverteilung *f*
crack-tip stress distribution Spannungsverteilung *f* an der Rißspitze
dislocation distribution Versetzungsverteilung *f*
dynamic stress distribution dynamische Spannungsverteilung *f*
elastic-plastic stress distribution elastisch-plastische Spannungsverteilung *f*
homogeneous distribution of stresses homogene Spannungsverteilung *f*
inhomogeneous slip distribution inhomoge Gleitverteilung *f*
inhomogeneous stress distribution inhomogene Spannungsverteilung *f*
linear load distribution lineare Lastverteilung *f*
linear strain distribution lineare Dehnungsverteilung *f*
load distribution Lastverteilung *f*, Verteilung *f* der Belastung
normal stress distribution Normalspannungsverteilung *f*
residual stress distribution Eigenspannungsverteilung *f*

shear stress distribution Schubspannungsverteilung *f*
strain distribution Dehnungsverteilung *f*
stress distribution, distribution of stress[es] {e.g. at crack tip} Spannungsverteilung *f*, Spannungsverlauf *m* {z.B. vor der Rißspitze}
stress-intensity distribution Spannungsintensitätsverteilung *f*
stress-intensity factor distribution Spannungsfaktorverteilung *f*
temperature distribution Temperaturverteilung *f*
three-dimensional stress distribution dreidimensionale Spannungsverteilung *f*
dog-bone model {of the plastic zone} Hundeknochen-Modell *n*, dog-bone-Modell *n* {der plastischen Zone}
dominant crack, main crack Hauptriß *m*
dominant-crack front Hauptrißfront *f*
double doppelt, Doppel-
double-cantilever beam specimen <abb.: DCB> **specimen** Doppelbalken[biege]probe *f*, DCB-Probe *f*
double-edge crack symmetrischer Kantenriß *m*
double-edge crack {specimens} beidseitiger Riß *m* {Proben}
double-edge cracked tensile specimen zweiseitig angerissene Zugprobe *f*
double-edge notches *pl* Doppelkerbe *f*
double-edge-notched specimen Doppelkerbprobe *f*
double torsion <abb.: DT> **specimen** Doppeltorsionsprobe *f*, DT-Probe *f*
tapered double-cantilever beam <abb.: TDCB> **specimen** keilförmige Doppelbalkenprobe *f*, konische Doppelbalken[biege]probe *f*, TDCB-Probe *f*

drop test Fallversuch *m*
drop-weight Fallgewicht *n*
drop-weight energy Fallgewichtsenergie *f*
drop-weight tear test specimen Probe *f* für den Fallgewichtsscherversuch, Probe *f* für den DWTT-Versuch
drop-weight tear test <abb.: DWTT> Fallgewichtsscherversuch *m*, DWTT-Versuch *m*
drop-weight test <abb.: DWT> Fallgewichtsversuch *m*, DWT-Versuch *m*, Fallgewichtsprüfung *f*
drop-weight test apparatus Prüfeinrichtung *f* für den Fallgewichtsversuch, Prüfeinrichtung *f* für den DWT-Versuch
drop-weight test <abb.: DWT> **specimen** Probe *f* für den Fallgewichtsversuch, Probe *f* für den DWT-Versuch
standard drop-weight test <abb.: DWT> **specimen, standard DWT specimen** Standardprobe *f* für den Fallgewichtsversuch, Standardprobe *f* für DWT-Versuch
DT..., double torsion... Doppeltorsions-, DT-
double torsion <abb.: DT> **specimen** Doppeltorsions-Probe *f*, DT-Probe *f*
DTA → differential thermal analysis
DT test <syn.: dynamic tear test> dynamische Reißprobe *f*, DT-Prüfung *f*
ductile duktil, zäh, dehnbar, verformbar
ductile behavio[u]r {of materials} duktiles Verhalten *n*, zähes Verhalten *n* {von Werkstoffen}
ductile-brittle transition Zäh-Spröd[e]-Übergang *m*
ductile crack propagation duktile Rißausbreitung *f*
ductile fatigue fracture duktiler Schwingbruch *m*

ductility

ductile fracture duktiler Bruch *m*, zäher Bruch *m*, Zähbruch *m*
ductile fracture behavio[u]r zähes Bruchverhalten *n*
ductile iron duktiles Eisen *n*
ductile material duktiler Werkstoff *m*, zäher Werkstoff *m*
ductile matrix duktile Matrix *f*
ductile overload fracture duktiler Gewaltbruch *m*
ductile state duktiler Zustand *m*
ductile tensile fracture duktiler Zugbruch *m*
ductile-to-brittle transition temperature Zäh-Spröd[e]-Übergangstemperatur *f*
ductile-to-brittle-transition Duktil-Spröd[e]-Übergang *m*
  anisotropic ductile material anisotroper duktiler Werkstoff *m*
  isotropic ductile material isotroper duktiler Werkstoff *m*
  pearlitic ductile iron perlitisches duktiles Eisen *n*
  rate-sensitive ductile material geschwindigkeitsempfindlicher duktiler Werkstoff *m*
ductility Duktilität *f*, Dehnbarkeit *f*, Verformbarkeit *f*
  fracture ductility Ermüdungsduktilität *f*
  measurement of ductility Duktilitätsmessung *f*
  nil ductility temperature < abb.: NDT > NDT-Temperatur *f* {Grenztemperatur, bei der ein Riß nicht mehr aufgehalten werden kann}
Dugdale
  Dugdale-Barenblatt model {elastic crack problem} Dugdale-Barenblatt-Modell {elastisches Rißproblem}
  Dugdale crack Dugdale-Riß *m*
  Dugdale crack model Dugdale-Rißmodell *n*
  Dugdale model {crack formation} Dugdale-Modell *n* {Rißbildung}
duplex specimen {bimaterial interface} Duplex-Probe *f*

DWT → drop-weight test
DWTT → drop-weight tear test...
Dy → dysprosion
dynamic dynamisch
  dynamic constant dynamische Konstante *f*
  dynamic crack behavio[u]r dynamisches Rißverhalten *n*
  dynamic crack growth dynamisches Rißwachstum *n*
  dynamic crack initiation dynamische Rißeinleitung *f*
  dynamic crack problem dynamisches Rißproblem *n*
  dynamic crack propagation dynamische Rißausbreitung *f*
  dynamic crack-propagation theory Theorie *f* der dynamischen Rißausbreitung
  dynamic crack resistance curve dynamische Rißwiderstandskurve *f*
  dynamic energy release dynamische Energiefreisetzung *f*
  dynamic energy release rate dynamische Energiefreisetzungsrate *f*
  dynamic fracture dynamischer Bruch *m*
  dynamic fracture testing dynamische Bruchprüfung *f*
  dynamic fracture toughness dynamische Bruchzähigkeit *f*
  dynamic fracture toughness value dynamischer Bruchzähigkeitswert *m*
  dynamic loading dynamische Beanspruchung *f*, dynamische Belastung *f*
  dynamic photoelasticity dynamische Spannungsoptik *f*
  dynamic singularity dynamische Singularität *f*
  dynamic stress analysis dynamische Spannungsanalyse *f*
  dynamic stress distribution dynamische Spannungsverteilung *f*
  dynamic stress intensity dynamische Spannungsintensität *f*
  dynamic stress-intensity factor dynamischer Spannungsintensitätsfaktor *m*

dynamic tear test dynamische Reißprüfung f, DT-Prüfung f
dynamic tear test specimen dynamische Reißprobe f, DT-Probe f
dynamic test method dynamische Prüfmethode f, Prüfmethode f mit dynamischer Beanspruchung
dynamic theory of elasticity dynamische Elastizitätstheorie f
concept of dynamic crack arrest dynamisches Rißarrest-Konzept n
two-dimensional dynamic photoelasticity ebene dynamische Spannungsoptik f
Dynstat equipment Dynstat-Prüfmaschine f
dysprosium, Dy Dysprosium, Dy

E

eddy-current method {detection of cracks} Wirbelstromverfahren n {Nachweis von Rissen}
edge Kante f, Rand m {von Proben}
edge crack Kantenriß m, Randriß m
edge defect Kantenfehler m
edge dislocation Stufenversetzung f
edge notch Randkerbe f
edge of the specimen Probenrand m, Probenberandung f
crack edge Rißkante f
radial edge crack radialer Kantenriß m
single edge crack Einzelrandriß m
through-the-thickness edge crack durchgehender Randriß m
transitional edge crack durchgehender Randriß m
EDX → energy-dispersive x-ray spectrometry
effect Effekt m; Einfluß m
 Bauschinger effect Bauschinger-Effekt m
 effect of geometry Geometrieeinfluß m
 effect of hardening Verfestigungseffekt m
 effect of notch Kerbeinfluß m, Kerbwirkung f
 notch effect Kerbwirkung f
 overload effect Überlastwirkung f
 permanent effect of heat {on plastics} Dauerwärmeeinwirkung f, Langzeitwärmeeinwirkung f
 temperature effect Temperatureinfluß m
 thickness effect {specimens} Dickeneinfluß m {Proben}
effective effektiv, wirksam
effective crack effektiver Riß m
effective crack extension effektive Rißerweiterung f
effective crack extension force effektive Rißerweiterungskraft f
effective crack-intensity effektive Spannungsintensität f
effective crack length effective Rißlänge f, wirksame Rißlänge f
effective crack size effektive Rißgröße f
effective cyclic stress-intensity effektive zyklische Spannungsintensität f
effective depth of crack effektive Rißtiefe f
effective plastic zone effektive plastische Zone f
effective radius wirksamer Radius m
effective stress effektive Spannung f
effective stress-intensity factor effektiver Spannungsintensitätsfaktor m
effective surface energy effektive Oberflächenenergie f
effects pl Einflüsse mpl
 environmental effects pl Umgebungseinflüsse mpl
eigenfunction of crack Rißeigenfunktion f
elastic elastisch
 elastic body elastischer Körper m
 elastic boundary-value problem elastisches Grenzwertproblem n
 elastic brittle fracture elastischer Sprödbruch m

elastic compliance elastische Nachgiebigkeit f
elastic constants pl Elastizitätskonstanten fpl
elastic constraint elastische Behinderung f
elastic crack elastischer Riß m
elastic crack problem elastisches Rißproblem n
elastic crack propagation elastische Rißausbeitung f
elastic crack-tip extension elastische Rißspitzenaufweitung f
elastic deformation elastische Verformung f
elastic deformation energy elastische Verformungsenergie f
elastic energy elastische Energie f
elastic energy of deformation elastische Formänderungsenergie f
elastic failure elastisches Versagen n
elastic fracture elastischer Bruch m
elastic fracture mechanics elastische Bruchmechanik f
elastic instability elastische Instabilität f
elastic limit Elastizitätsgrenze f
elastic limit load elastische Grenzlast f
elastic loading elastische Belastung f
elastic material elastischer Werkstoff m
elastic material behavio[u]r elastisches Werkstoffverhalten n
elastic modulus in bend Elastizitätsmodul m aus dem Biegeversuch
elastic-plastic analysis elastischplastische Analyse f
elastic-plastic analysis of fracture elastisch-plastische Bruchanalyse f
elastic-plastic behavio[u]r elastisch-plastisches Verhalten n
elastic-plastic body elastisch-plastischer Körper m
elastic-plastic boundary value problem elastisch-plastisches Randwertproblem n
elastic-plastic crack problem elastisch-plastisches Rißproblem n
elastic-plastic deformation elastisch-plastische Verformung f
elastic-plastic fracture elastischplastischer Bruch m
elastic-plastic fracture criterion elastisch-plastisches Bruchkriterium n
elastic-plastic fracture instability elastisch-plastische Inkompressibilität f
elastic-plastic fracture mechanics <abb.: EPFM> elastisch-plastische Bruchmechanik f, EPBM
elastic-plastic material elastischplastischer Werkstoff m
elastic-plastic material behavio[u]r elastisch-plastisches Werkstoffverhalten n
elastic-plastic state elastisch-plastischer Zustand m
elastic-plastic stress distribution elastisch-plastische Spannungsverteilung f
elastic-plastic stress-strain behavio[u]r elastisch-plastisches Spannungs-Dehnungs-Verhalten n
elastic singularity elastische Singularität f
elastic strain elastische Dehnung f
elastic strain energy elastische Dehnungsenergie f
elastic stress elastische Spannung f
elastic stress analysis elastische Spannungsanalyse f
elastic stress concentration elastische Spannungskonzentration f
elastic stress-concentration factor elastischer Spannungskonzentrationsfaktor m
elastic stress field elastisches Spannungsfeld n
elastic zone elastische Zone f
anisotropic elastic body anisotroper elastischer Körper m
concept of elastic-plastic fracture mechanics Fließbruchmechanik-Konzept n
equivalent elastic crack äquivalenter elastischer Riß m

isotropic elastic material isotroper elastischer Werkstofff *m*
linear elastic deformation field linear-elastisches Verformungsfeld *n*
linear elastic fracture criterion linear-elastisches Bruchkriterium *n*
linear elastic hardening linear-elastische Verfestigung *f*
linear elastic stress field linear-elastisches Spannungsfeld *n*
nonlinear elastic fracture mechanics nichtlinear-elastische Bruchmechanik *f*
plane elastic crack problem ebenes elastisches Rißproblem *n*
rate of elastic straining elastische Dehnungsgeschwindigkeit *f*, Geschwindigkeit *f* der elastischen Dehnung
three-dimensional elastic stress analysis dreidimensionale elastische Spannungsanalyse *f*
elastically-deformed elastisch verformt
elastically-deformed steel elastisch verformter Stahl *m*
elasticity Elastizität *f*
anisotropic elasticity anisotrope Elastizität *f*
dynamic theory of elasticity dynamische Elastizitätstheorie *f*
isotropic elasticity isotrope Elastizität *f*
limit of elasticity Elastizitätsgrenze *f*
modulus of elasticity Elastizitätsmodul *m*, E-Modul *m*
nonlinear elasticity nichtlineare Elastizität *f*
theory of elasticity Elastizitätstheorie *f*
three-dimensional elasticity dreidimensionale Elastizität *f*
volumetric modulus of elasticity Kompressionsmodul *m*
elasto-plastic elasto-plastisch
elasto-plastic crack problem elasto-plastisches Rißproblem *n*
elasto-plastic fracture behavio[u]r elasto-plastisches Bruchverhalten *n*
elasto-plastic parameter elasto-plastischer Kennwert *m*
elasto-plastic stress elasto-plastische Spannung *f*
elasto-dynamic problem elasto-dynamisches Problem *n*
electric potential method {determination of crack depth} Potentialsondenverfahren *n* {Rißtiefenbestimmung}
electrical test method elektrische Prüfmethode *f*
electrolytic corrosion elektrolytische Korrosion *f*
electron Elektron *n* Elektronen-
electron fractography Elektronenfraktographie *f*
electron microscopy Elektronenmikroskopie *f*
electron probe microanalysis <abb.: EPMA> Mikrosondenanalyse *f*
electron spectroscopy for chemical analysis <abb.: ESCA> Elektronenspektroskopie *f* für die chemische Analyse
Auger electron spectroscopy <abb.: AES> Auger-Elektronenspektroskopie *f*, AES
scanning electron microscope Rasterelektronenmikroskop *n*, REM
scanning electron microscopy Rasterelektronenmikroskopie *f*, REM
transmission electron microscope <abb.: TEM> Transmissions-Elektronenmikroskop *n*, TEM
transmission electron microscopy <abb.: TEM> Transmissions-Elektronenmikroskopie *f*, TEM
element Bauteil *n*; Element *n*
element geometry Bauteilgeometrie *f*
element of singularity Singularitätselement *n*
element strength Bauteilfestigkeit *f*

alloying element Legierungselement *n*
crack-tip element Rißspitzenelement *n*
finite element method <abb.: **FEM**> Finite-Element-Methode *f*, FEM
fracture mechanics element {e.g. **element of singularity**} Bruchmechanikelement *n* {z.B. Singularitätselement}
stiffening element Versteifungselement *n*
testing of element Bauteilprüfung *f*
thickness of element Bauteildicke *f*
volume element Volumenelement *n*
width of element Bauteilbreite *f*
elevate/to erhöhen
elevated temperature erhöhte Temperatur *f*
elevated-temperature failure Ausfall *m* bei erhöhten Temperaturen
short-time stability at elevated temperature Kurzzeitbeständigkeit *f* bei erhöhter Temperatur
ellipse Ellipse *f*
ellipsoidal ellipsoidisch, ellipsoidförmig
ellipsoidal void ellipsoidförmiger Hohlraum *m*
elliptical elliptisch, ellipsenförmig
elliptical defect ellipsenförmiger Fehler *m*, elliptischer Fehler *m*
elliptical flaw ellipsenförmiger Fehler *m*, elliptischer Fehler *m*
elliptical hole elliptische Bohrung *f*
elliptical internal crack ellipsenförmiger Innenriß *m*, elliptischer Innenriß *m*
elliptical notch elliptische Kerbe *f*
elliptical surface crack elliptischer Oberflächenriß *m*
elongated dimples *pl* {dimple fracture} langgestreckte Grübchen *npl*, längliche Grübchen *npl* {Grübchenbruch}
elongation Verlängerung *f*

plastic-zone elongation Verlängerung *f* der plastischen Zone
embedded crack eingeschlossener Riß *m*
embrittle/to verspröden, spröd[e] werden
embrittled specimen versprödete Probe *f*
embrittled steel versprödeter Stahl *m*
embrittlement Versprödung *f*
adsorption-induced embrittlement adsorptionsinduzierte Versprödung *f*
caustic embrittlement Laugenrissigkeit *f* {Spannungsrißkorrosion}
environmentally assisted embrittlement umgebungsbegünstigte Versprödung *f*
hydrogen embrittlement Wasserstoffversprödung *f*
liquid-metal embrittlement <abb.: **LME**> Versprödung *f* bei Kontakt mit schmelzflüssigen Metallen
material embrittlement Werkstoffversprödung *f*
neutron embrittlement Versprödung *f* durch Neutronenstrahlung
radiation-induced embrittlement Strahlungsversprödung *f*
solid-metal embrittlement <abb.: **SME**> Versprödung *f* mit festen (nichtschmelzflüssigen) Metallen
temper embrittlement Anlaßversprödung *f*
emission Emission *f*
acoustic emission Schallemission *f*
acoustic emission analysis Schallemissionsanalyse *f*, SEA
acoustic emission inspection Schallemissionsprüfung *f*
stress wave emission Spannungswellenemission *f*
empirical empirisch
end Ende *n*
end face of the specimen Probenstirnseite *f*
end of the crack Rißende *n*
end of the notch Kerbende *n*
end of the specimen Probenende *n*

end-region size of crack Größe ƒ der Rißspitze
endurance Dauerhaftigkeit ƒ, Dauer-
endurance test Dauerversuch m
thermal endurance Dauerwärmebeständigkeit ƒ
energy Energie ƒ
energy absorption Energieaufnahme ƒ
energy balance Energiegleichgewicht n {bei der Rißausbreitung}
energy concept {concept of fracture mechanics} Energie-Konzept n {Konzept der Bruchmechanik}
energy consumption Energieverbrauch m
energy criterion Energiekriterium n
energy dissipation Energieverlust m
energy generation {at crack tip} Energieerzeugung ƒ {an der Rißspitze}
energy of crack extension Rißerweiterungsenergie ƒ
energy of deformation Verformungsenergie ƒ
energy of fracture Bruchenergie ƒ
energy of plastic deformation plastische Verformungsenergie ƒ
energy release Energiefreisetzung ƒ
energy release rate Energieanlieferungsrate ƒ
activation energy Aktivierungsenergie ƒ
crack-closure energy Energie ƒ des Rißschließens
crack-growth energy release rate Rißwachstums-Energiefreisetzungsrate ƒ
crack-propagation energy Rißausbreitungsenergie ƒ
critical energy release rate kritische Energiefreisetzungsrate ƒ
critical specific fracture energy kritische spezifische Bruchenergie ƒ
damaging energy Schädigungsarbeit ƒ
distortion energy criterion Verzerrungsenergiekriterium n

drop-weight energy Fallgewichtsenergie ƒ
dynamic energy release dynamische Energiefreisetzung ƒ
dynamic energy release rate dynamische Energiefreisetzungsrate ƒ
effective surface energy effektive Oberflächenenergie ƒ
elastic deformation energy elastische Verformungsenergie ƒ
elastic energy elastische Energie ƒ
elastic energy of deformation elastische Formänderungsenergie ƒ
elastic strain energy elastische Dehnungsenergie ƒ
factor of deformation energy density {fracture criterion} Verformungsenergiedichtefaktor m {Bruchkriterium}
formation energy of crack Rißbildungsenergie ƒ
fracture energy Bruchenergie ƒ
impact energy {Izod test, Charpy test} Schlagenergie ƒ {Izod-Versuch, Charpy-Versuch}
internal energy innere Energie ƒ
kinetic energy kinetische Energie ƒ
low energy fracture energiearmer Bruch m
potential energy potentielle Energie ƒ
specific fracture energy < syn.: **specific energy of fracture** > spezifische Bruchenergie ƒ
specific surface energy spezifische Oberflächenenergie ƒ
stacking fault energy {crystal} Stapelfehlerenergie ƒ {Kristall}
strain energy Dehnungsenergie ƒ, Verzerrungsenergie ƒ
strain energy density Verzerrungsenergiedichte ƒ
strain energy release rate Verzerrungsenergie-Freisetzungsrate ƒ
strain rate energy Dehnungsgeschwindigkeitsenergie ƒ
surface energy Oberflächenenergie ƒ
true surface energy wahre Oberflächenenergie ƒ

energy-dispersive x-ray spectrometry <abb.: EDX> energiedispersive Röntgenspektrometrie *f*
engineering fracture mechanics Ingenieur-Bruchmechanik *f*
enthalpy Enthalpie *f*
entropy Entropie *f*
environment Umgebung *f*
environmental Umgebungs-
environmental cracking Rißbildung *f* durch Umgebungseinflüsse
environmental effects *pl* Umgebungseinflüsse *mpl*
environmental temperature Umgebungstemperatur *f*
environmentally assisted embrittlement umgebungsbegünstigte Versprödung *f*
EPFM → elastic-plastic fracture mechanics
EPMA → electron probe microanalysis
equally spaced cracks *pl* gleichmäßig angeordnete Risse *mpl*
equation Gleichung *f*
  basic equation Grundgleichung *f*
  fracture mechanics equation Bruchmechanik-Gleichung *f*
  wave equation Wellengleichung *f*
equilibrium Gleichgewicht *n*
  equilibrium crack Gleichgewichtsriß *m* {freigesetzte Energie Oberflächenenergie des Risses}
  state equilibrium statisches Gleichgewicht *n*
equivalence Äquivalenz *f*
equivalent äquivalent, Ersatz-
  equivalent crack Ersatzriß *m* {bei theoretischen Betrachtungen}
  equivalent crack length äquivalente Rißlänge *f*
  equivalent elastic crack äquivalenter elastischer Riß *m*
  equivalent stationary crack äquivalenter ruhender Riß *m*
  equivalent stress äquivalente Spannung *f*, Ersatzspannung *f*
  circular equivalent crack kreisrunder Ersatzriß *m*
Er → erbium
erbium, Er Erbium *n*, Er
erosion {destruction of materials} Erosion *f* {Werkstoffzerstörung}
  brittle erosion behavio[u]r sprödes Erosionsverhalten *n*
  cavitation erosion Kavitationserosion *f*
erosion-corrosion Strömungskorrosion *f*, Erosionskorrosion *f*
error {computation} Fehler *m* {Berechnung}
ESCA → electron spectroscopy for chemical analysis
estimate/to einschätzen
estimation Einschätzung *f*
ETT → explosion tear test
europium, Eu Europium *n*, Eu
evaluate/to abschätzen
evaluation Abschätzung *f*
  evaluation of safety Sicherheitsabschätzung *f*, Sicherheitsbewertung *f*
  macroscopic evaluation of fracture surface makroskopische Bruchflächenbewertung *f*
exact genau
exfoliate/to abblättern
exfoliation Abblättern *n*
expansion Ausdehnung *f*
  average coefficient of linear thermal expansion mittlerer linearer Wärmeausdehnungskoeffizient *m*
  coefficient of cubic expansion kubischer Ausdehnungskoeffizient *m*
  coefficient of cubical expansion kubischer Ausdehnungskoeffizient *m*
  coefficient of cubical thermal expansion kubischer Wärmeausdehnungskoeffizient *m*
  coefficient of expansion Ausdehnungskoeffizient *m*
  coefficient of linear expansion linearer Ausdehnungskoeffizient *m*

coefficient of linear thermal expansion linearer Wärmeausdehnungskoeffizient m
linear expansion apparatus Gerät n zur Bestimmung der linearen Ausdehnung
linear expansion measurement Messung f der linearen Ausdehnung
thermal expansion Wärmeausdehnung f, thermische Ausdehnung f
experiment Experiment n, Versuch m
blank experiment Blindversuch m
crack-arrest experiment Rißarrestexperiment n
experimental experimentell
experimental determination experimentelle Bestimmung f
experimental method of measurement experimentelles Meßverfahren n
experimental arrangement, test arrangement Versuchsanordnung f
explosion tear test <abb.: ETT> Explosions-Ausbeul-Versuch m
explosion tear test <abb.: ETT> **specimen** Probe f für den Explosions-Beulungsversuch
exponent Exponent m
crack growth exponent Rißwachstumsexponent m
hardening exponent Verfestigungsexponent m
extend/to erweitern
extending crack sich erweiternder Riß m
extensibility Dehnbarkeit f
extensibility after heat ag[e]ing Dehnbarkeit f nach Wärmealterung
extension {cracks} Erweiterung f, Aufweitung f, Breitenwachstum n {Risse}
angle of crack extension Rißausbreitungswinkel m
catastrophic crack extension katastrophenartige Rißerweiterung f
crack extension Rißaufweitung f, Rißvergrößerung f

crack extension force Rißausbreitungskraft f, Rißerweiterungskraft f, Rißvergrößerungskraft f
crack-tip extension Rißspitzenaufweitung f
criterion for crack extension force Rißerweiterungskraft-Kriterium n
criterion of crack extension Rißerweiterungskriterium n
current crack extension aktuelle Rißerweiterung f
direction of crack extension Rißerweiterungsrichtung f
effective crack extension effektive Rißerweiterung f
effective crack extension force effektive Rißerweiterungskraft f
elastic crack-tip extension elastische Rißspitzenaufweitung f
energy of crack extension Rißerweiterungsenergie f
normalized crack extension normierte Rißöffnung f
notch extension Kerbaufweitung f, Kerböffnung f
plastic crack-tip extension plastische Rißspitzenaufweitung f
process of crack extension Rißerweiterungsvorgang m
quasi-static crack extension quasistatische Rißerweiterung f
rate of extension Dehn[ungs]geschwindigkeit f
spontaneous crack extension spontane Rißerweiterung f
stable crack extension stabile Rißerweiterung f
steady-state crack extension stationäre Rißaufweitung f, stationäre Rißerweiterung f
stress-crack extension diagram Spannungsrißaufweitungsdiagramm n, Spannungsrißaufweitungskurve f
unstable crack extension instabile Rißerweiterung f
virtual crack extension <abb.: VCE> scheinbare Rißerweiterung f
extensometer Dehnungsmeßgerät n

external

external äußere, Außen-
external compressive load äußere Druckbelastung f
external crack äußerer Riß m
external force äußere Kraft f
external load äußere Last f
  circular external crack kreisförmiger Außenriß m
  sharp external notch scharfer Außenkerb m
extrapolate/to extrapolieren
extrapolation Extrapolation f
extrusion {fatigue fracture} Herauspressung f {Ermüdungsbruch}
eyebar {test specimen} Augenstab m {Prüfkörper}
  single-edge cracked eyebar {type of specimen} einseitig angerissener Augenstab m {Probenform}

F

F → fluorine
face Fläche f
  face-centered cubic < abb.: fcc > kubisch-flächenzentriert, kfz {Metall}
  face temperature Flächentemperatur f
  crack face Rißfläche f
  end face of the specimen Probenstirnseite f
facet Facette f
  intercrystalline facet interkristalline Facette f
  quasi-cleavage facet {fracture surface} Quasi-Spaltbruch-Facette f {Bruchfläche}
  transcrystalline facet transkristalline Facette f
factor Faktor m, Beiwert m
  factor of deformation energy density {fracture criterion} Verformungsenergiedichtefaktor m {Bruchkriterium}
  factor of safety Sicherheitsbeiwert m
  bending stress-intensity factor Biegespannungsintensitätsfaktor m
  constraint factor Behinderungsfaktor m
  corrective factor Korrekturfaktor m
  crack initiation stress-intensity factor Rißinitiierungs-Spannungsintensitätsfaktor m
  crack opening factor Rißöffnungsfaktor m
  crack-tip stress-intensity factor Spannungsintensitätsfaktor m an der Rißspitze
  critical stress-intensity factor kritischer Spannungsintensitätsfaktor m
  cyclic stress-intensity factor zyklischer Spannungsintensitätsfaktor m {Rißwachstum bei schwingender Beanspruchung}
  dimensionless stress intensity factor dimensionsloser Spannungsintensitätsfaktor m
  dynamic stress-intensity factor dynamischer Spannungsintensitätsfaktor m
  effective stress-intensity factor effektiver Spannungsintensitätsfaktor m
  elastic stress-concentration factor elastischer Spannungskonzentrationsfaktor m
  fatigue notch factor {unnotched specimen/notched specimen} Kerbwirkungszahl f {ungekerbte Probe/gekerbte Probe}
  fictitious stress-intensity factor fiktiver Spannungsintensitätsfaktor m
  load concentration factor Lastkonzentrationsfaktor m
  local stress factor örtlicher Spannungsfaktor m
  macroscopic stress-intensity factor makroskopischer Spannungsintensitätsfaktor m
  plastic strain concentration factor plastischer Dehnungskonzentrationsfaktor m
  plastic stress-concentration factor plastischer Spannungskonzentrationsfaktor m

reference stress-intensity factor Referenzspannungsintensitätsfaktor *m*
retention factor Verzögerungsfaktor *m*
safety factor Sicherheitsbeiwert *m*
shape factor Formfaktor *m*
static stress-intensity factor statischer Spannungsintensitätsfaktor *m*
strain concentration factor Dehnungskonzentrationsfaktor *m*
strain-intensity factor Dehnungsintensitätsfaktor *m*
stress concentration factor Spannungskonzentrationsfaktor *f*
stress-intensity factor Spannungs[intensitäts]faktor *m*
stress-intensity factor curve Spannungsintensitätsfaktorkurve *f*
stress-intensity factor distribution Spannungsfaktorverteilung *f*
stress-intensity factor value Spannungsintensitätsfaktorwert *m*
theoretical stress concentration factor theoretischer Spannungskonzentrationsfaktor *m*
FAD → failure analysis diagram
FAD → failure assessment diagram
FAD → fracture analysis diagram
fail-safe Versagenssicherheit *f*
fail/to versagen, ausfallen, zu Bruch gehen
failure Ausfall *m*, Versagen *n*, Schaden[sfall] *m*; Fehler *m* {im Sinne von Schaden}; Bruch *m*
failure analysis Schadens[fall]analyse *f*, Fehleranalyse *f*
failure-analysis diagram < abb.: FAD > Versagensanalyse-Diagramm *n*, VAD
failure assessment Versagensbeurteilung *f*
failure-assessment-diagram < abb.: FAD > Fehler-Abschätzungs-Diagramm *n*, FAD
failure conditions *pl* Versagensbedingungen *fpl*

failure criterion Versagenskriterium *n*
failure hypothesis Versagenshypothese *f*
failure load Versagenslast *f*
failure probability Versagenswahrscheinlichkeit *f*, Ausfallwahrscheinlichkeit *f*
failure research Schadensforschung *f*
angle of failure Bruchwinkel *m*
brittle failure Sprödbruch *m*
catastrophic failure katastrophenartiger Bruch *m*
cause of failure Schadensursache *f*
cleavage failure Spaltbruch *m*
corrosion failure Ausfall *m* durch Korrosion
corrosion-fatigue failure Ausfall *m* durch Korrosionsermüdung
crack failure Rißschaden *m*
crushing failure Bruch *m* durch Stauchung
elastic failure elastisches Versagen *n*
elevated-temperature failure Ausfall *m* bei erhöhten Temperaturen
fatigue failure Versagen *n* durch Ermüdung, Dauerschwingungsbruch *m*
initiation of failure Versagenseinleitung *f*
low-temperature failure Kältebruchtemperatur *f* {bei Biegebeanspruchung}
oblique failure schräger Bruch *m*
particles failure Teilchenbruch *m* {das Brechen von z.B. harten Teilchen}
percentage shear failure Scherbruchanteil *m*
plastic failure plastisches Versagen *n*
random failure zufälliger Ausfall *m*, zufälliger Bruch *m*
service failure analysis Betriebsschadensanalyse *f*
service failure {of structures} Betriebsversagen *n* {von Konstruktionen}, Betriebsschaden *m*
stress corrosion failure Spannungskorrosionsbruch *m*

falling

time to failure Zeit *f* bis zum Bruch
falling weight impact strength apparatus Kugelfallprüfmaschine *f* {zur Bestimmung der Schlagzähigkeit}
impact energy Schlagenergie *f*
falling-weight test Kugelfallprobe *f*
family of curves Kurvenschar *f*
fasten/to befestigen
fastening Befestigung *f*, Befestigen *n*
fastening device Befestigungselement *n*
fatigue Ermüdung *f*
fatigue behavio[u]r Ermüdungsverhalten *n*
fatigue bending test Dauerbiegeversuch *m*
fatigue condition Ermüdungsbedingung *f*
fatigue crack Dauerriß *m*, Dauerschwingriß *m*, Ermüdungsriß *m*, Schwingungsriß *m*
fatigue crack acceleration Ermüdungsrißbeschleunigung *f*
fatigue crack closure Schließen *n* des Ermüdungsrisses
fatigue crack delay Ermüdungsrißverzögerung *f*
fatigue crack growth Ermüdungsrißwachstum *n*
fatigue crack growth rate Ermüdungsrißgeschwindigkeit *f*
fatigue crack length Ermüdungsrißlänge *f*
fatigue crack prediction Ermüdungsrißvorhersage *f*
fatigue crack production Ermüdungsrißerzeugung *f*
fatigue crack propagation test Ermüdungsrißausbreitungsversuch *m*
fatigue crack propagation <abb.: FCP> Ermüdungsrißausbreitung *f*
fatigue crack surface Ermüdungsrißfläche *f*
fatigue crack test Ermüdungsrißversuch *m*
fatigue crack threshold Ermüdungsrißschwellwert *m*

fatigue crack transition Ermüdungsrißübergang *m*
fatigue cracking Ermüdungsrißbildung *f*
fatigue curve Ermüdungskurve *f*
fatigue failure Versagen *n* durch Ermüdung, Dauerschwingungsbruch *m*
fatigue fracture Schwing[ungs]bruch *m*, Dauerbruch *m*, Ermüdungsbruch *m*
fatigue fracture surface Schwingungsbruchfläche *f*, Dauerbruchfläche *f* Ermüdungsbruchfläche *f*
fatigue fracture zone Ermüdungsbruchzone *f*
fatigue limit Ermüdungsgrenze *f*
fatigue load Ermüdungsbelastung *f*
fatigue loading Ermüdungsbeanspruchung *f*
fatigue mechanism Ermüdungsmechanismus *m*
fatigue notch factor {unnotched specimen/notched specimen} Kerbwirkungszahl *f* {ungekerbte Probe/gekerbte Probe}
fatigue of materials Werkstoffermüdung *f*
fatigue pre-crack Dauerschwinganriß *m*, Dauerbruchanriß *m*, Ermüdungsanriß *m*
fatigue pre-crack length Ermüdungsanrißlänge *f*
fatigue strength Dauerfestigkeit *f*, Dauerschwingfestigkeit *f*, Ermüdungsfestigkeit *f*
fatigue test Ermüdungsversuch *m*
fatigue wear Verschleiß *m* durch Werkstoffermüdung
bending fatigue Dauerbiegebeanspruchung *f*
bending fatigue test Dauerbiegeprüfung *f*
biaxial fatigue zweiachsige Ermüdung *f*
blunt fatigue crack abgestumpfter Ermüdungsriß *m*
brittle fatigue spröder Bruch *m*
brittle fatigue fracture spröder Schwingungsbruch *m*

corrosion fatigue Korrosionsermüdung *f*
corrosion fatigue crack Korrosionsermüdungsriß *m*
corrosion fatigue crack growth Korrosionsermüdungsrißwachstum *n*
corrosion fatigue cracking Schwingungsrißkorrosion *f*
ductile fatigue fracture duktiler Schwingbruch *m*
fretting fatigue Ermüdung *f* durch Reibverschleiß
intercrystalline-transcrystalline fatigue fracture interkristallinertranskristalliner Ermüdungsbruch *m*
intergranular fatigue fracture intergranularer Ermüdungsbruch *m*
low-cycle fatigue niederzyklische Ermüdung *f*
mechanism of fatigue Ermüdungsmechanismus *m*
rate of fatigue crack propagation Ermüdungsrißausbreitungsgeschwindigkeit *f*
short fatigue crack kurzer Ermüdungsriß *m*
static fatigue statische Ermüdung *f*
symmetrical fatigue fracture symmetrischer Ermüdungsbruch *m*
thermal fatigue thermische Ermüdung *f*, Ermüdung *f* durch Wärmebeanspruchung
thermal fatigue strength thermische Dauerfestigkeit *f*
torsion fatigue fracture Torsionsschwingbruch *m*
fatigue/to {materials} ermüden {Werkstoffe}
FATT → fracture appearance transition temperature
fault Fehler *m*
  stacking fault {crystal} Stapelfehler *m* {Kristall}
  stacking fault energy {crystal} Stapelfehlerenergie *f* {Kristall}
fcc → face-centered cubic
FCP → fatigue crack propagation
Fe → iron

FEM → finite element method
ferrite Ferrit *m*
ferritic ferritisch
  ferritic iron-alumin[i]um alloy ferritische Eisen-Aluminium-Legierung *f*
  ferritic stainless steel ferritischer nichtrostender Stahl *m*
  ferritic steel ferritischer Stahl *m*
ferrous metals *pl* Eisenmetalle *npl*
fiber {US}, **fibre** {GB} Faser *f*
  fiber-reinforced composite faserverstärkter Werkstoff *m*
  fiber stress Faserspannung *f*
  glass fiber Fiberglas *n*, Glasfaser *f*
  outer fiber {materials} Außenfaser *f* {Werkstoffe}
fibers *pl* Fasern *fpl*
  nominal stress of outer fibers Randfaser-Nennspannung *f*
  stress of outer fibers Randfaserspannung *f*
fibrous fas(e)rig
  fibrous fracture Faserbruch *m*, fas[e]riger Bruch *m*
  fibrous structure {wrought iron} Faserstruktur *f* {Schmiedeeisen}
fictitious fiktiv
  fictitious crack fiktiver Riß *m*, Fiktivriß *m*
  fictitious crack length fiktive Rißlänge *f*
  fictitious crack tip fiktive Rißspitze *f*
  fictitious fracture toughness fiktive Bruchzähigkeit *f*
  fictitious stress-intensity factor fiktiver Spannungsintensitätsfaktor *m*
field Feld *n*
  biaxial tensile stress field zweiachsiges Zugspannungsfeld *n*
  compressive residual stress field Druckeigenspannungsfeld *n*
  crack field Rißfeld *n*
  crack-tip field Rißspitzenfeld *n*
  deformation field Verformungsfeld *n*
  displacement field Verschiebungsfeld *n*

elastic stress field elastisches Spannungsfeld *n*
homogeneous field of stress homogenes Spannungsfeld *n*
inhomogeneous stress field inhomogenes Spannungsfeld *n*
isotropic stress field isotropes Spannungsfeld *n*
linear elastic deformation field linear-elastisches Verformungsfeld *n*
linear elastic stress field linear-elastisches Spannungsfeld *n*
local stress field lokales Spannungsfeld *n*
non-uniform stress field ungleichförmiges Spannungsfeld *n*
residual stress field Eigenspannungsfeld *n*
slip-line field Gleitlinienfeld *n*
static stress field statisches Spannungsfeld *n*
strain field Dehnungsfeld *n*
stress deformation field Spannungsverformungsfeld *n*
stress-displacement field Spannungs-Verschiebungsfeld *n*
stress field Spannungsfeld *n*
two-dimensional deformation field zweidimensionales Verformungsfeld *n*
two-dimensional linear-elastic deformation field zweidimensionales linear-elastisches Verformungsfeld *n*
two-dimensional stress field zweidimensionales Spannungsfeld *n*
filler metal Zusatzmetall *n*
final letzte(r,s); End-
  final crack length Endrißlänge *f*
  final thickness {of specimen} Enddicke *f* {der Probe nach Beendigung der Prüfung}
finishing {metals} Feinbearbeitung *f*, Fertigbearbeitung *f* {Metalle}
finite endlich
  finite crack Riß *m* mit endlicher Länge, endlicher Riß *m*
  finite deformation endliche Verformung *f*

finite element method < abb.:
FEM > Finite-Element-Methode *f*, FEM
finite stress {at crack tip} endliche Spannung *f* {an der Rißspitze}
fire Feuer *n*, Brand *m*
fire-crack {metals} Brandriß *m* {Metalle}
fire propagation test Prüfung *f* der Brandausbreitung
fire test Brennbarkeitsprüfung *f*
fisheye {defect on fracture surface} Fischauge *n* {Fehler auf Bruchflächen}
fishmouthing {metal surface} "Krokodilhaut" *f* {Metalloberfläche}
fissure Riß *m*
  crack fissure Rißspalt *m*
fix/to befestigen
fixing Befestigung *f*, Befestigen *n*
flake {ferrous metals} Haarriß *m* {Eisenmetalle}
flame Flamme *f*
  flame resistance Flammfestigkeit *f*
  flame spread distance Flammenausbreitung *f*
  flame test Flammprüfung *f*, Flammprobe *f*, Flammtest *m*, Flammversuch *m*
  resistance to flame propagation Flammenausbreitungswiderstand *m*
  resistant to flame propagation beständig gegenüber Flammenausbreitung *f*
  spread of flame Brennlänge *f* {bei der Flammenausbreitung}
  test for flame resistance Flammfestigkeitsprüfung *f*
flame/to beflammen {eine Probe}
flaming Beflammen *n*, Flammbehandlung *f*
flammability Entflammbarkeit *f*
flammability apparatus Entflammbarkeits-Prüfgerät *n*
flammability test Entflammbarkeitsprüfung *f*

degree of flammability Entflammbarkeitsgrad *m*
surface flammability {of materials} Entflammbarkeit *f* der Oberfläche {von Werkstoffen}
flank Flanke *f*
crack flank Rißflanke *f*
crack flank displacement Rißflankenverschiebung *f*
rotation of crack flank Rißflankendrehung *f*
stress-free crack flank spannungsfreie Rißflanke *f*
flash ignition temperature Selbstentzündungstemperatur *f*
flat flach
flat fracture ebener Bruch *m*
flat specimen Flachprobe *f*
center-cracked flat specimen Flachprobe *f* mit Mittelriß
center-cracked flat tensile specimen Flachzugprobe *f* mit Mittelriß
single-edge cracked flat tensile specimen Flachzugprobe *f* mit einseitigem Randriß
single-edge notched flat tensile specimen einseitig gekerbte Flachzugprobe *f*
single-edge-cracked flat specimen Flachprobe *f* mit einseitigem Randriß
flaw {in materials} Fehler *m* {in Werkstoffen}
flaw-free fehlerfrei
flaw position {in materials} Fehlerstelle *f* {in Werkstoffen}
flaw size {flaw in materials} Fehlergröße *f* {Fehler in Werkstoffen}
flaw source {in materials} Fehlerquelle *f* {in Werkstoffen}
elliptical flaw ellipsenförmiger Fehler *m*, elliptischer Fehler *m*
material flaw Werkstoffehler *m*
quarter-elliptical flaw Viertelellipsenfehler *m*
semi-elliptical surface flaw halbelliptischer Oberflächenfehler *m*
surface flaw Oberflächenfehler *m*

surface flaw specimen Probe *f* mit Oberflächenfehler
flex cracking method Rißbiegeprüfung *f*
flex/to {the specimen} biegen {eine Probe}
flexibility Biegsamkeit *f*, Flexibilität *f*
flexibility test Prüfung *f* der Biegsamkeit
flexible biegsam, flexibel
flexible plastic biegsamer Kunststoff *m*
flexing tester Biegeprüfgerät *n*
flexural impact strength measurement Messung *f* der Schlagbiegefestigkeit
flexural modulus Biegemodul *m*
flexural strength Biegefestigkeit *f*
impact flexural test Schlagbiegeprüfung *f*, Schlagbiegeversuch *m*
fluid Flüssigkeit *f*
flow/to fließen
flow {element of material} Fließen *n* {Werkstoffelement}
flow lines *pl* {materials} Fließlinien *fpl* {Werkstoffe}
heat flow Wärmeströmung *f*
heat flow meter Wärmeströmungsmeßgerät *n*
plastic flow plastisches Fließen *n*
fluorine, F Fluor *n*, F
flutes *pl* {metal surface} Riefen *fpl*, Rillen *fpl* {Metalloberfläche}
fluting {metal surface} Riefenbildung *f*, Rillenbildung *f* {Metalloberfläche}
fold {defect in metal} Falte *f* {Metallfehler}
force Kraft *f*
force at fracture Bruchkraft *f*
cohesive force Kohäsionskraft *f*
concentrated force punktförmig angreifende Kraft *f*
constant force konstante Kraft *f*
crack-arrest force Rißauffangkraft *f*

crack-driving force Rißausbreitungskraft *f*
crack extension force Rißerweiterungskraft *f*, Rißaufweitungskraft *f*, Rißvergrößerungskraft *f*
criterion for crack-driving force Rißausbreitungskraft-Kriterium *n*
criterion for crack extension force Rißaufweitungskraft-Kriterium *n*
damaging force Schädigungskraft *f*
deformation force Verformungskraft *f*
effective crack extension force effektive Rißerweiterungskraft *f*
external force äußere Kraft *f*
internal force innere Kraft *f*
normal force Normalkraft *f*
point force Einzelkraft *f*
shear force Schubkraft *f*
split force Spaltkraft *f*
surface force Oberflächenkraft *f*
tangential force Tangentialkraft *f*
tensile force Zugkraft *f*
wedge force Aufkeilungskraft *f*
forging crack Schmiederiß *m*
form Form *f*, Gestalt *f*
form of specimen Probenform *f*
plastic zone form Form *f* der plastischen Zone
formation Bildung *f*, Herausbildung *f*, Formierung *f*, Entstehung *f*, Ausbildung *f*
formation energy of crack Rißbildungsenergie *f*
formation of bridges {in materials} Stegbildung *f* {in Werkstoffen}
formation of cracks Rißerzeugung *f*
formation of fracture Bruchausbildung *f*, Bruchentstehung *f*
formation of microcracks Mikrorißbildung *f*
formation of shear lips Scherlippenbildung *f*
cleavage fracture formation Spaltbruchbildung *f*
crack formation Riß[aus]bildung *f*, Rißentstehung *f*

mechanisms of striation formation Riefenmechanismus *m*
microcrack formation Mikrorißbildung *f*
pre-crack formation Anrißbildung *f*
shear lip formation Scherlippenbildung *f*
slip-line formation Gleitlinienbildung *f*
striation formation Riefenbildung *f*
twinning < syn.: twin formation > Zwillingsbildung *f*
void formation Hohlraumbildung *f*, Porenbildung *f*
four-point bend test Vierpunkt-Biegeversuch *m*
four-point bend test specimen Vierpunkt-Biegeprobe *f*
four-point bending Vier-Punkt-Biegung *f*
four-point bending technique Vierpunkt-Biegeverfahren *f*
four-point bending test Vierpunkt-Biegeprüfung *f*, Vierpunkt-Biegeversuch *m*
Fr → francium
fractographic fraktographisch
fractographic analysis fraktographische Analyse *f*
fractographic investigation fraktographische Untersuchung *f*
fractographic observation fraktographische Betrachtung *f*
fractographic study fraktographische Untersuchung *f*
fractography {fracture surface} Fraktographie *f* {Bruchflächen}
electron fractography Elektronenfraktographie *f*
fracture < syn.: rupture > Bruch *m*
fracture by cleavage Spaltbruch *m*
fracture toughness properties *pl* Bruchzähigkeitseigenschaften *fpl*
fracture toughness specimen Bruchzähigkeitsprobe *f*
fracture toughness testing Bruchzähigkeitsprüfung *f*

fracture toughness testing method Bruchzähigkeits-Prüfverfahren n
fracture toughness value Bruchzähigkeitswert m
fracture transition Bruchübergang m, Bruchdurchgang m
fracture type Bruchart f
fracture velocity Bruchgeschwindigkeit f
fracture work Brucharbeit f
brittle fracture Sprödbruch m, spröder Bruch m
brittle fracture theory Sprödbruchtheorie f
cleavage fracture Spaltbruch m
cleavage fracture zone Spaltbruchbereich m
crystalline fracture Trennbruch m
dynamic fracture toughness value dynamischer Bruchzähigkeitswert m
granular fracture körniger Bruch m
measurement of fracture velocity Bruchgeschwindigkeitsmessung f
minimum fracture toughness Minimalbruchzähigkeit f, minimale Bruchzähigkeit f
quasi-static fracture toughness quasistatische Bruchzähigkeit f
reference fracture toughness Referenzbruchzähigkeit f
rosette fracture Rosettenbruch m
static fracture toughness statische Bruchzähigkeit f
theory of brittle fracture Sprödbruchtheorie f
transcrystalline fracture, transgranular fracture transkristalliner Bruch m
fracture-mechanical bruchmechanisch
fracture-mechanical assessment bruchmechanische Beurteilung f
fracture-mechanical behavio[u]r bruchmechanisches Verhalten n
fracture-safe bruchsicher
fracture/to {e.g. specimen} [zer]brechen {z.B. eine Probe}

fractured surface gebrochene Oberfläche f, Bruchfläche f
francium, Fr Francium n, Fr
free length {of the clamped specimen} freie Länge f {der eingespannten Probe}
free surface freie Oberfläche f
freezing Einfrieren n
stress freezing {photoelasticity} Einfrierverfahren n {Spannungsoptik}
frequency Frequenz f
loading frequency Beanspruchungsfrequenz f
test frequency Versuchsfrequenz f
fretting {materials} Reibverschleiß m {Werkstoffe}
fretting corrosion Reibkorrosion f
fretting fatigue Ermüdung f durch Reibverschleiß
friction Reibung f
friction stress Reibungsspannung f
internal friction innere Reibung f
sliding friction Gleitreibung f
front Front f
area of crack front Rißfrontbereich f
crack front Rißfront f
crack front curvature Rißfrontkrümmung f, Krümmung f der Rißfront
crack front displacement Rißfrontverlagerung f
crack front geometry Rißfrontgeometrie f
crack front orientation Rißfrontorientierung f
curved crack front gekrümmte Rißfront f
dominant-crack front Hauptrißfront f
straight crack front gerade Rißfront f
wave front Wellenfront f
frozen stress eingefrorene Spannung f
function Funktion f
angular function Winkelfunktion f

complex stress function komplexe Spannungsfunktion *f*
correction function Korrekturfunktion *f*
displacement function Verschiebungsfunktion *f*
load function Belastungsfunktion *f*
normalized correction function normierte Korrekturfunktion *f*
strain-energy function Dehnungsenergiefunktion *f*
stress function Spannungsfunktion *f*
yield function Fließfunktion *f*

G

Ga → gallium
gadolinium, Gd Gadolinium, Gd
galling {materials} Festfressen *n* {Werkstoff}
gallium, Ga Gallium *n*, Ga
galvanic corrosion galvanische Korrosion *f*, Kontaktkorrosion *f*
galvanometer Galvanometer *n*
gas Gas *n*
 gas hole {metals} Gaseinschluß *m* {Metalle}
 gas porosity {metals} Gasporosität *f* {Metalle}
ga[u]ge Meßgerät *n*; Meß-
 ga[u]ge mark {in specimens} Meßmarke *f* {an Proben}
 crack-velocity ga[u]ge Dehnungsmeßstreifen *m* für die Rißgeschwindigkeitsmessung *f*
 strain ga[u]ge Dehnungsmeßstreifen *m*
Gd → gadolinium
Ge → germanium
general corrosion Flächenkorrosion *f*
generalized stress normierte Spannung *f*
generation Erzeugung *f*
 energy generation Energieerzeugung *f*
 energy generation {at crack tip} Energieerzeugung *f* {an der Rißspitze}

geometry Geometrie *f*
 geometry change Geometrieänderung *f*
 geometry-dependent geometrieabhängig
 geometry-dependent constant geometrieabhängige Konstante *f*
 component geometry Bauteilgeometrie *f*
 crack front geometry Rißfrontgeometrie *f*
 crack geometry Rißgeometrie *f*
 crack-tip geometry Rißspitzengeometrie *f*
 effect of geometry Geometrieeinfluß *m*
 element geometry Bauteilgeometrie *f*
 initial geometry Ausgangsgeometrie *f*
 notch geometry Kerbgeometrie *f*
 slip geometry Gleitgeometrie *f*
 specimen geometry Probengeometrie *f*
germanium, Ge Germanium *n*, Ge
glass Glas *n*
 glass fiber Fiberglas *n*, Glasfaser *f*
globular {structure} globular {Gefüge}
 globular structure Globulargefüge *n*, globulares Gefüge *n*
gold, Au Gold *n*, Au
gold palladium alloy Gold-Palladium-Legierung *f*
gradient Gradient *m*
 deformation gradient Verformungsgradient *m*
 displacement gradient Verschiebungsgradient *m*
 stress gradient Spannungsgradient *m*
 temperature gradient Temperaturgradient *m*
gradual stufenweise, schrittweise
 gradual loading stufenweise Belastung *f*, schrittweise Belastung *f*
grain Korn *n*
 grain boundary Korngrenze *f*

grain-boundary cavity {crystal} Korngrenzenhohlraum *m*, Hohlraum *m* an Korngrenzen {Kristall}
grain-boundary corrosion Korngrenzenkorrosion *f*, interkristalline Korrosion *f*
grain-boundary crack Korngrenzenriß *m*
grain-boundary enrichment Korngrenzenanreicherung *f*, Anreicherung *f* an den Korngrenzen
grain-boundary segregation Korngrenzenseigerung *f*
grain-boundary sliding Korngrenzengleiten *n*
grain size Korngröße *f*
segregation in grain boundary Korngrenzenausscheidung *f*
small-angle grain boundary Kleinwinkelkorngrenze *f*
granular körnig
granular fracture körniger Bruch *m*
graphitic corrosion graphitische Korrosion *f*
gray cast iron Grauguß *m*
hypereutectic gray cast iron hypereutektischer Grauguß *m*
Griffith crack Griffith-Riß *m*
Griffith model Griffith-Modell *n*
Griffith-Orowan-Irwin criterion {crack propagation} Griffith-Orowan-Irwin-Kriterium *n* {Rißausbreitung}
Griffith
  Griffith theory {brittle fracture} Griffithsche Theorie *f* {Sprödbruch}
grinding crack Schleifriß *m*
grip conditions *pl* {specimen} Einspannbedingungen *f pl* {Probe}
grow/to {cracks} wachsen {Risse}
growth Wachstum *n*
  growth characteristic Wachstumscharakteristik *f*
  growth parameter Wachstumsparameter *m*
  growth rate Wachstumsgeschwindigkeit *f*

angle of crack growth Rißwachstumswinkel *m*
area of crack growth Rißwachstumsumfeld *n*, RW-Feld *n*
corrosion fatigue crack growth Korrosionsermüdungsrißwachstum *n*
crack growth Rißwachstum *n*, Rißwachsen *n*
crack growth analysis Rißwachstumsanalyse *f*
crack growth condition Rißwachstumsbedingung *f*
crack growth curve Rißwachstumskurve *f*
crack growth delay Rißwachstumsverzögerung *f*
crack growth energy release rate Rißwachstums-Energiefreisetzungsrate *f*
crack growth exponent Rißwachstumsexponent *m*
crack growth rate Rißwachstumsrate *f*, Rißwachstumsgeschwindigkeit *f*
crack growth resistance Rißausbreitungswiderstand *m*
crack growth stage Rißwachstumsstadium *n*
crack growth velocity Rißwachstumsgeschwindigkeit *f*
creep crack growth Kriechrißwachstum *n*
deep crack growth Tiefenrißwachstum *n*
direction of crack growth Rißwachstumsrichtung *f*
dynamic crack growth dynamisches Rißwachstum *n*
fatigue crack growth Ermüdungsrißwachstum *n*
fatigue crack growth rate Ermüdungsrißgeschwindigkeit *f*
macroscopic crack growth makroskopisches Rißwachstum *n*
slow crack growth allmähliches Rißwachstum *n*, langsames Rißwachstum *n*
stable crack growth stabiles Rißwachstum *n*

static crack growth statisches Rißwachstum *n*
subcritical crack growth subkritisches Rißwachstum *n*
unstable crack growth instabiles Rißwachstum *n*
void growth Hohlraumwachstum *n*, Porenwachstum *n*

H

H → hydrogen
hafnium, Hf Hafnium *n*, Hf
hairline crack, shatter crack, flake {ferrous metals} Haarriß *m* {Eisenmetalle}
half-moon crack "sichelförmiger" Riß *m*
hardened steel gehärteter Stahl *m*
hardening Härtung *f*, Verfestigung *f*
 hardening surface Oberflächenverfestigung *f*
 hardening behavio[u]r Verfestigungsverhalten *n*
 hardening crack Härteriß *m*
 hardening curve Verfestigungskurve *f*
 hardening exponent Verfestigungsexponent *m*
 effect of hardening Verfestigungseffekt *m*
 inhomogeneous state of hardening inhomogener Verfestigungszustand *m*
 isotropic hardening isotrope Verfestigung *f*
 linear elastic hardening linear-elastische Verfestigung *f*
 state of hardening Verfestigungszustand *m*
 strain hardening Dehnungsverfestigung *f*, Kaltverfestigung *f*
 work hardening Umformverfestigung *f*, Verfestigen *n* {Metalle}
hardness Härte *f*
 hardness test Härteprüfung *f*
 Brinell hardness number < abb.: HB > Brinellhärte *f*
 Brinell hardness test {indentation test} Brinellhärteprüfung *f* {Eindringprüfung}
 Knoop hardness number < abb.: HK > {indentation hardness} Knoop-Härte *f* {Eindringhärte}
 Rockwell hardness number Rockwellhärte *f*
 Rockwell hardness test Rockwellhärteprüfung *f*
 Scleroscope hardness number Rücksprunghärte *f*
 Scleroscope hardness testing Rücksprunghärteprüfung *f*
 surface hardness Oberflächenhärte *f*
 Vickers hardness number < abb.: VH > Vickershärte *f*
 Vickers hardness test {indentation hardness} Vickershärteprüfung *f* {Eindringhärte}
Hartmann lines *pl* Lüderssche Linien *fpl*, Lüders-Streifen *mpl*, Fließlinien *fpl* {inhomogenes Fließen}
HAZ heat-affected zone
HB → Brinell hardness number
He → helium
Hf → hafnium
HK → Knoop hardness number
heat Wärme *f*
 heat-affected zone < abb.: HAZ > Wärmeeinflußzone *f*, WEZ
 heat ag[e]ing Wärmealterung *f*, thermische Alterung *f*
 heat deflection temperature Formbeständigkeit *f* in der Wärme
 heat distortion point < syn.: heat distortion temperature > Formbeständigkeit *f* in der Wärme
 heat flow Wärmeströmung *f*
 heat flow meter Wärmeströmungsmeßgerät *n*
 heat resistance Wärmebeständigkeit *f*
 heat-resistant wrought alloy warmfeste Knetlegierung *f*
 heat-treated specimen wärmebehandelte Probe *f*, temperierte Probe *f*

heat treatment {steel} Wärmebehandlung f {Stahl}
arc-welded heat-resistant alloy lichtbogengeschweißte hitzebeständige Legierung f
deformation under heat Formbeständigkeit f in der Wärme
extensibility after heat ag[e]ing Dehnbarkeit f nach Wärmealterung
heat distortion point, heat distortion temperature Formbeständigkeit f in der Wärme
latent heat Umwandlungswärme f
permanent effect of heat {on plastics} Dauerwärmeeinwirkung f, Langzeitwärmeeinwirkung f
specific heat spezifische Wärme[kapazität] f
specific heat at constant pressure spezifische Wärme f bei konstantem Druck
specific heat at constant volume spezifische Wärme f bei konstantem Volumen
heat/to erwärmen
heating Erwärmung f, Aufheizen n
heating chamber Wärmekammer f
heating rate Aufheizgeschwindigkeit f
heating temperature Aufheiztemperatur f
loss in weight on heating {in percent} Masseverlust m bei Erwärmung {in Prozent}
transverse heating crack querverlaufender Warmriß m
helium, He Helium n, He
heterogeneity Heterogenität f, Ungleichartigkeit f
heterogeneous heterogen, ungleichartig
heterogeneous material heterogener Werkstoff m
Hg → mercury
high hoch, Hoch-
high-alloy steel hochlegierter Stahl m

high-carbon steel kohlenstoffreicher Stahl m
high-duty cast iron hochfestes Gußeisen n
high-energy fracture energiereicher Bruch m
high-nickel cast iron hochnickelhaltiges Gußeisen n
high-purity copper hochreines Kupfer n
high-purity iron Reinsteisen n
high-purity metals pl hochreine Metalle npl
high-silicon cast iron hochsiliziumhaltiges Gußeisen n
high-speed loading Hochgeschwindigkeits-Belastung f
high-speed properties pl Eigenschaften fpl bei hohen Prüfgeschwindigkeiten
high-speed steel Schnellarbeitsstahl m
high-speed tensile impact machine Hochgeschwindigkeits-Prüfmaschine f zur Bestimmung der Schlagzugfestigkeit
high-speed tension testing machine Hochgeschwindigkeits-Zugprüfmaschine f
high-speed test Hochgeschwindigkeitsprüfung f, Hochgeschwindigkeitsversuch m
high-strength alumin[i]um alloy hochfeste Aluminiumlegierung f
high-strength material hochfester Werkstoff m
high-strength steel hochfester Stahl m
high-temperature alloy hochwarmfeste Legierung f
high-temperature material hochtemperaturbeständiger Werkstoff m
high-temperature test Prüfung f bei hohen Temperaturen
Hill specimen {a flat tensile specimen} Hill-Probe f {eine flache Zugprobe}

hinge-type deformation scharnierförmige Verformung f
history "Geschichte" f, "Vorgeschichte" f
  loading history Belastungsvorgeschichte f, Belastungshergang m
  stress history {of materials} Spannungsgeschichte f {von Werkstoffen}
hole {e.g. in specimens} Bohrung f {z.B. in Proben}, Loch n
  circular hole kreisrunde Bohrung f
  elliptical hole elliptische Bohrung f
  gas hole {metals} Gaseinschluß m {Metalle}
holmium, Ho Holmium n, Ho
homogeneity Homogenität f, Gleichartigkeit f
  degree of homogeneity Homogenitätsgrad m
homogeneous homogen, gleichartig
  homogeneous body homogener Körper m
  homogeneous deformation homogene Verformung f
  homogeneous distribution of stress[es] homogene Spannungsverteilung f
  homogeneous field of stress homogenes Spannungsfeld n
  homogeneous loading homogene Belastung f
  homogeneous state of stress homogener Spannungszustand m
Hooke's law Hookesches Gesetz n
hoop stress Tangentialspannung f
hot heiß; Warm-
hot brittleness Warmbrüchigkeit f
  hot crack Warmriß m
  hot tear Warmriß m
  internal hot tear innerer Wärmeriß m
hydrogen, H Wasserstoff m, H
hydrogen blistering {metal surface} Wasserstoffblasenbildung f {Metalloberfläche}
hydrogen cracking wasserstoffinduzierte Rißbildung f

hydrogen damage {embrittlement, cracking, blistering} Wasserstoffschädigung f, Schädigung f durch Wasserstoff {Versprödung, Rißbildung, Blasenbildung}
hydrogen-embrittled wasserstoffversprödet, versprödet durch Wasserstoff m
hydrogen embrittlement Wasserstoffversprödung f
hydrogen embrittleness Wasserstoffsprödigkeit f
hydrogen-induced cracking, HIC wasserstoffinduzierte Rißbildung f
hydrogen-induced delayed cracking wasserstoffinduzierte verzögerte Rißbildung f
hydrostatic hydrostatisch
  hydrostatic compression hydrostatische Druckbeanspruchung f
  hydrostatic modulus Kompressionsmodul m
  hydrostatic pressure hydrostatischer Druck m
  hydrostatic stress hydrostatische Spannung f
hypereutectic cast iron hypereutektisches Gußeisen n
hypereutectic gray cast iron hypereutektischer Grauguß m
hypothesis Hypothese f
  hypothesis of normal stresses Normalspannungshypothese f
  failure hypothesis Versagenshypothese f
  fracture hypothesis Bruchhypothese f
  strength hypothesis Festigkeitshypothese f

I

ideal, ideal, vollkommen, vollständig
  ideal brittle material ideal-spröder Werkstoff m
  ideal plasticity ideale Plastizität f
ignitability Zündbarkeit f

ignitability test Prüfung *f* der Zündbarkeit
ignite/to zünden
ignition properties *pl* {of plastic} Zündverhalten *n*, Zündeigenschaften *fpl*
ignition source Zündquelle *f*
ignition temperature Zündtemperatur *f*
ignition test Zündversuch *m*
flash ignition temperature Selbstentzündungstemperatur *f*
immerse/to {a specimen} [ein]tauchen {eine Probe}
impact Aufschlag *m*, Schlag *m*, Aufprall *m*, Stoß *m*
impact brittleness temperature Kältebruchtemperatur *f* bei Schlagbeanspruchung
impact energy {Izod test, Charpy test} Schlagenergie *f* {Izod-Versuch, Charpy-Versuch}
impact flexural test Schlagbiegeprüfung *f*, Schlagbiegeversuch *m*
impact fracture Stoßbruch *m*
impact loading schlagartige Beanspruchung *f*, Schlagbeanspruchung *f*, Schlagbelastung *f*, Stoßbelastung *f*
impact mechanism Schlagvorrichtung *f*
impact method Schlagprüfung *f*
impact pendulum Pendelhammer *m*
impact resistance measurement Schlagfestigkeitsmessung *f*, Messung *f* der Schlagfestigkeit
impact strength Kerbschlagfestigkeit *f*
impact strength data *pl* Schlagfestigkeitsangaben *fpl*
impact tensile test Schlagzugversuch *m*
impact test Schlagversuch *m*, Schlagprüfung *f*
impact test method Prüfmethode *f* mit Schlagbeanspruchung, Prüfmethode *f* mit schlagartiger Beanspruchung

impact testing Schlagprüfung *f*, Prüfung *f* mit Schlagbeanspruchung
impact testing machine Schlagprüfmaschine *f*, Schlagprüfgerät *n*, Pendelschlagwerk *n*
impact torsion test Schlagverdrehversuch *m*
impact velocity Schlaggeschwindigkeit *f*
brittleness temperature by impact Kältebruchtemperatur *f* bei Schlagbeanspruchung
Charpy impact resistance Charpy-Schlagfestigkeit *f*, Schlagfestigkeit *f* nach Charpy
falling weight impact strength apparatus Kugelfallprüfmaschine *f* {zur Bestimmung der Schlagzähigkeit}
flexural impact strength measurement Messung *f* der Schlagbiegefestigkeit
high-speed tensile impact machine Hochgeschwindigkeits-Prüfmaschine *f* zur Bestimmung der Schlagzugfestigkeit
instrumented notched-bar impact test instrumentierter Kerbschlagbiegeversuch *m*
Izod impact strength specimen Izod-Probe *f* {zur Bestimmung der Schlagfestigkeit}
Izod impact testing machine Schlagprüfgerät *n* nach Izod, Izod-Schlagprüfgerät *n*
notch impact test specimen Kerbschlagprobe *f*
notch impact toughness Kerbschlagzähigkeit *f*
notch impact toughness-temperature curve Kerbschlagzähigkeits-Temperatur-Kurve *f*, Kerbschlagzähigkeits-Temperaturverlauf *m*
notch impact toughness value Kerbschlagzähigkeitswert *m*
notched-bar impact test Kerbschlagbiegeversuch *m*
notched-bar impact test specimen Kerbschlagbiegeprobe *f*

notched-bar impact testing Kerbschlagbiegeprüfung f
pendulum impact tester Pendelschlagwerk n
tensile impact specimen Schlagzugprobe f, Prüfkörper m für den Schlagzugversuch
tensile impact strength measurement Messung f für Schlagzugfestigkeit
tensile impact testing machine Schlagzugfestigkeits-Prüfmaschine f, Prüfmaschine f für die Bestimmung der Schlagzugfestigkeit
impact/to [auf]schlagen, aufprallen, auftreffen
imperfection {in materials} Fehler m {in Werkstoffen}
imperfection of crystal Kristallbaufehler m
impingement attack {corrosion turbulent flow of liquid} Angriff m durch Flüssigkeitsschlag {Korrosion turbulente Flüssigkeitsströmungen}
impurity {metals} Verunreinigung f {Metalle}
In → Indium
inclined <syn.: slanting, oblique> schräg
inclined crack schräg[liegend]er Riß m
include/to einschließen
inclusion {in materials} Einschluß m, Einlagerung f
brittle inclusion spröder Einschluß m
nonmetallic inclusion nichtmetallischer Einschluß m
incompressibility Inkompressibilität f
incompressible inkompressibe
incompressible deformation inkompressible Deformation f
increase/to ansteigen, zunehmen, erhöhen
increase Anstieg m, Zunahme f, Erhöhung f

increase of load Belastungsanstieg m
increase of stress Spannungsanstieg m
temperature increase {during testing} Temperaturerhöhung f {bei der Prüfung}
increment Inkrement n
strain increment Dehnungsinkrement n
crack increment Rißinkrement n
load increment Laststufe f
strain increment Dehnungsinkrement n
stress increment Spannungsinkrement n
incremental inkremental
incubation time {crack initiation} Inkubationszeit f {Rißleitung}
indefinitely thin crack unbestimmt schmaler Riß m
indium, In Indium n, In
induce/to {a fracture} induzieren {einen Bruch}
induced anisotropy induzierte Anisotropie f
industrial atmosphere {corrosion} Industrieatmosphäre f {Korrosion}
inelastic unelastisch
inelastic behavio[u]r unelastisches Verhalten n
inelastic deformation unelastische Verformung f
inelasticity Unelastizität f
infinite unendlich
infinite body unendlicher Körper m
infinite loading unendliche Belastung f
infinite plate unendlich ausgedehnte Scheibe f, unendliche Scheibe f
infinitesimal deformation infinitesimale Verformung f
influence Einfluß m
influence of temperature Temperatureinfluß m
inherent anisotropy natürliche Anisotropie f

inherent fracture toughness Eigen-Bruchzähigkeit f
inhomogeneity Inhomogenität f, Ungleichartigkeit f
inhomogeneous inhomogen, ungleichartig
inhomogeneous deformation inhomogene Verformung f
inhomogeneous material inhomogener Werkstoff m
inhomogeneous slip distribution inhomogene Gleitverteilung f
inhomogeneous state of hardening inhomogener Verfestigungszustand m
inhomogeneous strain inhomogene Dehnung f
inhomogeneous stress distribution inhomogene Spannungsverteilung f
inhomogeneous stress field inhomogenes Spannungsfeld n
inhomogeneous yielding inhomogenes Fließen n
initial Ausgangs-, Anfangs-
initial crack Ausgangsriß m
initial crack length Ausgangsrißlänge f
initial depth {surface crack} Anfangstiefe f {Oberflächenriß}
initial dimensions *pl* Anfangsabmessungen fpl
initial geometry Ausgangsgeometrie f
initial stress Vorspannung f
initial thickness {of specimen} Anfangsdicke f {der Probe zu Beginn der Prüfung}
initial yielding Fließbeginn m
initiate/to {cracks} initiieren, auslösen {Risse}
initiated crack eingebrachter Riß m
initiation Initiierung f, Einleitung f, Auslösung f
initiation {of cracks} Initiation f, Initiierung f, Auslösung f {von Rissen}
initiation of failure Versagenseinleitung f
initiation of fracture Brucheinleitung f

circular-crack initiation Kreisrißbildung f
crack initiation Rißauslösung f, Rißeinleitung f, Rißinitiierung f Rißbildung f
crack initiation concept Rißinitiierungskonzept n
crack initiation condition Rißinitiierungsbedingung f
crack initiation process Rißinitiierungsprozeß m
crack initiation stress-intensity factor Rißinitiierungs-Spannungsintensitätsfaktor m
crack initiation toughness Rißinitiierungszähigkeit f
crack start Rißstart m
dynamic crack initiation dynamische Rißeinleitung f
fracture initiation Bruchauslösung f, Brucheinleitung f, Bruchinitiierung f
fracture initiation zone Bruucheinleitungszone f
intercrystalline fracture initiation interkristalline Brucheinleitung f
location of crack initiation Rißeinleitungsort m
pre-crack initiation Anrißerzeugung f
quasistatic crack initiation quasistatische Rißeinleitung f
unstable crack initiation instabile Rißauslösung f
inner innere, Innen-
inner zone {crack tip} innerer Bereich m {Rißspitze}
inner zone of specimen Probeinneres n
crack at the inner surface Riß m auf der Innenfläche
inside diameter {of the specimen} Innendurchmesser m {von Proben}
inspection Inspektion f, Kontrolle f, Überprüfung f
inspection interval Inspektionsintervall n
inspection technique Inspektionsverfahren n

instability

acoustic emission inspection Schallemissionsprüfung f
penetrant inspection {detection of cracks} Eindringprüfung f {Rißnachweis}
instability Instabilität f
instability analysis Instabilitätsanalyse f
instability parameter Instabilitäts-Kennwert m
crack instability Rißinstabilität f
elastic instability elastische Instabilität f
elastic-plastic fracture instability elastisch-plastische Bruchinstabilität f
fracture instability Bruchinstabilität f
mechanical instability mechanische Instabilität f {z.B. Knicken oder Einschnüren}
plastic instability plastische Instabilität f
shear instability Scherungsinstabilität f
instrumented {test} instrumentiert {Versuch}
instrumented Charpy test instrumentierter Charpy-Versuch m
instrumented notched-bar impact test instrumentierter Kerbschlagbiegeversuch m
integral Integral
critical J integral kritisches J-Integral n
cyclic J integral zyklisches J-Integral n
J integral concept {linear-elastic fracture mechanics} J-Integral-Konzept n {Fließbruchmechanik}
J integral design curve J-Integral-Auslegungskurve f
intensity Intensität f
average stress intensity mittlere Spannungsintensität f
concept of stress intensity Spannungsintensitätskonzept n {Bruchmechanik}
cyclic stress intensity zyklische Spannungsintensität f
dimensionless stress intensity factor dimensionsloser Spannungsintensitätsfaktor m
dynamic stress intensity dynamische Spannungsintensität f
linear-elastic stress intensity linear-elastische Spannungsintensität f
stress intensity Spannungsintensität f, S.I.
stress intensity range Spannungsintensitätsbereich m
threshold stress intensity Schwellspannungsintensität f
intercrystalline interkristallin
intercrystalline brittle fracture interkristalliner Sprödbruch m
intercrystalline cleavage fracture interkristalliner Spaltbruch m
intercrystalline corrosion Korngrenzenkorrosion f, interkristalline Korrosion f
intercrystalline crack propagation interkristalline Rißausbreitung f
intercrystalline cracking interkristalline Rißbildung f
intercrystalline facet interkristalline Facette f
intercrystalline fracture interkristalliner Bruch m
intercrystalline fracture initiation interkristalline Brucheinleitung f
intercrystalline microcrack interkristalliner Mikroriß m
intercrystalline, intergranular {between crystals, grains, along the grain boundaries} interkristallin, intergranular {zwischen Kristallen, Körnern, entlang der Korngrenzen}
intercrystalline-transcrystalline fatigue fracture interkristalliner-transkristalliner Ermüdungsbruch m
interdendritic corrosion {alloy castings} Korrosion f zwischen Dendriten {Gußlegierungen}

interdendritic crack interdendritischer Riß *m*
interface {matrix/particle} Grenzfläche *f* {Matrix/Teilchen}
interface {of plastic zone} Berandung *f* {der plastischen Zone}
interface crack {material A/material B} Grenzflächenriß *m* {Werkstoff A/Werkstoff B}
intergranular intergranular
intergranular corrosion Korngrenzenkorrosion *f*, interkristalline Korrosion *f*
intergranular cracking interkristalline Rißbildung *f*
intergranular creep rupture intergranularer Kriechbruch *m*
intergranular dimple fracture intergranularer Grübchenbruch *m*
intergranular fatigue fracture intergranularer Ermüdungsbruch *m*
intergranular fracture Korngrenzbruch *m*, intergranularer Bruch *m*
intergranular quenching crack intergranularer Härteriß *m*
intergranular stress-corrosion cracking interkristalline Spannungsrißkorrosion *f*
intermetallic compound intermetallische Verbindung *f*
internal innen, Innen-
internal compressive load innere Druckbelastung *f*
internal crack Innenriß *m*
internal energy innere Energie *f*
internal force innere Kraft *f*
internal friction innere Reibung *f*
internal hot tear innerer Wärmeriß *m*
internal notch Innenkerbe *f*
internal oxidation, subsurface corrosion {corrosion products} innere Oxidation *f* {Korrosionsprodukte}
circular internal crack kreisförmiger Innenriß *m*
elliptical internal crack ellipsenförmiger Innenriß *m*, elliptischer Innenriß *m*

sharp internal notch scharfer Innenkerb *m*
intersection point Schnittpunkt *m*
intracrystalline intrakristallin
iridium, Ir Iridium *n*, Ir
iron, Fe Eisen *n*, Fe
iron alloy Eisenlegierung *f*
iron-alumin[i]um alloy Eisen-Aluminium-Legierung *f*
iron casting Eisenguß *m*
iron-chromium alloy Eisen-Chrom-Legierung *f*
iron-chromium-alumin[i]um alloy Eisen-Chrom-Aluminium-Legierung *f*
ductile iron duktiles Eisen *n*
ferritic iron-alumin[i]um alloy ferritische Eisen-Aluminium-Legierung *f*
gray cast iron Grauguß *m*
high-duty cast iron hochfestes Gußeisen *n*
high-nickel cast iron hochnickelhaltiges Gußeisen *n*
high-purity iron Reinsteisen *n*
high-silicon cast iron hochsiliziumhaltiges Gußeisen *n*
hypereutectic cast iron hypereutektisches Gußeisen *n*
hypereutectic gray cast iron hypereutektischer Grauguß *m*
malleable iron Temperguß *m*
pearlitic ductile iron perlitisches duktiles Eisen *n*
irreversible irreversibel, nicht umkehrbar
ISO ISO -
ISO-V-notch ISO-Spitzkerb *m*, ISO-V-Kerb *m*
ISO-V-specimen {notched} ISO-V-Probe *f* {gekerbt}
isochromatic line {photoelasticity} Isochromate *f* {Spannungsoptik}
isocline {photoelasticity} Isokline *f* {Spannungsoptik}
isolated isoliert; Einzel-
isolated crack Einzelriß *m*

isothermal

isolated defect Einzelfehler *m*
isothermal isothermisch
isotropic isotrop, richtungsunabhängig
isotropic cylinder isotroper Zylinder *m*
isotropic ductile material isotroper duktiler Werkstoff *m*
isotropic elastic material isotroper elastischer Werkstofff *m*
isotropic elasticity isotrope Elastizität *f*
isotropic fracture isotroper Bruch *m*
isotropic hardening isotrope Verfestigung *f*
isotropic material isotroper Werkstoff *m*
isotropic state of stress isotroper Spannungszustand *m*
isotropic stress field isotropes Spannungsfeld *n*
isotropic strip isotroper Streifen *m*
isotropy Isotropie *f*
Izod
Izod impact strength specimen Izod-Probe *f* {zur Bestimmung der Schlagfestigkeit}
Izod impact testing machine Schlagprüfgerät *n* nach Izod, Izod-Schlagprüfgerät *n*
Izod-test {determination of impact strength} Izod-Prüfung *f* {Bestimmung der Schlagfestigkeit}
Izod test {impact toughness} Izod-Prüfung *f* {Kerbschlagzähigkeit}

J

J integral J-integral *n*
J integral concept {linear-elastic fracture mechanics} J-Integral-Konzept *n* {Fließbruchmechanik}
J integral design curve J-Integral-Auslegungskurve *f*
J integral {mathematical expression: fracture toughness} J-Integral *n* {mathematischer Ausdruck: Bruchzähigkeit}
critical J integral kritisches J-Integral *n*
cyclic J integral zyklisches J-Integral *n*
J-testing J-Prüfung *f*
joint {materials} Verbindung *f* {Werkstoffe}

K

K → potassium
keyhole-notch specimen {Charpy test} Probe *f* mit "Schlüsselloch"-Kerb {Charpy-Versuch}
kinetic kinetisch
kinetic energy kinetische Energie *f*
Knoop hardness number < abb.: HK > {indentation hardness} Knoop-Härte *f* {Eindringhärte}
Kr → krypton
krypton, Kr Krypton *n*, Kr

L

laboratory specimen Probe *f* für Laborversuche
lamellar lamellar
lamellar structure lamellares Gefüge *n*
lamination Lamellierung *f*, Schichtung *f*
lanthanum, La Lanthan *n*, La
lap Walzgrat *m*
large-area specimen großflächige Probe *f*
latent heat Umwandlungswärme *f*
lead, Pb Blei *n*, Pb
lead alloy Bleilegierung *f*
leak-before-break Leck-vor-Bruch-
 leak-before-break behavio[u]r Leck-vor-Bruch-Verhalten *n*

leak-before-break condition Leck-vor-Bruch-Bedingung f
leak-before-break criterion Leck-vor-Bruch-Kriterium n
leak-before-break test Leck-vor-Bruch-Prüfung f
LEFM → linear-elastic fracture mechanics
length Länge f
length of plastic zone Länge f der plastischen Zone
arrest-crack length Arrestrißlänge f
average crack length mittlere Rißlänge f
bending length {bending test} Biegelänge f {Biegeprüfung}
branching crack length Nebenrißlänge f
change in crack length Rißlängenänderung f, Rißzuwachs m
crack length Rißlänge f
critical crack length kritische Rißlänge f
current crack length aktuelle Rißlänge f
dependence from the crack length Rißlängenabhängigkeit f
determination of the crack length Rißlängenbestimmung f
effective crack length effektive Rißlänge f, wirksame Rißlänge f
equivalent crack length äquivalente Rißlänge f
fatigue crack length Ermüdungsrißlänge f
fatigue pre-crack length Ermüdungsanrißlänge f
fictitious crack length fiktive Rißlänge f
final crack length Endrißlänge f
fracture length Bruchlänge f
free length {of the clamped specimen} freie Länge f {der eingespannten Probe}
initial crack length Ausgangsrißlänge f
measurement of crack length Rißlängenmessung f
notch length Kerblänge f
optical measurement of crack length optische Rißlängenmessung f
physical crack length physikalische Rißlänge f
pre-crack length Anrißlänge f
range of crack length Rißlängenbereich m
relative crack length relative Rißlänge f
secondary-crack length Nebenrißlänge f
starter crack length Ausgangsrißlänge f
surface-crack length Oberflächenrißlänge f
total crack length Gesamtrißlänge
wave length Wellenlänge f
level Niveau n, Stufe f
constant stress level konstantes Spannungsniveau n
load level Lastniveau n, Laststufe f
working stress level Betriebsspannungsniveau n
Li → lithium
life Lebensdauer f
calculation of service life Lebensdauerberechnung f
determination of service life Lebensdauerermittlung f
service life Betriebslebensdauer f, Lebensdauer f
total service life {of structures} Gesamtlebensdauer f {von Konstruktionen}
ligament Ligament n
ligament-independent ligamentunabhängig
ligament size Ligamentgröße f
ligament width Ligamentbreite f
crack ligament Rißligament f
uncracked ligament rißfreies Ligament n
light alloy Leichtmetallegierung f
limit Grenze f
limit load Grenzlast f
limit of elasticity Elastizitätsgrenze f

limit/to

creep limit Kriechgrenze *f*
elastic limit Elastizitätsgrenze *f*
elastic limit load elastische Grenzlast *f*
fatigue limit Ermüdungsgrenze *f*
load limit Belastungsgrenze *f*, Lastgrenze *f*
local load limit lokale Belastungsgrenze *f*
plastic limit load plastische Grenzlast *f*
proportional limit Proportionalitätsgrenze *f*
shear limit Schergrenze *f*
temperature limit Temperaturgrenze *f*
limit/to begrenzen, einschränken
limitation Begrenzung *f*, Einschränkung *f*
stress limitation Spannungsbegrenzung *f*
limiting temperature Grenztemperatur *f*
limiting transition temperature range Übergangstemperaturgrenzbereich *m*
limiting velocity {crack propagation} Grenzgeschwindigkeit *f* {Rißausbreitung}
concept of limiting temperature {determination of toughness} Grenztemperatur-Konzept *n* {Zähigkeitsnachweis}
line Linie *f*; Gerade *f*
blunting line {cracks} Wölbungsgerade *f*, Rißabstumpfungsgerade *f* {Risse}
center line shrinkage Mittellinienlunkerung *f*
crack line Rißlinie *f*
crack line loading Belastung *f* quer zur Rißlänge
dislocation line Versetzungslinie *f*
isochromatic line {photoelasticity} Isochromate *f* {Spannungsoptik}
notch line Kerblinie *f*
stress line Spannungslinie *f*

unloading line Entlastungsgerade *f*, Entlastungslinie *f*
yield line theory Fließlinientheorie *f*
linear linear; eindimensional
linear-elastic linear-elastisch
linear-elastic behavio[u]r linear-elastisches Verhalten *n*
linear-elastic body linear-elastischer Körper *m*
linear-elastic continuum linear-elastisches Kontinuum *n*
linear-elastic deformation linear-elastische Verformung *f*
linear elastic deformation field linear-elastisches Verformungsfeld *n*
linear-elastic fracture behavio[u]r linear-elastisches Bruchverhalten *n*
linear elastic fracture criterion linear-elastisches Bruchkriterium *n*
linear-elastic fracture mechanics <abb.: LEFM> linear-elastische Bruchmechanik *f*, LEBM
linear-elastic fracture mechanics <abb.: LEFM> concept LEBM-Konzept *n*, Konzept *n* der linear-elastischen Bruchmechanik
linear elastic hardening linear-elastische Verfestigung *f*
linear-elastic material linear-elastischer Werkstoff *m*
linear-elastic solution linear-elastische Lösung *f*
linear elastic stress field linear-elastisches Spannungsfeld *n*
linear-elastic stress intensity linear-elastische Spannungsintensität *f*
linear elasticity lineare Elastizität *f*
linear expansion apparatus Gerät *n* zur Bestimmung der linearen Ausdehnung
linear expansion measurement Messung *f* der linearen Ausdehnung
linear load distribution lineare Lastverteilung *f*
linear shrinkage Längsschwindung *f*
linear strain distribution lineare Dehnungsverteilung *f*

average coefficient of linear thermal expansion mittlerer linearer Wärmeausdehnungskoeffizient *m*
coefficient of linear expansion linearer Ausdehnungskoeffizient *m*
coefficient of linear thermal expansion linearer Wärmeausdehnungskoeffizient *m*
concept of linear-elastic fracture mechanics Konzept *n* der linear-elastischen Bruchmechanik
two-dimensional linear-elastic deformation field zweidimensionales linear-elastisches Verformungsfeld *n*
lines *pl* Linien *fpl*
arrest lines *pl* Rastlinien *fpl* {Bruchfläche}
flow lines *pl* {materials} Fließlinien *fpl* {Werkstoffe}
Hartmann lines *pl* Lüderssche Linien *fpl*, Lüders-Streifen *mpl*, Fließlinien *fpl* {inhomogenes Fließen}
Lüders lines *pl* Lüderssche Linien *fpl*, Lüders-Streifen *mpl*, Fließlinien *fpl* {inhomogenes Fließen}
Piobert lines *pl* Lüderssche Linien *fpl*, Lüders-Streifen *mpl*, Fließlinien *fpl* {inhomogenes Fließen}
Wallner lines *pl* {fracture surface} Wallner-Linien *fpl* {Bruchfläche}
lips *pl* Lippen *fpl*
formation of shear lips *pl* Scherlippenbildung *f*
percentage shear lips *pl* Scherlippenanteil *m*
shear lips *pl* Scherlippen *fpl*
liquid Flüssigkeit *f*
liquid-metal embrittlement, LME Versprödung *f* bei Kontakt mit schmelzflüssigen Metallen
liquid shrinkage Flüssigkeitsschwindung *f*
lithium, Li Lithium *n*, Li
LME → liquid-metal embrittlement
load Last *f*, Beanspruchung *f*
load amplitude Lastamplitude *f*
load application Lastaufbringung *f*

load-application point Lastangriffspunkt *m*
load COD diagram Belastung-COD-Diagramm *n*
load component Lastkomponente *f* {z.B. eine Spannung}
load concentration Lastkonzentration *f*
load concentration factor Lastkonzentrationsfaktor *m*
load configuration Belastungskonfiguration *f*
load control Belastungskontrolle *f*
load cycle Lastspiel *n*, Lastwechsel *m*, Lastzyklus *m*
load cycles *pl* Lastwechsel *mpl*
load cycles at fracture Bruchlastspielzahl *f*
load-deformation curve Last-Verformungs-Kurve *f*
load-deformatioon diagram Last-Verformungs-Diagramm *n*
load distribution Lastverteilung *f*, Verteilung *f* der Belastung
load-displacement curve Lastverschiebungskurve *f*
load-extension curve Kraftverlängerungskurve *f*
load function Belastungsfunktion *f*
load increment Laststufe *f*
load level Lastniveau *n*, Laststufe *f*
load limit Belastungsgrenze *f*, Lastgrenze *f*
load peak Lastspitze *f*
load system Belastungssystem *n*
load vector Belastungsvektor *m*
action of load Lastangriff *m*
alternating load Wechsellast *f*
average load Mittellast *f*
bending load Biegebeanspruchung *f*, Biegelast *f*
compressive load Drucklast *f*
constant load konstante Last *f*
constant load amplitude konstante Lastamplitude *f*
critical load kritische Last *f*
cyclic load Wechsellast *f*
elastic limit load elastische Grenzlast *f*

external compressive load äußere Druckbelastung *f*
external load äußere Belastung *f*, äußere Last *f*
failure load Versagenslast *f*
fatigue load Ermüdungsbelastung *f*
fracture load Bruchlast *f*
increase of load Belastungsanstieg *m*
internal compressive load innere Druckbelastung *f*
limit load Grenzlast *f*
linear load distribution lineare Lastverteilung *f*
local load limit lokale Belastungsgrenze *f*
local load rate lokale Belastungsgeschwindigkeit *f*
maximum load Höchstlast *f*, Lastmaximum *n*, Maximalbeanspruchung *f*
minimum load {for fracture} Mindestbruchlast *f*
multiaxial tensile load mehrachsige Zugbeanspruchung *f*
multiple load path Mehrfachlastweg *m*
non-linear load-displacement curve nichtlineare Lastverschiebungskurve *f*
number of load cycles Lastwechselfrequenz *f*, Lastspielfrequenz *f*, Lastspielzahl *f*
partial load Teillast *f*
peak load Spitzenlast *f*
peak load Spitzenlast *f*
penetrative load Durchstoßbelastung *f*, Durchstoßlast *f*
permissible load Beanspruchbarkeit *f*
plastic limit load plastische Grenzlast *f*
point load Einzellast *f*
positive peak load positive Spitzenlast *f*
service load Betriebslast *f*
shear load Schubbeanspruchung *f*
shock load Stoßbelastung *f*
temperature of deflection under load Formbeständigkeit *f* in der Wärme
tensile load Zuglast *f*
test load Prüflast *f*
threshold tensile load Zugschwellbelastung *f*
torsional load Verdrehungsbeanspruchung *f*, Verdrehungsbelastung *f*
yield load Fließlast *f*
load/to beanspruchen, belasten
loaded unter Last *f*, beansprucht, belastet
loaded body beanspruchter Körper *m*, belasteter Körper *m*
loaded in tension zugbelastet
axially loaded axial beansprucht
symmetrically loaded crack system symmetrisch belastetes Rißsystem *n*
load[ing] Beanspruchung *f*, Belastung *f*; Belastungsvorgang *m*
loading amplitude Beanspruchungsamplitude *f*
loading analysis Beanspruchungsanalyse *f*
loading case Beanspruchungsfall *m*
loading characteristics *pl* Belastungskennlinien *fpl*
loading conditions *pl* Beanspruchungsbedingungen *f*, Belastungsbedingungen *fpl*, Lastbedingungen *fpl*, Beanspruchungsverhältnisse *npl*
loading curve Beanspruchungsverlauf *m*
loading cycle Beanspruchungswechsel *m*
loading direction Belastungssituation *f*
loading frequency Beanspruchungsfrequenz *f*
loading history Belastungsvorgeschichte *f*, Belastungshergang *m*
loading mechanism Belastungseinrichtung *f*, Belastungsvorrichtung *f*
loading of crack Rißbeanspruchung *f*, Rißbelastung *f*

loading of specimen Probenbelastung f
loading parameter Beanspruchungsparameter m, Beanspruchungskenngröße f
loading process Belastungsablauf m
loading program Belastungsfolge f, Belastungsprogramm n
loading rate Beanspruchungsgeschwindigkeit f, Belastungsgeschwindigkeit f
loading situation Beanspruchungssituation f
loading stage Belastungsstufe f
loading state Beanspruchungszustand m
loading test Belastungsversuch m
loading time Beanspruchungsdauer f, Belastungszeit f
loading value Beanspruchungswert m
alternating loading Wechselbeanspruchung f
boundary loading Grenz[flächen]belastung f; Randbelastung f
characterization of loading Beanspruchungscharakterisierung f
constant amplitude cyclic loading zyklische Beanspruchung f mit konstanter Amplitude
crack line loading Belastung f quer zur Rißlänge
cyclic loading zyklische Beanspruchung f, zyklische Belastung f
direction of loading Beanspruchungsrichtung f, Lastrichtung f
dynamic loading dynamische Beanspruchung f, dynamische Belastung f
elastic loading elastische Belastung f
fatigue loading Ermüdungsbeanspruchung f
gradual loading stufenweise Belastung f, schrittweise Belastung f
high-speed loading Hochgeschwindigkeits-Belastung f
homogeneous loading homogene Belastung f

impact loading schlagartige Beanspruchung f, Schlagbeanspruchung f, Schlagbelastung f, Stoßbelastung f
infinite loading unendliche Belastung f
method of loading Belastungsverfahren n
mixed-mode loading gemischte Beanspruchungsart f
mode of crack loading Rißbeanspruchungsart f
modulation of loading Beanspruchungsmodulation f
monotonic loading monotone Beanspruchung f, monotone Belastung f
pre-history of loading Belastungsvorgeschichte f
principal loading direction Hauptbelastungsrichtung f
pure shear loading reine Scherbeanspruchung f
random stress loading Zufallsbelastung f
rate of loading Belastungsgeschwindigkeit f
scew-symmetric loading asymmetrische Belastung f
service loading Betriebsbelastung f
shear loading Scherbeanspruchung f, Scherbelastung f
single-stage loading Einstufenbeanspruchung f, Einstufenbelastung f
spontaneous loading spontane Belastung f
static loading ruhende Belastung f, statische Belastung f
stepwise loading stufenweise Belastung f
symmetric loading symmetrische Belastung f
tensile loading Zugbeanspruchung f, Zugbelastung f
three-point loading Dreipunkt-Belastung f
transient loading instationäre Belastung f
trial loading Probebelastung f, probeweise Belastung f

local 74

type of loading Beanspruchungsart f, Belastungsart f
uniaxial compression loading einachsige Druckbelastung f
uniaxial loading einachsige Belastung f
uniaxial tensile loading einachsige Zugbeanspruchung f, einachsige Zugbelastung f
vibration loading Schwingbeanspruchung f, schwingende Beanspruchung f, Schwingbelastung f, schwingende Belastung f
wedge loading Keilbelastung f
wedge-opening loading <abb.: WOL> **specimen** Spaltkeilprobe f, WOL-Probe f
local lokal, örtlich
local crack propagation lokale Rißausbreitung f
local crack resistance lokaler Rißwiderstand m, örtlicher Rißwiderstand m
local displacement lokale Verschiebung f
local fracture strain lokale Bruchdehnung f
local load limit lokale Belastungsgrenze f
local load rate lokale Belastungsgeschwindigkeit f
local stress component lokale Spannungskomponente f
local stress factor örtlicher Spannungsfaktor m
local stress field lokales Spannungsfeld n
local stress relaxation örtliche Spannungsrelaxation f
local yielding lokales Fließen n, örtliches Fließen n
location Lage f, Ort m, Stelle f, Anordnung f
location of crack initiation Rißeinleitungsort m
location of specimen Probenlage f
location of the crack Rißlage f
location of the notch Kerblage f

fracture location Bruchstelle f
locked dislocation blockierte Versetzung f
long lang
long crack langer Riß m
longitudinal in Längsrichtung, longitudinal; Längs-
longitudinal crack Längsriß m
longitudinal direction Längsrichtung f
longitudinal fracture properties pl Brucheigenschaften fpl in Längsrichtung
longitudinal shear Längsscherung f
longitudinal wave Longitudinalwelle f
loss {energy, weight} Verlust m {Energie, Masse}
loss in weight on heating {in percent} Masseverlust m bei Erwärmung {in Prozent}
weight loss test Masseverlustprüfung f
low niedrig, gering
low-alloy steel niedriglegierter Stahl m
low-carbon steel kohlenstoffarmer Stahl m
low-conductivity material Material n mit geringer Leitfähigkeit
low-cycle niederzyklisch
low-cycle fatigue niederzyklische Ermüdung f
low-energy brittle fracture energiearmer Sprödbruch m
low energy fracture energiearmer Bruch m
low-melting alloy niedrigschmelzende Legierung f
low-pressure deformation tester Niederdruck-Verformungsprüfgerät n
low-stress fracture Niedrigspannungsbruch m
low-temperature apparatus Tieftemperaturprüfgerät n

low-temperature brittleness Kältebrüchigkeit *f*, Brüchigkeit *f* bei tiefen Temperaturen
low-temperature failure Kältebruchtemperatur *f* {bei Biegebeanspruchung}
low-temperature measurement Tieftemperaturmessung *f*
low-temperature mechanical testing Tieftemperatur-Prüfung *f* der mechanischen Eigenschaften
low-temperature testing Tieftemperaturprüfung *f*
low-temperature working chamber Tieftemperaturprüfraum *m*
arc-welded low-carbon steel lichtbogengeschweißter kohlenstoffarmer Stahl *m*
resistance to low temperature Tieftemperaturbeständigkeit *f*
lower yield point untere Fließgrenze *f*
lubricate/to {the specimen to prevent sticking} einfetten {eine Probe}

M

machine Maschine *f*, (i.e.S.) Prüfmaschine *f*
Charpy machine Charpy-Prüfmaschine *f*
compression testing machine Druckprüfmaschine *f*
deformation testing machine Verformungs-Prüfmaschine *f*, Maschine *f* zur Prüfung der Verformung
high-speed tensile impact machine Hochgeschwindigkeits-Prüfmaschine *f* zur Bestimmung der Schlagzugfestigkeit
high-speed tension testing machine Hochgeschwindigkeits-Zugprüfmaschine *f*
impact testing machine Schlagprüfmaschine *f*, Schlagprüfgerät *n*, Pendelschlagwerk *n*
Izod impact testing machine Schlagprüfgerät *n* nach Izod, Izod-Schlagprüfgerät *n*

pendulum machine Pendelschlagwerk *n*
soft testing machine weiche Prüfmaschine *f*
tensile impact testing machine Schlagzugfestigkeits-Prüfmaschine *f*, Prüfmaschine *f* für die Bestimmung der Schlagzugfestigkeit
tensile testing machine Zugprüfmaschine *f*
testing machine Prüfmaschine *f*
machined bearbeitet
machined notch Kerbeinfräsung *f*
machined specimen (mechanisch) bearbeiteter Probekörper *m*
macrocrack {pre-cracks, notches, cracks} Makroriß *m* {Anrisse, Kerbe, Risse}
macrodefect, macroflaw Makrofehler *m*
macrodeformation Makroverformung *f* {Verformung im Makrobereich}
macrofailure Makrobruch *m*
macroflaw Makrofehler *m*
macrofractography Makrofraktographie *f*
macromorphology {fracture surface} Makromorphologie *f* {Bruchfläche}
macroscopic makroskopisch
macroscopic characteristic of fracture makroskopisches Bruchmerkmal *n*
macroscopic crack makroskopischer Riß *m*
macroscopic crack growth makroskopisches Rißwachstum *n*
macroscopic criterion makroskopisches Kriterium *n*
macroscopic direction of crack propagation makroskopische Rißausbreitungsrichtung *f*
macroscopic direction of fracture propagation makroskopische Bruchausbreitungsrichtung *f*

macroshrinkage

macroscopic evaluation of fracture surface makroskopische Bruchflächenbewertung f
macroscopic fracture appearance makroskopische Brucherscheinung f, makroskopisches Bruchbild n
macroscopic fracture criterion makroskopisches Bruchkriterium n
macroscopic notch makroskopischer Kerb m
macroscopic state of stress makroskopischer Spannungszustand m
macroscopic stress-intensity factor makroskopischer Spannungsintensitätsfaktor m
macroshrinkage Makrolunker m
macrostructure {metal} Makrogefüge f, makroskopisches Gefüge n {Metall}
magnesium, Mg Magnesium n, Mg
magnesium alloy Magnesiumlegierung f
magnetic powder testing {detection of cracks} Magnetpulverprüfung f
magnification Vergrößerung f
major axis {ellipse} Hauptachse f {Ellipse}
malleability Verformbarkeit f unter Druckbelastung, Umformbarkeit f
malleable iron Temperguß m
mandrel Biegedorn m
manganese, Mn Mangan n, Mn
mapping {mathematics} Abbildung f {Mathematik}
marine atmosphere {corrosion} Meeresatmosphäre f, Seeatmosphäre f {Korrosion}
mark Marke f, Markierung f, Kennzeichnung f
ga[u]ge mark {on specimens} Meßmarke f {an Proben}
mark {on the specimen} Markierung f, Kennzeichnung f {auf der Probe}
marks pl Linien fpl, Streifen mpl

beach marks pl Rastlinien fpl {Bruchfläche}
clambshell marks pl Rastlinien fpl {Bruchfläche}
crack-arrest marks pl Rißarreststreifen mpl
tide marks pl {fracture surface} Rastlinien fpl {Bruchfläche}
Marten
Marten's temperature Martens-Zahl f {zur Kennzeichnung der Formbeständigkeit in der Wärme}
Marten's test Martens-Prüfung f {Prüfung der Formbeständigkeit in der Wärme}
martensite {steel} Martensite m {Stahl}
martensitic martensitisch
martensitic stainless steel martensitischer nichtrostender Stahl m
material Material n, Werkstoff m
material behavio[u]r Werkstoffverhalten n
material condition Werkstoffzustand m, Werkstoffbeschaffenheit f
material constant Werkstoffkonstante f
material defect Werkstoffehler m
material-dependent werkstoffabhängig
material embrittlement Werkstoffversprödung f
material flaw Werkstoffehler m
material-independent werkstoffunabhängig
material of construction Konstruktionswerkstoff m
material properties pl Werkstoffeigenschaften fpl
material selection Werkstoffauswahl f
material structure Werkstoffstruktur f
material toughness Werkstoffzähigkeit f
material without pre-crack anrißfreier Werkstoff m

anisotropic ductile material anisotroper duktiler Werkstoff *m*
anisotropic material anisotroper Werkstoff *m*
basis material Grundwerkstoff *m*
brittle material spröder Werkstoff *m*
ceramic material keramischer Werkstoff *m*
constructional material Konstruktionswerkstoff *m*
ductile material duktiler Werkstoff *m*
ductile material zäher Werkstoff *m*
elastic material elastischer Werkstoff *m*
elastic material behavio[u]r elastisches Werkstoffverhalten *n*
elastic-plastic material elastisch-plastischer Werkstoff *m*
elastic-plastic material behavio[u]r elastisch-plastisches Werkstoffverhalten *n*
heterogeneous material heterogener Werkstoff *m*
high-strength material hochfester Werkstoff *m*
high-temperature material hochtemperaturbeständiger Werkstoff *m*
ideal brittle material ideal-spröder Werkstoff *m*
inhomogeneous material inhomogener Werkstoff *m*
isotropic ductile material isotroper duktiler Werkstoff *m*
isotropic elastic material isotroper elastischer Werkstoff *m*
isotropic material isotroper Werkstoff *m*
linear-elastic material linear-elastischer Werkstoff *m*
low-conductivity material Material *n* mit geringer Leitfähigkeit
matrix of material Werkstoffmatrix *f*
metallic material metallischer Werkstoff *m*
non-metallic material nichtmetallischer Werkstoff *m*
plastics material Kunststoff *m*
polycrystalline material polykristalliner Werkstoff *m*
rate-sensitive ductile material geschwindigkeitsempfindlicher duktiler Werkstoff *m*
reference material {for testing} Vergleichsmaterial *n* {für Prüfungen}
separation of material Werkstofftrennung *f*
sheet material Plattenwerkstoff *m*
test material Prüfmaterial *n*
work-hardenable material verfestigungsfähiger Werkstoff *m*
materials *pl* Werkstoffe *mpl*, Materialmaterials data *pl* Werkstoffdaten *fpl*
materials science Werkstoffwissenschaft *f*, Werkstoffkunde *f*
materials testing Materialprüfung *f*, Werkstoffprüfung *f*
anisotropy of materials Werkstoffanisotropie *f*
composite materials *pl* Verbundwerkstoffe *mpl*
damage of materials Werkstoffschädigung *f*
fatigue of materials Werkstoffermüdung *f*
material defect Werkstoffehler *m*
testing of materials Materialprüfung *f*, Werkstoffprüfung *f*
matrix Matrix *f*
matrix of material Werkstoffmatrix *f*
ductile matrix duktile Matrix *f*
maximum maximal, höchst-, Maximum *n*
maximum compressive strength maximale Druckfestigkeit *f*
maximum crack resistance maximaler Rißwiderstand *m*
maximum crack velocity maximale Rißgeschwindigkeit *f*
maximum fracture speed Bruchhöchstgeschwindigkeit *f*
maximum load Höchstlast *f*, Lastmaximum *n*, Maximalbeanspruchung *f*
maximum stress Maximalspannung *f*

maximum stress {fatigue test} Oberspannung f {Dauerbiegeversuch}
mean mittlerer
mean Mittel n; Mittelwert m {Mathematik}; Mittel-
mean strain Mitteldehnung f
mean stress Mittelspannung f
measure {of properties} Maß n {für Eigenschaften}
measure/to messen
measured fracture stress gemessene Bruchspannung f
measurement Messung f
measurement of crack depth Rißtiefenmessung f
measurement of crack length Rißlängenmessung f
measurement of crack propagation Rißausbreitungsmessung f
measurement of crack speed Rißgeschwindigkeitsmessung f
measurement of ductility Duktilitätsmessung f
measurement of fracture velocity Bruchgeschwindigkeitsmessung f
bearing measurement Messung f der Tragfähigkeit
bending measurement Messung f unter Biegebeanspruchung
comparison measurement Vergleichsmessung f
compliance measurement Nachgiebigkeitsmessung f
conductivity measurement Leitfähigkeitsmessung f
crack opening measurement Rißöffnungsmessung f
crack toughness measurement Rißzähigkeitsmessung f
direct measurement direkte Messung f
displacement measurement Verschiebungsmessung f
experimental method of measurement experimentelles Meßverfahren n

flexural impact strength measurement Messung f der Schlagbiegefestigkeit
impact resistance measurement Schlagfestigkeitsmessung f, Messung f der Schlagfestigkeit
linear expansion measurement Messung f der linearen Ausdehnung
low-temperature measurement Tieftemperaturmessung f
optical measurement of crack length optische Rißlängenmessung f
residual stress measurement Eigenspannungsmessung f
roentgenographic measurement of stresses röntgenographische Spannungsmessung f
shear measurement Messung f unter Scherbeanspruchung
simultaneous measurement Parallelmessung f, gleichzeitige Messung f
steady-state measurement {of conductivity} stationäre Messung f {der Leitfähigkeit}
strain measurement Dehnungsmessung f
tensile impact strength measurement Messung f für Schlagzugfestigkeit
thermal conductivity measurement Wärmeleitfähigkeitsmessung f
time measurement Zeitmessung f
ultrasonic measurement {crack velocity} Ultraschallmessung f {Rißgeschwindigkeit}
measuring Messen n
measuring technique Meßverfahren n
mechanical mechanisch
mechanical behavio[u]r mechanisches Verhalten n
mechanical crack Kaltriß m
mechanical degradation mechanischer Abbau m
mechanical instability mechanische Instabilität f {z.B. Knicken oder Einschnüren}
mechanical overload mechanische Überlastung f

mechanical properties *pl* mechanische Eigenschaften *fpl*
mechanical stress mechanische Spannung *f*
mechanical test mechanische Prüfung *f*
mechanical test method mechanische Prüfmethode *f*
short term mechanical testing Kurzzeitprüfung *f* der mechanischen Eigenschaften
mechanics Mechanik *f*
mechanics of fracture Bruchmechanik *f*
concept of elastic-plastic fracture mechanics Fließbruchmechanik-Konzept *n*
concept of fracture mechanics Konzept *n* der Bruchmechanik
concept of linear-elastic fracture mechanics Konzept *n* der linear-elastischen Bruchmechanik
continuum mechanics Kontinuumsmechanik *f*
criterion for fracture mechanics bruchmechanisches Kriterium *n*
elastic fracture mechanics elastische Bruchmechanik *f*
elastic-plastic fracture mechanics Fließbruchmechanik *f*, FBM, Zähbruchmechanik *f*
engineering fracture mechanics Ingenieur-Bruchmechanik *f*
fracture mechanics Bruchmechanik *f*
fracture mechanics concept Bruchmechanik-Konzept *n*, Konzept *n* der Bruchmechanik
fracture mechanics criterion bruchmechanisches Kriterium *n*
fracture mechanics element {e.g. element of singularity} Bruchmechanikelement *n* {z.B. Singularitätselement}
fracture mechanics equation Bruchmechanik-Gleichung *f*
fracture mechanics method bruchmechanische Methode *f*
fracture mechanics parameter bruchmechanischer Kennwert *m*
fracture mechanics principle Bruchmechanik-Prinzip *n*
fracture mechanics test Bruchmechanik-Versuch *m*
fracture mechanics testing Bruchmechanik-Prüfung *f*
linear-elastic fracture mechanics linear-elastische Bruchmechanik *f*, LEBM
method of fracture mechanics bruchmechanische Methode *f*
nonlinear elastic fracture mechanics nichtlinear-elastische Bruchmechanik *f*
parameter of fracture mechanics bruchmechanischer Kennwert *m*
probabilistic fracture mechanics probabilistische Bruchmechanik *f*
subcritical fracture mechanics <abb: SCFM> subkritische Bruchmechanik *f*
mechanism Mechanismus *m* {Vorgang}; Vorrichtung *f*
mechanism of fatigue Ermüdungsmechanismus *m*
mechanism of fracture Bruchmechanismus *m*
mechanism of separation Trennmechanismus *m*
crack-propagation mechanism Rißausbreitungsmechanismus *m*
cracking mechanism Mechanismus *m* der Rißbildung
fatigue mechanism Ermüdungsmechanismus *m*
fracture mechanism Bruchmechanismus *m*
impact mechanism Schlagvorrichtung *f*
loading mechanism Belastungseinrichtung *f*
mechanisms of striation formation Riefenmechanismus *m*
medium Medium *n*, Medien *npl*
medium-carbon steel mittelgekohlter Stahl *m*

anisotropic medium anisotropes Medium *n*
melt/to schmelzen
melting temperature Schmelztemperatur *f*
mercury, Hg Quecksilber *n*, Hg
metal Metall *n*
metal coating Metallbeschichtung *f*
babbitt metal Babbitt-Metall *n*
filler metal Zusatzmetall *n*
white metal Weißmetall *n*
metallic metallisch; Metall-
metallic material metallischer Werkstoff *m*
metallography Metallographie *f*
metals *pl* Metalle *npl*
ferrous metals *pl* Eisenmetalle *npl*
nonferrous metals *pl* Nichteisenmetalle *npl*, NE-Metalle *npl*
method Methode *f*
method of ag[e]ing Alterungsmethode *f*, Alterungsverfahren *n*
method of caustics Kaustik-Methode *f*
method of fracture mechanics bruchmechanische Methode *f*
method of loading Belastungsverfahren *n*
method of superposition Superpositionsmethode *f*
boundary value method {dropweight test} Grenzwertverfahren *n* {Fallgewichtsprüfung}
comparison method Vergleichsmethode *f*
compliance method {method of crack length measurement} Compliance-Methode *f* {Rißlängenmeßmethode}
dynamic test method dynamische Prüfmethode *f*, Prüfmethode *f* mit dynamischer Beanspruchung
eddy-current method {detection of cracks} Wirbelstromverfahren *n* {Nachweis von Rissen}
electrial test method thermische Prüfmethode *f*

electric potential method {determination of crack depth} Potentialsondenverfahren *n* {Rißtiefenbestimmung}
experimental method of measurement experimentelles Meßverfahren *n*
flex cracking method Rißbiegeprüfung *f*
fracture mechanics method bruchmechanische Methode *f*
fracture toughness testing method Bruchzähigkeits-Prüfverfahren *n*
impact method Schlagprüfung *f*
impact test method Prüfmethode *f* mit Schlagbeanspruchung, Prüfmethode *f* mit schlagartiger Beanspruchung
mechanical test method mechanische Prüfmethode *f*
non-standard method nicht genormte Prüfmethode *f*
non-steady state method of determining instationäres Bestimmungsverfahren *n*
optical test method optische Prüfmethode *f*
penetrometer method Eindringverfahren *n*
photoelastic method photoelastische (spannungsoptische) Methode *f*
quasi-dynamic method {for determining conductivity} quasi-dynamisches Prüfverfahren *n* {Zur Bestimmung der Leitfähigkeit}
quasi-steady state method quasistationäre Prüfmethode *f*
shear-difference method Schubdifferenzmethode *f*
static test method statische Prüfmethode *f*, Prüfmethode *f* mit statischer Beanspruchung
testing method Prüfmethode *f*
thermal test method thermisches Prüfverfahren *n*
torsional stiffening test method Torsionssteifheits-Prüfmethode *f*
Mg → magnesium

micro-cleavage crack Mikrospaltriß *m*
microanalysis Mikroanalyse *f*
  electron probe microanalysis <abb.: EPMA> Mikrosondenanalyse *f*
microcrack Mikroriß *m*
  microcrack formation Mikrorißbildung *f*
  arrested microcrack aufgefangener Mikroriß *m*
  intercrystalline microcrack interkristalliner Mikroriß *m*
  stable microcrack stabiler Mikroriß *m*
  stopped microcrack aufgefangener Mikroriß *m*
  surface microcrack Oberflächenmikroriß *m*
  transcrystalline microcrack transkristalliner Mikroriß *m*
  unstable microcrack instabiler Mikroriß *m*
microdefect, microflaw Mikrofehler *m*
microdeformation Mikroverformung *f* {Verformung im Mikrobereich}
  microdeformation tensor Mikroverformungstensor *m*
microdilatometer Mikro-Dilatometer *n*
microductile mikroduktil
  microductile crack propagation mikroduktile Rißausbreitung *f*
  microductile fracture mikroduktiler Bruch *m*
microflaw Mikrofehler *m*
microfractography Mikrofraktographie *f*
microfracture Mikrobruch *m*
  microfracture surface Mikrobruchfläche *f*
micromorphology {fracture surface} Mikromorphologie *f* {Bruchfläche}
micropore Mikropore *f*

microporosity Mikroporosität *f*
microscale Mikrobereich *m*
microscope Mikroskop *n*
  scanning electron microscope Rasterelektronenmikroskop *n*, REM
microscopic mikroskopisch
  microscopic characteristic of fracture mikroskopisches Bruchmerkmal *n*
  microscopic cleavage-fracture strength mikroskopische Spaltbruchfestigkeit *f*
  microscopic crack mikroskopischer Riß *m*
  microscopic crack branching mikroskopische Rißverzweigung *f*
  microscopic criterion mikroskopisches Kriterium *n*
  microscopic fracture behavio[u]r mikroskopisches Bruchverhalten *n*
  microscopic fracture criterion mikroskopisches Bruchkriterium *n*
  microscopic fracture stress mikroskopische Bruchspannung *f*
  microscopic notch mikroskopischer Kerb *m*
  microscopic type of fracture mikroskopische Bruchform *f*
microscopy Mikroskopie *f*
  electron microscopy Elektronenmikroskopie *f*
  scanning electron microscopy Rasterelektronenmikroskopie *f*, REM
microshrinkage Mikrolunker *m*
microstrain Mikrodehnung *f*
microstructure Mikrogefüge *n*, Feinstruktur *f*; Mikrostruktur *f*
microvoid Mikrohohlraum *m*
middle plane of specimen Probenmittelebene *f*
minimal minimal, Minimal-
minimum Minimum *n*, Mindest-
  minimum crack speed {for branching} Mindestrißgeschwindigkeit *f* {für die Verzweigung}

minor

minimum dimensions *pl* {specimens} Mindestabmessungen *fpl* {Proben}
minimum fracture toughness Minimalbruchzähigkeit *f*
minimum fracture toughness minimale Bruchzähigkeit *f*
minimum load for fracture Mindestbruchlast
minimum service temperature minimale Betriebstemperatur *f*
minimum specimen thickness Mindestprobendicke *f*
minimum specimen width Mindestprobenbreite *f*
minimum stress {fatigue test} Unterspannung *f* {Dauerbiegeversuch}
minimum thickness {specimens} Mindestdicke *f* {Proben}
minimum width {specimens} Mindestbreite *f* {Proben}
minor axis {ellipse} Nebenachse *f* {Ellipse}
misrun {metals, alloys} Fehlguß *m* {Metalle, Legierungen}
mixed mode gemischt, Misch-
  mixed-mode fracture Mischbruch *m*
  mixed-mode loading gemischte Beanspruchungsart *f*
  mixed-mode stress state gemischter Spannungszustand *m*
Mn → manganese
Mo → molybdenum
mode Modus *m* {z.B. Art und Weise der Beanspruchung}
  mode of crack loading Rißbeanspruchungsart *f*
  crack-propagation mode Rißausbreitungsart *f*
  fracture mode Bruchmodus *m*, Bruchtyp *m*
  fracture mode transition Bruchmoduswechsel *m*, Bruchmodenübergang *m*
  shearing mode Schermodus *m*
model Modell *n*
  model test Modellversuch *m*
  crack model Rißmodell *n*
  crack-propagation model Rißausbreitungsmodell *n*
  crystallographic crack-propagation model kristallographisches Rißausbreitungsmodell *n*
  dislocation model Versetzungsmodell *n*
  dog-bone model {of the plastic zone} Hundeknochen-Modell *n*, dog-bone-Modell *n* {der plastischen Zone}
  Dugdale-Barenblatt model {elastic crack problem} Dugdale-Barenblatt-Modell {elastisches Rißproblem}
  Dugdale crack model Dugdale-Rißmodell *n*
  Dugdale model {crack formation} Dugdale-Modell *n* {Rißbildung}
  Griffith model Griffith-Modell *n*
  nonlinear model nichtlineares Modell *n*
  slip-band model Gleitbandmodell *n*
modification Modifikation *f*, Abänderung *f*
modify/to modifizieren, abändern
modulation of loading Beanspruchungsmodulation *f*
modulus, moduli *pl* Modul *m*, Moduln *mpl*
  modulus in flexure Biegemodul *m*
  modulus of bending Biegemodul *m*
  modulus of cohesion Kohäsionsmodul *m*
  modulus of elasticity Elastizitätsmodul *m*, E-Modul *m*
  modulus of rigidity Scherungsmodul *m*, Schubmodul *m*
  modulus of rupture Bruchmodul *m*
  modulus of rupture in torsion Bruchmodul *m* bei Torsionsbeanspruchung
  bending modulus Biegemodul *m*
  bulk modulus {of elasticity} Kompressionsmodul *m*
  compression modulus Kompressionsmodul *m*
  elastic modulus in bend Elastizitätsmodul *m* aus dem Biegeversuch
  flexural modulus Biegemodul *m*

hydrostatic modulus Kompressionsmodul *m*
rigidity modulus Schub[elasitzitäts]modul *m*
rupture modulus Bruchmodul *m*
rupture modulus in bending Bruchmodul *m* bei Biegebeanspruchung
secant modulus Sekantenmodulus *m*
shear modulus Scher[ungs]modul *m*, Schubmodul *m*
tearing modulus Reißmodul *m*
torsion modulus Torsionsmodul *m*
volumetric modulus of elasticity Kompressionsmodul *m*
Young's modulus (of elasticity) Elastizitätsmodul *m*
modus Modus *m*, Art *f*
  crack opening modus Rißöffnungsart *f*, Rißöffnungsmodus *m*
moiré fringes Moiré-Linienmuster *n* {Spannungsoptik}
moiré pattern Moiré-Muster *n* {Spannungsoptik}
moiré technique Moiré-Verfahren *n* {Spannungsoptik}
molybdenum, Mo Molybdän *n*, Mo
moment {mechanics} Moment *n* {Mechanik}
  bending moment Biegemoment *n*
  torsional moment Verdrehmoment *n*
monotonic monoton
  monotonic loading monotone Beanspruchung *f*, monotone Belastung *f*
mounted specimen befestigte Probe *f*, befestigter Probekörper *m*
movement {of the specimen} Bewegen *n*, Verfahren *n* {einer Probe}
movement of dislocations Versetzungsbewegung *f*
moving crack in Bewegung befindlicher Riß *m*, laufender Riß *m*
multiaxial mehrachsig
  multiaxial state of stress mehrachsiger Spannungszustand *m*
  multiaxial stress mehrachsige Spannung *f*
  multiaxial stress state mehrachsiger Spannungszustand *m*
  multiaxial tensile load mehrachsige Zugbeanspruchung *f*
multiaxiality Mehrachsigkeit *f*
multiple mehrfach, vielfach; Mehrfach-
  multiple load path Mehrfachlastweg *m*
  multiple slip Mehrfachgleitung *f*
multiplication of dislocations Versetzungsvervielfältigung *f*
multistage test Mehrstufenversuch *m*

N

N → nitrogen
Na → sodium
natural crack realer Riß *m*
Nb → niobium
Nd → neodynium
NDE → non-destructive evaluation
NDT → nil ductility temperature
NDT → non-destructive testing
Ne → neon
near nahe
  near crack tip in der Nähe der Rißspitze
necking Einschnürung *f*, Einschnüren *n*, Verengung *f*
  necking in tension Brucheinschnürung *f*
neighbo[u]rhood of crack tip <syn.: **crack tip vicinity**> Rißspitzenumgebung *f*
neodymium, Nd Neodym *n*, Nd
neon, Ne Neon *n*, Ne
neutron embrittlement Versprödung *f* durch Neutronenstrahlung
new specimen "jungfräuliche" Probe *f*
Ni → nickel
Niblink test {crack-initiation temperature} Niblink-Versuch *m* {Rißeinleitungstemperatur}

nickel

nickel, Ni Nickel *n*, Ni
nickel alloy Nickellegierung *f*
nickel-chromium-molybdenum-vanadium steel Nickel-Chrom-Molybdän-Vanadium-Stahl *m*
nickel-copper alloy Nickel-Kupfer-Legierung *f*
nickel-molybdenum-vanadium alloy Nickel-Molybdän-Vanadium-Legierung *f*
nil ductility temperature <abb.: NDT> NDT-Temperatur *f* {Grenztemperatur, bei der ein Riß nicht mehr aufgehalten werden kann}
niobium, Nb, columbium, Cb Niob *n*, Nb
niobium alloy Niobiumlegierung *f*
nitrided steel nitrierter Stahl *m*, nitriergehärteter Stahl *m*
nitrogen, N Stickstoff *m*, N
node Knoten *m* {Versetzung}
dislocation node Versetzungsknoten *m*
node {finite-element method} Knoten *m* {Methode der finiten Elemente}
nominal nominell; Nenn-, Nominal-
nominal cross-section of the crack Rißnennquerschnitt *m*
nominal shear stress Nennscherspannung *f*
nominal strain Nenndehnung *f*
nominal strength Nennfestigkeit *f*
nominal stress Nennspannung *f*, Nominalspannung *f*
nominal stress of outer fibers Randfaser-Nennspannung *f*
nominal tensile strength Nennzugfestigkeit *f*
non nicht -
non-ag[e]ing steel alterungsbeständiger Stahl *m*
non-ambient temperature test Prüfung *f* bei außergewöhnlichen Temperaturen {abweichend von der Raumtemperatur}

non-combustibility test Prüfung *f* der Nichtbrennbarkeit (Unbrennbarkeit)
non-combustible unbrennbar, nicht brennbar
non-crystalline nichtkristallin
non-cumulative fracture nichtkumulativer Bruch *m*
non-cumulative rupture isolierter Bruch *m*
non-destructive zerstörungsfrei
non-destructive evaluation <abb.: NDE> zerstörungsfreie Bewertung *f*
non-destructive testing <abb.: NDT> zerstörungsfreie Prüfung *f*, ZfP
non-linear nichtlinear
non-linear load-displacement curve nichtlineare Lastverschiebungskurve *f*
non-linearity Nichtlinearität *f*
non-metallic material nichtmetallischer Werkstoff *m*
non-propagating crack stehender Riß *m*, ruhender Riß *m*
non-propagating crack tip ruhende Rißspitze *f*
non-rigid plastic weicher Kunststoff *m*
non-standard method nicht genormte Prüfmethode *f*
non-steady crack propagation instationäre Rißausbreitung *f*
non-steady state method of determining instationäres Bestimmungsverfahren *n*
non-uniform stress field ungleichförmiges Spannungsfeld *n*
nonaustenitic steel nichtaustenitischer Stahl *m*
nonembrittled specimen nicht versprödete Probe *f*
nonextending crack stehender Riß *m*
nonferrous alloys *pl* Nichteisenmetallegierungen *fpl*
nonferrous metals *pl* Nichteisenmetalle *npl*, NE-Metalle *npl*

nonlinear crack problem nichtlineares Rißproblem n
nonlinear elastic fracture mechanics nichtlinear-elastische Bruchmechanik f
nonlinear elasticity nichtlineare Elastizität f
nonlinear fracture nichtlineare Bruchmechanik f
nonlinear model nichtlineares Modell n
nonmetallic inclusion nichtmetallischer Einschluß m
nonmetallic material nichtmetallischer Werkstoff m
nonsingular stress nichtsinguläre Spannung f
normal Normale f, Senkrechte f
normal normal; senkrecht
normal component of stress Normalspannungskomponente f
normal force Normalkraft f
normal strain Normaldehnung f
normal stress Normalspannung f
normal stress component Normalspannungskomponente f
normal stress distribution Normalspannungsverteilung f
normal temperature Normaltemperatur f
criterion of normal stresses Normalspannungskriterium n
hypothesis of normal stresses Normalspannungshypothese f
principal normal stress Hauptnormalspannung f
principal normal stress criterion Hauptnormalspannungskriterium n
principal normal tensile stress Hauptnormalzugspannung f
normalization {mathematics} Normierung f {Mathematik}
normalize/to {mathematics} normieren {Mathematik}
normalized normiert
normalized circumferential stress normierte Umfangsspannung f
normalized compliance normierte Nachgiebigkeit f
normalized correction function normierte Korrekturfunktion f
normalized crack extension normierte Rißöffnung f
notch Kerb m, Kerbe f,
notch acuity Kerbschärfe f
notch bend test Kerbbiegeversuch m
notch bend test specimen Kerbbiegeprobe f
notch configuration Kerbkonfiguration f
notch depth Kerbtiefe f
notch dimensions pl Kerbabmessungen fpl
notch effect Kerbwirkung f
notch extension Kerbaufweitung f, Kerböffnung f
notch geometry Kerbgeometrie f
notch impact test specimen Kerbschlagprobe f
notch impact toughness Kerbschlagzähigkeit f
notch impact toughness-temperature curve Kerbschlagzähigkeits-Temperatur-Kurve f, Kerbschlagzähigkeits-Temperaturverlauf m
notch impact toughness value Kerbschlagzähigkeitswert m
notch length Kerblänge f
notch line Kerblinie f
notch on outer surface Außenkerb m
notch plane Kerbenebene f
notch problem Kerbproblem n
notch radius Kerbradius m
notch root Kerbgrund m
notch root radius Kerbgrundradius m
notch root radius of curvature Kerbgrund-Krümmungsradius m
notch sensitive {materials} kerbempfindlich {Werkstoffe}
notch sensitivity Kerbempfindlichkeit f
notch sensitivity ratio <abb.: NSR> Kerbempfindlichkeitszahl f
notch sharpness Kerbschärfe f

notch stress Kerbspannung *f*
notch surface Kerb[ober]fläche *f*
notch tensile strength Kerbzugfestigkeit *f*
notch tension test Kerbzugversuch *m*
notch thickness Kerbdicke *f*
notch tip Kerbspitze *f*
notch-unnotch ratio Kerbfestigkeitsverhältnis *n*
blunt notch abgestumpfte Kerbe *f*, abgestumpfter Kerb *m*
Chevron crack starter notch Chevron-Rißstarterkerbe *f*
Chevron notch Chevron-Kerbe *f* {Kerb in Proben}
circular notch runder Kerb *m*
circumferential notch Umfangskerb *m*
circumferential notch {of a round test specimen} Umlaufkerbe *f* {einer Rundprobe}
crack starter notch Rißstarterkerbe *f*
edge notch Randkerbe *f*
effect of notch Kerbeinfluß *m*, Kerbwirkung *f*
elliptical notch elliptische Kerbe *f*
end of the notch Kerbende *n*
fatigue notch factor {unnotched specimen/notched specimen} Kerbwirkungszahl *f* {ungekerbte Probe/gekerbte Probe}
internal notch Innenkerbe *f*
location of the notch Kerblage *f*
machined notch Kerbeinfräsung *f*
macroscopic notch makroskopischer Kerb *m*
microscopic notch mikroskopischer Kerb *m*
notch-unnotch ratio, notch sensitivity ratio, NSR Kerbempfindlichkeitszahl *f*
parabolic notch Parabelkerbe *f*
semi-infinite notch halbunendlicher Kerb *m*
shallow notch flacher Kerb *m*
sharp external notch scharfer Außenkerb *m*

sharp internal notch scharfer Innenkerb *m*
sharpness of the notch Kerbschärfe *f*
sharp notch scharfer Kerb *m*, Spitzkerbe *f*
single-edge notch specimen Probe *f* mit einseitigem Kerb
single-edge notch tensile specimen einseitig gekerbte Zugprobe *f*
smooth-ended notch glatte Kerbe *f*
starter notch Ausgangskerbe *f*
surface notch Oberflächenkerb *m*
theory of notch stresses Kerbspannungslehre *f*, Kerbtheorie *f*
type of notch Kerbform *f*
notch/to einkerben, kerben
notched {specimens} gekerbt {Proben}
notched bar gekerbter Stab *m*, Kerbstab *m*
notched-bar impact test Kerbschlagbiegeversuch *m*
notched-bar impact test specimen Kerbschlagbiegeprobe *f*
notched-bar impact testing Kerbschlagbiegeprüfung *f*
notched-bar tensile strength Kerbzugfestigkeit *f*
notched-bar tensile test Kerbzugversuch *m*
notched-bar tensile test specimen Kerbzugprobe *f*
notched bend test specimen gekerbte Biegeprobe *f*
notched body gekerbter Körper *m*
notched plate gekerbte Platte *f*, gekerbtes Blech *n*
notched specimen gekerbte Probe *f*
notched surfase {of the specimen} gekerbte Oberfläche *f* {von Proben}
notched tear test specimen gekerbte Aufreißprobe *f*
notched tensile test Kerbzugversuch *m*
notched tension-test specimen gekerbte Zugprobe *f*

notched {test} specimen gekerbte Probe *f*, gekerbter Probekörper *m*
centrally notched specimen Probe *f* mit Mittelkerb
circumferentially notched round bar specimen Rundprobe *f* mit Umdrehungskerbe
instrumented notched-bar impact test instrumentierter Kerbschlagbiegeversuch *m*
single-edge notched bend <abb.: SENB> specimen Einfachkantenriß-Biegeprobe *f*, SENB-Probe *f*
single-edge notched flat tensile specimen einseitig gekerbte Flachzugprobe *f*
single-edge notched <abb.: SEN> specimen {notch + crack} Einfachkantenrißprobe *f*, SEN-Probe *f* {Kerb Riß}
notching {of the specimen} Einkerben *n*, Kerben *n*, Einkerbung *f* {von Proben}
nucleation Keimbildung *f*
nucleation of cracks Rißkeimbildung *f*
crack nucleation Rißkeimbildung *f*
nucleus Kern *m* Keim *m*, Keimstelle *f*
nucleus {cracks, fracture} Keimstelle *f*, Ausgangsstelle *f* {Risse, Bruch}
crack nucleus Rißkeim *m*
fracture nucleus Bruchausgangspunkt *m*
number Zahl *f*, Anzahl *f*
number of flexings Anzahl *f* (Zahl *f*) der Biegungen
number of load cycles Lastwechselfrequenz *f*
number of stress cycles Lastspielfrequenz *f*, Lastspielzahl *f*
Brinell hardness number <abb.: HB> Brinellhärte *f*
Knoop hardness number <abb.: HK> {indentation hardness} Knoop-Härte *f* {Eindringhärte}
Rockwell hardness number Rockwellhärte *f*
Scleroscope hardness number Rücksprunghärte *f*
Vickers hardness number, VH Vickershärte *f*

O

oblique schräg (liegend), schräg verlaufend
oblique crack Schrägriß *m*
oblique failure schräger Bruch *m*
oblique fracture schräg verlaufender Bruch *m*
open offen
open crack offener Riß *m*
opening Öffnung *f*
crack opening Rißöffnung *f*
crack opening displacement criterion, COD criterion Rißöffnungsverschiebungskriterium *n*, COD-Kriterium *n*
crack opening displacement <abb.: COD> Rißöffnungsverschiebung *f*, COD
crack opening factor Rißöffnungsfaktor *m*
crack opening measurement Rißöffnungsmessung *f*
crack opening modus Rißöffnungsmodus *m*, Rißöffnungsart *f*
crack-tip opening Rißspitzenöffnung *f*
crack tip opening displacement <abb.: CTOD> Rißspitzenöffnungsverschiebung *f*, CTOD
critical crack opening displacement kritische Rißöffnungsverschiebung *f*
critical crack tip opening kritische Rißspitzenöffnung *f*
surface crack opening displacement <abb.: SCOD> Oberflächen-Rißöffnungs-Verschiebung *f*, SCOD
operating Betriebs-
operating temperature Betriebstemperatur *f*
optical optisch

optical measurement of crack length optische Rißlängenmessung f
optical test method optische Prüfmethode f
orange peel {surface roughening} Apfelsinenschaleneffekt m {Oberflächenfehler}
orientation Orientierung f
   orientation of specimen Probenorientierung f
   crack front orientation Rißfrontorientierung f
   crack orientation Rißorientierung f
   crack plane orientation Orientierung f der Rißebene
   preferred orientation {crystal} Vorzugsrichtung f, Hauptrichtung f {Kristall}
orthotropic orthotrop
   orthotropic crack system orthotropes Rißsystem n
   orthotropic plate orthotrope Platte f
orthotropy Orthotropie f
osmium, Os Osmium n, Os
out-of-plane shear Längsscherung f
outer äußere(r,s); Außen-
   outer fiber {materials} Außenfaser f {Werkstoffe}
   outer zone {crack tip} äußerer Bereich {Rißspitze}
   crack at the outer surface Riß m auf der m Außenfläche
   nominal stress of outer fibers Randfaser-Nennspannung f
   stress of outer fibers Randfaserspannung f
outside außen; Außen-
   outside diameter {of the specimen} Außendurchmesser m {von Proben}
oval oval; langgestreckt
   oval crack ovaler Riß m
   oval dimple {dimple rupture} ovales Grübchen n {Grübchenbruch}
oven with fan circulation of the air Wärmeschrank m mit zwängsläufiger Durchlüftung

overall crack rate Gesamtrißgeschwindigkeit f
overload Überlast f, Überlastung f, Überbeanspruchung f, Lastüberhöhung f
   overload effect Überlastwirkung f
   overload fracture Gewaltbruch m
   overload fracture surface Gewaltbruchfläche f
   overload stress Überlastspannung f
   brittle overload fracture spröder Gewaltbruch m
   ductile overload fracture duktiler Gewaltbruch m
   mechanical overload mechanische Überlastung f
   torsion overload fracture Torsionsgewaltbruch m
overload/to überlasten, überbeanspruchen
oxidation Oxidation f
   oxidation of the crack surface Rißflächenoxidation f
oxidative oxidativ
   oxidative wear {oxide film} oxidativer Verschleiß m {Oxidfilm}
oxygen, O Sauerstoff m, O

P

Pa → palladium
palladium, Pd Palladium n, Pd
parabolic parabolisch, parabelförmig, Parabel-
   parabolic notch Parabelkerbe f
parallel parallel
   parallel crack paralleler Riß m
parameter Parameter m, Kennwert m, Kenngröße f
   parameter of fracture Bruchkennwert m
   parameter of fracture mechanics bruchmechanischer Kennwert m
   correlation parameter Korrelationsparameter m
   crack-arrest parameter Rißarrestparameter m

elasto-plastic parameter elasto-plastischer Kennwert *m*
fracture mechanics parameter bruchmechanischer Kennwert *m*
fracture parameter Bruchparameter *m*, Bruchkennwert *m*
growth parameter Wachstumsparameter *m*
instability parameter Instabilitäts-Kennwert *m*
loading parameter Beanspruchungsparameter *m*, Beanspruchungskenngröße *f*
stress-intensity parameter Spannungsintensitätsparameter *m*
test parameter Versuchsparameter *m*
toughness parameter Zähigkeitsparameter *m*
part Teil *n*, Teil *m*
part-circular crack Kreisabschnittriß *m*
part-through crack Teildurchriß *m*, teilweise durchgehender Riß *m*
partial partiell, teilweise
partial load Teillast *f*
partial unloading partielle Entlastung *f*
particle Teilchen *n*
particles failure Teilchenbruch *m* {das Brechen von z.B. harten Teilchen}
path Bahn *f*, Weg *m*, Pfad *m*
crack path Rißlaufweg *m*
crack path Rißpfad *m*
fracture path Bruchbahn *f*
path of rupture Bruchverlauf *m*
multiple load path Mehrfachlastweg *m*
pattern Muster *n*; Bild *n*, Anordnung *f*
crack pattern Rißmuster *n*
crack-propagation pattern Rißausbreitungsschema *n*
moiré pattern Moiré-Muster *n*
river pattern Flußmuster *n*
patterns *pl* **of dislocation** Versetzungsanordnung *f*
Pb → lead

peak Peak *n*, Spitze *f*
peak load Spitzenlast *f*
load peak Lastspitze *f*
positive peak load positive Spitzenlast *f*
stress peak Spannungsspitze *f*
pearlite Perlit *m*
pearlitic perlitisch
pearlitic ductile iron perlitisches duktiles Eisen *n*
pearlitic steel perlitischer Stahl *m*
pendulum {of the pendulum impact tester} Pendel *n* {eines Pendelschlagwerkes}
pendulum impact tester Pendelschlagwerk *n*
pendulum machine Pendelschlagwerk *n*
impact pendulum Pendelhammer *m*
penetrant inspection {detection of cracks} Eindringprüfung *f* {Rißnachweis}
penetrate/to eindringen
penetrative load Durchstoßbelastung *f*, Durchstoßlast *f*
penetrometer method Eindringverfahren *n*
penetrometer technique Eindringtechnik *f*
penny-shaped crack münzförmiger Riß *m*, pfennigförmiger Riß *m*
percentage Prozentsatz *m*; Bruchanteil *m*
percentage of fracture Bruchanteil *m*
percentage shear fracture Schubbruchanteil *m*, Scherbruchanteil *m*
percentage shear lips Scherlippenanteil *m*
perfectly vollkommen, voll-
perfectly plastic behavio[u]r vollplastisches Verhalten *n*
perfectly plastic state vollplastischer Zustand *m*
periphery {e.g. of cracks} Umfeld *n* {z.B. von Rissen}

permanent

crack periphery Rißumgebung f, Randgebiet n des Risses
permanent dauerhaft, bleibend, Dauer-, Langzeit-
  permanent damage bleibende Schädigung f, dauerhafte Schädigung f
  permanent deformation bleibende Verformung f
  permanent effect of heat {on plastics} Dauerwärmeeinwirkung f, Langzeitwärmeeinwirkung f
  permanent strain bleibende Dehnung f
permissible zulässig
  permissible load Beanspruchbarkeit f
  permissible stress Beanspruchbarkeit f
phase Phase f; Stadium n
  phase boundary Phasengrenze f
  phase of fracture Bruchstadium n
  unloading phase Entlastungsphase f
phenomenology Phänomenologie f
phenomenon Phänomen n, Erscheinung f
  fracture phenomenon Bruchphänomen n
phosphorus, P Phosphor m, P
photoelastic photoelastisch, spannungsoptisch
  photoelastic method photoelastische (spannungsoptische) Methode f
photoelasticity Photoelastizität f, Spannungsoptik f
  dynamic photoelasticity dynamische Spannungsoptik f
  plane static photoelasticity ebene statische Spannungsoptik f
  scattered light photoelasticity Streulichtverfahren n {Spannungsoptik}
  stress freezing photoelasticity Einfrierverfahren n {Spannungsoptik}
  three-dimensional photoelasticity räumliche Spannungsoptik f
  two-dimensional dynamic photoelasticity ebene dynamische Spannungsoptik f
physical physikalisch
  physical conditions pl {of the test} physikalische Bedingungen fpl {einer Prüfung}
  physical crack physikalischer Riß m
  physical crack length physikalische Rißlänge f
  physical properties pl physikalische Eigenschaften fpl
pickling crack Beizriß m
piece Körper m, Prüfkörper m
  shape of test piece Prüfkörperform f
  tensile test piece Zugprobe f, Prüfkörper m für den Zugversuch
  test piece Prüfkörper m
  test piece thickness Prüfkörperdicke f
pile-up {dislocations} Aufstau m {Versetzungen}
  pile-up of dislocations Versetzungsaufstauung f
  pile-up {dislocations} Aufstau m {Versetzungen}
pinhole {metal surface} Nadelstichpore f {Metalloberfläche}
Piobert lines pl Lüderssche Linien fpl, Lüders-Streifen mpl, Fließlinien fpl {inhomogenes Fließen}
pitting {corrosion} Lochfraß m {Korrosion}
place/to {a specimen} anordnen {eine Probe}
plain eben
  plain carbon steel unlegierter Kohlenstoffstahl m
  plain strain compression ebene (zweiachsige) Druckbeanspruchung f
  plain strain compression test ebene (zweidimensionale) Druckfestigkeitsprüfung f
plane eben; Ebene f
  plane crack problem ebenes Rißproblem n

plane deformation state ebener Verformungszustand *m*
plane elastic crack problem ebenes elastisches Rißproblem *n*
plane of crystalline fracture Trennbruchebene *f*
plane of separation Trennebene *f*
plane of the crack Rißebene *f*
plane problem of crack ebenes Rißproblem *n*
plane shear ebener Schub *m*
plane static photoelasticity ebene statische Spannungsoptik *f*
plane strain ebene Dehnung *f*, ebene Verzerrung *f*
plane strain fracture EVZ-Bruch *m*
plane strain fracture toughness EVZ-Bruchzähigkeit *f* {EVZ ebener Verzerrungszustand}
plane strain testing EVZ-Prüfung *f* {EVZ ebener Verzerrungszustand}
plane stress ebene Spannung *f*, E.S.
plane stress fracture ESZ-Bruch *m*
plane stress fracture toughness ESZ-Bruchzähigkeit *f* {ESZ ebener Spannungszustand}
plane stress state ebener Spannungszustand *m*, ESZ
plane stress testing ESZ-Prüfung *f* {ESZ ebener Spannungszustand}
cleavage plane Spalt[bruch]ebene *f*
crack plane orientation Orientierung *f* der Rißebene
crack-tip plane strain ebene Dehnung *f* an der Rißspitze
crystallographic plane Kristallebene *f*
fracture plane Bruchebene *f*
middle plane of specimen Probenmittelebene *f*
notch plane Kerbebene *f*
preferred cleavage plane bevorzugte Spaltebene *f*
principal slip plane Hauptgleitebene *f*
principal-stress plane Hauptspannungsebene *f*
reference plane Bezugsebene *f*
secondary slip plane Sekundärgleitebene *f*
shear plane Scherebene *f*
slip plane Gleitebene *f*
specimen fracture plane Bruchebene *f* der Probe
state of plane deformation ebener Verformungszustand *m*
state of plane strain ebener Dehnungszustand *m*, EDZ
state of plane strain ebener Verzerrungszustand *m*, EVZ
state of plane stress ebener Spannungszustand *m*, ESZ
planimetry Planimetrie *f* {Flächenmessung}
plastic Kunststoff *m*
flexible plastic biegsamer Kunststoff *m*
non-rigid plastic weicher Kunststoff *m*
rigid plastic harter Kunststoff *m*
unfilled plastic nicht gefüllter Kunststoff *m*
plastic {material} plastisch {Werkstoff}
plastic behavio[u]r plastisches Verhalten *n*
plastic collaps plastischer Kollaps *m*, plastisches Versagen *n*
plastic crack propagation plastische Rißausbreitung *f*
plastic crack-tip extension plastische Rißspitzenaufweitung *f*
plastic deformation plastische Deformation *f*, Verformung *f*
plastic failure plastisches versagen *n*
plastic flow plastisches Fließen *n*
plastic fracture Verformungsbruch *m*
plastic instability plastische Instabilität *f*
plastic limit load plastische Grenzlast *f*
plastic region plastischer Bereich *m*
plastic singularity plastische Singularität *f*
plastic strain plastische Dehnung *f*

plasticity

plastic strain concentration factor plastischer Dehnungskonzentrationsfaktor m
plastic strain constraint plastische Dehnungsbehinderung f
plastic stress plastische Spannung f
plastic stress-concentration factor plastischer Spannungskonzentrationsfaktor m
plastic yield Wärmebeständigkeit f, Formbeständigkeit f in der Wärme
plastic yield test Prüfung f der Formbeständigkeit in der Wärme
plastic yielding plastisches Fließen n
plastic zone plastische Zone f
plastic zone elongation Verlängerung f der plastischen Zone
plastic zone form Form f der plastischen Zone
plastic zone size Größe f der plastischen Zone
cyclic plastic deformation zyklische plastische Verformung f
dimensionless plastic zone dimensionslose plastische Zone f
effective plastic zone effektive plastische Zone f
energy of plastic deformation plastische Verformungsenergie f
length of plastic zone Länge f der plastischen Zone
perfectly plastic behavio[u]r vollplastisches Verhalten n
perfectly plastic state vollplastischer Zustand m
radius of the plastic zone Radius m der plastischen Zone
rate of plastic straining plastische Dehnungsgeschwindigkeit f, Geschwindigkeit f der plastischen Dehnung
plasticity Plastizität f
plasticity correction {crack length} Plastizitätskorrektur f {Rißlänge}
plasticity theory Plastizitätstheorie f
  ideal plasticity ideale Plastizität f
plastics Plast-

plastics material Kunststoff m
cellular plastics Schaumkunststoff m
plate Platte f; Blech n; Scheibe f
plate specimen plattenförmige Probe f
plate thickness Plattendicke f; Blechdicke f; Scheibendicke f
plate width Plattenbreite f, Scheibenbreite f
cracked plate gerissene Platte f
infinite plate unendlich ausgedehnte Scheibe f, unendliche Scheibe f
notched plate gekerbte Platte f, gekerbtes Blech n
orthotropic plate orthotrope Platte f
rectangular plate rechteckige Platte f
test plate Prüfplatte f
through-cracked plate Platte f mit durchgehendem Riß
welded plate geschweißte Platte f
platinum, Pt Platin n, Pt
platinum-carbon alloy Platin-Kohlenstoff-Legierung f
platinum-gallium alloy Platin-Gallium-Legierung f
platinum-rhodium alloy Platin-Rhodium-Legierung f
point Punkt m; Temperatur f; Grenze f; Einzel-
point force Einzelkraft f
point load Einzellast f
automatic Vicat softening point apparatus automatisches Prüfgerät n zur Bestimmung der Vicat-Erweichungstemperatur
brittle point Versprödungstemperatur f, Sprödigkeitstemperatur f
intersection point Schnittpunkt m
load-application point Lastangriffspunkt m
lower yield point untere Fließgrenze f
soft point determination Erweichungspunktbestimmung f, Bestimmung f des Erweichungspunktes

softening point Erweichungstemperatur f, Erweichungspunkt m
stress point Spannungspunkt m
tensile yield strength, tensile yield point Streckgrenze f
test point Versuchspunkt m
upper yield point obere Fließgrenze f
Vicat softening point Vicat-Erweichungstemperatur f
Vicat softening point apparatus Gerät n zur Bestimmung der Vicat-Erweichungstemperatur f
yield point Fließgrenze f
zero point Nullpunkt m
Poisson's ratio Poissonsche Konstante f, Querkontraktionszahl f
polar coordinates pl {mathematics} Polarkoordinaten fpl {Mathematik}
polar {mathematics} polar, Polar- {Mathematik}
polish/to {a specimen} polieren {eine Probe}
polycrystalline polykristallin
polycrystalline material polykristalliner Werkstoff m
polymer Polymer n, Polymeres n
polymeric sample Kunststoffprobe f
pop-in {the first discrete crack extension} pop-in {plötzliche Rißinitiation, Rißeinbruch}
pore Pore f {in Werkstoffen}
cylindrical pore zylindrische Pore f
spherical pore kugelförmige Pore f
porosity Porosität f, Porigkeit f
gas porosity {metals} Gasporosität {Metalle}
porous porös, porig
porportional proportional, Proportional-
position Position f, Lage f, Stelle f
flaw position {in materials} Fehlerstelle f {in Werkstoffen}
zero position Nullage f, Nullstellung f
positive positiv

positive compression positive Druckbeanspruchung f
positive peak load positive Spitzenlast f
potassium, K Kalium n, K
potential potentiell
potential crack potentieller Riß m
potential energy potentielle Energie f
potential... Potential-
electric potential method {determination of crack depth} Potentialsondenverfahren n {Rißtiefenbestimmung}
potentiometer Potentiometer m
poultice corrosion Korrosion f unter Ablagerungen {z.B. Karosserieteile von Kraftfahrzeugen}
pre-crack/to anreißen
pre An-, Vor-
pre-crack Anriß m
pre-crack formation Anrißbildung f
pre-crack initiation Anrißerzeugung f
pre-crack length Anrißlänge f
pre-crack production Anrißerzeugung f
pre-crack-size Anrißgröße f
cleavage pre-crack Spaltanriß m
critical pre-crack size kritische Anrißgröße f
fatigue pre-crack Dauerschwinganriß m, Dauerbruchanriß m
fatigue pre-crack length Ermüdungsanrißlänge f
fatigue pre-crack Ermüdungsanriß m
material without pre-crack anrißfreier Werkstoff m
without pre-crack anrißfrei
pre-cracked angerissen
pre-cracked specimen {testing} angerissene Probe f, Probe f mit Anriß {Prüfung}
pre-cracking Anrißbildung f
pre-heated specimen vorgewärmte (angewärmte) Probe f

precipitation

pre-history of loading Belastungsvorgeschichte f
precipitation-hardening stainless steel ausscheidungshärtender nichtrostender Stahl m
precision <syn.: accuracy> {of the apparatus} Meßgenauigkeit f {eines Gerätes}
predetermination Vorausbestimmung f
predetermine/to vorherbestimmen, im voraus bestimmen
predict/to {fracture, failure} voraussagen, vorhersagen {Bruch, Ausfall}
predicted fracture stress vorhergesagte Bruchspannung f
prediction {fracture, failure} Voraussage f, Vorhersage f {Bruch, Ausfall}
fatique crack prediction Ermüdungsrißvorhersage f
preferred cleavage plane bevorzugte Spaltebene f
preferred orientation {crystal} Vorzugsrichtung f, Hauptrichtung f {Kristall}
preload Vorbeanspruchung f
pressure Druck m
pressure dependence Druckabhängigkeit f
pressure-dependent druckabhängig
pressure vessel Druckbehälter m
bursting pressure Berstdruck m
clamping pressure {for a specimen} Einspanndruck m, Spanndruck m {Proben}
hydrostatic pressure hydrostatischer Druck m
specific heat at constant pressure spezifische Wärme f bei konstantem Druck
primary creep primäres Kriechen n
principal hauptsächlich, Haupt-
principal loading direction Hauptbelastungsrichtung f

principal normal stress Hauptnormalspannung f
principal normal stress criterion Hauptnormalspannungskriterium n
principal normal tensile stress Hauptnormalzugspannung f
principal shear stress Hauptschubspannung f
principal slip plane Hauptgleitebene f
principal stress Hauptspannung f
principal-stress plane Hauptspannungsebene f
principle Prinzip n
fracture mechanics principle Bruchmechanik-Prinzip n
superposition principle Superpositionprinzip n
prismatic prismatisch
prismatic void prismatische Pore f
probabilistic probabilistisch {auf der Wahrscheinlichkeitstheorie beruhend}
probabilistic fracture mechanics probabilistische Bruchmechanik f
probability Wahrscheinlichkeit f
probability of fracture Bruchwahrscheinlichkeit f
failure probability Ausfallwahrscheinlichkeit f, Versagenswahrscheinlichkeit f
fracture probability Bruchwahrscheinlichkeit f
problem Problem n
problem solution Problemlösung f
boundary-value problem Grenzwertproblem n, Randwertproblem n
branched crack problem Rißverzweigungsproblem n
crack problem Rißproblem n
crack-propagation problem Rißausbreitungsproblem n
dynamic crack problem dynamisches Rißproblem n
elastic boundary-value problem elastisches Grenzwertproblem n
elastic crack problem elastisches Rißproblem n

elastic-plastic boundary value problem elastisch-plastisches Randwertproblem n
elastic-plastic crack problem elastisch-plastisches Rißproblem n
elasto-plastic crack problem elasto-plastisches Rißproblem n
elasto-dynamic problem elasto-dynamisches Problem n
fracture problem Bruchproblem n
nonlinear crack problem nichtlineares Rißproblem n
notch problem Kerbproblem n
plane crack problem ebenes Rißproblem n
plane elastic crack problem ebenes elastisches Rißproblem n
plane problem of crack ebenes Rißproblem n
three-dimensional boundary-value problem dreidimensionales Grenzwertproblem n
three-dimensional crack problem dreidimensionales Rißproblem n, räumliches Rißproblem n
two-dimensional crack problem zweidimensionales Rißproblem n
process Prozeß m, Vorgang m
process of crack extension Rißerweiterungsvorgang m
process zone Prozeßzone f
crack-arrest process Rißarrestprozeß m, Rißarrestvorgang m
crack initiation process Rißinitiierungsprozeß m
crack-propagation process Rißausbreitungsvorgang m
damage process Schädigungsprozeß m
fracture process Bruchprozeß m, Bruchvorgang m, Bruchablauf m
fracture process zone Bruchprozeßzone f
loading process Belastungsablauf m
produce/to {a crack} erzeugen {einen Riß}

production {of cracks} Produktion f, Erzeugung f, Herstellung f {von Rissen}
production control Produktionskontrolle f, Produktionsüberwachung f
production of cracks {in specimens} Rißeinbringung f, Rißerzeugung f {in Proben}
fatigue crack production Ermüdungsrißerzeugung f
pre-crack production Anrißerzeugung f
profile Profil n, Verlauf m
crack profile Rißprofil n
crack-tip profile Rißspitzenprofil n
fracture strength profile Bruchflächenprofil n
temperature profile Temperaturverlauf m
program Programm n, Ablauf m, Abfolge f
loading program Belastungsfolge f
test program Versuchsprogramm n
propagate/to {cracks} ausbreiten {Risse}
propagating Ausbreiten n Fortschreiten n
crack propagating Rißfortschreiten n
propagating crack sich ausbreitender Riß m, sich ausbreitender Riß m
slowly propagating crack sich langsam ausbreitender Riß m
propagation {of cracks} Ausbreitung f, Fortpflanzung f {von Rissen}
propagation velocity {of cracks} Ausbreitungsgeschwindigkeit f {von Rissen}
propagation {of cracks} Ausbreitung f, Fortpflanzung f {von Rissen}
accelerated crack propagation beschleunigte Rißausbreitung f
border of crack propagation Rißausbreitungsgrenze f
brittle crack propagation spröde Rißausbreitung f

properties

crack propagation Rißausbreitung *f*, Rißentwicklung *f*, Rißfortschritt *m*
criterion for fracture propagation Bruchausbreitungskriterium *n*
cryogenic crack propagation test Tieftemperaturrißausbreitungsversuch *m*
ductile crack propagation duktile Rißausbreitung *f*
dynamic crack propagation dynamische Rißausbreitung *f*
elastic crack propagation elastische Rißausbeitung *f*
fatigue crack propagation test Ermüdungsrißausbreitungsversuch *m*
fire propagation test Prüfung *f* der Brandausbreitung
fracture propagation Bruchausbreitung *f*
fracture propagation data *pl* Bruchausbreitungsangaben *fpl*
fracture propagation direction Bruchausbreitungsrichtung *f*
intercrystalline crack propagation interkristalline Rißausbreitung *f*
local crack propagation lokale Rißausbreitung *f*
macroscopic direction of crack propagation makroskopische Rißausbreitungsrichtung *f*
macroscopic direction of fracture propagation makroskopische Bruchausbreitungsrichtung *f*
measurement of crack propagation Rißausbreitungsmessung *f*
microductile crack propagation mikroduktile Rißausbreitung *f*
non-steady crack propagation instationäre Rißausbreitung *f*
plastic crack propagation plastische Rißausbreitung *f*
rapid crack propagation schnelle Rißausbreitung *f*
rate of fatigue crack propagation Ermüdungsrißausbreitungsgeschwindigkeit *f*
region of crack propagation Rißausbreitungsbereich *m*

resistance to flame propagation Flammenausbreitungswiderstand *m*
resistant to flame propagation beständig gegenüber Flammenausbreitung *f*
slip-band crack propagation Gleitbandrißausbreitung *f*
stable crack propagation stabile Rißausbreitung *f*
stage of crack propagation Rißausbreitungsstadium *n*
steady-state crack propagation stationäre Rißausbreitung *f*
subcritical crack propagation unterkritische Rißausbreitung *f*, vorkritische Rißausbreitung *f*
transcrystalline crack propagation transkristalline Rißausbreitung *f*
unstable propagation of fracture instabile Bruchausbreitung *f*
unstable crack propagation instabile Rißausbreitung *f*
velocity of crack propagation Rißausbreitungsgeschwindigkeit *f*
properties *pl* Eigenschaften *fpl*
bending properties *pl* Biegeeigenschaften *fpl*, Eigenschaften *fpl* bei Biegebeanspruchung
deformation properties *pl* Verformungseigenschaften *fpl*
fracture properties *pl* Brucheigenschaften *fpl*
fracture toughness properties *pl* Bruchzähigkeitseigenschaften *fpl*
high-speed properties *pl* Eigenschaften *fpl* bei hohen Prüfgeschwindigkeiten
ignition properties *pl* {of plastic} Zündverhalten *n*, Zündeigenschaften *fpl*
longitudinal fracture properties *pl* Brucheigenschaften *fpl* in Längsrichtung
material properties *pl* Werkstoffeigenschaften *fpl*
material properties *pl* Werkstoffeigenschaften *fpl*
mechanical properties *pl* mechanische Eigenschaften *fpl*

physical properties *pl* physikalische Eigenschaften *fpl*
shear properties *pl* Schereigenschaften *fpl*, Eigenschaften *fpl* bei Scherbeanspruchung
strength properties *pl* Festigkeitseigenschaften *fpl*
stress-strain properties *pl* Spannungs-Dehnungs-Eigenschaften *fpl*
thermal properties *pl* thermische Eigenschaften *fpl*
thermodynamic properties *pl* thermodynamische Eigenschaften *fpl*
transverse fracture properties *pl* Brucheigenschaften *fpl* in Querrichtung
proportional proportional
  proportional (test) specimen Proportionalprobe {alle Maße stehen in festen Verhältnissen zueinander}
  proportional limit Proportionalitätsgrenze *f*
proportionality Proportionalität *f*
Pt → platinum
pure {loading: Material} rein {Belastung: Werkstoff}
  pure bending reine Biegung *f*
  pure shear reiner Schub *m*
  pure shear loading reine Schubbeanspruchung *f*
  pure {loading; material} rein {Belastung; Werkstoff}

Q

qualitative qualitativ
quality Qualität *f*
  quality control Qualitätskontrolle *f*, Qualitätsüberwachung *f*
  quality control test Qualitätsprüfung *f*
quantification Quantifizierung *f*
quantify/to {fracture surfaces} quantifizieren {Bruchflächen}
quantitative quantitativ
quarter Viertel *n*; Viertel-

quarter-elliptical crack viertelelliptischer Riß *m*
quarter-elliptical flaw Viertelellipsenfehler *m*
quasi Quasi-
  quasi-brittle fracture Quasisprödbruch *m*
  quasi-cleavage facet {fracture surface} Quasi-Spaltbruch-Facette *f* {Bruchfläche}
  quasi-cleavage fracture Quasispaltbruch *m*
  quasi-dynamic method {for determining conductivity} quasi-dynamisches Prüfverfahren *n* {zur Bestimmung der Leitfähigkeit}
  quasi-static crack extension quasi-statische Rißerweiterung *f*
  quasi-static crack initiation quasi-statische Rißeinleitung *f*
  quasi-static crack velocity quasi-statische Rißgeschwindigkeit *f*
  quasi-static fracture toughness quasistatische Bruchzähigkeit *f*
  quasi-steady state method quasistationäre Prüfmethode *f*
quench-cracking susceptibility Härterißanfälligkeit *f*
quenching Härten *n*, Härtung *f*
  quenching crack Härteriß *m*
  intergranular quenching crack intergranularer Härteriß *m*

R

R → crack resistance
R curve concept {R crack resistance} R-Kurven-Konzept *n* {R Rißwiderstand}
R curve {RH} crack resistance R-Kurve *f*, Rißwiderstandskurve *f*
radial radial
  radial edge crack radialer Kantenriß *m*
  radial stress Radialspannung *f*
radiate/to strahlen, Strahlung aussenden

radiation

radiation Strahlung f
radiation damage {materials} Strahlenschaden m {Werkstoffe}
radiation-induced embrittlement Strahlungsversprödung f
radiographic testing {of materials} Durchstrahlungsprüfung f {Werkstoffe}
radium, Ra Radium n, Ra
radius Radius m
radius of curvature {at the end of a crack} Krümmungsradius m {Rißende}
radius of the crack tip Rißspitzenradius m
radius of the plastic zone Radius m der plastischen Zone
effective radius wirksamer Radius m
notch radius Kerbradius m
notch root radius Kerbgrundradius m
notch root radius of curvature Kerbgrund-Krümmungsradius m
radius/to {a specimen} abrunden {eine Probe}
rail steel Schienenstahl m
raise/to erhöhen, steigern
random Zufall m
random zufällig, Zufalls-
random failure zufälliger Ausfall m, zufälliger Bruch m
random stress loading Zufallsbelastung f
range {temperature, pressure...} Bereich m, Intervall n {Temperatur, Druck-}
range of crack length Rißlängenbereich m
limiting transition temperature range Übergangstemperaturgrenzbereich m
stress intensity range Wechselspannungsintensitätsfaktor m, Spannungsintensitätsbereich m
temperature range Temperaturbereich m
transition range Übergangsbereich m
transition temperature range Übergangstemperaturbereich m
yielding range Fließbereich m
rapid schnell
rapid crack propagation schnelle Rißausbreitung f
rate {process} Geschwindigkeit f {Vorgang}; Rate f
rate-dependent geschwindigkeitsabhängig
rate-dependent fracture toughness geschwindigkeitsabhängige Bruchzähigkeit f
rate-independent geschwindigkeitsunabhängig
rate of burning Verbrennungsgeschwindigkeit f
rate of elastic straining elastische Dehnungsgeschwindigkeit f, Geschwindigkeit f der elastischen Dehnung
rate of evaporation Verdunstungsgeschwindigkeit f
rate of extension Dehn[ungs]geschwindigkeit f
rate of fatigue crack propagation Ermüdungsrißausbreitungsgeschwindigkeit f
rate of loading Belastungsgeschwindigkeit f
rate of plastic straining plastische Dehnungsgeschwindigkeit f
rate of plastic straining plastische Dehnungsgeschwindigkeit f, Geschwindigkeit f der plastischen Dehnung
rate of straining Dehnungsgeschwindigkeit f
rate-sensitive geschwindigkeitsempfindlich
rate-sensitive ductile material geschwindigkeitsempfindlicher duktiler Werkstoff m
average burning rate mittlere Verbrennungsgeschwindigkeit f

burning rate Verbrennungsgeschwindigkeit *f*
coolig rate Abkühlungsgeschwindigkeit *f*
crack growth energy release rate Rißwachstums-Energiefreisetzungsrate *f*
crack growth rate Rißwachstumsrate *f*
crack growth velocity, crack growth rate Rißwachstumsgeschwindigkeit *f*
crack-propagation rate Rißfortschrittsrate *f*
creep rate Kriechgeschwindigkeit *f*
critical energy release rate kritische Energiefreisetzungsrate *f*
deformation rate Deformationsgeschwindigkeit *f*, Verformungsgeschwindigkeit *f*
dynamic energy release rate dynamische Energiefreisetzungsrate *f*
energy release rate Energiefreisetzungsrate *f*, Energieanlieferungsrate *f*
fatigue crack growth rate Ermüdungsrißgeschwindigkeit *f*
growth rate Wachstumsgeschwindigkeit *f*
heating rate Aufheizgeschwindigkeit *f*
loading rate Beanspruchungsgeschwindigkeit *f*, Belastungsgeschwindigkeit *f*
local load rate lokale Belastungsgeschwindigkeit *f*
overall crack rate Gesamtrißgeschwindigkeit *f*
rate of burning Verbrennungsgeschwindigkeit *f*
shear rate Schergeschwindigkeit *f*
strain energy release rate Verzerrungsenergie-Freisetzungsrate *f*
strain rate Verzerrungsgeschwindigkeit *f*, Dehnungsgeschwindigkeit *f*
strain rate energy Dehnungsgeschwindigkeitsenergie *f*
wear rate Verschleißgeschwindigkeit *f*
ratio Verhältnis *n*; Zahl *f*, Konstante *f*

notch sensitivity ratio <abb.: NSR> Kerbempfindlichkeitszahl *f*
notch-unnotch ratio Kerbfestigkeitsverhältnis *n*
Poisson's ratio Poissonsche Konstante *f*, Querkontraktionszahl *f*
slenderness ratio {test bar} Schlankheitsgrad *m* {Probestab}
stress ratio {alternating stress amplitude/mean stress or minimum stress/maximum stress} Spannungsverhältnis *n* {Wechselspannungsamplitude/Mittelspannung oder Minimalspannung/Maximalspannung}
yield point-to-tensile strength ratio Streckgrenzenverhältnis *n*
Rayleigh wave velocity Rayleighwellengeschwindigkeit *f*
RCT → round compact tension...
R-curve → crack resistance curve
Re → rhenium
reach/to erreichen
record/to aufzeichnen
recovery {after removal of the load} Rückverformung *f* {nach der Entlastung}
rectangular rechteckig
rectangular cross section rechteckiger Querschnitt *m*
rectangular plate rechteckige Platte *f*
rectangular surface crack rechteckiger Oberflächenriß *m*
rectilinear geradlining
rectilinear crack geradliniger Riß *m*
rectilinearity Geradlinigkeit *f*
reduced reduziert, verringert, gemindert, verkleinert
reduced stress reduzierte Spannung *f*
reduction Reduzierung *f*, Verminderung *f*, Verkleinerung *f*, Verringerung *f*
reduction in area Querschnittsabnahme *f*, Querschnittsverringerung *f*

reduction

reduction in cross section Querschnittsreduzierung f, Querschnittsverringerung f
reduction of area Querschnittsabnahme, Querschnittsverringerung f
stress reduction Spannungsabbau m
reduction {chemical} Reduktion f {chemisch}
reference Referenz-, Bezugs-, Vergleichs-
reference curve Referenzkurve f
reference fracture toughness Referenzbruchzähigkeit f
reference material {for testing} Vergleichsmaterial n {für Prüfungen}
reference plane Bezugsebene f
reference specimen Vergleichsprobe f
reference stress-intensity factor Referenzspannungsintensitätsfaktor m
reference temperature Bezugstemperatur f, Referenztemperatur f
reflection Reflexion f
reflexion Reflexion f
refraction Brechung f
region Bereich m, Region f
region of crack propagation Rißausbreitungsbereich m
crack region Rißbereich m
plastic region plastischer Bereich m
regression curve Regressionskurve f
reinitiation {of cracks} Wiedereinleitung f {von Rissen}
relative relativ
relative crack depth relative Rißtiefe f
relative crack length relative Rißlänge f
relative crack size relative Rißabmessungen fpl, relative Rißgröße f
relaxation Relaxation f
local stress relaxation örtliche Spannungsrelaxation f
stress relaxation Spannungsrelaxation f
release Freisetzung f

crack growth energy release rate Rißwachstums-Energiefreisetzungsrate f
critical energy release rate kritische Energiefreisetzungsrate f
dynamic energy release dynamische Energiefreisetzung f
dynamic energy release rate dynamische Energiefreisetzungsrate f
energy release Energiefreisetzung f
energy release rate Energiefreisetzungsrate f, Energieanlieferungsrate f
strain energy release rate Verzerrungsenergie-Freisetzungsrate f
reloading Wiederbelastung f, wiederholte Belastung f, erneutes Belasten n
repeat test Wiederholungsprüfung f
repeat/to {a test} wiederholen {eine Prüfung}
replace/to {a specimen} entfernen {eine Probe}
replica Abdruck m
research Untersuchung f, Forschung f
failure research Schadenforschung f
fracture research Bruchuntersuchung f, Bruchforschung f
fracture research results pl Bruchuntersuchungsergebnisse npl
residual Rest-, Eigen-
compressive residual stress Druckeigenspannung f
residual stress Eigenspannung f
residual stress curve Eigenspannungsverlauf m
residual stress distribution Eigenspannungsverteilung f
residual stress field Eigenspannungsfeld n
residual stress measurement Eigenspannungsmessung f
residual stress state Eigenspannungszustand m
residual tensile stress Zugeigenspannung f
compressive residual stress curve Druckeigenspannungsverlauf m

compressive residual stress field Druckeigenspannungsfeld n
resistance Widerstand m
resistance-temperature characteristics *pl* Widerstand-Temperatur-Kennlinien *fpl*
resistance to ag[e]ing Alterungsbeständigkeit *f*
resistance to brittle fracture Sprödbruchwiderstand m
resistance to deformation, deformation resistance Verformungswiderstand m
resistance to flame propagation Flammenausbreitungswiderstand m
resistance to low temperature Tieftemperaturbeständigkeit *f*
absolute resistance to fracture absoluter Bruchwiderstand m
Charpy impact resistance Charpy-Schlagfestigkeit *f*, Schlagfestigkeit *f* nach Charpy
cold resistance Kältebeständigkeit *f*
corrosion resistance Korrosionsbeständigkeit *f*
crack growth resistance Rißausbreitungswiderstand m
crack resistance Rißwiderstand m, R
crack resistance curve <syn.: R-curve> Rißwiderstandskurve *f*, R-Kurve *f*
creep resistance Zeitstandfestigkeit *f*
deformation resistance Verformungswiderstand m
determination of crack resistance curve R-Kurvenbestimmung *f*
dynamic crack resistance curve dynamische Rißwiderstandskurve *f*
flame resistance Flammfestigkeit *f*
fracture resistance Bruchwiderstand m
fracture resistance curve Bruchwiderstandskurve *f*
fracture resistance value Bruchwiderstandswert m
heat resistance Wärmebeständigkeit *f*

impact resistance measurement Schlagfestigkeitsmessung *f*, Messung *f* der Schlagfestigkeit
local crack resistance lokaler Rißwiderstand m, örtlicher Rißwiderstand m
maximum crack resistance maximaler Rißwiderstand m
shock resistance {of materials} Stoßfestigkeit *f* {von Materialien}
test for flame resistance Flammfestigkeitsprüfung *f*
torsion resistance Torsionswiderstand, Verdrehwiderstand m
weld-crack resistance Schweißrißbeständigkeit *f*
resistant beständig
resistant to flame propagation beständig gegenüber Flammenausbreitung *f*
chemical resistant steel chemikalienbeständiger Stahl m
steel resistant to caustic cracking laugenrißbeständiger Stahl m
results *pl* Ergebnisse *npl*
fracture research results *pl* Bruchuntersuchungsergebnisse *npl*
test results *pl* Versuchsergebnisse *f*
retention factor Verzögerungsfaktor m
reversibility Reversibilität *f*
reversible reversibel, umkehrbar
Rh → rhodium
rhenium, Re Rhenium n, Re
rhodium, Rh Rhodium n, Rh
rigid starr, steif
rigid body starrer Körper m
rigid-body deformation Starrkörperverformung *f*
rigid-body displacement Starrkörperverschiebung *f*
rigid plastic harter Kunststoff m
rigid specimen harte (starre) Probe *f*
rigidity Starrheit *f*, Steifheit *f*
rigidity modulus Schub[elastizitäts]modul m, Scherungsmodul m
river pattern Flußmuster n

Robertson

Robertson
Robertson specimen {tensile test specimen} Robertson-Probe f {Zugprobe}
Robertson test {crack arrest} Robertson-Versuch m {Rißstopp}
Rockwell
Rockwell hardness number Rockwellhärte f
Rockwell hardness test Rockwellhärteprüfung f
rod {for testing} Stab m {für Prüfungen}
roentgenographic röntgenographisch
roentgenographic measurement of stresses röntgenographische Spannungsmessung f
rolling crack Walzriß m
room temperature Raumtemperatur f
root Wurzel f Grund-
root of the crack Rißgrund m
notch root Kerbgrund m
notch root radius Kerbgrundradius m
notch root radius of curvature Kerbgrund-Krümmungsradius m
rosette fracture Rosettenbruch m
rotation of crack flank Rißflankendrehung f
roughness Rauhigkeit f, Rauheit f
fracture surface roughness Bruchflächenrauhigkeit f
surface roughness Oberflächenrauheit f
round rund, Rund-
round compact tension <abb.: RCT> specimen Rund-Kompakt-Zugprobe f, RCT-Probe f
round specimen Rundprobe f
circumferentially cracked round bar specimen Rundstab m mit konzentrischem Außenriß
circumferentially notched round bar specimen Rundprobe f mit Umdrehungskerbe
concentric round bar konzentrischer Rundstab m

sharp-notched round tension specimen scharf gekerbter Zugstab m
rubidium, Rb Rubidium n, Rb
run/to {cracks} laufen {Risse}
running crack laufender Riß m
rupture Bruch m, Gewaltbruch m
rupture modulus Bruchmodul m
rupture modulus in bending Bruchmodul m bei Biegebeanspruchung
rupture strength Trennfestigkeit f
creep rupture Kriechbruch m, Zeitstandbruch m
decohesive rupture Trennbruch m
dimple rupture Grübchenbruch m
path of rupture Bruchverlauf m
rupture stress Bruchspannung f
intergranular creep rupture intergranularer Kriechbruch m
modulus of rupture Bruchmodul m
modulus of rupture in torsion Bruchmodul m bei Torsionsbeanspruchung
transgranular creep rupture transkristalliner Kriechbruch m
rural atmosphere {corrosion} Landatmosphäre f {Korrosion}
rust {corrosion product} Rost m {Korrosionsprodukt}
ruthenium, Ru Ruthenium n, Ru

S

S → sulphur
sulphur (GB), sulfur (US), S Schwefel m, S
S-N curve <syn.: S-N diagram {S stress, N number of cycles to failure}, Wöhler curve> Wöhler-Kurve f, Dauerfestigkeitskurve f
safe sicher
safety Sicherheit f
safety analysis Sicherheitsanalyse f
safety concept Sicherheitskonzept n
safety factor Sicherheitsbeiwert m, Sicherheitsfaktor m
brittle fracture safety Sprödbruchsicherheit f

crack-arrest safety analysis Rißarrestsicherheitsanalyse *f*
criterion for fracture safety Bruchsicherheitskriterium *n*
evaluation of safety Sicherheitsbewertung *f*, Sicherheitsabschätzung *f*
factor of safety Sicherheitsfaktor *m*, Sicherheitsbeiwert *m*
fracture safety Bruchsicherheit *f*
fracture safety criterion Bruchsicherheitskriterium *n*
fracture safety diagram Bruchsicherheits-Diagramm *n*
samarium, Sm Samarium *n*, Sm
sample Probe *f*
  sample holder Probenhalter *m*, Probenhalterung *f*
  sample thickness Probendicke *f*
  polymeric sample Kunststoffprobe *f*
  temperature of the sample Probentemperatur *f*
  test sample Probe *f*
saw cut gesägter Riß *m*
Sb → antimony
Sc → scandium
scan/to abtasten, zerlegen {elektronisch}
scandium, Sc Scandium *n*, Sc
scanning Abtasten *n*, Abtast *m*, Zerlegung *f* {elektronisch}
  scanning electron microscope Rasterelektronenmikroskop *n*, REM
  scanning electron microscopy Rasterelektronenmikroskopie *f*, REM
scatter/to streuen
scatterband Streuband *n*
scattered light photoelasticity Streulichtverfahren *n* {Spannungsoptik}
scattering Streuung *f*, Streuen *n*
SCC → stress corrosion cracking
SCC → subcritical crack growth
SCFM → subcritical fracture mechanics
science Wissenschaft *f*
  materials science Werkstoffwissenschaft *f*, Werkstoffkunde *f*

Scleroscope hardness number Rücksprunghärte *f*
Scleroscope hardness testing Rücksprunghärteprüfung *f*
SCOD → surface crack opening displacement
scoring {metal surface} Kratzerbildung *f*, Riefenbildung *f* {Metalloberfläche}
screw dislocation Schraubenversetzung *f*
SCT → surface-crack tensile...
scuffing {adhesive war} Abnutzung *f* {adhäsiver Verschleiß}
seasoning cracking {brass: corrosion + internal stress} Spannungsrißkorrosion *f* {Messing: Korrosion + innere Spannung}
secant modulus Sekantenmodul *m*
secondary sekundär, untergeordnet; Sekundär-, Neben-
  secondary crack Sekundärriß *m*, Nebenriß *m*
  secondary-crack length Nebenrißlänge *f*
  secondary slip plane Sekundärgleitebene *f*
  secondary cracking Rißverzweigung *f*
  secondary creep stationäres Kriechen *n*
section Querschnitt *m*; Querschnittsfläche *f*
  crack section Rißquerschnitt *m*
  cross section Querschnitt *m*
  rectangular cross section rechteckiger Querschnitt *m*
  reduction in cross section Querschnittsreduzierung *f*, Querschnittsverringerung *f*
secure/to {one end of the specimen} fixieren, sichern {ein Ende eines Probenkörpers}
segregate/to {metallography} seigern {Metallographie}

segregation

segregation Segregation *f*, Ausscheidung *f*
segregation at grain boundary Korngrenzenausscheidung *f*
segregation zone Seigerungszone *f*
grain-boundary segregation Korngrenzenseigerung *f*
selctive selektiv
selective corrosion selektive Korrosion *f*
selective leaching {corrosion} selektives Herauslösen *n* {Korrosion}
selenium, Se Selen *n*, Se
self-extinguishing selbst[ver]löschend {Eigenschaft eines Materials}
semi halb-
  semi-circular crack halbkreisförmiger Riß *m*
  semi-elliptical halbelliptisch
  semi-elliptical crack halbelliptischer Riß *m*
  semi-elliptical surface crack halbelliptischer Oberflächenriß *m*
  semi-elliptical surface flaw halbelliptischer Oberflächenfehler *m*
  semi-empirical halbempirisch
  semi-infinite halbunendlich
  semi-infinite crack halbunendlicher Riß *m*
  semi-infinite notch halbunendlicher Kerb *m*
  semi-infinite tensile specimen halbunendliche Zugprobe *f*
SEN → single-edge notched...
SENB → single-edge notched bend...
sensitivity Empfindlichkeit *f*
  notch sensitivity Kerbempfindlichkeit *f*
  notch sensitivity ratio < abb.: NSR > Kerbempfindlichkeitszahl *f*
sensitization {steel: corrosion} Sensibilisierung *f* {Stahl: Korrosion}
separate/to trennen
separation < syn.: decohesion > Trennung *f*

separation of material Werkstofftrennung *f*
mechanism of separation Trennmechanismus *m*
plane of separation Trennebene *f*
service Betrieb *m*, Betriebs-, Dienst; Wartung *f*
service conditions *pl* Betriebsbedingungen *fpl*
service failure Betriebsschaden *m*
service failure analysis Betriebsschadensanalyse *f*
service failure {of structures} Betriebsversagen *n* {von Konstruktionen}
service life Betriebslebensdauer *f*, Lebensdauer *f*
service load Betriebslast *f*
service loading Betriebsbelastung *f*
service temperature Betriebstemperatur *f*, Anwendungstemperatur *f*
service tensile stress Betriebszugspannung *f*
calculation of service life Lebensdauerberechnung *f*
determination of service life Lebensdauerermittlung *f*
minimum service temperature minimale Betriebstemperatur *f*
total service life {of structures} Gesamtlebensdauer *f* {von Konstruktionen}
shallow flach
  shallow crack flacher Riß *m*
  shallow dimples *pl* {fracture surface} muldenförmige Grübchen *npl* {Bruchfläche}
  shallow notch flache Kerbe *f*
  shallow surface crack flacher Oberflächenriß *m*
shape Form *f*, Gestalt *f*
shape factor Formfaktor *m*
shape of crack tip Rißspitzenform *f*, Form *f* der Rißspitze
shape of dimples {dimple rupture} Grübchenform *f*, Gestalt *f* der Grübchen {Grübchenbruch}
shape of test piece Prüfkörperform *f*

analysis of crack shape Rißformanalyse *f*
crack shape Rißform *f*
crack-tip shape Form *f* der Rißspitze, Rißspitzenform *f*
shape/to formen
sharp crack scharfer Riß *m*
sharp external notch scharfer Außenkerb *m*
sharp internal notch scharfer Innenkerb *m*
sharp notch scharfer Kerb *m*, Spitzkerbe *f*
sharp-notched round tension specimen scharf gekerbter Zugstab *m*
shattering {under impact shock} Zersplittern *n*, Zerspringen *n* {bei Schlagbeanspruchung}
shear Scherung *f*, Schub *m*
shear band Scherband *n*
shear component Schub-Komponente *f*
shear-difference method Schubdifferenzmethode *f*
shear failure Scherbruch *m*, Schubbruch *m*
shear force Schubkraft, Scherkraft *f*
shear fracture Scherbruch *m*, Schubbruch *m*
shear instability Scherungsinstabilität *f*
shear limit Schergrenze *f*
shear lip formation Scherlippenbildung *f*
shear-lip zone Scherlippenzone *f*
shear lips *pl* Scherlippen *fpl*
shear load Schubbeanspruchung *f*, Scherbeanspruchung *f*
shear-loaded crack schubbeanspruchter Riß *m*, scherbeanspruchter Riß *m*
shear-loaded surface crack schubbeanspruchter Oberflächenriß *m*, scherbeanspruchter Oberflächenriß *m*
shear loading Schubbeanspruchung *f*

shear measurement Messung *f* unter Scherbeanspruchung
shear modulus Scher[ungs]modul *m*, Schubmodul *m*
shear plane Scherebene *f*
shear properties *pl* Schereigenschaften *fpl*, Eigenschaften *fpl* bei Scherbeanspruchung
shear rate Schergeschwindigkeit *f*
shear strain Scherdehnung *f*, Schubverzerrung *f*
shear strength Scherfestigkeit *f*; Schubfestigkeit *f*
shear stress Schubspannung *f*, Scherspannung *f*
shear stress component Schubspannungskomponente *f*, Scherspannungskomponente *f*
shear stress concentration Schubspannungskonzentration *f*, Scherspannungskonzentration *f*
shear stress distribution Schubspannungsverteilung *f*, Scherspannungsverteilung *f*
shear stress vektor Schubspannungsvektor *m*
shear test Scherversuch *m*, Schubversuch *m*
shear-wave speed Scherungswellengeschwindigkeit *f*
shear-wave velocity Scherungswellengeschwindigkeit *f*
formation of shear lips Scherlippenbildung *f*
longitudinal shear Längsscherung *f*
nominal shear stress Nennscherspannung *f*
out-of-plane shear Längsscherung *f*
percentage shear failure Scherbruchanteil *m*
percentage shear fracture Schubbruchanteil *m*
percentage shear lips Scherlippenanteil *m*
plane shear ebener Schub *m*
principal shear stress Hauptschubspannung *f*
pure shear reiner Schub *m*

shear/to

pure shear loading reine Schubbeanspruchung *f*
theoretical shear strength theoretische Scherfestigkeit *f*, theoretische Schubfestigkeit *f*
shear/to abscheren
shearing Abscherung *f*, Abschervorgang *m*, Scherung *f*
shearing mode Schermodus *m*
sheet Platte *f*, Tafel *f*, Blech *n*
sheet material Plattenwerkstoff *m*
stiffening sheet Versteifungsblech *n*
shell Schale *f*
shock Schock *m*, Stoß *m*
shock load Stoßbelastung *f*
shock resistance {of materials} Stoßfestigkeit *f* {von Materialien}
thermal shock Thermoschock *m*, Wärmeschock *m*
short kurz, Kurz-
short bar specimen Kurzstabprobe *f*
short crack kurzer Riß *m*
short fatigue crack kurzer Ermüdungsriß *m*
short term mechanical testing Kurzzeitprüfung *f* der mechanischen Eigenschaften
short-time stability at elevated temperature Kurzzeitbeständigkeit *f* bei erhöhter Temperatur
shrink/to {crack tip} zusammenschrumpfen {Rißspitze}
shrinkage Schrumpfung *f*, Schrumpfen *n*, Schwindung *f*, Schwinden *n*
shrinkage cavity Lunker *m*
shrinkage crack Schrumpfriß *m*, Schwindungsriß *m*
axial shrinkage axiale Schwindung *f*
center line shrinkage Mittellinienlunkerung *f*
solidification shrinkage crack Warmriß *m*
linear shrinkage Längsschwindung *f*
liquid shrinkage Flüssigkeitsschwindung *f*
solid shrinkage {metals} Schrumpfung *f* {Metalle}
solidification shrinkage Erstarrungsschrumpfung *f*
side {specimen} Seite *f*; Seitenfläche *f* {von Proben}
side groove {specimen} Seitenkerbe *f* {Proben}
side surface of the specimen Probenseite *f*
silicon, Si Silizium *n*, Silicium *n*, Si
silky fracture seidenartiger Bruch *m*
silver, Ag Silber *n*, Ag
simulate/to modellieren
simulation Modellierung *f*
computer simulation Computer-Modellierung *f*
simultaneous measurement Parallelmessung *f*, gleichzeitige Messung *f*
single Einzel-; Ein-
single crystal Einkristall *m*
single defect Einzelfehler *m*
single edge crack Einzelrandriß *m*
single-edge cracked eyebar {type of specimen} einseitig angerissener Augenstab *m* {Probenform}
single-edge-cracked flat specimen Flachprobe *f* mit einseitigem Randriß
single-edge cracked flat tensile specimen Flachzugprobe *f* mit einseitigem Randriß
single-edge cracked strip Streifen *m* mit einseitigem Randriß
single-edge cracked tensile specimen einseitig angerissene Zugprobe *f*, Zugprobe *f* mit Einzelrandriß *m*
single-edge notch specimen Probe *f* mit einseitigem Kerb
single-edge notch tensile specimen einseitig gekerbte Zugprobe *f*
single-edge notched bend <abb.: SENB> **specimen** Einfachkantenriß-Biegeprobe *f*, SENB-Probe *f*
single-edge notched flat tensile specimen einseitig gekerbte Flachzugprobe *f*
single-edge notched specimen, SEN specimen {notch + crack} Einfachkantenrißprobe *f*, SEN-Probe *f* {Kerb + Riß}

single specimen Einzelprobe *f*
single-stage loading Einstufenbeanspruchung *f*, Einstufenbelastung *f*
single-stage test Einstufenversuch *m*
single test Einzelversuch *m*
singularity Singularität *f*
crack-tip singularity Rißspitzensingularität *f*
dynamic singularity dynamische Singularität *f*
elastic singularity elastische Singularität *f*
element of singularity Singularitätselement *n*
plastic singularity plastische Singularität *f*
stress singularity Spannungssingularität *f*
size Größe *f*; Abmessungen *fpl*
absolute crack size absolute Rißgröße *f*
crack size Rißabmessungen *fpl*; Rißgröße *f*
critical crack size kritische Rißgröße *f*
critical defect size kritische Fehlergröße *f*
critical pre-crack size kritische Anrißgröße *f*
critical size {of a crack} kritische Größe *f* {eines Risses}
dimple size Grübchengröße *f*
effective crack size effektive Rißgröße *f*
end-region size of crack Größe *f* der Rißspitze
flaw size {flaw in materials} Fehlergröße *f* {Fehler in Werkstoffen}
grain size Korngröße *f*
ligament size Ligamentgröße *f*
plastic zone size Größe *f* der plastischen Zone
precrack size Anrißgröße *f*
relative crack size relative Rißabmessungen *fpl*, relative Rißgröße *f*
specimen size Probengröße *f*, Probenabmessungen *fpl*

skew-symmetric loading asymmetrische Belastung *f*
slant fracture schräg verlaufender Bruch *m*
slant fracture surface schräge Bruchfläche *f*
slenderness ratio {test bar} Schlankheitsgrad *m* {Probestab}
slide/to gleiten
sliding Gleiten *n*, Gleitung *f*
sliding friction Gleitreibung *f*
sliding surface Gleitoberfläche *f*
grain-boundary sliding Korngrenzengleiten *n*
slip {sometimes called: slide} Gleiten *n*, Gleitung *f*
slip band Gleitband *n*
slip-band crack Gleitbandriß *m*
slip-band crack propagation Gleitbandrißausbreitung *f*
slip-band model Gleitbandmodell *n*
slip deformation Gleitdeformation *f*
slip geometry Gleitgeometrie *f*
slip-line field Gleitlinienfeld *n*
slip-line formation Gleitlinienbildung *f*
slip-line theory Gleitlinientheorie *f*
slip plane Gleitebene *f*
slip-plane fracture Gleitebenenbruch *m*
slip step Gleitstufe *f*
slip system Gleitsystem *n*
slip {sometimes called: slide} Gleiten *n*
cross slip {crystal} Quergleitung *f* {Kristall}
fracture of slip bands Gleitbandbruch *m*
inhomogeneous slip distribution inhomogene Gleitverteilung *f*
multiple slip Mehrfachgleitung *f*
principal slip plane Hauptgleitebene *f*
secondary slip plane Sekundärgleitebene *f*
slip/to gleiten
slip off/to abgleiten

slipping off

slipping off Abgleiten n, Abgleitung f
slow crack growth allmähliches Rißwachstum n, langsames Rißwachstum n
slowly propagating crack sich langsam ausbreitender Riß m
small {crack} klein {crack}
small crack kleiner Riß m
small-angle grain boundary Kleinwinkelkorngrenze f
small-scale yielding Kleinbereichsfließen n
SME → solid-metal embrittlement
smooth {surface} glatt {Oberfläche}
smooth-ended notch glatte Kerbe f
smooth fracture surface glatte Bruchfläche f
smooth specimen {unnotched} glatte Probe f {ungekerbt}
smooth tensile bar glatter Zugstab m
smooth tensile specimen {unnotched} glatte Zugprobe f {ungekerbt}
Sn → tin
S-N diagram → S-N curve
sodium, Na Natrium n, Na
soft weich
soft point determination Erweichungspunktbestimmung f, Bestimmung f des Erweichungspunktes
soft testing machine weiche Prüfmaschine f
softening Erweichung f, Erweichen n, Entfestigung f
softening point Erweichungstemperatur f, Erweichungspunkt m
automatic Vicat softening point apparatus automatisches Prüfgerät n zur Bestimmung der Vicat-Erweichungstemperatur
Vicat softening point Vicat-Erweichungstemperatur f
Vicat softening point apparatus Gerät n zur Bestimmung der Vicat-Erweichungstemperatur f
solid fest

solid body fester Körper m
solid-metal embrittlement < abb.: SME > Versprödung f mit festen (nichtschmelzflüssigen) Metallen
solid shrinkage {metals} Schrumpfung f {Metalle}
solidification Erstarrung f, Erstarren n; Festwerden n
solidification shrinkage Erstarrungsschrumpfung f
solidification shrinkage crack Warmriß m
solution Lösung f
approximation solution Näherungslösung f
linear-elastic solution linear-elastische Lösung f
problem solution Problemlösung f
source Quelle f
flaw source {in materials} Fehlerquelle f {in Werkstoffen}
ignition source Zündquelle f
space Raum m
space/to anordnen, [sich] befinden
spalling Abplatzen n
special speziell, besonders; Spezial-
special case Spezialfall m
special steel Sonderstahl m
specific spezifisch, kennzeichnend
specific energy of fracture spezifische Bruchenergie f
specific fracture energy spezifische Bruchenergie f
specific heat spezifische Wärmekapazität f
specific heat at constant pressure spezifische Wärme f bei konstantem Druck
specific heat at constant volume spezifische Wärme f bei konstantem Volumen
specific surface energy spezifische Oberflächenenergie f
critical specific fracture energy kritische spezifische Bruchenergie f
specimen Probe f, Probekörper m, Prüfkörper m

specimen area Probenfläche f, Probenbereich m
specimen configuration Probenkonfiguration f
specimen cross-section Probenquerschnitt m
specimen depth Probentiefe f
specimen design Probenform f
specimen dimensions pl Probenabmessungen fpl
specimen fracture plane Bruchebene f der Probe
specimen geometry Probengeometrie f
specimen ligament Probenligament n
specimen preparation Probenvorbereitung f
specimen size Probengröße f
specimen surface Probenoberfläche f
specimen thickness Probendicke f
specimen width Probenbreite f
bend specimen Biegeprobe f
bimaterial specimen aus zwei Werkstoffen bestehende Probe f
C specimen Kompaktprobe f, C-Probe f
CCT specimen {tensile specimen} Mittelrißprobe f, CCT-Probe f {Zugprobe}
cellular specimen zellige (porige) Probe f
center-cracked flat specimen Flachprobe f mit Mittelriß
center-cracked flat tensile specimen Flachzugprobe f mit Mittelriß
center-cracked specimen {tensile specimen} Probe f mit Mittelriß {Zugprobe}
center-cracked tensile specimen mittig angerissene Zugprobe f, Zugprobe f mit Mittelriß
center-cracked tensile <abb.: CCT> specimen Zugprobe f mit Mittelriß, Mittelrißprobe f, CCT-Probe f {Zugprobe}
center-notched specimen Probe f mit Mittelkerb
center-notched tensile specimen in der Mitte gekerbte Zugprobe f
center of specimen Probenmitte f, Probenmittelpunkt m
central specimen mittlere Probe f {von mehreren nebeneinander angeordneten Proben}
centrally notched specimen Probe f mit Mittelkerb
Charpy specimen {with notch} Charpy-Probe f {mit Kerb}
Chevron-notch specimen Probe f mit Chevron-Kerbe
circumferentially cracked round bar specimen Rundstab m mit konzentrischem Außenriß
circumferentially notched round bar specimen Rundprobe f mit Umdrehungskerbe
clamped specimen eingespannte Probe f
compact specimen, CS Kompakt-Probe f, C-Probe f
compact tension specimen Kompakt-Zug-Probe f, CT-Probe f
compression specimen Probe f für den Druckversuch
crack-arrest specimen Rißarrestprobe f
crack-line-wedge-loaded <abb.: CLWL> specimen CLWL-Probe f
CT specimen Kompakt-Zug-Probe f, CT-Probe f
DCB specimen Doppelbalken[biege]probe f, DCB-Probe f
DCT specimen scheibenförmige Kompaktzugprobe f, DCT-Probe f
deformation of specimen Probenverformung f
disk-shaped compact [tensile] specimen scheibenförmige Kompaktzugprobe f, DCT-Probe f
disk-shaped tensile specimen Rundscheiben-Zugprobe f
double-cantilever beam specimen Doppelbalken[biege]probe f, DCB-Probe f

specimen

double-cantilever beam <abb.: DCB> specimen Doppelbalken[biegel]probe *f*, DCB-Probe *f*
double-edge cracked tensile specimen zweiseitig angerissene Zugprobe *f*
double-edge-notched specimen Doppelkerbprobe *f*
double torsion <abb.: DT> specimen Doppeltorsions-Probe *f*, DT-Probe *f*
drop-weight tear test <abb.: DWTT> specimen Probe *f* für den Fallgewichtsscherversuch, Probe *f* für den DWTT-Versuch
drop-weight test <abb.: DWT> specimen Probe *f* für den Fallgewichtsversuch, Probe *f* für den DWT-Versuch
DT specimen Doppeltorsionsprobe *f*, DT-Probe *f*
duplex specimen {bimaterial interface} Duplex-Probe *f*
DWT specimen Probe *f* für den Fallgewichtsversuch, Probe *f* für den DWT-Versuch
DWTT specimen Probe *f* für den Fallgewichtsscherversuch, Probe *f* für den DWTT-Versuch
dynamic tear test specimen dynamische Reißprobe *f*
edge of the specimen Probenrand *m*, Probenberandung *f*
embrittled specimen versprödete Probe *f*
end face of the specimen Probenstirnseite *f*
end of the specimen Probenende *n*
ETT specimen Probe *f* für den Explosions-Beulungsversuch
explosion tear test <abb.: ETT> specimen Probe *f* für den Explosions-Beulungsversuch
flat specimen Flachprobe *f*
form of specimen Probenform *f*
four-point bend test specimen Vierpunkt-Biegeprobe *f*
fracture of the specimen Probenbruch *m*, Bruch *m* der Probe
fracture specimen {for testing} Bruchmechanik-Probe *f* {für Prüfungen}
fracture toughness specimen Bruchzähigkeitsprobe *f*
heat-treated specimen wärmebehandelte Probe *f*, temperierte Probe *f*
Hill specimen {a flat tensile specimen} Hill-Probe *f* {eine flache Zugprobe}
inner zone of specimen Probeninneres *n*
Izod impact strength specimen Izod-Probe *f* {zur Bestimmung der Schlagfestigkeit}
keyhole-notch specimen {Charpy test} Probe *f* mit "Schlüsselloch"-Kerb {Charpy-Versuch}
laboratory specimen Probe *f* für Laborversuche
large-area specimen großflächige Probe *f*
loading of specimen Probenbelastung *f*
location of specimen Probenlage *f*
machined specimen (mechanisch) bearbeiteter Probekörper *m*
middle plane of specimen Probenmittelebene *f*
minimum specimen thickness Mindestprobendicke *f*
minimum specimen width Mindestprobenbreite *f*
mounted specimen befestigte Probe *f*, befestigter Probekörper *m*
new specimen "jungfräuliche" Probe *f*
non-embrittled specimen nicht versprödete Probe *f*
notch bend test specimen Kerbbiegeprobe *f*
notch impact test specimen Kerbschlagprobe *f*
notched (test) specimen gekerbte Probe *f*, gekerbter Probekörper *m*
notched-bar impact test specimen Kerbschlagbiegeprobe *f*
notched-bar tensile test specimen Kerbzugprobe *f*

notched bend test specimen gekerbte Biegeprobe *f*
notched specimen gekerbte Probe *f*
notched tension-test specimen gekerbte Zugprobe *f*
notched tear test specimen gekerbte Aufreißprobe *f*
orientation of specimen Probenorientierung *f*
plate specimen plattenförmige Probe *f*
pre-heated specimen vorgewärmte (angewärmte) Probe *f*
precracked specimen {testing} angerissene Probe *f*, Probe *f* mit Anriß {Prüfung}
proportional (test) specimen Proportionalprobe *f* {alle Maße stehen in festen Verhältnissen zueinander}
RCT specimen Rund-Kompakt-Zugprobe *f*, RCT-Probe *f*
reference specimen Vergleichsprobe *f*
rigid specimen harte (starre) Probe *f*
Robertson specimen {tensile test specimen} Robertson-Probe *f* {Zugprobe}
round compact tension < abb.: RCT > specimen Rund-Kompakt-Zugprobe *f*, RCT-Probe *f*
round specimen Rundprobe *f*
SCT specimen zugbeanspruchte Probe *f* mit Oberflächenriß, SCT-Probe *f*
semi-infinite tensile specimen halbunendliche Zugprobe *f*
SEN specimen {notch + crack} Einfachkantenrißprobe *f*, SEN-Probe *f* {Kerb + Riß}
SENB specimen {notch crack} Einfachkantenriß-Biegeprobe *f*, SENB-Probe *f* {Kerb + Riß}
sharp-notched round tension specimen scharf gekerbter Zugstab *m*
short bar specimen Kurzstabprobe *f*
side surface of the specimen Probenseite *f*

single-edge cracked flat tensile specimen Flachzugprobe *f* mit einseitigem Randriß
single-edge cracked tensile specimen einseitig angerissene Zugprobe *f*, Zugprobe *f* mit Einzelrandriß *m*
single-edge notch specimen Probe *f* mit einseitigem Kerb
single-edge notch tensile specimen einseitig gekerbte Zugprobe *f*
single-edge notched bend specimen Einfachkantenriß-Biegeprobe *f*, SENB-Probe *f*
single-edge notched flat tensile specimen einseitig gekerbte Flachzugprobe *f*
single-edge notched specimen {notch + crack} Einfachkantenrißprobe *f*, SEN-Probe *f* {Kerb + Riß}
single-edge-cracked flat specimen Flachprobe *f* mit einseitigem Randriß
single specimen Einzelprobe *f*
smooth specimen {unnotched} glatte Probe *f* {ungekerbt}
smooth tensile specimen {unnotched} glatte Zugprobe *f* {ungekerbt}
standard arc-shaped (tension) specimen Standard-C-Form-Zugprobe *f*
standard bend specimen Standard-Biegeprobe *f*
standard compact tension < abb.: CT > specimen Standard-Kompakt-Zugprobe *f*
standard disk-shaped compact (tension) specimen Standard-Rundscheiben-Zugprobe *f*
standard drop-weight test < abb.: DWT > specimen Standardprobe *f* für den Fallgewichtsversuch, Standardprobe für DWT-Versuch
standard fracture specimen Standard-Bruchmechanik-Probe *f*
standard specimen {for testing} Standardprobe *f* {für Prüfungen}
standard [test] specimen Norm-Probe *f*, genormte Probe *f*

spectroscopy

strip specimen streifenförmige Probe *f*, Streifenprobe *f*
surface-crack tensile <abb.: SCT> **specimen** zugbeanspruchte Probe *f* mit Oberflächenriß, SCT-Probe *f*
surface flaw specimen Probe *f* mit Oberflächenfehler
tapered double-cantilever beam <abb.: TDCB> **specimen** konische Doppelbalken[biege]probe *f*, keilförmige Doppelbalkenprobe *f*, TDCB-Probe *f*
temperature of specimen Probentemperatur *f*
tensile impact specimen Schlagzugprobe *f*, Prüfkörper *m* für den Schlagzugversuch
tensile specimen zugbeanspruchte Probe *f*, Zugprobe *f*
test specimen Prüfkörper *m*
test specimen assembly Prüfkörperanordnung *f*
thickness of specimen Probendicke *f*
thin specimen dünne Probe *f*
three-point bend specimen Dreipunkt-Biegeprobe *f*, 3PB-Probe *f*
through-thickness crack specimen Probe *f* mit durchgehendem Riß
transparent specimen transparente Probe *f*
type of specimen Probentyp *m*, Probenart *f*
unnotched (test) specimen ungekerbte Probe *f*, ungekerbter Probekörper *m*
unnotched tensile specimen ungekerbte Zugprobe *f*
wedge-loaded compact test specimen keilbelastete Kompakt-Probe *f*
wedge-opening loading <abb.: WOL> **specimen** Spaltkeilprobe *f*, WOL-Probe *f*
width of specimen Probenbreite *f*
spectroscopy Spektroskopie *f*
  Auger electron spectroscopy <abb.: AES> Auger-Elektronenspektroskopie *f*
  electron spectroscopy for chemical analysis <abb.: ESCA> Elektronenspektroskopie *f* für die chemische Analyse
  X-ray photoelectron spectroscopy <abb.: XPS> Röntgen-Photoelektronen-Spektroskopie *f*
speed Geschwindigkeit *f*
  crack speed Rißgeschwindigkeit *f*
  fracture speed Bruchgeschwindigkeit *f*
  maximum fracture speed Bruchhöchstgeschwindigkeit *f*
  measurement of crack speed Rißgeschwindigkeitsmessung *f*
  minimum crack speed {for branching} Mindestrißgeschwindigkeit *f* {für die Verzweigung}
  shear-wave speed Scherungswellengeschwindigkeit *f*
  testing speed Prüfgeschwindigkeit *f*
spherical kugelförmig, Kugel-
spherical pore kugelförmige Pore *f*
split force Spaltkraft *f*
spontaneous spontan
  spontaneous crack extension spontane Rißerweiterung *f*
  spontaneous fracture spontan einsetzender Bruch *m*
  spontaneous loading spontane Belastung *f*
spread/to {cracks} auseinanderlaufen, (sich) ausbreiten
  flame spread distance Flammenausbreitung *f*
  spread of flame Brennlänge *f* {bei der Flammenausbreitung}
spring steel Federstahl *m*
square quadratisch
square fracture ebener Bruch *m*
stability Stabilität *f*
  stability criterion {Griffith crack} Stabilitätskriterium *n* {Griffith-Riß}
  crack stability Rißstabilität *f*
  dimensional stability test Formstabilitätsprüfung *f*, Prüfung *f* der Formstabilität

short-time stability at elevated temperature Kurzzeitbeständigkeit f bei erhöhter Temperatur
temperature stability Temperaturbeständigkeit f
thermal stability Wärmebeständigkeit f, thermische Beständigkeit f
stable stabil
stable crack extension stabile Rißerweiterung f
stable crack growth stabiles Rißwachstum n
stable crack propagation stabile Rißausbreitung f
stable microcrack stabiler Mikroriß m
stacking fault {crystal} Stapelfehler m {Kristall}
stacking fault energy {crystal} Stapelfehlerenergie f {Kristall}
stage Stadium n
stage of crack propagation Rißausbreitungsstadium n
crack growth stage Rißwachstumsstadium n
loading stage Belastungsstufe f
stainless nichtrostend, rostfrei
stainless steel nichtrostender Stahl m
arc-welded stainless steel lichtbogengeschweißter nichtrostender Stahl m
austenitic stainless steel austenitischer nichtrostender Stahl m
ferritic stainless steel ferritischer nichtrostender Stahl m
martensitic stainless steel martensitischer nichtrostender Stahl m
precipitation-hardening stainless steel ausscheidungshärtender nichtrostender Stahl m
superplastic stainless steel superplastischer nichtrostender Stahl m
standard Norm f, Standard m
standard arc-shaped (tension) specimen Standard-C-Form-Zugprobe f

standard bend specimen Standard-Biegeprobe f
standard compact tension <abb.: CT>specimen Standard-Kompakt-Zugprobe f
standard CT-specimen Standard-Kompakt-Zugprobe f
standard deviation Standardabweichung f
standard disk-shaped compact (tension) specimen Standard-Rundscheiben-Zugprobe f
standard drop-weight test <abb.: DWT>specimen Standardprobe f für den Fallgewichtsversuch, Standardprobe f für DWT-Versuch
standard DWT specimen Standardprobe f für den Fallgewichtsversuch, Standardprobe f für DWT-Versuch
standard fracture specimen Standard-Bruchmechanik-Probe f
standard specimen {for testing} Standardprobe f {für Prüfungen}
standard steel Standard-Stahl m
standard temperature Normtemperatur f
standard test Norm-Prüfverfahren n, Norm-Versuch m, genormter Versuch m genormtes Prüfverfahren n
standard [test] specimen Norm-Probe f, genormte Probe f
standardization Normung f
standardized test genormtes Prüfverfahren n
start of fracture Bruchein tritt m
starter Starter m; Ausgangs-, Anfangs-
starter crack Anfangsriß m, Ausgangsriß m
starter crack configuration Anfangsrißkonfiguration f
starter crack length Ausgangsrißlänge f
starter notch Ausgangskerbe f
Chevron crack starter notch Chevron-Rißstarterkerbe f
crack starter Rißstarter m {Ausgangsstelle des Bruch[e]s}

crack starter notch Rißstarterkerbe *f*
state Zustand *m*
state equilibrium statisches Gleichgewicht *n*
state of hardening Verfestigungszustand *m*
state of plane deformation ebener Verformungszustand *m*
state of plane strain ebener Dehnungszustand *m*, EDZ, ebener Verzerrungszustand *m*, EVZ
state of plane stress ebener Spannungszustand *m*, EDZ
state of strain Dehnungszustand *m*, Verzerrungszustand *m*
biaxial stress state zweiachsiger Spannungszustand *m*
brittle state spröder Zustand *m*
current stress state aktueller Spannungszustand *m*
deformation state Verformungszustand *m*, Deformationszustand *m*
ductile state duktiler Zustand *m*
elastic-plastic state elastisch-plastischer Zustand *m*
homogeneous state of stress homogener Spannungszustand *m*
inhomogeneous state of hardening inhomogener Verfestigungszustand *m*
isotropic state of stress isotroper Spannungszustand *m*
loading state Beanspruchungszustand *m*
macroscopic state of stress makroskopischer Spannungszustand *m*
mixed-mode stress state gemischter Spannungszustand *m*
multiaxial state of stress mehrachsiger Spannungszustand *m*
multiaxial stress state mehrachsiger Spannungszustand *m*
non-steady state method of determining instationäres Bestimmungsverfahren *n*
perfectly plastic state vollplastischer Zustand *m*
plane deformation state ebener Verformungszustand *m*
plane stress state ebener Spannungszustand *m*
quasi-steady state method quasistationäre Prüfmethode *f*
residual stress state Eigenspannungszustand *m*
steady state conditions *pl* stationäre Bedingungen *fpl*
steady state measurement {of conductivity} stationäre Messung *f* {der Leitfähigkeit}
stress state, state of stress[es] Spannungszustand *m*
three-dimensional state of stress dreidimensionaler Spannungszustand *m*
triaxial state of stress dreiachsiger Spannungszustand *m*
triaxial stress state dreiachsiger Spannungszustand *m*
uniaxial stress state einachsiger Spannungszustand *m*
yield state Fließzustand *m*
static statisch, ruhend
static crack growth statisches Rißwachstum *n*
static deformation statische Verformung *f*
static fatigue statische Ermüdung *f*
static fracture toughness statische Bruchzähigkeit *f*
static loading statische Belastung *f*, ruhende Belastung *f*
static stress analysis statische Spannungsanalyse *f*
static stress field statisches Spannungsfeld *n*
static stress-intensity factor statischer Spannungsintensitätsfaktor *m*
static tensile strength statische Zugfestigkeit *f*
static test method statische Prüfmethode *f*, Prüfmethode *f* mit statischer Beanspruchung
concept of static crack arrest statisches Rißarrestkonzept *n*

plane static photoelasticity ebene statische Spannungsoptik *f*
statics Statik *f* {Mechanik ruhender Körper}
stationary stationär, ruhend
equivalent stationary crack äquivalenter ruhender Riß *m*
stationary crack ruhender Riß *m*
steady state stationär
steady state conditions *pl* stationäre Bedingungen *fpl*
steady state crack extension stationäre Rißerweiterung *f*, stationäre Rißaufweitung *f*
steady state crack propagation stationäre Rißausbreitung *f*
steady state creep stationäres Kriechen *n*
steady state measurement {of conductivity} stationäre Messung *f* {der Leitfähigkeit}
steel Stahl *m*
steel casting Stahlguß *m*
steel resistant to caustic cracking laugenrißbeständiger Stahl *m*
acid brittle steel beizspröder Stahl *m*
acid-proof steel säurebeständiger Stahl *m*, säurefester Stahl *m*
alloy steel Legierungsstahl *m*, legierter Stahl *m*
arc-welded alloy steel lichtbogengeschweißter legierter Stahl *m*
arc-welded hardenable carbon steel lichtbogengeschweißter härtbarer Kohlenstoffstahl *m*
arc-welded low-carbon steel lichtbogengeschweißter kohlenstoffarmer Stahl *m*
arc-welded stainless steel lichtbogengeschweißter nichtrostender Stahl *m*
austenitic manganese steel austenitischer Manganstahl *m*
austenitic stainless steel austenitischer nichtrostender Stahl *m*
austenitic steel austenitischer Stahl *m*
boiler steel Kesselstahl *m*
carbon-molybdenum steel Kohlenstoff-Molybdän-Stahl *m*
chemical resistant steel chemikalienbeständiger Stahl *m*
chisel steel Meißelstahl *m*
chromium-nickel-molybdenum steel Chrom-Nickel-Molybdän-Stahl *m*
cold-brittle steel kaltspröder Stahl *m*, kaltbrüchiger Stahl *m*
corrosion-resistant steel korrosionsbeständiger Stahl *m*
elastically-deformed steel elastisch verformter Stahl *m*
embrittled steel versprödeter Stahl *m*
ferritic stainless steel ferritischer nichtrostender Stahl *m*
ferritic steel ferritischer Stahl *m*
hardened steel gehärteter Stahl *m*
high-alloy steel hochlegierter Stahl *m*
high-carbon steel kohlenstoffreicher Stahl *m*
high-speed steel Schnellarbeitsstahl *m*
high-strength steel hochfester Stahl *m*
low-alloy steel niedriglegierter Stahl *m*
low-carbon steel kohlenstoffarmer Stahl *m*
martensitic stainless steel martensitischer nichtrostender Stahl *m*
medium-carbon steel mittelgekohlter Stahl *m*
nickel-chromium-molybdenum-vanadium steel Nickel-Chrom-Molybdän-Vanadium-Stahl *m*
nitrided steel nitrierter Stahl *m*, nitriergehärteter Stahl *m*
non-ag[e]ing steel alterungsbeständiger Stahl *m*
non-austenitic steel nichtaustenitischer Stahl *m*
pearlitic steel perlitischer Stahl *m*
plain carbon steel unlegierter Kohlenstoffstahl *m*

precipitation-hardening stainless steel ausscheidungshärtender nichtrostender Stahl *m*
rail steel Schienenstahl *m*
special steel Sonderstahl *m*
spring steel Federstahl *m*
stainless steel nichtrostender Stahl *m*
standard steel Standard-Stahl *m*
structural steel Baustahl *m*
superplastic stainless steel superplastischer nichtrostender Stahl *m*
titanium steel Titanstahl *m*
tool steel Werkzeugstahl *m*
tough steel zäher Stahl *m*
ultrahigh-strength steel ultrahochfester Stahl *m*
vanadium steel Vanadiumstahl *m*
step Schritt *m*; Stufe *f*
  cleavage step {cleavage fracture} Spaltstufe *f* {Spaltbruch}
  slip step Gleitstufe *f*
stepwise stufenweise, schrittweise
  stepwise cracking stufenweise Rißbildung *f*
  stepwise loading stufenweise Belastung *f*
stereography Stereographie
stiffen/to versteifen
stiffening Versteifung *f*
  stiffening element Versteifungselement *n*
  stiffening sheet Versteifungsblech *n*
  stiffening test Prüfung *f* der Steifigkeit, Steifigkeitsprüfung *f*
  torsional stiffening test method Torsionssteifheits-Prüfmethode *f*
stiffness Steifigkeit *f*
  total stiffness Gesamtsteifigkeit *f*
stochastic stochastisch
stopped {crack} gestoppt, aufgefangen {Riß}
  stopped crack aufgefangener Riß *m*
  stopped microcrack aufgefangener Mikroriß *m*
straight gerade, geradlinig
  straight crack gerader Riß *m*

straight crack front gerade Rißfront *f*
straight-through crack gerade (geradlinig) durchgehender Riß *m*
strain Dehnung *f*, Verzerrung *f*
  strain ag[e]ing Verzerrungsalterung *f*
  strain component Dehnungskomponente *f*
  strain concentration Dehnungskonzentration *f*, Verzerrungskonzentration *f*
  strain concentration factor Dehnungskonzentrationsfaktor *m*
  strain constraint Dehnungsbehinderung *f*
  strain distribution Dehnungsverteilung *f*
  strain energy Dehnungsenergie *f*
  strain energy density Dehnungsenergiedichte *f*, Verzerrungsenergiedichte *f*
  strain energy function Dehnungsenergiefunktion *f*
  strain energy release rate Verzerrungsenergie-Freisetzungsrate *f*
  strain field Dehnungsfeld *n*
  strain toughness EVZ-Bruchzähigkeit *f* {EVZ ebener Verzerrungszustand}
  strain ga[u]ge Dehnungsmeßstreifen *m*
  strain hardening Dehnungsverfestigung *f*, Kaltverfestigung *f*
  strain increment Dehnungsinkrement *n*
  strain-induced dehnungsinduziert
  strain-induced anisotropy dehnungsinduzierte Anisotropie *f*
  strain-intensity factor Dehnungsintensitätsfaktor *m*
  strain measurement Dehnungsmessung *f*
  strain rate Dehnungsgeschwindigkeit *f*, Verzerrungsgeschwindigkeit *f*
  strain rate energy Dehnungsgeschwindigkeitsenergie *f*
  strain tensor Dehnungstensor *m*, Verzerrungstensor *m*

analysis of strain Dehnungsanalyse *f*
axial strain axiale Dehnung *f*, Dehnung *f* in axialer Richtung
crack-tip plane strain ebene Dehnung *f* an der Rißspitze
creep strain Kriechdehnung *f*
criterion for strain Dehnungskriterium *n*
critical strain kritische Dehnung *f*
elastic strain elastische Dehnung *f*
elastic strain energy elastische Dehnungsenergie *f*
fracture strain Bruchdehnung *f*
inhomogeneous strain inhomogene Dehnung *f*
linear strain distribution lineare Dehnungsverteilung *f*
local fracture strain lokale Bruchdehnung *f*
mean strain Mitteldehnung *f*
nominal strain Nenndehnung *f*
normal strain Normaldehnung *f*
permanent strain bleibende Dehnung *f*
plain strain compression ebene (zweiachsige) Druckbeanspruchung *f*
plain strain compression test ebene (zweidimensionale) Druckfestigkeitsprüfung *f*
plane strain ebene Dehnung *f*, ebene Verzerrung *f*
plane strain fracture EVZ-Bruch *m* {EVZ ebener Verzerrungszustand}
plane strain fracture toughness EVZ-Bruchzähigkeit *f* {EVZ ebener Verzerrungszustand}
plane strain testing EVZ-Prüfung *f* {EVZ ebener Verzerrungszustand}
plastic strain plastische Dehnung *f*
plastic strain concentration factor plastischer Dehnungskonzentrationsfaktor *m*
plastic strain constraint plastische Dehnungsbehinderung *f*
shear strain Scherdehnung *f*, Schubverzerrung *f*
state of plane strain ebener Dehnungszustand *m*, EDZ, ebener Verzerrungszustand *m*, EVZ
state of strain Dehnungszustand *m*, Verzerrungszustand *m*
tensile strain Zugdehnung *f*
transverse strain Querdehung *f*
true fracture strain wahre Bruchdehnung *f*
strain/to dehnen
straining Dehnen *n*, Dehnung *f*
rate of elastic straining elastische Dehnungsgeschwindigkeit *f*, Geschwindigkeit *f* der elastischen Dehnung
rate of plastic straining plastische Dehnungsgeschwindigkeit *f*, Geschwindigkeit *f* der plastischen Dehnung
stray-current corrosion Streustromkorrosion *f*
strength Festigkeit *f*
strength behavio(u)r Festigkeitsverhalten *n*
strength hypothesis Festigkeitshypothese *f*
strength properties *pl* Festigkeitseigenschaften *fpl*
strength test Festigkeitsprüfung *f*
strength value Festigkeitswert *m*
bearing strength Tragfähigkeit *f*
bending strength Biegefestigkeit *f*
buckling strength Knickfestigkeit *f*
cleavage fracture strength Spaltbruchfestigkeit *f*
coefficient of bending strength Biegefestigkeit[sbeiwert] *f*[*m*]
cohesion strength Kohäsionsfestigkeit *f*
cold bend strength Kältebiegefestigkeit *f*
component strength Bauteilfestigkeit *f*
compressive strength Druckfestigkeit *f*
creep-rupture strength Kriechbruchfestigkeit *f*
creep strength Kriechfestigkeit *f*

stress

cross-breaking strength Knickfestigkeit *f*
element strength Bauteilfestigkeit *f*
falling weight impact strength apparatus Kugelfallprüfmaschine *f* {zur Bestimmung der Schlagzähigkeit}
fatigue strength Ermüdungsfestigkeit *f*, Dauerschwingfestigkeit *f*, Dauerfestigkeit *f*
flexural impact strength measurement Messung *f* der Schlagbiegefestigkeit
flexural strength Biegefestigkeit *f*
fracture strength profile Bruchflächenprofil *n*
impact strength Kerbschlagfestigkeit *f*
impact strength data *pl* Schlagfestigkeitsangaben *fpl*
Izod impact strength specimen Izod-Probe *f* zur Bestimmung der Schlagfestigkeit
maximum compressive strength maximale Druckfestigkeit *f*
microscopic cleavage-fracture strength mikroskopische Spaltbruchfestigkeit *f*
nominal strength Nennfestigkeit *f*
nominal tensile strength Nennzugfestigkeit *f*
notch tensile strength Kerbzugfestigkeit *f*
notched-bar tensile strength Kerbzugfestigkeit *f*
rupture strength Trennfestigkeit *f*
shear strength Scherfestigkeit *f*; Schubfestigkeit *f*
static tensile strength statische Zugfestigkeit *f*
tearing strength Reißfestigkeit *f*, Zerreißfestigkeit *f*
tensile impact strength Schlagzugfestigkeit *f*, Zugfestigkeit *f* bei Schlagbeanspruchung
tensile impact strength measurement Messung *f* für Schlagzugfestigkeit
tensile strength Zugfestigkeit *f*

theoretical fracture strength theoretische Bruchfestigkeit *f*
theoretical shear strength theoretische Scherfestigkeit *f*, theoretische Schubfestigkeit *f*
theoretical strength theoretische Festigkeit *f*
theoretical tensile strength theoretische Zugfestigkeit *f*
thermal fatigue strength thermische Dauerfestigkeit *f*
thermal yield strength Wärmestreckgrenze *f*
torsion strength Torsionsfestigkeit *f*
torsional strength Verdreh[ungs]festigkeit *f*
transverse strength Biegefestigkeit *f*
yield point-to-tensile strength ratio Streckgrenzenverhältnis *n*
yield strength Fließfestigkeit *f*
stress {mechanics}; < syn.:voltage > {electrical engineering} Spannung *f* {Mechanik, Elektronik}
stress amplitude Spannungsamplitude *f*
stress analysis Spannungsanalyse *f*
stress component Spannungskomponente *f*
stress concentration Spannungskonzentration *f*
stress concentration factor Spannungskonzentrationsfaktor *f*
stress condition Spannungsbedingung *f*
stress corrosion cracking < abb.: SCC > Spannungsrißkorrosion *f*, SRK, Spannungskorrosionsrißbildung *f*
stress corrosion failure Spannungskorrosionsbruch *m*
stress corrosion threshold Spannungskorrosionsschwellwert *m*
stress criterion Spannungskriterium *n*
stress cycle Lastspiel *n*
stress deformation field Spannungsverformungsfeld *n*

stress detection Spannungsnachweis *m*
stress deviation Spannungsumlagerung *f*
stress distribution {e.g. at crack tip} Spannungsverlauf *m*, Spannungsverteilung *f* {z.B. vor der Rißspitze}
stress elevation Spannungserhöhung *f*
stress field Spannungsfeld *n*
stress freezing {photoelasticity} Einfrierverfahren *n* {Spannungsoptik}
stress function Spannungsfunktion *f*
stress gradient Spannungsgradient *m*
stress history {of materials} Spannungsgeschichte *f* {von Werkstoffen}
stress increment Spannungsinkrement *n*
stress intensification Spannungserhöhung *f*
stress intensity Spannungsintensität *f*, S.I.
stress intensity range Spannungsintensitätsbereich *m*
stress limitation Spannungsbegrenzung *f*
stress line Spannungslinie *f*
stress of outer fibers Randfaserspannung *f*
stress peak Spannungsspitze *f*
stress point Spannungspunkt *m*
stress ratio {alternating stress amplitude/mean stress or minimum stress/maximum stress} Spannungsverhältnis *n* {Wechselspannungsamplitude/Mittelspannung oder Minimalspannung/Maximalspannung}
stress reduction Spannungsabbau *m*
stress relaxation Spannungsrelaxation *f*
stress singularity Spannungssingularität *f*
stress state Spannungszustand *m*
stress symmetry Spannungssymmetrie *f*
stress system Spannungssystem *n*
stress tensor Spannungstensor *m*
stress trajectory Spannungstrajektorie *f*
stress vector Spannungsvektor *m*
stress wave emission Spannungswellenemission *f*
average stress intensity mittlere Spannungsintensität *f*
axial stress Axialspannung *f*
bending stress Biegespannung *f*
bending stress distribution Biegespannungsverteilung *f*
biaxial stress zweiachsige Spannung *f*
biaxial stress state zweiachsiger Spannungszustand *m*
biaxial tensile stress field zweiachsiges Zugspannungsfeld *n*
boundary stress Randspannung *f*
breaking stress Zerreißspannung *f*; Bruchspannung *f*
calculated fracture stress theoretische Bruchspannung *f*
circumferential stress Umfangsspannung *f*
cleavage fracture stress Spaltbruchspannung *f*
cleavage stress Spaltspannung *f*
complex stress komplexe Spannung *f*
complex stress function komplexe Spannungsfunktion *f*
compressive residual stress Druckeigenspannung *f*
compressive residual stress curve Druckeigenspannungsverlauf *m*
compressive residual stress field Druckeigenspannungsfeld *n*
compressive stress Druckspannung *f*
concept of stress intensity Spannungsintensitätskonzept *n* {Bruchmechanik}
constant stress konstante Spannung *f*
constant stress level konstantes Spannungsniveau *n*

stress

crack-tip stress Spannung f an der Rißspitze
crack-tip stress distribution Spannungsverteilung f an der Rißspitze
critical stress kritische Spannung f
critical stress of fracture kritische Bruchspannung f
critical tensile stress kritische Zugspannung f
current stress state aktueller Spannungszustand m
cyclic stress intensity zyklische Spannungsintensität f
dimensionless stress dimensionslose Spannung f
dimensionless stress intensity factor dimensionsloser Spannungsintensitätsfaktor m
dynamic stress analysis dynamische Spannungsanalyse f
dynamic stress distribution dynamische Spannungsverteilung f
dynamic stress intensity dynamische Spannungsintensität f
effective stress effektive Spannung f
elastic-plastic stress distribution elastisch-plastische Spannungsverteilung f
elastic stress elastische Spannung f
elastic stress analysis elastische Spannungsanalyse f
elastic stress concentration elastische Spannungskonzentration f
elastic stress field elastisches Spannungsfeld n
elasto-plastic stress elasto-plastische Spannung f
equivalent stress Ersatzspannung f, äquivalente Spannung f
fiber stress Faserspannung f
finite stress {at crack tip} endliche Spannung f {an der Rißspitze}
fracture stress Bruchspannung f
fracture tensile stress Bruchzugspannung f
friction stress Reibungsspannung f
frozen stress eingefrorene Spannung f

generalized stress normierte Spannung f
homogeneous field of stress homogenes Spannungsfeld n
homogeneous state of stress homogener Spannungszustand m
hoop stress Tangentialspannung f
hydrostatic stress hydrostatische Spannung f
increase of stress Spannungsanstieg m
inhomogeneous stress distribution inhomogene Spannungsverteilung f
inhomogeneous stress field inhomogenes Spannungsfeld n
initial stress Vorspannung f
isotropic state of stress isotroper Spannungszustand m
isotropic stress field isotropes Spannungsfeld n
linear-elastic stress field linear-elastisches Spannungsfeld n
linear-elastic stress intensity linear-elastische Spannungsintensität f
local stress component lokale (örtliche) Spannungskomponente f
local stress factor lokaler (örtlicher) Spannungsfaktor m
local stress field lokales (örtliches) Spannungsfeld n
local stress relaxation lokale (örtliche) Spannungsrelaxation f
macroscopic state of stress makroskopischer Spannungszustand m
maximum stress {fatigue test} Oberspannung f {Dauerbiegeversuch}, Maximalspannung f
mean stress Mittelspannung f
measured fracture stress gemessene Bruchspannung f
mechanical stress mechanische Spannung f
microscopic fracture stress mikroskopische Bruchspannung f
minimum stress {fatigue test} Unterspannung f {Dauerbiegeversuch}, Minimalspannung f
mixed-mode stress state gemischter Spannungszustand m

multiaxial state of stress mehrachsiger Spannungszustand *m*
multiaxial stress mehrachsige Spannung *f*
multiaxial stress state mehrachsiger Spannungszustand *m*
nominal shear stress Nennscherspannung *f*
nominal stress Nennspannung *f*, Nominalspannung *f*
nominal stress of outer fibers Randfaser-Nennspannung *f*
non-uniform stress field ungleichförmiges Spannungsfeld *n*
nonsingular stress nichtsingulare Spannung *f*
normal component of stress Normalspannungskomponente *f*
normal stress Normalspannung *f*
normal stress component Normalspannungskomponente *f*
normal stress distribution Normalspannungsverteilung *f*
normalized circumferential stress normierte Umfangsspannung *f*
notch stress Kerbspannung *f*
overload stress Überlastspannung *f*
permissible stress Beanspruchbarkeit *f*
plane stress ebene Spannung *f*, E.S.
plane stress fracture ESZ-Bruch *m* {ESZ ebener Spannungszustand}
plane stress fracture toughness ESZ-Bruchzähigkeit *f* {ESZ ebener Spannungszustand}
plane stress state ebener Spannungszustand *m*
plane stress testing ESZ-Prüfung *f*; Prüfung *f* bei ebenem Spannungszustand
plastic stress plastische Spannung *f*
predicted fracture stress vorhergesagte Bruchspannung *f*
principal normal stress Hauptnormalspannung *f*
principal normal stress criterion Hauptnormalspannungskriterium *n*
principal normal tensile stress Hauptnormalzugspannung *f*
principal shear stress Hauptschubspannung *f*
principal stress Hauptspannung *f*
radial stress Radialspannung *f*
random stress loading Zufallsbelastung *f*
reduced stress reduzierte Spannung *f*
residual stress Eigenspannung *f*
residual stress curve Eigenspannungsverlauf *m*
residual stress distribution Eigenspannungsverteilung *f*
residual stress field Eigenspannungsfeld *n*
residual stress measurement Eigenspannungsmessung *f*
residual stress state Eigenspannungszustand *m*
residual tensile stress Zugeigenspannung *f*
rupture stress Bruchspannung *f*
service tensile stress Betriebszugspannung *f*
shear stress Scherspannung *f*, Schubspannung *f*
shear stress component Schubspannungskomponente *f*
shear stress concentration Schubspannungskonzentration *f*
shear stress distribution Schubspannungsverteilung *f*
shear stress vector Schubspannungsvektor *m*
state of plane stress ebener Spannungszustand *m*, ESZ
static stress analysis statische Spannungsanalyse *f*
static stress field statisches Spannungsfeld *n*
tangential stress Tangentialspannung *f*
tangential stress component Tangentialspannungskomponente *f*
tensile stress Zugspannung *f*
theoretical stress concentration factor theoretischer Spannungskonzentrationsfaktor *m*

thermal stress Wärmespannung f, thermische Spannung f
three-dimensional elastic stress analysis dreidimensionale elastische Spannungsanalyse f
three-dimensional state of stress dreidimensionaler Spannungszustand m
three-dimensional stress analysis dreidimensionale Spannungsanalyse f
three-dimensional stress distribution dreidimensionale Spannungsverteilung f
threshold stress intensity Schwellspannungsintensität f
torsion stress Torsionsspannung, f Verdrehspannung f
triaxial state of stress dreiachsiger Spannungszustand m
triaxial stress state dreiachsiger Spannungszustand m
triaxial tensile stress dreiachsige Zugspannung f
triaxial yield stress dreiachsige Fließspannung f
two-dimensional stress field zweidimensionales Spannungsfeld n
uniaxial stress einachsige Spannung f
uniaxial stress state einachsiger Spannungszustand m
uniaxial yield stress einachsige Fleißspannung f
working stress level Betriebsspannungsniveau n
yield stress Fließspannung f
yield stress curve Fließspannungskurve f
stress-corrosion crack Spannungskorrosionsriß m
stress-corrosion fracture Spannungskorrosionsbruch m
stress-crack extension diagram Spannungsrißaufweitungsdiagramm n, Spannungsrißaufweitungskurve f
stress-displacement field Spannungs-Verschiebungsfeld n
stress-free crack flank spannungsfreie Rißflanke f
stress-free crack surface spannungsfreie Riß[ober]fläche f
stress-intensity distribution Spannungsintensitätsverteilung f
stress-intensity factor Spannungsfaktor m
stress-intensity factor Spannungsintensitätsfaktor m
stress-intensity factor curve Spannungsintensitätsfaktorkurve f
stress-intensity factor distribution Spannungsfaktorverteilung f
stress-intensity factor value Spannungsintensitätsfaktorwert m
stress-intensity parameter Spannungsintensitätsparameter m
stress-relief crack Relaxationsriß m
stress-strain behavio[u]r Spannungs-Dehnungs-Verhalten n
stress-strain curve Spannungs-Dehnungs-Kurve f
stress-strain diagram Spannungs-Dehnungs-Diagramm n
stress-strain properties pl Spannungs-Dehnungs-Eigenschaften fpl
stress-strain relation Spannungs-Dehnungs-Beziehung f
bending stress-intensity factor Biegespannungsintensitätsfaktor m
crack initiation stress-intensity factor Rißinitiierungs-Spannungsintensitätsfaktor m
crack-tip stress-intensity factor Spannungsintensitätsfaktor m an der Rißspitze
critical stress-intensity factor kritischer Spannungsintensitätsfaktor m
cyclic stress-intensity factor zyklischer Spannungsintensitätsfaktor m {Rißwachstum bei schwingender Beanspruchung}
cyclic stress-strain behavio[u]r zyklisches Spannungs-Dehnungs-Verhalten n
dynamic stress-intensity factor dynamischer Spannungsintensitätsfaktor m

effective cyclic stress-intensity effektive zyklische Spannungsintensität f
effective stress-intensity factor effektiver Spannungsintensitätsfaktor m
elastic-plastic stress-strain behavio[u]r elastisch-plastisches Spannungs-Dehnungs-Verhalten n
elastic stress-concentration factor elastischer Spannungskonzentrationsfaktor m
fictitious stress-intensity factor fiktiver Spannungsintensitätsfaktor m
intergranular stress-corrosion cracking interkristalline Spannungsrißkorrosion f
macroscopic stress-intensity factor makroskopischer Spannungsintensitätsfaktor m
plastic stress-concentration factor plastischer Spannungskonzentrationsfaktor m
reference stress-intensity factor Referenzspannungsintensitätsfaktor m
static stress-intensity factor statischer Spannungsintensitätsfaktor m
sulfide stress-cracking, SSC Sulfid-Spannungsrißkorrosion f
stresses pl Spannungen fpl
   criterion of normal stresses Normalspannungskriterium n
   homogeneous distribution of stresses homogene Spannungsverteilung f
   hypothesis of normal stresses Normalspannungshypothese f
   roentgenographic measurement of stresses röntgenographische Spannungsmessung f
   theory of notch stresses Kerbspannungslehre f, Kerbtheorie f
stressfree spannungsfrei
stretch zone Dehnzone f, Stretch-Zone f {vor der Rißfront}
stretchability Dehnbarkeit f

stretches strains pl {inhomogeneous yielding} Lüderssche Linien fpl, Lüders-Streifen mpl, Fließlinien fpl {inhomogenes Fließen}
striation formation Riefenbildung f
striation spacing Riefenbreite f
   mechanisms of striation formation Riefenmechanismus m
striations pl {fatigue fracture} Schwingungsstreifen mpl, Riefen fpl {Schwingungsbruch}
striker Schlagpendel n, Pendel n
striking surface Schlagfläche f
stringer zeilenartiger Einschluß m
strip Streifen m
strip specimen streifenförmige Probe f, Streifenprobe f
   arrest strip Rißstoppstreifen m
   cracked strip Streifen m mit Riß
   isotropic strip isotroper Streifen m
   single-edge cracked strip Streifen m mit einseitigem Randriß
   uncracked strip ungerissener Streifen m
strontium, Sr Strontium n, Sr
structural steel Baustahl m
structure Gefüge n {Werkstoffe}; Struktur f
structure anisotropy Gefügeanisotropie f
structure {materials} Gefüge n {Werkstoffe}
   bainitic structure bainitisches Mikrogefüge n
   banded structure {metals} Zeilengefüge n {Metalle}
   columnar structure stengeliges Gefüge n
   crystal structure Kristallstruktur f
   dislocation structure {e.g. at crack tip} Versetzungsstruktur f {z.B. an der Rißspitze}
   fibrous structure {wrought iron} Faserstruktur f {Schmiedeeisen}
   globular structure Globulargefüge f, globulares Gefüge f

lamellar structure lamellares Gefüge n
material structure Werkstoffstruktur f
subgrain structure, sub-boundary structure Subkornstruktur f
study Untersuchung f
crack-propagation study Rißausbreitungsuntersuchung f
fractographic investigation, fractographic study fraktographische Untersuchung f
fracture surface study Bruchflächenuntersuchung f
study/to untersuchen
subcritical unterkritisch, vorkritisch, subkritisch
subcritical crack subkritischer Riß m
subcritical crack growth subkritisches Rißwachstum n
subcritical crack growth < abb.: SCC > unterkritisches Rißwachstum n
subcritical crack propagation unterkritische Rißausbreitung f, vorkritische Rißausbreitung f
subcritical fracture mechanics < abb.: SCFM > subkritische Bruchmechanik f
subgrain Subkorn n
subgrain boundary Subkorngrenze f
subgrain structure Subkornstruktur f
sulfide stress-cracking, SSC Sulfid-Spannungsrißkorrosion f
Sulfur → sulphur
superplastic {materials} superplastisch {Werkstoffe}
superplastic stainless steel superplastischer nichtrostender Stahl m
superposition Superposition f
superposition principle Superpositionsprinzip n
method of superposition Superpositionsmethode f

superalloy Superlegierung f
surface Oberfläche f
surface burning characteristics pl Brandverhalten n der Oberfläche
surface coating Oberflächenbeschichtung f
surface crack Oberflächenriß m
surface-crack behavio[u]r Oberflächenrißverhalten n
surface-crack length Oberflächenrißlänge f
surface crack opening displacement < abb.: SCOD > Oberflächen-Rißöffnungs-Verschiebung f
surface-crack tensile < abb.: SCT > specimen zugbeanspruchte Probe f mit Oberflächenriß, SCT-Probe f
surface cracking {of the specimen} Rißbildung f auf der Oberfläche {von Proben}
surface defect Oberflächendefekt,
surface energy Oberflächenenergie f
surface flammability {of materials} Entflammbarkeit f der Oberfläche
surface flaw Oberflächenfehler m
surface flaw specimen Probe f mit Oberflächenfehler
surface force Oberflächenkraft f
surface hardness Oberflächenhärte f
surface microcrack Oberflächenmikroriß m
surface notch Oberflächenkerb m
surface roughness Oberflächenrauheit f
surface temperature Oberflächentemperatur f
surface tension Oberflächenspannung f
surface treatment Oberflächenbehandlung f
surface wave Oberflächenwelle f
brittle fracture surface Sprödbruchfläche f
cleavage fracture surface Spaltbruchfläche f
corroded surface korrodierte Oberfläche f

crack at the inner surface Riß *m* auf der Innenfläche
crack at the outer surface Riß *m* auf der Außenfläche
crack surface Riß[ober]fläche *f*
crack surface displacement Rißflächenverschiebung *f*
defect surface fehlerhafte Oberfläche *f*
effective surface energy effektive Oberflächenenergie *f*
elliptical surface crack elliptischer Oberflächenriß *m*
fatigue crack surface Ermüdungsrißfläche *f*
fatigue fracture surface Dauerbruchfläche *f*, Ermüdungsbruchfläche *f*, Schwingungsbruchfläche *f*
fracture surface Bruch[ober]fläche *f*
fracture surface analysis Bruchflächen-Analyse *f*, Analyse *f* von Bruchflächen
fracture surface roughness Bruchflächenrauhigkeit *f*
fracture surface study Bruchflächenuntersuchung *f*
fracture surface topography Bruchflächentopographie *f*
fractured surface gebrochene Oberfläche *f*, Bruchfläche *f*
free surface freie Oberfläche *f*
macroscopic evaluation of fracture surface makroskopische Bruchflächenbewertung *f*
microfracture surface Mikrobruchfläche *f*
notch surface Kerb[ober]fläche *f*
overload fracture surface Gewaltbruchfläche *f*
oxidation of the crack surface Rißflächenoxidation *f*
rectangular surface crack rechteckiger Oberflächenriß *m*
semi-elliptical surface crack halbelliptischer Oberflächenriß *m*
semi-elliptical surface flaw halbelliptischer Oberflächenfehler *m*
shallow surface crack flacher Oberflächenriß *m*

shear-loaded surface crack scherbeanspruchter Oberflächenriß *m*
side surface of the specimen Probenseite *f*
slant fracture surface schräge Bruchfläche *f*
sliding surface Gleitoberfläche *f*
smooth fracture surface glatte Bruchfläche *f*
specific surface energy spezifische Oberflächenenergie *f*
specimen surface Probenoberfläche *f*
stress-free crack surface spannungsfreie Riß[ober]fläche *f*
striking surface Schlagfläche *f*
tensile fracture surface Zugbruchfläche *f*
tensile-loaded surface crack zugbelasteter Oberflächenriß *m*
through-the-thickness surface crack durchgehender Oberfächenriß *m*
true surface energy wahre Oberflächenenergie *f*
valuation of fracture surface Bruchflächenbewertung *f*
zone of fracture surface Bruchflächenbereich *m*
symmetric loading symmetrische Belastung *f*
symmetrical fatigue fracture symmetrischer Ermüdungsbruch *m*
symmetrically loaded crack system symmetrisch belastetes Rißsystem *n*
symmetry Symmetrie *f*
  axis of symmetry Symmetrieachse *f*
system System *n*
  Cartesian coordinate system kartesisches Koordinatensystem *n*
  crack system Rißgruppe *f*, Rißsystem *n*
  load system Belastungssystem *n*
  orthotropic crack system orthotropes Rißsystem *n*
  slip system Gleitsystem *n*
  stress system Spannungssystem *n*

symmetrically loaded crack system symmetrisch belastetes Rißsystem n
three-dimensional crack system dreidimensionales Rißsystem n
two-dimensional crack system zweidimensionales Rißsystem n

T

Ta → tantalum
tangential tangential, Tangential-
tangential force Tangentialkraft f
tangential stress Tangentialspannung f
tangential stress component Tangentialspannungskomponente f
tantalum, Ta Tantal n, Ta
tapered {specimens} keilförmig {Proben}
tapered double-cantilever beam specimen < abb.: TDCB > konische Doppelbalken[biege]probe f, keilförmige Doppelbalkenprobe f, TDCB-Probe f
Tb → terbium
TDCB → tapered double-cantilever beam...
Te → tellurium
tear/to reißen, zerreißen
tear Reißen m Zerreißen n
  drop-weight tear test specimen Probe f für den Fallgewichtsscherversuch, Probe f für den DWTT-Versuch
  drop-weight tear test < abb.: DWTT > Fallgewichtsscherversuch m, DWTT-Versuch m
  dynamic tear test dynamische Reißprüfung f, DT-Prüfung f
  dynamic tear test specimen dynamische Reißprobe f, DT-Probe f
  explosion tear test < abb.: ETT > specimen Probe f für den Explosions-Beulungsversuch
  explosion tear test < abb.: ETT > Explosions-Ausbeul-Versuch m
  hot tear Heißriß m
  internal hot tear innerer Wärmeriß m
  notched tear test specimen gekerbte Aufreißprobe f
tear/to {materials} zerreißen {Werkstoff}
tearing Reißen n, Zerreißen n
tearing modulus Reißmodul m
tearing strength Reißfestigkeit f, Zerreißfestigkeit f
technique Technik f, Verfahren n
  four-point bending technique Vierpunkt-Biegeprüfung f
  inspection technique Inspektionsverfahren n
  measuring technique Meßverfahren n
  moiré technique Moiré-Verfahren n {Spannungsoptik}
  penetrometer technique Eindringprüfung f
  tensile technique Zug[festigkeits]prüfung f
  test technique Prüfverfahren n
  three-point bending technique Dreipunkt-Biegeprüfung f
technetium, Tc Technetium n, Tc
tellurium, Te Tellur n, Te
TEM → transmission electron microscopy
temper Anlaß-
temper-brittle anlaßversprödet
temper-brittle fracture Anlaßsprödbruch m
temper brittleness Anlaßsprödigkeit f
temper embrittlement Anlaßversprödung f
temperature Temperatur f
temperature bath Temperierbad n
temperature behavio[u]r {of plastics} Temperaturverhalten n {von Kunststoffen}
temperature dependence {of properties} Temperaturabhängigkeit f {von Eigenschaften}

temperature difference Temperaturdifferenz *f*, Temperaturunterschied *m*
temperature distribution Temperaturverteilung *f*
temperature effect Temperatureinfluß *m*
temperature gradient Temperaturgradient *m*
temperature increase {during testing} Temperaturerhöhung *f* {bei der Prüfung}
temperature limit Temperaturgrenze *f*
temperature of deflection under load Formbeständigkeit *f* in der Wärme
temperature of specimen Probentemperatur *f*
temperature of the sample Probentemperatur *f*
temperature profile Temperaturverlauf *m*
temperature range Temperaturbereich *m*
temperature shift Temperaturverschiebung *f*
temperature stability Temperaturbeständigkeit *f*
air temperature Lufttemperatur *f*
ambient temperature Raumtemperatur *f*, Umgebungstemperatur *f*
bath temperature {conditioning of the specimen} Badtemperatur *f* {Temperieren von Proben}
brittleness temperature Kältebruchtemperatur *f*, Versprödungstemperatur *f*, Sprödigkeitstemperatur *f*
brittleness temperature by impact Kältebruchtemperatur *f* bei Schlagbeanspruchung
brittleness temperature test Kältebruchtemperaturprüfung *f*
chamber temperature Kammertemperatur *f*
cold bend temperature Kältebiegefestigkeit *f*

concept of limiting temperature {determination of toughness} Grenztemperatur-Konzept *n* {Zähigkeitsnachweis}
concept of transition temperature {brittle fracture behavio[u]r} Übergangstemperaturkonzept *n* {Sprödbruchverhalten}
crack-arrest temperature Rißauffangtemperatur *f*
crack-arrest temperature curve Rißauffangtemperatur *f*
crack-initiation temperature Rißeinleitungstemperatur *f*
crack-tip temperature Rißspitzentemperatur *f*
creep temperature Kriechtemperatur *f*
decomposition temperature Zersetzungstemperatur *f*
ductile-to-brittle transition temperature Zäh-Spröd[e]-Übergangstemperatur *f*
elevated temperature erhöhte Temperatur *f*
environment temperature Umgebungstemperatur *f*
face temperature Flächentemperatur *f*
flash ignition temperature Selbstentzündungstemperatur *f*
fracture appearance transition temperature Brucherscheinungsübergangstemperatur *f*, FATT
heat deflection temperature Formbeständigkeit *f* in der Wärme
heat distortion point Formbeständigkeit *f* in der Wärme
heat distortion temperature Formbeständigkeit *f* in der Wärme
heating temperature Aufheiztemperatur *f*
ignition temperature Zündtemperatur *f*
influence of temperature Temperatureinfluß *m*
limiting temperature Grenztemperatur *f*

temperatures

limiting transition temperature range Übergangstemperaturgrenzbereich *m*
Marten's temperature Martens-Zahl {zur Kennzeichnung der Formbeständigkeit in der Wärme}
melting temperature Schmelztemperatur *f*
minimum service temperature minimale Betriebstemperatur *f*
nil ductility temperature < abb.: NDT > NDT-Temperatur *f* {Grenztemperatur, bei der ein Riß nicht mehr aufgehalten werden kann}
non-ambient temperature test Prüfung *f* bei außergewöhnlichen Temperaturen {abweichend von der Raumtemperatur}
normal temperature Normaltemperatur *f*
operating temperature Betriebstemperatur *f*
reference temperature Bezugstemperatur *f*, Referenztemperatur *f*
resistance to low temperature Tieftemperaturbeständigkeit *f*
room temperature Raumtemperatur *f*
service temperature Betriebstemperatur *f*, Anwendungstemperatur *f*
standard temperature Normtemperatur *f*
surface temperature Oberflächentemperatur *f*
test temperature Versuchstemperatur *f*
testing temperature Prüftemperatur *f*
transition temperature Übergangstemperatur *f*, Umwandlungstemperatur *f*
transition temperature range Übergangstemperaturbereich *m*
temperatures *pl* Temperaturen *f*
cryogenic temperatures Temperaturen *fpl* im Bereich der Temperatur des flüssigen Stickstoffs

short-time stability at elevated temperatures Kurzzeitbeständigkeit *f* bei erhöhter Temperatur
tendency Neigung *f*
tendency for cracking Rißneigung *f*
tendency to brittle fracture Sprödbruchneigung *f*
tendency to cracking Rißbildungsneigung *f*
tensibility Zugbelastbarkeit *f*
tensile zugbelastbar, auf Zug(beanspruchung) belastbar, Zug...
tensile bar runde Zugprobe *f*
tensile bar dimensions *pl* Zugstabmessungen *fpl*
tensile bar {tensile test} Zugstab *m* {Zugversuch}
tensile-compression test Zug-Druck-Versuch *m*
tensile deformation Zugverformung *f*
tensile force Zugkraft *f*
tensile fracture Zugbruch *m*, Bruch *m* durch Zugbelastung
tensile fracture surface Zugbruchfläche *f*
tensile impact specimen Schlagzugprobe *f*, Prüfkörper *m* für den Schlagzugversuch
tensile impact strength Schlagzugfestigkeit *f*, Zugfestigkeit *f* bei Schlagbeanspruchung
tensile impact strength measurement Messung *f* für Schlagzugfestigkeit
tensile impact testing machine Schlagzugfestigkeits-Prüfmaschine *f*, Prüfmaschine *f* für die Bestimmung der Schlagzugfestigkeit
tensile load Zuglast *f*
tensile-loaded surface crack zugbelasteter Oberflächenriß *m*
tensile loading Zugbeanspruchung *f*, Zugbelastung *f*
tensile specimen Zugprobe *f*, zugbeanspruchte Probe *f*
tensile strain Zugdehnung *f*
tensile strength Zugfestigkeit *f*

tensile strength value Zugfestigkeitswert *m*
tensile stress Zugspannung *f*
tensile stress criterion Zugspannungskriterium *n*
tensile technique Zug[festigkeits]prüfung *f*
tensile test Zugversuch *m*, Zerreißversuch *m*
tensile test piece Zugprobe *f*, Prüfkörper *m* für den Zugversuch
tensile testing machine Zugprüfmaschine *f*
tensile yield point Streckgrenze *f*
tensile yield strength Streckgrenze *f*
biaxial tensile stress field zweiachsiges Zugspannungsfeld *n*
center-cracked flat tensile specimen Flachzugprobe *f* mit Mittelriß
center-cracked tensile <abb.: CCT> specimen Zugprobe *f* mit Mittelriß, mittig angerissene Zugprobe *f*
center-notched tensile specimen in der Mitte gekerbte Zugprobe *f*
critical tensile stress kritische Zugspannung *f*
disk-shaped tensile specimen Rundscheiben-Zugprobe *f*
double-edge cracked tensile specimen zweiseitig angerissene Zugprobe *f*
ductile tensile fracture duktiler Zugbruch *m*
fracture tensile stress Bruchzugspannung *f*
high-speed tensile impact machine Hochgeschwindigkeits-Prüfmaschine *f* zur Bestimmung der Schlagzugfestigkeit
impact tensile test Schlagzugversuch *m*
multiaxial tensile load mehrachsige Zugbeanspruchung *f*
nominal tensile strength Nennzugfestigkeit *f*
notch tensile strength Kerbzugfestigkeit *f*
notched-bar tensile strength Kerbzugfestigkeit *f*
notched-bar tensile test Kerbzugversuch *m*
notched-bar tensile test specimen Kerbzugprobe *f*
notched tensile test Kerbzugversuch *m*
principal normal tensile stress Hauptnormalzugspannung *f*
residual tensile stress Zugeigenspannung *f*
semi-infinite tensile specimen halbunendliche Zugprobe *f*
service tensile stress Betriebszugspannung *f*
single-edge cracked flat tensile specimen Flachzugprobe *f* mit einseitigem Randriß
single-edge cracked tensile specimen einseitig angerissene Zugprobe *f*, Zugprobe *f* mit Einzelrandriß *m*
single-edge notched tensile specimen einseitig gekerbte Zugprobe *f*
single-edge notched flat tensile specimen einseitig gekerbte Flachzugprobe *f*
smooth tensile bar glatter Zugstab *m*
smooth tensile specimen {unnotched} glatte Zugprobe *f* {ungekerbt}
static tensile strength statische Zugfestigkeit *f*
surface-crack tensile <abb.: SCT> specimen zugbeanspruchte Probe *f* mit Oberflächenriß, SCT-Probe *f*
theoretical tensile strength theoretische Zugfestigkeit *f*
threshold tensile load Zugschwellbelastung *f*
triaxial tensile stress dreiachsige Zugspannung *f*
uniaxial tensile loading einachsige Zugbelastung *f*, einachsige Zugbeanspruchung *f*
uniaxial tensile test einachsiger Zugversuch *m*
unnotched tensile specimen ungekerbte Zugprobe *f*

tension

tension Zug m; Zugspannung f
biaxial tension zweiachsiger Zug m
center-cracked tension specimen Mittelrißprobe f, CCT-Probe f {Zugprobe}
compact tension <abb.: CT> **specimen** CT-Probe f, Kompakt-Zug-Probe f
high-speed tension testing machine Hochgeschwindigkeits-Zugprüfmaschine f
loaded in tension zugbelastet
necking in tension Brucheinschnürung f
notch tension test Kerbzugversuch m
notched tension-test specimen gekerbte Zugprobe f
round compact tension <abb.: RCT> **specimen** Rund-Kompakt-Zugprobe f, RCT-Probe f
sharp-notched round tension specimen scharf gekerbter Zugstab m
standard compact <abb.: CT> **tension specimen** Standard-Kompakt-Zugprobe f
surface tension Oberflächenspannung f
tensile loading, tension Zugbelastung f
uniaxial tension einachsiger Zug m
tensor Tensor m
deformation tensor Verformungstensor m
microdeformation tensor Mikroverformungstensor m
strain tensor Dehnungstensor m, Verzerrungstensor m
stress tensor Spannungstensor m
terbium, Tb Terbium n, Tb
terminal crack velocity Endgeschwindigkeit f des Risses
test Versuch m, Prüfung f, Test m
test apparatus Prüfeinrichtung f
test arrangement, experimental arrangement Versuchsanordnung f
test assembly Prüfaufbau m, Prüfanordnung f

test bar Probestab m, Prüfstab m
test conditions pl {e.g. temperature, pressure, loading rate} Prüfbedingungen fpl {z.B Temperatur, Druck, Belastungsgeschwindigkeit}
test data pl Prüfergebnisse npl
test duration Versuchsdauer f
test for flame resistance Flammfestigkeitsprüfung f
test frequency Versuchsfrequenz f
test load Prüflast f
test material Prüfmaterial n
test parameter Versuchsparameter m
test piece Prüfkörper m
test piece thickness Prüfkörperdicke f
test plate Prüfplatte f
test point Versuchspunkt m
test procedure Versuchsdurchführung f
test program Versuchsprogramm n
test report Versuchsprotokoll n
test results pl Versuchsergebnisse f
test sample Probe f
test specimen assembly Prüfkörperanordnung f
test technique Prüfverfahren n
test temperature Versuchstemperatur f
absolute test absolute Prüfung f
accelerated ag[e]ing test beschleunigte Alterungsprüfung f
ag[e]ing test Alterungsprüfung f
bend test fixture Spannvorrichtung f für den Biegeversuch
bending fatigue test Dauerbiegeprüfung f
bending test Biegeversuch m
bending test Biegeversuch m, Biegeprüfung f
boundary value test {maximum notch sharpness and loading rate} Grenzwertprüfung f {größtmögliche Kerbschärfe und Belastungsgeschwindigkeit}

Brinell hardness test {indentation test} Brinellhärteprüfung *f* {Eindringprüfung}
brittle fracture test Sprödbruchprüfung *f*
brittleness temperature test Kältebruchtemperaturprüfung *f*
brittleness test Prüfung *f* der Sprödigkeit
burning test Brennbarkeitsprüfung *f*
burst test Berstversuch *m*
Charpy (impact) test Charpy-Pendelschlagversuch *m*, Pendelschlagversuch *m* nach Charpy
Charpy test {notch sensitivity} Charpy-Versuch *m* {Kerbempfindlichkeit}
cold bend test Kaltbiegeversuch *m*, Kältebiegeversuch *m*
comparison test, comparative test Vergleichsprüfung *f*
compression test Druckversuch *m*
control test Kontrollversuch *m*, Kontrolltest *m*
crack-arrest test Rißauffangversuch *m*
crack-propagation test Rißausbreitungsversuch *m*
crack toughness test Rißzähigkeitsversuch *m*
creep-rupture test Zeitstandversuch *m*
creep test Kriechversuch *m*
cross-breaking (strength) test Knickfestigkeitsprüfung *f*
crush test Stauchprobe *f*
cryogenic crack propagation test Tieftemperaturrißausbreitungsversuch *m*
cryogenic test Tieftemperaturversuch *m*
dimensional stability test Formstabilitätsprüfung *f*, Prüfung *f* der Formstabilität
drop test Fallversuch *m*
drop-weight tear test <abb.: DWTT> Fallgewichtsscherversuch *m*, DWTT-Versuch *m*
drop-weight tear test specimen Probe *f* für den Fallgewichtsscherversuch, Probe *f* für den DWTT-Versuch
drop-weight test <abb.: DWT> Fallgewichtsprüfung *f*, DWT-Prüfung *f*, Fallgewichtsversuch *m*
drop-weight test apparatus Prüfeinrichtung *f* für den Fallgewichtsversuch, Prüfeinrichtung *f* für den DWT-Versuch
drop-weight test specimen Probe *f* für den Fallgewichtsversuch, Probe *f* für den DWT-Versuch
dynamic tear test dynamische Reißprüfung *f*, DT-Prüfung *f*
dynamic tear test specimen dynamische Reißprobe *f*, DT-Probe *f*
dynamic test method dynamische Prüfmethode *f*, Prüfmethode *f* mit dynamischer Beanspruchung
electrical test method elektrische Prüfmethode *f*
endurance test Dauerversuch *m*
explosion tear test <abb.: ETT> Explosions-Ausbeul-Versuch *m*
explosion tear test <abb.: ETT> **specimen** Probe *f* für den Explosions-Beulungsversuch
falling weight test Kugelfallprobe *f*
fatigue bending test Dauerbiegeversuch *m*
fatigue crack propagation test Ermüdungsrißausbreitungsversuch *m*
fatigue crack test Ermüdungsrißversuch *m*
fatigue test Ermüdungsversuch *m*
fire propagation test Prüfung *f* der Brandausbreitung
fire test Brennbarkeitsprüfung *f*
flame test Flammtest *m*, Flammversuch *m*, Flammprüfung *f*, Flammprobe *f*
flammability test Entflammbarkeitsprüfung *f*
flexibility test Prüfung *f* der Biegsamkeit
four-point bend test Vierpunkt-Biegeversuch *m*

four-point bend test specimen Vierpunkt-Biegeprobe f
four-point bending test Vierpunkt-Biegeprüfung f, Vierpunkt-Biegeversuch m
fracture mechanics test Bruchmechanik-Versuch m
fracture test Bruchversuch m
hardness test Härteprüfung f
high-speed test Hochgeschwindigkeitsprüfung f, Hochgeschwindigkeitsversuch m
high-temperature test Prüfung f bei hohen Temperaturen
ignitability test Prüfung f der Zündbarkeit
ignition test Zündversuch m
impact flexural test Schlagbiegeprüfung f, Schlagbiegeversuch m
impact tensile test Schlagzugversuch m
impact test Schlagversuch m, Schlagprüfung f
impact test method Prüfmethode f mit Schlagbeanspruchung, Prüfmethode f mit schlagartiger Beanspruchung
impact torsion test Schlagverdrehversuch m
instrumented Charpy test instrumentierter Charpy-Versuch m
instrumented notched-bar impact test instrumentierter Kerbschlagbiegeversuch m
Izod test {impact toughness} Izod-Prüfung f {Kerbschlagzähigkeit}
leak-before-break test Leck-vor-Bruch-Prüfung f
loading test Belastungsversuch m
Marten's test Martens-Prüfung f {Prüfung der Formbeständigkeit in der Wärme}
mechanical test mechanische Prüfung f
mechanical test method mechanische Prüfmethode f
model test Modellversuch m
multistage test Mehrstufenversuch m

Niblink test {crack-initiation temperature} Niblink-Versuch m {Rißeinleitungstemperatur}
non-ambient temperature test Prüfung f bei außergewöhnlichen Temperaturen {abweichend von der Raumtemperatur}
non-combustibility test Prüfung f der Nichtbrennbarkeit (Unbrennbarkeit)
notch bend test Kerbbiegeversuch m
notch bend test specimen Kerbbiegeprobe f
notch impact test specimen Kerbschlagprobe f
notch tension test Kerbzugversuch m
notched-bar impact test Kerbschlagbiegeversuch m
notched-bar impact test specimen Kerbschlagbiegeprobe f
notched-bar tensile test Kerbzugversuch m
notched-bar tensile test specimen Kerbzugprobe f
notched bend test specimen gekerbte Biegeprobe f
notched tensile test Kerbzugversuch m
notched tear test specimen gekerbte Aufreißprobe f
optical test method optische Prüfmethode f
plain strain compression test ebene (zweidimensionale) Druckfestigkeitsprüfung f
plastic yield test Prüfung f der Formbeständigkeit in der Wärme
quality control test Qualitätsprüfung f
repeat test Wiederholungsprüfung f
Robertson test {crack arrest} Robertson-Versuch m {Rißstopp}
Rockwell hardness test Rockwellhärteprüfung f
shape of test piece Prüfkörperform f
shear test Scherversuch m, Schubversuch m

single-stage test Einstufenversuch *m*
single test Einzelversuch *m*
standard drop-weight test <abb.: DWT> **specimen** Standardprobe *f* für den Fallgewichtsversuch, Standardprobe für DWT-Versuch
standard test Norm-Versuch *m*, genormter Versuch *m*, Norm-Prüfverfahren *n*
standard test specimen genormte Probe *f*, Norm-Probe *f*
standardized test genormtes Prüfverfahren *n*
static test method statische Prüfmethode *f*, Prüfmethode *f* mit statischer Beanspruchung
stiffening test Prüfung *f* der Steifigkeit, Steifigkeitsprüfung *f*
strength test Festigkeitsprüfung *f*
tensile-compression test Zug-Druck-Versuch *m*
tensile test Zugversuch *m*, Zerreißversuch *m*
tensile test piece Zugprobe *f*, Prüfkörper *m* für den Zugversuch
thermal conductivity test apparatus Wärmeleitfähigkeits-Prüfgerät *n*
thermal test method thermisches Prüfverfahren *n*
three-point bend test Dreipunkt-Biegeversuch *m*
three-point bending test apparatus Dreipunkt-Biegevorrichtung *f*
torsion test Verdrehversuch *m*
torsional stiffening test method Torsionssteifheits-Prüfmethode *f*
torsional test Verdrehversuch *m*
type of test bar Probestabform *f*
uniaxial tensile test einachsiger Zugversuch *m*
Vickers hardness test {indentation hardness} Vickershärteprüfung *f* {Eindringhärte}
wedge-loaded compact test specimen keilbelastete Kompakt-Probe *f*
weight loss test Masseverlustprüfung *f*

wide-plate test Großplattenversuch *m*
test/to prüfen, testen
tester Prüfgerät *n*, Prüfvorrichtung *f*
flexing tester Biegeprüfgerät *n*
low-pressure deformation tester Niederdruck-Verformungsprüfgerät *n*
pendulum impact tester Pendelschlagwerk *n*
testing Prüfung *f*, Prüfen *n*, Prüf-
testing machine Prüfmaschine *f*
testing method Prüfmethode *f*
testing of component Bauteilprüfung *f*
testing of element Bauteilprüfung *f*
testing of materials Materialprüfung *f*, Werkstoffprüfung *f*
testing speed Prüfgeschwindigkeit *f*
testing temperature Prüftemperatur *f*
climatic testing Klimaprüfung *f*
compression testing machine Druckprüfmaschine *f*
compressive testing Druckprüfung *f*
deformation testing machine Verformungs-Prüfmaschine *f*, Maschine zur Prüfung der Verformung
dynamic fracture testing dynamische Bruchprüfung *f*
fracture mechanics testing Bruchmechanik-Prüfung *f*
fracture testing Bruchprüfung *f*
fracture toughness testing Bruchzähigkeitsprüfung *f*
fracture toughness testing method Bruchzähigkeits-Prüfverfahren *n*
high-speed tension testing machine Hochgeschwindigkeits-Zugprüfmaschine *f*
impact testing Schlagprüfung *f*, Prüfung *f* mit Schlagbeanspruchung
impact testing machine Schlagprüfmaschine *f*, Schlagprüfgerät *n*, Pendelschlagwerk *n*
Izod impact testing machine Schlagprüfgerät *n* nach Izod, Izod-Schlagprüfgerät *n*

texture

low-temperature mechanical testing Tieftemperatur-Prüfung f der mechanischen Eigenschaften
low-temperature testing Tieftemperaturprüfung f
magnetic powder testing {detection of cracks} Magnetpulverprüfung f {Rißnachweis}
materials testing Materialprüfung f, Werkstoffprüfung f
notched-bar impact testing Kerbschlagbiegeprüfung f
plane strain testing EVZ-Prüfung f {EVZ ebener Verzerrungszustand}
plane stress testing ESZ-Prüfung f {ESZ ebener Spannungszustand}
radiographic testing {of materials} Durchstrahlungsprüfung f {Werkstoffe}
Scleroscope hardness testing Rücksprunghärteprüfung f
short-term mechanical testing Kurzzeitprüfung f der mechanischen Eigenschaften
soft testing machine weiche Prüfmaschine f
speed of testing Prüfgeschwindigkeit f
tensile impact testing machine Schlagzugfestigkeits-Prüfmaschine f, Prüfmaschine f für die Bestimmung der Schlagzugfestigkeit
tensile testing machine Zugprüfmaschine f
testing speed Prüfgeschwindigkeit f
ultrasonic testing Ultraschallprüfung f
weldment testing Schweißprüfung f {von geschweißten Bauteilen}
texture Textur f
TGA → thermogravimetric analysis
Th → thorium
thallium, Tl Thallium n, Tl
theoretical theoretisch
  theoretical angle of crack extension theoretischer Rißausbreitungswinkel m
  theoretical compliance theoretische Nachgiebigkeit f
  theoretical crack angle theoretischer Rißausbreitungswinkel m
  theoretical fracture strength theoretische Bruchfestigkeit f
  theoretical shear strength theoretische Scherfestigkeit f, theoretische Schubfestigkeit f
  theoretical strength theoretische Festigkeit f
  theoretical stress concentration factor theoretischer Spannungskonzentrationsfaktor m
  theoretical tensile strength theoretische Zugfestigkeit f
theory Theorie f
  theory of brittle fracture, brittle fracture theory Sprödbruchtheorie f
  theory of deformation Deformationstheorie f
  theory of elasticity Elastizitätstheorie f
  theory of notch stresses Kerbspannungslehre f, Kerbtheorie f
  Barenblatt theory {crack extension} Barenblatt-Theorie f {Rißerweiterung}
  brittle fracture theory Sprödbruchtheorie f
  concept of brittle fracture theory Konzept n der Sprödbruchtheorie
  continuum theory Kontinuumstheorie f
  crack-propagation theory Rißausbreitungstheorie f
  dislocation theory Versetzungstheorie f
  dynamic crack-propagation theory Theorie f der dynamischen Rißausbreitung
  dynamic theory of elasticity dynamische Elastizitätstheorie f
  fracture theory Bruchtheorie f
  Griffith theory {brittle fracture} Griffithsche Theorie f {Sprödbruch}
  plasticity theory Plastizitätstheorie f

slip-line theory Gleitlinientheorie *f*
yield line theory Fließlinientheorie *f*
thermal thermisch, Wärme-
thermal analysis thermische Analyse *f*
thermal conductivity Wärmeleitfähigkeit *f*, Wärmeleitvermögen *n*
thermal conductivity measurement Wärmeleitfähigkeitsmessung *f*
thermal conductivity test apparatus Wärmeleitfähigkeits-Prüfgerät *n*
thermal endurance Dauerwärmebeständigkeit *f*
thermal expansion Wärmeausdehnung *f*, thermische Ausdehnung *f*
thermal fatigue thermische Ermüdung *f*, Ermüdung *f* durch Wärmebeanspruchung
thermal fatigue strength thermische Dauerfestigkeit *f*
thermal insulation Wärmedämmung *f*, Wärmeisolierung *f*
thermal method thermisches Prüfverfahren *n*
thermal properties *pl* thermische Eigenschaften *fpl*
thermal shock Thermoschock *m*, Wärmeschock *m*
thermal-shock crack Thermoschockriß *m*
thermal stability Wärmebeständigkeit *f*, thermische Beständigkeit *f*
thermal stress Wärmespannung *f*, thermische Spannung *f*
thermal test method thermisches Prüfverfahren *n*
thermal yield strength Wärmestreckgrenze *f*
average coefficient of linear thermal expansion mittlerer linearer Wärmeausdehnungskoeffizient *m*
coefficient of cubical thermal expansion kubischer Wärmeausdehnungskoeffizient *m*
coefficient of linear thermal expansion linearer Wärmeausdehnungskoeffizient *m*

differential thermal analysis <abb.: DTA> Differentialthermoanalyse *f*, DTA
thermocouple Thermoelement *n*
thermodynamic properties *pl* thermodynamische Eigenschaften *fpl*
thermogravimetric analysis <abb.: TGA> thermogravimetrische Analyse *f*, TGA
thermogravimetry Thermogravimetrie *f*
thick-walled dickwandig
thick-walled cylinder dickwandiger Zylinder *m*
thickness Dicke *f*
thickness effect {specimens} Dickeneinfluß *m* {Proben}
thickness of component Bauteildicke *f*
thickness of element Bauteildicke *f*
thickness of specimen Probendicke *f*
final thickness {of specimen} Enddicke *f* {der Probe nach Beendigung der Prüfung}
initial thickness {of specimen} Anfangsdicke *f* {der Probe zu Beginn der Prüfung}
minimum specimen thickness Mindestprobendicke *f*
minimum thickness {specimens} Mindestdicke *f* {Proben}
notch thickness Kerbdicke *f*
plate thickness Blechdicke *f*, Plattendicke *f*, Scheibendicke *f*
sample thickness Probendicke *f*
specimen thickness Probendicke *f*
test piece thickness Prüfkörperdicke *f*
total thickness {of the specimen} Gesamtdicke *f* {der Probe}
thin dünn, schmal
indefinitely thin crack unbegrenzt schmaler Riß *m*
thin specimen dünne Probe *f*
thorium, Th Thorium *n*, Th
three-dimensional dreidimensional, räumlich

three-point   136

three-dimensional body dreidimensionaler Körper m
three-dimensional boundary-value problem dreidimensionales Grenzwertproblem n
three-dimensional continuum dreidimensionales Kontinuum n
three-dimensional crack dreidimensionaler Riß m
three-dimensional crack problem dreidimensionales Rißproblem n, räumliches Rißproblem n
three-dimensional crack system dreidimensionales Rißsystem n
three-dimensional deformation dreidimensionale Verformung f
three-dimensional elastic stress analysis dreidimensionale elastische Spannungsanalyse f
three-dimensional elasticity dreidimensionale Elastizität f
three-dimensional photoelasticity räumliche Spannungsoptik f
three-dimensional state of stress dreidimensionaler Spannungszustand m
three-dimensional stress analysis dreidimensionale Spannungsanalyse f
three-dimensional stress distribution dreidimensionale Spannungsverteilung f
three-point bend specimen Dreipunkt-Biegeprobe f, 3PB-Probe f
three-point bend test Dreipunkt-Biegeversuch m
three-point bending Dreipunkt-Biegung f
three-point bending technique Dreipunkt-Biegeprüfung f
three-point bending test apparatus Dreipunkt-Biegevorrichtung f
three-point loading Dreipunkt-Belastung f
threshold Schwelle f, Schwellwert m
threshold stress intensity Schwellspannungsintensität f
threshold tensile load Zugschwellbelastung f
threshold value Schwellenwert m, Schwelle f
fatigue crack threshold Ermüdungsrißschwellwert m
stress corrosion threshold Spannungskorrosionsschwellwert m
through durchgehend
through-cracked plate Platte f mit durchgehendem Riß
through-the-thickness crack durchgehender Riß m
through-the-thickness edge crack durchgehender Randriß m
through-the-thickness surface crack durchgehender Oberfächenriß m
through-thickness crack specimen Probe f mit durchgehendem Riß
thulium, Tm Thulium n, Tm
thumbnail crack {bend specimen} Daumennagel-Riß m {Biegeprobe}
Ti → titanium
tide marks pl {fracture surface} Rastlinien fpl {Bruchfläche}
tilt boundary {crystal} Kippgrenze f {Kristall}
time Zeit f
time-dependent zeitabhängig
time-dependent deformation zeitabhängige Verformung f
time-dependent fracture zeitabhängiger Bruch m
time-dependent fracture behavio[u]r zeitabhängiges Bruchverhalten n
time-independent zeitunabhängig
time measurement Zeitmessung f
time of operation Betriebsdauer f
time-to-failure Zeit f bis zum Ausfall, Zeit f bis zum Bruch
burning time {the period in seconds that the specimen burns after removal of the ignition source} Brenndauer f
crack-propagation time Rißausbreitungszeit f

incubation time {crack initiation} Inkubationszeit *f* {Rißleitung}
loading time Beanspruchungsdauer *f*, Belastungszeit *f*
tin, Sn Zinn *n*, Sn
tin alloy Zinnlegierung *f*
tin bronze Zinnbronze *f*
tip {of a crack}; <syn.: peak {load}> Spitze *f* {Rißspitze; Belastung}
area around the crack tip Rißspitzenumfeld *n*
blunt crack tip abgestumpfte Rißspitze *f*
crack tip Rißspitze *f*
crack tip blunting Abstumpfung *f* (Abstumpfen *n*) der Rißspitze
crack tip opening displacement <abb.: CTOD> Rißspitzenöffnungsverschiebung *f*, CTOD
crack-tip region, area around the crack tip Rißspitzenbereich *m*
crack tip vicinity Rißspitzenumgebung *f*
critical crack tip opening kritische Rißspitzenöffnung *f*
distance from crack tip Abstand *m* von der Rißspitze
fictitious crack tip fiktive Rißspitze *f*
near crack tip in der Nähe der Rißspitze
neighbo[u]rhood of crack tip Rißspitzenumgebung *f*
non-propagating crack tip ruhende Rißspitze *f*
notch tip Kerbspitze *f*
radius of the crack tip Rißspitzenradius *m*
shape of crack tip Form *f* der Rißspitze, Rißspitzenform *f*
shape of crack tip Rißspitzenform *f*
titanium, Ti Titan *n*, Ti
arc-welded titanium lichtbogengeschweißtes Titan *n*
titanium alloy Titanlegierung *f*
titanium steel Titanstahl *m*
Tl → thallium

tool Werkzeug *n*
tool steel Werkzeugstahl *m*
topography Topographie *f*
fracture surface topography Bruchflächentopographie *f*
torque Drehmoment *n*; Drehtorque pulley {for torsion tests} Drehscheibe *f* {für Drehversuche}
torsion Torsion *f*, Verdrehung *f*
torsion fatigue fracture Torsionsschwingbruch *m*
torsion fracture Torsionsbruch *m*
torsion fracture Verdrehungsbruch *m*
torsion modulus Torsionsmodul *m*
torsion overload fracture Torsionsgewaltbruch *m*
torsion resistance Torsionswiderstand *m*, Verdrehwiderstand *m*
torsion strength Torsionsfestigkeit *f*
torsion stress Torsionsspannung *f*, Verdrehspannung *f*
torsion test Verdrehversuch *m*
double torsion <abb.: DT> specimen Doppeltorsions-Probe *f*, DT-Probe *f*
impact torsion test Schlagverdrehversuch *m*
modulus of rupture in torsion Bruchmodul *m* bei Torsionsbeanspruchung
torsional... Torsions- Verdrehungs- Verdreh-
torsional load Verdrehungsbelastung *f* Verdrehungsbeanspruchung *f*
torsional moment Verdrehmoment *n*, Drehmoment *n*
torsional moment; <syn.: torque> Drehmoment *n*
torsional stiffening test method Torsionssteifheits-Prüfmethode *f*
torsional strength Verdreh[ungs]festigkeit *f*
torsional test Verdrehversuch *m*
total vollständig; Gesamt-
total crack length Gesamtrißlänge

tough

total immersion {of the specimen} vollständiges Eintauchen *n* {einer Probe}
total service life {of structures} Gesamtlebensdauer *f* {von Konstruktionen}
total stiffness Gesamtsteifigkeit *f*
total thickness {of the specimen} Gesamtdicke *f* {der Probe}
tough, < syn.: **ductile** > zäh, duktil
tough steel zäher Stahl *m*
toughness Zähigkeit *f*
toughness behavio[u]r Zähigkeitsverhalten *n*
toughness parameter Zähigkeitsparameter *m*
arrest toughness {cracks} Arrestzähigkeit *f* {Risse}
crack-arrest toughness Rißarrestzähigkeit *f*, Rißauffangzähigkeit *f*
crack-initiation toughness Rißeinleitungsszähigkeit *f*, Rißinitiierungszähigkeit *f*
crack toughness Rißzähigkeit *f*
crack toughness behavio[u]r Rißzähigkeitsverhalten *n*
crack toughness measurement Rißzähigkeitsmessung *f*
crack toughness test Rißzähigkeitsversuch *m*
crack toughness value Rißzähigkeitswert *m*
dynamic fracture toughness dynamische Bruchzähigkeit *f*
dynamic fracture toughness value dynamischer Bruchzähigkeitswert *m*
fictitious fracture toughness fiktive Bruchzähigkeit *f*
fracture toughness Bruchzähigkeit *f*
fracture toughness properties *pl* Bruchzähigkeitseigenschaften *fpl*
fracture toughness specimen Bruchzähigkeitsprobe *f*
fracture toughness testing Bruchzähigkeitsprüfung *f*
fracture toughness testing method Bruchzähigkeits-Prüfverfahren *n*
fracture toughness value Bruchzähigkeitswert *m*
inherent fracture toughness Eigen-Bruchzähigkeit *f*
material toughness Werkstoffzähigkeit *f*
minimum fracture toughness Minimalbruchzähigkeit *f*, minimale Bruchzähigkeit *f*
notch impact toughness Kerbschlagzähigkeit *f*
notch impact toughness-temperature curve Kerbschlagzähigkeits-Temperaturverlauf *m*, Kerbschlagzähigkeits-Temperatur-Kurve *f*
notch impact toughness value Kerbschlagzähigkeitswert *m*
plane-strain fracture toughness Bruchzähigkeit *f* bei ebenem Spannungszustand, ESZ-Bruchzähigkeit *f*
quasi-static fracture toughness quasistatische Bruchzähigkeit *f*
strain fracture toughness Bruchzähigkeit *f* bei ebenem Verzerrungszustand, EVZ-Bruchzähigkeit *f*
rate-dependent fracture toughness geschwindigkeitsabhängige Bruchzähigkeit *f*
reference fracture toughness Referenzbruchzähigkeit *f*
static fracture toughness statische Bruchzähigkeit *f*
transcrystalline < syn.: **intracrystalline, transgranular** > {through the grains} transkristallin, intrakristallin, transgranular {durch Kristallkörner hindurch}
transcrystalline cleavage fracture transkristalliner Spaltbruch *m*
transcrystalline crack propagation transkristalline Rißausbreitung *f*
transcrystalline cracking < syn.: **transgranular cracking** > transkristalline Rißbildung *f*, transkristalline Rißbildung *f*
transcrystalline facet transkristalline Facette *f*

transcrystalline fracture <syn.: **transgranular fracture**> transkristalliner Bruch *m*
transcrystalline microcrack transkristalliner Mikroriß *m*
transgranular {through the grains} transgranular, transkristallin, intrakristallin {durch Kristallkörner hindurch}
transgranular fracture transgranularer (transkristalliner, interkristalliner) Bruch *m*
transient instationär; Übergangs-; Einschwing-
transient creep Übergangskriechen *n*
transient loading instationäre Belastung *f*
transition Übergang *m*, Durchgang *m*
transition behavio[u]r Übergangsverhalten *n*
transition range Übergangsbereich *m*
transition temperature Übergangstemperatur *f*, Umwandlungstemperatur *f*
transition temperature range Übergangstemperaturbereich *m*
brittle-ductile transition spröd-duktiler Übergang *m*, Spröd[e]-Zäh-Übergang *m*, Übergang *m* "spröd[e]-zäh"
concept of transition temperature {brittle-fracture behavio[u]r} Übergangstemperaturkonzept *n* {Sprödbruchverhalten}
ductile-brittle transition Zäh-Spröd[e]-Übergang *m*, zäh-spröder Übergang *m*, Übergang *m* "zäh-spröd[e]"
ductile-to-brittle transition temperature Zäh-Spröd[e]-Übergangstemperatur *f*
fatigue crack transition Ermüdungsrißübergang *m*
fracture appearance transition temperature <abb.: FATT> Brucherscheinungsübergangstemperatur *f*, FATT
fracture mode transition Bruchmoduswechsel *m*, Bruchmodenübergang *m*
fracture transition Bruchübergang *m*, Bruchdurchgang *m*
limiting transition temperature range Übergangstemperaturgrenzbereich *m*
zone of transition, transition zone Übergangszone *f*
transition-temperature behavio[u]r Übergangstemperaturverhalten *n*
transitional crack Durchriß *m*, durchgehender Riß *m*
transitional edge crack durchgehender Randriß *m*
transmission Übertragung *f*, Transmissions-
transmission electron microscope <abb.: TEM> Transmissions-Elektronenmikroskop *n*, TEM
transmission electron microscopy <abb.: TEM> Transmissions-Elektronenmikroskopie *f*, TEM
transparency Transparenz *f*, Durchlässigkeit *f*
transparent transparent, lichtdurchlässig
transparent specimen transparente Probe *f*
transversal, transverse transversal, quer, Quer-, in Querrichtung
transversal wave Transversalwelle *f*
transversal wave velocity Transversalwellengeschwindigkeit *f*
transverse transversal, quer, Quer-, in Querrichtung *f*
transverse direction Querrichtung *f*
transverse displacement Verschiebung *f* in Querrichtung, transversale Verschiebung *f*
transverse fracture properties *pl* Brucheigenschaften *fpl* in Querrichtung
transverse heating crack querverlaufender Warmriß *m*
transverse strain Querdehnung *f*

trapezoidal 140

transverse strength Biegefestigkeit *f*
trapezoidal trapezförmig
trapezoidal crack trapezförmiger Riß *m*
treatment Behandlung *f*; Bearbeitung *f*
  heat treatment {steel} Wärmebehandlung *f* {Stahl}
  surface treatment Oberflächenbehandlung *f*
treat/to behandeln; bearbeiten
Tresca's criterion Fließkriterium *n* nach Tresca, Tresca-Fließkriterium *n*
Tresca's yield criterion Fließkriterium *n* nach Tresca, Tresca-Fließkriterium *n*
trial loading Probebelastung *f*, probeweise Belastung *f*
triaxial dreiachsig
  triaxial state of stress dreiachsiger Spannungszustand *m*
  triaxial stress state dreiachsiger Spannungszustand *m*
  triaxial tensile stress dreiachsige Zugspannung *f*
  triaxial yield stress dreiachsige Fließspannung *f*
triaxiality {stress} Dreiachsigkeit *f* {Spannung}
tribology Tribologie *f*
true wahr, wirklich
  true fracture strain wahre Bruchdehnung *f*
  true surface energy wahre Oberflächenenergie *f*
truncation {of loading} Abbruch *m* {der Belastung}
truncation {of stress-factor distribution} Abflachung *f* {der Spannungsfaktorverteilung}
tuberculation {corrosion} Knollenbildung *f* {Korrosion}
tubular void {fracture surface} röhrenförmiger Hohlraum *m* {Bruchfläche}
tungsten, W Wolfram *n*, W

tungsten alloy Wolframlegierung *f*
tunnel crack Tunnelriß *m*
twin Zwilling *m*
twin band Zwillingsband *n*
  annealing twin {metals} Glühzwilling *m* {Metalle}
twin formation < syn.: twinning > Zwillingsbildung *f*
twinning fracture Bruch *m* an Zwillingsbildungen
twinning, < syn.: twin formation > Zwillingsbildung *f*
twist boundary {crystal} Verschränkungs[korn]grenze *f* {Kristall}
twist Verdrehung *f*, Torsion *f*
twist/to verdrehen, auf Verdrehung *f* beanspruchen
two-dimensional eben, zweidimensional
  two-dimensional crack zweidimensionaler Riß *m*
  two-dimensional crack problem zweidimensionales Rißproblem *n*
  two-dimensional crack system zweidimensionales Rißsystem *n*
  two-dimensional deformation zweidimensionale Verformung *f*, ebene Verformung *f*
  two-dimensional deformation field zweidimensionales Verformungsfeld *n*
  two-dimensional dynamic photoelasticity ebene dynamische Spannungsoptik *f*
  two-dimensional linear-elastic deformation field zweidimensionales linear-elastisches Verformungsfeld *n*
  two-dimensional stress field zweidimensionales Spannungsfeld *n*
type Typ *m*, Art *f*, Form *f*
  type of crack Rißart *f*
  type of fracture Bruchart *f*, Bruchform *f*
  type of fracture appearance Brucherscheinungsform *f*
  type of loading Beanspruchungsart *f*, Belastungart *f*
  type of notch Kerbform *f*

type of specimen Probenart f, Probentyp m
type of test bar Probestabform f
crack type Rißart f
fracture type Bruchart f
microscopic type of fracture mikroskopische Bruchform f

U

U → uranium
ultrahigh-strength steel ultrahochfester Stahl m
ultrasonic Ultraschall-
ultrasonic measurement {crack velocity} Ultraschallmessung f {Rißgeschwindigkeit}
ultrasonic testing Ultraschallprüfung f
unbroken {specimen} nicht gebrochen {Probe}
uncracked ungerissen, rißfrei
uncracked ligament rißfreies Ligament n
uncracked strip ungerissener Streifen m
unfilled ungefüllt, nicht gefüllt
unfilled plastic nicht gefüllter Kunststoff m
uniaxial einachsig
uniaxial compression einachsige Druckbeanspruchung f
uniaxial compression loading einachsige Druckbelastung f
uniaxial loading einachsige Belastung f
uniaxial stress einachsige Spannung f
uniaxial stress state einachsiger Spannungszustand m
uniaxial tensile loading einachsige Zugbeanspruchung f, einachsige Zugbelastung f
uniaxial tensile test einachsiger Zugversuch m
uniaxial tension einachsiger Zug m
uniaxial yield stress einachsige Fließspannung f

unidirectional einseitig {in eine Richtung}
unidirectional bending einseitige Biegung f
unload/to entlasten
unloaded lastfrei, unbelastet
unloaded body unbelasteter Körper m
unloaded central crack lastfreier Zentralriß m
unloaded crack unbelasteter Riß m
unloading Entlastung f, Entlastungsvorgang m
unloading line Entlastungsgerade f, Entlastungslinie f
unloading phase Entlastungsphase f
partial unloading partielle Entlastung f
unnotched (test) specimen ungekerbte Probe f, ungekerbter Probekörper m
unnotched tensile specimen ungekerbte Zugprobe f
unstable instabil
unstable crack instabiler Riß m
unstable crack extension instabile Rißerweiterung f
unstable crack growth instabiles Rißwachstum n
unstable crack initiation instabile Rißauslösung f
unstable crack propagation instabile Rißausbreitung f
unstable fracture instabiler Bruch m
unstable microcrack instabiler Mikroriß m
unstable propagation of fracture instabile Bruchausbreitung f
upper yield point obere Fließgrenze f
uranium, U Uran n, U

V

V → vanadium
valuate/to bewerten
valuation Bewertung f

value

valuation of fracture surface Bruchflächenbewertung *f*
value Wert *m*
boundary value Randwert *m*, Grenzwert *m*
boundary value method {drop-weight test} Grenzwertverfahren *n* {Fallgewichtsprüfung}
boundary value test {maximum notch sharpness and loading rate} Grenzwertprüfung *f* {größtmögliche Kerbschärfe und Belastungsgeschwindigkeit}
crack toughness value Rißzähigkeitswert *m*
dynamic fracture toughness value dynamischer Bruchzähigkeitswert *m*
elastic-plastic boundary value problem elastisch-plastisches Randwertproblem *n*
fracture resistance value Bruchwiderstandswert *m*
fracture toughness value Bruchzähigkeitswert *m*
loading value Beanspruchungswert *m*
notch impact toughness value Kerbschlagzähigkeitswert *m*
strength value Festigkeitswert *m*
stress-intensity factor value Spannungsintensitätsfaktorwert *m*
tensile strength value Zugfestigkeitswert *m*
vanadium, V Vanadium *n*, V
vanadium-niobium alloy Vanadium-Niob-Legierung *f*
vanadium steel Vanadiumstahl *m*
VCE → virtual crack extension
vector Vektor *m*
displacement vector Verschiebungsvektor *m*
load vector Belastungsvektor *m*
stress vector Spannungsvektor *m*
velocity Geschwindigkeit *f*
velocity of crack propagation Rißausbreitungsgeschwindigkeit *f*
branching velocity Verzweigungsgeschwindigkeit *f*
crack velocity < syn.: speed > Rißgeschwindigkeit *f*
crack-tip velocity Rißspitzengeschwindigkeit *f*
critical velocity kritische Geschwindigkeit *f*
diffusion velocity < syn.: rate > Diffusionsgeschwindigkeit *f*
dislocation velocity Versetzungsgeschwindigkeit *f*
fracture velocity Bruchgeschwindigkeit *f*
impact velocity Schlaggeschwindigkeit *f*
limiting velocity {crack propagation} Grenzgeschwindigkeit *f* {Rißausbreitung}
maximum crack velocity maximale Rißgeschwindigkeit *f*
measurement of fracture velocity Bruchgeschwindigkeitsmessung *f*
propagation velocity {of cracks} Ausbreitungsgeschwindigkeit *f* {von Rissen}
quasi-static crack velocity quasi-statische Rißgeschwindigkeit *f*
Rayleigh wave velocity Rayleighwellengeschwindigkeit *f*
shear-wave velocity < syn.: speed > Scherungswellengeschwindigkeit *f*
terminal crack velocity Endgeschwindigkeit *f* des Risses
transversal wave velocity Transversalwellengeschwindigkeit *f*
wave velocity Wellengeschwindigkeit *f*
vertical vertikal, senkrecht; Vertikale *f*, Senkrechte *f*
vertical Vertikale *f*, Senkrechte *f*
vertical crack-front curvature vertikale Rißfrontkrümmung *f*
VH → Vickers hardness number
vibrate/to schwingen
vibration Schwingung *f*
vibration loading Schwingbeanspruchung *f*, Schwingbelastung *f*, schwingende Beanspruchung *f*, schwingende Belastung *f*

Vicat
Vicat apparatus {determination of softening point} Vicat-Prüfgerät *n* {zur Bestimmung der Vicat-Erweichungstemperatur}
Vicat needle Vicat-Nadel *f*
Vicat softening point Vicat-Erweichungstemperatur *f*
Vicat softening point apparatus Gerät *n* zur Bestimmung der Vicat-Erweichungstemperatur
automatic Vicat softening point apparatus automatisches Prüfgerät *n* zur Bestimmung der Vicat-Erweichungstemperatur
vicinity, neighbo[u]rhood; environment Umgebung *f*, Nähe *f*, Umfeld *n*
Vickers
Vickers hardness number <abb.: VH> Vickershärte *f*
Vickers hardness test {indentation hardness} Vickershärteprüfung *f* {Eindringhärte}
virtual virtuell, scheinbar
virtual crack extension <abb.: VCE> scheinbare Rißerweiterung *f*
viscoelastic viskoelastisch
viscoelasticity Viskoelastizität *f*
viscoplastic viskoplastisch
viscoplasticity Viskoplastizität *f*
visual visuell
visual control Sichtprüfung *f*
void {in materials} Hohlraum *m*, Pore *f* {in Werkstoffen}
void coalescence Hohlraumvereinigung *f*, Hohlraumzusammenschluß *m*
void diameter Porendurchmesser *m*
void formation Hohlraumbildung *f*, Porenbildung
void growth Hohlraumwachstum *n*, Porenwachstum *n*
ellipsoidal void ellipsoidförmiger Hohlraum *m*
prismatic void prismatische Pore *f*
tubular void {fracture surface} röhrenförmiger Hohlraum *m* {Bruchfläche}
volume Volumen *n*
volume change Volumenänderung *f*
volume element Volumenelement *n*
specific heat at constant volume spezifische Wärme *f* bei konstantem Volumen
volumetric volumetrisch
volumetric modulus of elasticity Kompressionsmodul *m*
von Mises' yield criterion Fließkriterium *n* nach von Mises, von Mises-Fließkriterium *n*

W

W → tungsten
wall Wand *f*
Wallner lines *pl* {fracture surface} Wallner-Linien *fpl* {Bruchfläche}
warping Verwerfung *f*
water Wasser *n*
wave Welle *f*
wave equation Wellengleichung *f*
wave front Wellenfront *f*
wave length Wellenlänge *f*
wave velocity Wellengeschwindigkeit *f*
longitudinal wave Longitudinalwelle *f*
Rayleigh wave velocity Rayleighwellengeschwindigkeit *f*
stress wave emission Spannungswellenemission *f*
surface wave Oberflächenwelle *f*
transversal wave Transversalwelle *f*
transversal wave velocity Transversalwellengeschwindigkeit *f*
wear Verschleiß *m*
wear rate Verschleißgeschwindigkeit *f*
abrasive wear abrasiver Verschleiß *m*
adhesive wear adhäsiver Verschleiß *m*

wedge

catastrophic wear katastrophenartiger Verschleiß *m*
corrosive wear korrosiver Verschleiß *m*
fatigue wear Verschleiß *m* durch Werkstoffermüdung
oxidative wear {oxide film} oxidativer Verschleiß *m* {Oxidfilm}
wedge Keil *m*
wedge force Aufkeilungskraft *f*
wedge-loaded keilbelastet
wedge-loaded compact test specimen keilbelastete Kompakt-Probe *f*
wedge loading Keilbelastung *f*
wedge-opening loading <abb.: WOL> **specimen** Spaltkeilprobe *f*, WOL-Probe *f*
wedge-type deformation keilförmige Verformung *f*
wedge/to [auf]spalten {mit einem Keil}
weight Gewicht *n*
weight change Masseänderung *f*
weight loss test Masseverlustprüfung *f*
drop weight Fallgewicht *n*
falling weight impact strength apparatus Kugelfallprüfmaschine *f* {zur Bestimmung der Schlagzähigkeit}
falling weight test Kugelfallprobe *f*
loss in weight on heating {in percent} Masseverlust *m* bei Erwärmung
weld-crack resistance Schweißrißbeständigkeit *f*
weld/to schweißen
weldability {materials} Schweißbarkeit *f* {Werkstoffe}
weldable {materials} schweißbar {Werkstoffe}
weldable alloy schweißbare Legierung *f*
welded plate geschweißte Platte *f*
weldment testing Schweißprüfung *f* {von geschweißten Bauteilen}
whisker Haarkristall *m*

white metal Weißmetall *n*
wide-plate test Großplattenversuch *m*
width Breite *f*
width of component Bauteilbreite *f*
width of element Bauteilbreite *f*
width of specimen Probenbreite *f*
crack width Rißbreite *f*
ligament width Ligamentbreite *f*
minimum specimen width Mindestprobenbreite *f*
minimum width {specimens} Mindestbreite *f* {Proben}
plate width Plattenbreite *f*, Scheibenbreite *f*
specimen width Probenbreite *f*
winder Wickelkörper *m* {zum Aufwickeln der Probe}
Wöhler curve → S-N curve
WOL → wedge-opening loading
work Arbeit *f*
fracture work Brucharbeit *f*
work-hardenable material verfestigungsfähiger Werkstoff *m*
work-hardenable {metals} verfestigungsfähig {Metalle}
work-hardening <syn.: hardening> {metals} Verfestigen, Umformverfestigung *f* {Metalle}
work-harden/to {metals} verfestigen {Metalle}
working Betrieb *m*, Betriebs-, Arbeit *f*, arbeitend
working stress level Betriebsspannungsniveau *n*
low-temperature working chamber Tieftemperaturprüfraum *m*
wrought alloy Knetlegierung *f*
wrought alumin[i]um alloy Aluminium-Knetlegierung *f*
heat-resistant wrought alloy warmfeste Knetlegierung *f*

X

Xe → xenon
XPS → X-ray photoelectron spectroscopy

X-ray Röntgenstrahl m Röntgen-
X-ray diffraction Röntgenstrahlenbeugung f
X-ray photoelectron spectroscopy <abb.: XPS> Röntgen-Photoelektronen-Spektroskopie f
X-ray spectrometer Röntgenspektrometer m
xenon, Xe Xenon n, Xe

Y

Y → yttrium
Yb → ytterbium
yield Fließen n, Fließ-
yield conditions pl Fließbedingungen fpl
yield constraint Fließbehinderung f
yield criteria pl Fließkriterien npl
yield function Fließfunktion f
yield line theory Fließlinientheorie f
yield load Fließlast f
yield point Fließgrenze f
yield point-to-tensile strength ratio Streckgrenzenverhältnis n
yield state Fließzustand m
yield strength Fließfestigkeit f
yield stress Fließspannung f
yield stress curve Fließspannungskurve f
anisotropic yield anisotropes Fließen n
lower yield point untere Fließgrenze f
plastic yield Wärmebeständigkeit f, Formbeständigkeit f in der Wärme
plastic yield test Prüfung f der Formbeständigkeit in der Wärme
(sharp-)notch-strength to yield-strength-ratio Kerbfestigkeits-Streckgrenzenverhältnis n
tensile yield point Streckgrenze f
tensile yield strength Streckgrenze f
thermal yield strength Wärmestreckgrenze f
Tresca's yield criterion Fließkriterium n nach Tresca, Tresca-Fließkriterium n
triaxial yield stress dreiachsige Fließspannung f
uniaxial yield stress einachsige Fließspannung f
upper yield point obere Fließgrenze f
von Mises' yield criterion Fließkriterium n nach von Mises, von Mises-Fließkriterium n
yield/to {materials} fließen {Werkstoffe}
yielding {materials} Fließen n, Fließ- {Werkstoffe}
yielding range Fließbereich m
yielding zone Fließzone
inhomogeneous yielding inhomogenes Fließen n
initial yielding Fließbeginn m
local yielding lokales Fließen n, örtliches Fließen n
plastic yielding plastisches Fließen n
small-scale yielding Kleinbereichsfließen n
Young's modulus (of elasticity) Elastizitätsmodul m
ytterbium, Yb Ytterbium n, Yb
yttrium, Y Yttrium n, Y

Z

zero Null f; Nullpunkt m
zero point Nullpunkt m
zero position Nullage f, Nullstellung f
zinc alloy Zinklegierung f
zinc, Zn Zink n, Zn
zirconium, Zr Zirkonium n, Zirconium n, Zr
Zn → zinc
zone {in materials} Zone f, Gebiet n, Bereich m {in Werkstoffen}
zone of brittle fracture Sprödbruchbereich m
zone of fracture surface Bruchflächenbereich m
zone of transition Übergangszone f

zinc

arrest zone {in materials: crack arrest} Arrestzone *f* {in Werkstoffen: Rißarrest}
cleavage fracture zone Spaltbruchbereich *m*
cohesion zone Kohäsionszone *f*
crack-arrest zone Rißarrestzone *f*
crack-tip zone Rißspitzenzone *f*
creep zone Kriechbereich *m*, Kriechzone *f*
deformation zone {crack} Verformungsgebiet *n* {Riß}
dimensionless plastic zone dimensionslose plastische Zone *f*
effective plastic zone effektive plastische Zone *f*
elastic zone elastische Zone *f*
fatigue-fracture zone Ermüdungsbruchzone *f*
fracture initiation zone Brucheinleitungszone *f*
fracture process zone Bruchprozeßzone *f*
inner zone {crack tip} innerer Bereich *m* {Rißspitze}
inner zone of specimen Probeninneres *n*
length of plastic zone Länge *f* der plastischen Zone
outer zone {crack tip} äußerer Bereich *m* {Rißspitze}
plastic zone plastische Zone *f*
plastic zone form Form *f* der plastischen Zone
plastic zone size Größe *f* der plastischen Zone
process zone Prozeßzone *f*
radius of the plastic zone Radius *m* der plastischen Zone
segregation zone Seigerungszone *f*
shear-lip zone Scherlippenzone *f*
stretch zone Dehnzone *f*, Stretch-Zone *f* {vor der Rißfront}
transition zone Übergangszone *f*
yielding zone Fließzone *f*
zone of transition Übergangszone *f*
zinc alloy Zinklegierung *f*
Zr → zirconium

Abkürzungen Englisch/Deutsch

Al s. aluminium
ESCA s. electron spectroscopy for chemical analysis
FAD s. fracture analysis diagram
TGA s. thermogravimetric analysis
DTA s. differential thermal analysis
Sb s. antimony
A s. argon
As s. arsenic
AES s. Auger electron spectroscopy
Ba s. barium
DCB s. double-cantilever beam
TDCB s. tapered double-cantilever beam
Be s. beryllium
Bi s. bismuth
B s. boron
HB s. Brinell hardness number
Br s. bromine
C s. carbon
C s. compact
Cd s. cadmium
Ca s. calcium
CCT s. center-cracked tensile ...
Cs s. cesium
Cl s. chlorine
Cr s. chromium
Co s. cobalt
COD s. crack opening displacement
Cb s. colubium
Nb s. niobium
CS s. compact specimen
CT s. compact tension ...
DCT s. disk-shaped compact ...
RCT s. round compact tension ...
R s. crack resistance
LEFM s. linear-elastic fracture mechanics
Cu s. copper
CF s. corrosion fatigue

SCC s. stress corrosion cracking
CTOD s. crack tip opening displacement
FCP s. fatigue crack propagation
SCOD s. surface crack opening displacement
CLWL s. crack-line-wegde-loaded ...
HIC s. hydrogen-induced cracking
DT s. double torsion
DWTT s. drop-weight tear test
NDT s. nil ductility temperature
DWT s. drop-weight test
DT s. dynamic tear ...
Dy s. dysprosium
EPFM s. elastic-plastic fracture mechanics
EPMA s. electron probe micoranalysis
TEM s. transmission electron microscope
TEM s. transmission electron microsopy
FEM s. finite element method
LME s. liquid-metal embrittlement
SME s. solid-metal embrittlement
EDX s. energy-dispersive x-ray spectrometry
Er s. erbium
Eu s. europium
VDE s. virtual crack extension
fcc s. face-centered cubic
FAD s. failure-analysis diagram
FAD s. failure-assessment diagram
FCP s. fatigue crack propagation
F s. fluorine
Gd s. gadolinium
Ga s. gallium
Fr s. francium
Ge s. germanium
Au s. gold
Hf s. hafnium

HK s. Knoop hardness number
VH s. Vickers hardness number
HAZ s. heat affected zone
He s. helium
Ho s. holmium
Fe s. iron
Pb s. lead
Mg s. magnesium
SCFM s. subcritical fracture mechanics
Hg s. mercury
Mo s. molybdenum
NDT s. non-destructive testing
Nd s. neodymium
Ne s. neon
N s. nitrogen
NDE s. non-destructive evaluation
NSR s. notch sensitivity ratio
SENB ... s. nigle-edge notched bend ...
SEN s. single-edge notched
Os s. osmium
O s. oxygen
Pa s. palladium
P s. phosphorus
Pt s. platinum
Ra s. radium
Re s. rhenium
Rh s. rhodium
Rb s. rubidium
Ru s. ruthenium
S s. sulpur
Sm s. samarium
Sc s. scandium
Se s. selenium
Ag s. silver

Na s. sodium
SCC s. sulfide stress-cracking
Sr s. strontium
SCC s. subcritical crack growth
SCFM s. subcritical fracture mechanics
S s. sulphur
sulphur s. sulphur
SCOD s. surface-crack opening displacement
SCT s. surface-crack tensile ...
Ta s. tantalum
ETT s. explosion tear test
Tc s. technetium
Te s. tellurium
SCT s. surface crack tensile ...
Tb s. terbium
Tl s. thallium
Th s. thorium
Tm s. thulium
Sn s. tin
Ti s. titanium
W s. tungsten
U s. uranium
V s. vanadium
VH s. Vickers hardness number
VCE s. virtual crack extension
WOL s. wegde-opening loading ...
XPS s. x-ray photoelectron spectroscopy
Xe s. xenon
Zn s. zinc
Yb s Ytterbium
Y s. yttrium
Zr s. zirconium

Abbreviations of several Organizations

AAR Association of American Railroads
AFS American Foundrymen's Society
AIME American Institute of Mining, Metallurgical and Petroleum Engineers
AISI American Iron and Steel Institute
AMS Aerospace Material Specification
ANSI American National Standards Institute
API American Petroleum Institute
ASM American Society for Metals
ASME American Society of Mechanical Engineers
ASTM American Society for Testing and Materials

CFTA Committee of Foundry Technical Associations
FHWA Federal Highway Association
IACS International Annealed Copper Standard
ISO International Organization for Standardization
NACE National Association of Corrosion Engineers
NASA National Aeronautics and Space Administration
NBS National Bureau of Standards
SAE Society of Automotive Engineers
SI Systme International d'Units
BSI British Standards Institute
DIN Deutsche Industrie-Norm

Abkürzungen

DIN Deutsche Industrie-Norm
EN Europische Norm
BSI British Standards Institute
IOS International Organization for Standardization
ASTM American Society for Testing and Materials

ANSI American National Standards Institute
NBS National Bureau of Standards
BAM Bundesanstalt für Materialprüfung
DVS Deutscher Verband für Schweißtechnik
VDI Verein Deutscher Ingenieure

parat Wörterbücher

Junge, H.-D.
parat Wörterbuch Informationstechnologie
parat Dictionary of Information Technology
Deutsch/Englisch
1990. Ca. X, 900 Seiten. Gebunden. Ca. DM 195,-. ISBN 3-527-26420-5

Junge, H.-D.
parat Dictionary of Information Technology
parat Wörterbuch Informationstechnologie
English/German
1989. VIII, 936 Seiten. Gebunden. DM 195,-. ISBN 3-527-26430-2

Jedes dieser beiden Wörterbücher enthält über 50 000 anglo-amerikanische Einträge aus dem gesamten Bereich der Informationstechnologie mit zahlreichen Hinweisen auf Spezialgebiete, zusätzlichen Erläuterungen, Phrasen, Synonymen, Beispielen für unterschiedliche Verwendung und Wortkombinationen. Wichtigste Gebiete sind Gewinnung (Meßtechnik und Sensoren), Wandlung, Codierung, Übertragung, Verarbeitung (EDV, Computertechnologie), Speicherung, Wiedergewinnung, Darstellung und Nutzung (z.B. Steuerungs- und Regelungstechnik, Robotertechnik, KI) von Information, ferner andere wissenschaftlich-technische Gebiete, wie Logik, Zuverlässigkeitstechnik, Statistik, sowie die in der Informationstechnologie verwendeten Bauelemente, Geräte, Verfahren usw.

Jakobi, G. / Löhr, A.
parat Dictionary of Washing
Wörterbuch Waschen
English/German - Deutsch/Englisch
1989. X, 174 Seiten. Gebunden. DM 68,-. ISBN 3-527-26982-7

parat Dictionary of Plastics Technology
parat Wörterbuch Kunststofftechnologie
English/German
Junge, H.-D. (Hrsg.)
1987. VI, 318 Seiten. Gebunden. DM 178,-. ISBN 3-527-26432-9

Preisänderung vorbehalten.
Stand der Daten: August 1989

parat Wörterbücher

Junge, H.-D.
parat Pocket Dictionary of Laboratory Equipment
parat Taschenwörterbuch Laborausrüstung
English/German - Deutsch/Englisch
1987. VIII, 201 Seiten. DM 48,-. ISBN 3-527-26591-0

von Keitz, S. / von Keitz, W.
parat Dictionary of Library and Information Science
parat Wörterbuch Bibliotheks- und Informationswissenschaft
English/German/English - Deutsch/Englisch
1989. Ca. VIII, 408 Seiten. Gebunden. Ca. DM 84,-. ISBN 3-527-28002-2

Korzak, G.
parat Dictionary of Fracture Mechanics
parat Wörterbuch Bruchmechanik
English/German - Deutsch/Englisch
1989. Ca. VIII, 300 Seiten. Gebunden. Ca. DM 65,-. ISBN 3-527-27891-5

Schenk, H.
parat Dictionnaire de la Robotique
parat Wörterbuch Robotik
Français/Allemand - Deutsch/Französisch
1989. Ca. 200 Seiten. Gebunden. DM 68,-. ISBN 3-527-26940-1

Student-Bilharz, B.
parat Fachwörterbuch Sprengtechnologie
parat Dictionary of Blasting Technology
parat Dictionnaire de Technologie du Tir
Deutsch/Englisch/Französisch - English/German/French - Français/Allemand/Anglais
1988. XIII, 331 Seiten. DM 185,-. ISBN 3-527-26345-4

Preisänderung vorbehalten.
Stand der Daten: August 1989

parat

Adrian, J. / Legrand, G. / Frangne, R.
parat Dictionary of Food and Nutrition
1988. VIII, 233 Seiten mit 17 Abbildungen und 64 Tabellen. Gebunden.
DM 85,-. ISBN 3-527-26213-X

King, R.C. / Stansfield, W.D.
parat Encyclopedic Dictionary of Genetics with German Term Equivalents and Extensive German/English Index
1989. Ca. X, 900 Seiten mit ca. 65 Abbildungen. Gebunden. Ca. DM 260,-.
ISBN 3-527-26726-3

Englisch ist die internationale Wissenschaftssprache. Oft reichen aber 'normale' Englischkenntnisse nicht aus, wenn man Informationen, die man sich aus der Fachliteratur besorgt hat, in deutscher Sprache darstellen will: Fast alle neuen Fachworte haben sich im angelsächsischen Sprachraum entwickelt, die deutschen Begriffe fehlen. Das gilt besonders für ein so innovatives Gebiet wie die Genetik und Molekularbiologie.

Dieses Buch verfolgt daher ein neues Konzept: Das bewährte 'Dictionary of Genetics' von King und Stansfield mit seinen über 6000 Stichworten wurde um die entsprechenden deutschen Fachbegriffe ergänzt. So kann sich der Benutzer, der die englische Umgangssprache beherrscht, über alle Begriffe der Genetik informieren; darüber hinaus wird die deutsche Fachterminologie auf diesem Gebiet erschlossen, ja zum Teil auch neu etabliert. Umfangreiche deutsch-englische Wortlisten ermöglichen auch die Übersetzung in der umgekehrten Richtung. Damit ist das neue 'Wörterbuch Genetik' ein unentbehrliches Nachschlagewerk für Journalisten, Autoren, Übersetzer und Wissenschaftler - kurz für alle, die über Themen der Genetik, Molekularbiologie und Gentechnik in deutscher Sprache reden oder schreiben.

parat Index of Polymer Trade Names
Fachinformationszentrum Chemie, (Hrsg.)
1987. VI, 456 Seiten. Gebunden. DM 250,-. ISBN 3-527-26724-7

parat Index of Acronyms and Abbreviations in Electrical and Electronic Engineering
1989. V, 538 Seiten. Gebunden. DM 224,-. ISBN 3-527-26842-1

Preisänderung vorbehalten.
Stand der Daten: August 1989

parat Lexika

Durzok, J.
parat Fachlexikon Messung und Meßfehler
1989. VII, 172 Seiten mit 28 Abbildungen und 1 Tabelle. Gebunden. DM 68,-.
ISBN 3-527-26747-6

Die Grundbegriffe der Metrologie werden durch kurze Definitionen und Anwendungen erläutert und ihre englischen Äquivalente angegeben. Besonderen Wert wird auf die Erklärung der verschiedenartigen Meßfehler und deren Behandlung gelegt.

Henglein, E.
parat Lexikon Chemische Technik
1988. VII, 742 Seiten mit 369 Abbildungen und 107 Tabellen. Gebunden. DM 128,-. ISBN 3-527-26121-4

Die chemische Technik hat nicht nur in der chemischen Großindustrie herausragende Bedeutung, auch andere Industriezweige, wie die Metallurgie, die Energieumwandlung, die Lebensmittelindustrie oder der Bergbau, sowie viele andere industrielle Bereiche wenden chemisch-technische Verfahren an.
Der Autor hat in diesem Lexikon eine repräsentative Auswahl von Begriffen der chemischen Technik und ihrer Randgebiete zusammengestellt, definiert und erläutert, wobei er auf seine jahrzehntelange Tätigkeit und praktische Erfahrung in maßgeblichen Funktionen in der chemischen Industrie, unter anderem als Betriebsleiter und Werksdirektor innerhalb der Metallgesellschaft AG, Frankfurt am Main, sowie als Lehrbeauftragter und Honorarprofessor an der Technischen Universität Clausthal zurückgreifen konnte.

Hibbert, D.B. / James, A.M.
parat Lexikon Elektrochemie
1987. XI, 272 Seiten mit 130 Abbildungen und 18 Tabellen. Gebunden. DM 118,-. ISBN 3-527-26353-5

Unter rund 400 der wichtigsten Begriffe der Elektrochemie werden die neuesten Entwicklungen und die Bedeutung der Elektrochemie für andere Wissenschaftsgebiete definiert und erläutert. Das Lexikon ist durch die entsprechenden englischen Begriffe ergänzt.

Preisänderung vorbehalten.
Stand der Daten: August 1989

TexTerm Text und Terminologie

Herausgeber: P. Schmitt, Germersheim

Die Werke der TexTerm-Reihe sind Fachbuch und Wörterbuch zugleich. Jeder Band besteht aus zwei Hauptteilen: Eine fachliche Einführung liefert das didaktisch/logisch strukturierte Hintergrundwissen zu einem speziellen Fachgebiet. Ein Glossar liefert die Terminologie dieses Fachgebiets, alphabetisch sortiert, in beiden Übersetzungsrichtungen, mit mehr terminographischen Angaben als in üblichen Fachwörterbüchern. Das Glossar basiert ausschließlich auf der Auswertung eines umfangreichen Korpus typischer Fachliteratur der jeweiligen Sprache und reflektiert realen Sprachgebrauch. Ein Literaturverzeichnis dient nicht nur als Quellennachweis, sondern erleichtert auch die Suche nach weiterführender Literatur. Mit diesem Informationsangebot sind die TexTerm-Bände nicht nur das ideale Nachschlagemedium für Fachübersetzer und -dolmetscher, sondern sie richten sich an jeden, der sich effizient mit Grundlagen und Terminologie eines speziellen Fachgebiets vertraut machen will.

Donnevert, M.
TexTerm Four-Wheel Drive
TexTerm Allradantrieb
English/German - Deutsch/Englisch
1989. XI, 131 Seiten. Broschur. DM 124,-. ISBN 3-527-27869-9

Göpferich, S.
TexTerm Corrosion
TexTerm Korrosion
English/German - Deutsch/Englisch
1989. XVIII, 271 Seiten. Broschur. DM 128,-. ISBN 3-527-27868-0

Schwanhäuser, H.
TexTerm Fibres Optiques
TexTerm Lichtwellenleiter
Français/Allemand - Deutsch/Franzsösich
1989. X, 310 Seiten mit 52 Abbildungen und 3 Tabellen. Broschur. DM 124,-. ISBN 3-527-27867-2

Preisänderung vorbehalten.
Stand der Daten: August 1989

VCH

Deutsch – Englisch
German – English

A

A → Argon
Abänderung f, <syn.: Modifikation f > modification
Abbau m {Metalle: Oberflächen} degradation {metals: surface}
mechanischer Abbau m mechanical degradation
abbauen {Metalle: Oberflächen} degrade/to {metals: surface}
Abbauverhalten n degradation behavio[u]r
Abbildung f {Mathematik} mapping {mathematics}
abblättern exfoliate/to
Abblättern n exfoliation
Abbruch m {der Belastung} truncation {of loading}
Abdruck m replica
Abflachung f {der Spannungsfaktorverteilung} truncation {of stress-factor distribution}
Abfolge f program
abgerundeter Riß m blunt crack
abgestumpfter Riß m, <Syn.: stumpfer Riß m> blunt crack
abgleiten slip off/to
Abgleiten n slipping off
Abgleitung f slipping off
Abhängigkeit f dependence
Abkühlen n {Proben} cooling {specimens}
abkühlen {Proben} cool/to {specimens}
Abkühlungsgeschwindigkeit f cooling rate
Ablauf m program
Ablösung f delamination
Abmessungen fpl dimensions pl
Abnutzung f {adhäsiver Verschleiß} scuffing {adhesive wear}
Abplatzen n spalling
abrasiv abrasive

abrasiver Verschleiß m abrasive wear
Abrieb m abrasion {wear}
abrunden {eine Probe} radius/to {a specimen}
Abrundung f {Risse} blunting {cracks}
abschätzen evaluate/to
Abschätzung f evaluation
abscheren shear/to
Abscherung f, <Syn.: Scherung f > shearing
Abschervorgang m shearing
absenken {Belastung, Last} decrease/to
absolut absolute
absolute Prüfung f absolute test
absolute Rißgröße f absolute crack size
absoluter Bruchwiderstand m absolute resistance to fracture
Abstand m distance
Abstand m in Rißrichtung distance along the crack
Abstand m von der Rißspitze distance from crack tip
abstumpfen blunt/to
Abstumpfen n {Risse} blunting {cracks}
Abstumpfung f {Risse} blunting {cracks}
Abstumpfung f der Rißspitze crack tip blunting
Abtasten n {elektronisch} scanning
abtasten {elektronisch} scan/to
Abtastung f {elektronisch} scanning
abweichen deviate/to
Abweichung f deviation
Achse f axis
adhäsiv adhesive
adhäsiver Verschleiß m adhesive wear
adsorbieren adsorp/to
Adsorption f adsorption

adsorptionsinduzierte Versprödung f adsorption-induced embrittlement
AES → Auger-Elektronenspektroskopie f
Ag → Silber
Aktivieren n activation
Aktivierung f activation
Aktivierungsenergie f activation energy
aktuell <Syn.: laufend> current
aktuelle Rißerweiterung f current crack extension
aktuelle Rißlänge f current crack length
aktueller Spannungszustand m current stress state
akustisch, Schall- acoustic
Al → Aluminium
korrosionsbeständige Legierung f corrosion-resistant alloy
altern age/to
Alterung f ag[e]ing
Alterung f <Syn.: thermische Wärmealterung f> heat ag[e]ing
alterungsbeständiger Stahl m non-ag[e]ing steel
Alterungsbeständigkeit f resistance to ag[e]ing
alterungsfähige Legierung f age-hardenable alloy
Alterungsmethode f method of ag[e]ing, method for ag[e]ing
Alterungswiderstand m resistance to ag[e]ing
Alterungsprüfung f ag[e]ing test
beschleunigte Alterungsprüfung f accelerated ag[e]ing test
Alterungsverfahren n method for ag[e]ing, method of ag[e]ing
Aluminium n, Al aluminium (GB), aluminum (US), Al
Aluminium-Guß-Legierung f cast alumin[i]um alloy

Aluminium-Knetlegierung f wrought alumin[i]um alloy
Aluminium-Kupfer-Legierung f alumin[i]um-copper alloy
Aluminium-Kupfer-Silizium-Legierung f alumin[i]um-copper-silicon alloy
Aluminium-Lithium-Legierung f alumin[i]um-lithium alloy
Aluminium-Magnesium-Silizium-Legierung f alumin[i]um-magnesium-silicon alloy
Aluminium-Zink-Magnesium-Legierung f alumin[i]um-zinc-magnesium alloy
Aluminiumbronze f alumin[i]um bronze
Aluminiumlegierung f alumin[i]um alloy
hochfeste Aluminiumlegierung f high-strength alumin[i]um alloy
lichtbogengeschweißte Aluminiumlegierung f arc-welded alumin[i]um alloy
amorph {Werkstoff} amorphous {material}
Amplitude f amplitude
konstante Amplitude f constant amplitude
zyklische Beanspruchung f mit konstanter Amplitude f constant amplitude cyclic loading
Analyse f analysis
elastisch-plastische Analyse f elastic-plastic analysis
Elektronenspektroskopie f für die chemische Analyse f electron spectroscopy for chemical analysis ESCA
fraktrographische Analyse f fractrographic analysis
thermische Analyse f thermal analysis
thermogravimetrische Analyse f <Abk.: TGA> thermogravimetric analysis TGA

Analyse f von Bruchflächen fracture surface analysis
analysieren analyze/to
analytisch analytic
Änderung f, < Syn.: **Veränderung f** > change
Anfangs- < Syn.: **Ausgangs-** > initial
Anfangsabmessungen fpl initial dimensions
Anfangsdicke f {der Probe zu Beginn der Prüfung} initial thickness {of specimen}
Anfangsriß m < Syn.: **Anriß m** > incipient crack, starter crack
Anfangsrißkonfiguration f starter crack configuration
Anfangstiefe f {Oberflächenriß} initial depth {surface crack}
Angaben fpl < Syn.: **Daten pl** > data
angerissen pre-cracked
angerissene Probe f < Syn.: **Probe f mit Anriß** > {Prüfung} pre-cracked specimen {testing}
einseitig angerissene Zugprobe f < Syn.: **Zugprobe f mit Einzelrandriß m** > single-edge cracked tensile specimen
mittig angerissene Zugprobe f < Syn.: **Zugprobe f mit Mittelriß** > center-cracked tensile < abb.: CCT > specimen
zweiseitig angerissene Zugprobe f double-edge cracked tensile specimen
angerissener Augenstab m {Probenform} single-edge cracked eyebar {type of specimen} einseitig
angreifen {Werkstoff} attack/to {materials}
angreifende Kraft f concentrated force punktförmig
Angriff m {Werkstoff} attack {materials}
Angriff m durch Flüssigkeitsschlag {Korrosion + turbulente Flüssigkeitsströmungen} impingement attack {corrosion + turbulent flow of liquid}
Anhalten n < Syn.: **Arretieren n, Stoppen n** > {Risse} arresting {cracks}
anisotrop anisotropic
anisotrope Elastizität f anisotropic elasticity
anisotroper duktiler Werkstoff m anisotropic ductile material
anisotroper elastischer Körper m anisotropic elastic body
anisotroper Werkstoff m anisotropic material
anisotropes Fließen n anisotropic yield
anisotropes Medium n anisotropic medium
Anisotropie f anisotropy **dehnungsinduzierte Anisotropie f** strain-induced anisotropy
induzierte Anisotropie f induced anisotropy
natürliche Anisotropie f inherent anisotropy
Anlaßsprödbruch m temper-brittle fracture
Anlaßsprödigkeit f temper brittleness
anlaßversprödet temper-brittle
Anlaßversprödung f temper embrittlement
Anode f anode
Anomalie f {Gefüge} anomaly {structure}
anordnen {eine Probe} place/to {a specimen}
Anordnung f < Syn.: **Aufbau m; Mon-tage f** > assembly
Anordnung f < Syn.: **Lage f, Ort m, Stelle f** > location
Anreicherung f enrichment

anreißen

Anreicherung f an den Korngrenzen grain-boundary enrichment
anreißen pre-crack/ to
Anriß m pre-crack
Probe f mit Anriß {Prüfung} pre-cracked specimen {testing}
angerissene Probe f pre-cracked specimen
Anrißbildung f pre-crack formation, pre-cracking
Sb → Antimon
Anrißerzeugung f pre-crack production, pre-crack initiation
anrißfreier Werkstoff m material without pre-crack
Anrißgröße f pre-crack size
kritische Anrißgröße f critical pre-crack size
Anrißlänge f pre-crack length
ansteigen < Syn.: zunehmen, erhöhen > increase/to
Anstieg m < Syn.: Zunahme f, Erhöhung f> increase
Antimon n, Sb antimony, Sb
anwendbar < Syn.: übertragbar > applicable
Anwendbarkeit f applicability {of concepts, criteria}
anwenden apply/to
Anwendungstemperatur f < Syn.: Betriebstemperatur f> service temperature
Anzahl f, Zahl f number
Anzahl f (Zahl f) der Biegungen number of flexings
Anzeige f indication
automatische Anzeige f automatic indication
Apfelsinenschaleneffekt m {Oberflächenfehler} orange peel {surface roughening}
Apparat m, < Syn.: Gerät n, (i.e.s.) Prüfgerät n, Prüfvorrichtung f > apparatus

äquivalent < Syn.: Ersatz- > equivalent
äquivalente Rißlänge f equivalent crack length
äquivalente Spannung f < Syn.: Ersatzspannung f> equivalent stress
äquivalenter elastischer Riß m equivalent elastic crack
äquivalenter ruhender Riß m equivalent stationary crack
Äquivalenz f equivalence
Arbeit f work
arbeitend, < Syn.: Betriebs-> working
Argon n, A argon, A
Arrest m < Syn.: Stoppen n, Anhalten n> {Risse} arrest {cracks}
Arrestrißlänge f arrest-crack length
Arrestverhalten n {Risse} arrest behavio[u]r {cracks}
Arrestzähigkeit f {Risse} arrest toughness {cracks}
Arrestzone f {in Werkstoffen: Rißarrest} arrest zone {in materials: crack arrest}
Arretieren n < Syn.: Stoppen n, Anhalten n> {Risse} arresting {cracks}
arretierender Riß m arresting crack
arretierter Riß m arrest-crack
Arretierung f < Syn.: Stillstand m von Rissen > arresting of cracks
Arsen n, As arsenic, As
Art f type
As → Arsen
Asymmetrie f < Syn.: Unsymmetrie f> asymmetry
asymmetrisch < Syn.: unsymmetrisch> asymmetric
asymmetrische Belastung f skew-symmetric loading
Atmosphäre {Korrosion} atmosphere {corrosion}
Au → Gold

Aufbau *m*, **Anordnung** *f*, **Montage** *f* assembly
aufgefangen <Syn.: gestoppt> {Riß} stopped {crack}
aufgefangener Mikroriß *m* arrested microcrack, stopped microcrack
aufgefangener Riß *m* arrested crack, stopped crack
Aufheizgeschwindigkeit *f* heating rate
Aufheiztemperatur *f* heating temperature
Aufkeilungskraft *f* wedge force
Aufprall *m* <Syn.: Stoß *m*, Aufschlag *m*, Schlag *m*> impact
aufprallen <Syn.: auftreffen, [auf]schlagen> impact/to
Aufreißprobe *f* tear test specimen
  gekerbte Aufreißprobe *f* notched tear test specimen
Aufschlag *m* <Syn.: Schlag *m*, Aufprall *m*, Stoß *m*> impact
aufspalten cleave/to
Aufstau *m* {Versetzungen} pile-up {dislocations}
auftreffen <Syn.: [auf]schlagen, aufprallen> impact/to
Aufweitung *f* <Syn.: Breitenwachstum *n*, Erweiterung *f*> {Risse} extension {cracks} Erweiterung *f*
aufzeichnen record/to
Augenstab *m* {Prüfkörper} eyebar {test specimen}
  einseitig angerissener Augenstab *m* {Probenform} single-edge cracked eyebar {type of specimen}
Auger-Elektronenspektroskopie *f* <Abk.: AES> Auger electron spectroscopy <abb.: AES>
ausbeulen {Probe}; [aus]knicken {eines langen Stabes} buckle/to
Ausbildung *f*, <Syn.: Bildung *f*, Herausbildung *f*, Formierung *f*, Entstehung *f*> formation

ausbreiten, auseinanderlaufen spread/to {cracks}
ausbreiten {Risse} propagate/to {cracks}
  sich ausbreitender Riß *m* propagating crack
  sich langsam ausbreitender Riß *m* slowly propagating crack
Ausbreitung *f* <Syn.: Fortpflanzung *f*> {von Rissen} propagation {of cracks}
Ausbreitungsgeschwindigkeit *f* {von Rissen} propagation velocity {of cracks}
Ausbruch *m* {Fehler} burst {defect}
ausdehnen {Werkstoffe} dilate/to {materials}
Ausdehnung *f* {von Werkstoffen} dilatation {of materials}; expansion
  Gerät *n* **zur Bestimmung der linearen Ausdehnung** *f* linear expansion apparatus
  Messung *f* **der linearen Ausdehnung** *f* linear expansion measurement
  thermische Ausdehnung *f* <Syn.: Wärmeausdehnung *f*> thermal expansion
Ausdehnungskoeffizient *m* coefficient of expansion
  kubischer Ausdehnungskoeffizient *m* coefficient of cubic[al] expansion
  linearer Ausdehnungskoeffizient *m* coefficient of linear expansion
Ausdruck *m* {mathematischer} expression {mathematical}
auseinanderlaufen <Syn.: (sich) ausbreiten> spread/to {cracks}
außen <Syn.: Außen-> outside, external
Außendurchmesser *m* {von Proben} outside diameter {of the specimen}
Außenfaser *f* {Werkstoffe} outer fiber {materials}

Außenfläche

Außenfläche f outer surface
Außenkerb m notch on outer surface
scharfer Außenkerb m sharp external notch
Außenriß m external crack
kreisförmiger Außenriß m circular external crack
Rundstab m mit konzentrischem Außenriß m circumferentially cracked round bar specimen
äußere, < Syn.: Außen- > external; outside
äußere Druckbelastung f external compressive load
äußere Kraft f external force
äußere Last f external load
äußerer Bereich {Rißspitze} outer zone {crack tip}
äußerer Riß m external crack
Ausfall m {im Sinne von Schaden} failure
Ausfall m bei erhöhten Temperaturen elevated-temperature failure
Ausfall m durch Korrosion corrosion failure
Ausfall m durch Korrosionsermüdung corrosion-fatigue failure
zufälliger Ausfall m random failure
Zeit f bis zum Ausfall time-to-failure
ausfallen < Syn.: versagen > fail/to
Ausfallwahrscheinlichkeit f < Syn.: Versagenswahrscheinlichkeit f > failure probability
Ausgangs- < Syn.: Anfangs- > initial
Ausgangsgeometrie f initial geometry
Ausgangskerbe f starter notch
Ausgangsriß m initial crack, starter crack
Ausgangsrißlänge f initial crack length, starter crack length
Ausgangsstelle f < Syn.: Keimstelle f > {Risse, Bruch} nucleus {cracks, fracture}
Ausgleich m correction
ausgleichen correct/to
auslegen {Konstruktio < Syn.: entwerfen design/to {structure}
auslösen, < Syn.: initiieren > {Risse} initiate/to {cracks}
Auslösung f < Syn.:Initiierung f, Einleitung f > initiation
Auslösung f < Syn.: Initiation f, Initiierung f > {von Rissen} initiation {of cracks}
ausrichten align/to
Ausrichten n alignment
Ausrichtung f alignment
Ausscheidung f < Syn.: Segregation f > segregation
ausscheidungshärtender nichtrostender Stahl m precipitation-hardening stainless steel
Aussehen n < Syn.: Erscheinungsbild n > {Oberflächen} appearance {surfaces}
aussenden < Syn.: strahlen > radiate/to
Austenite m austenite
austenitisch austenitic
austenitische Legierung f austenitic alloy
austenitischer Manganstahl m austenitic manganese steel
austenitischer nichtrostender Stahl m austenitic stainless steel
austenitischer Stahl m austenitic steel
automatisch < Syn.: selbsttätig > automatic
automatische Anzeige f automatic indication
automatisches Prüfgerät n zur Bestimmung der Vicat-Erweichungstemperatur automatic Vicat softening point apparatus

axial axial
axial beansprucht axially loaded
axiale Dehnung f <Syn.: Dehnung f in axialer Richtung> axial strain
axiale Schwindung f axial shrinkage
Axialspannung f axial stress

B

B → Bor
Ba → Barium
Babbitt-Metall n babbitt metal
Bad n bath
Badtemperatur f {Temperieren von Proben} bath temperature {conditioning of the specimen}
Bahn f <Syn.: Weg m, Pfad m> path
bainitisch {Gefüge} bainitic {structure}
Balken m beam
Band n {z.B. auf Bruchflächen} band {e.g. on fracture surface}
Barenblatt-Theorie f {Rißerweiterung} Barenblatt theory {crack extension}
Barium n, Ba barium, Ba
Basis f <Syn.: Grundlage f; Hauptbestandteil m> basis
Bauschinger-Effekt m Bauschinger effect
Baustahl m structural steel
Bauteil n <Syn.: Element n> element; component
Bauteilbreite f width of component; width of element
Bauteildicke f thickness of component
Bauteilfestigkeit f component strength; element strength
Bauteilgeometrie f component geometry; element geometry
Bauteilprüfung f testing of component; testing of element
Bauwerk n <Syn.: Konstruktion f> construction

Be → Beryllium
Beanspruchbarkeit f permissible load; permissible stress
beanspruchen <Syn.: belasten> load/to
auf Verdrehung f beanspruchen <Syn.: verdrehen> twist/to
beansprucht <Syn.: belastet, unter Last f> loaded
axial beansprucht axially loaded
beanspruchter (belasteter) Körper m loaded body
Beanspruchung f <Syn.: Belastung f> load[ing]
dynamische Beanspruchung f <Syn.: dynamische Belastung f> dynamic loading
monotone Beanspruchung f <Syn.: monotone Belastung f> monotonic loading
schlagartige Beanspruchung f <Syn.: Schlagbeanspruchung f, Schlagbelastung f, Stoßbelastung f> impact loading
schwingende Beanspruchung f (Belastung) <Syn.: Schwingbeanspruchung f, Schwingbelastung f> vibration loading
zyklische Beanspruchung f <Syn.: zyklische Belastung> cyclic loading
zyklische Beanspruchung f mit konstanter Amplitude constant amplitude cyclic loading
Beanspruchungsamplitude f loading amplitude
Beanspruchungsanalyse f loading analysis
Beanspruchungsart f type of loading
gemischte Beanspruchungsart f mixed-mode loading
Beanspruchungsbedingungen fpl <Syn.: Belastungsbedingungen fpl, Lastbedingungen fpl, Beanspruchungsverhältnisse npl> loading conditions pl

Beanspruchungscharakterisierung f characterization of loading
Beanspruchungsdauer f <Syn.: **Belastungszeit** f> loading time
Beanspruchungsfall m loading case
Beanspruchungsfrequenz f loading frequency
Beanspruchungsgeschwindigkeit f <Syn.: **Belastungsgeschwindigkeit** f> loading rate
Beanspruchungskenngröße f <Syn.: **Beanspruchungsparameter** m> loading parameter
Beanspruchungsmodulation f modulation of loading
Beanspruchungsparameter m <Syn.: **Beanspruchungskenngröße** f> loading parameter
Beanspruchungsrichtung f <Syn.: **Lastrichtung** f> direction of loading
Beanspruchungssituation f loading situation
Beanspruchungsverhältnisse npl <Syn.: **Beanspruchungsbedingungen** fpl, **Belastungsbedingungen** fpl, **Lastbedingungen** fpl> loading conditions pl
Beanspruchungsverlauf m loading curve
Beanspruchungswechsel m loading cycle
Beanspruchungswert m loading value
Beanspruchungszustand m loading state
bearbeiten <Syn.: behandeln> treat/to
(mechanisch) bearbeiteter Probekörper m machined specimen
Bearbeitung f <Syn.: **Behandlung** f> treatment
Becherbruch m cup fracture
Bedingung f condition
Bedingungen fpl <Syn.: **Verhältnisse** npl> conditions pl
stationäre Bedingungen fpl steady state conditions pl
physikalische Bedingungen fpl {einer Prüfung} physical conditions pl {of the test}
befestigen fasten/to; fix/to
Befestigen n fastening, fixing
befestigte Probe f mounted specimen
befestigter Probekörper m mounted specimen
Befestigung f fastening; fixing
Befestigungselement n fastening device
Beflammen n <Syn.: **Flammbehandlung** f> flaming
beflammen {eine Probe} flame/to {a specimen}
begrenzen <Syn.: einschränken> limit/to
Begrenzung f <Syn.: **Einschränkung** f> limitation
behandeln <Syn.: bearbeiten> treat/to
Behandlung f <Syn.: **Bearbeitung** f> treat-ment
behindern {z.B. Dehnung} constrain/to {e.g. strain}
Behinderung f {z.B. Dehnungsbehinderung} constraint {e.g. strain constraint}
elastische Behinderung f elastic constraint
Behinderungsfaktor m constraint factor
beidseitiger Riß m {Proben} double-edge crack {specimens}
Beiwert m <Syn.: **Faktor** m> coefficient <syn.: factor>
Beizriß m pickling crack
beizspröder Stahl m acid brittle steel
belasten <Syn.: beanspruchen> load/to
belastet loaded unter Last f beansprucht

belasteter (beanspruchter) Körper *m* loaded body
Belastung *f* <Syn.: Belastungsvorgang *m*, Beanspruchung *f*> load[ing]
Belastung *f* quer zur Rißlänge crack line loading
asymmetrische Belastung *f* screwsymmetric loading
dynamische Belastung *f* <Syn.: dynamische Beanspruchung *f* dynamic loading
einachsige Belastung *f* uniaxial loading
elastische Belastung *f* elastic loading
homogene Belastung *f* homogeneous loading
instationäre Belastung *f* transient loading
monotone Belastung *f* <Syn.: monotone Beanspruchung *f*> monotonic loading
probeweise Belastung *f* <Syn.: Probebelastung *f*> trial loading
ruhende (statische) Belastung *f* static loading
schrittweise Belastung *f* gradual loading
schwingende Belastung *f* vibration loading
spontane Belastung *f* spontaneous loading
statische (ruhende) Belastung *f* static loading
stufenweise Belastung *f* stepwise loading
symmetrische Belastung *f* symmetric loading
unendliche Belastung *f* infinite loading
wiederholte Belastung *f* <Syn.: Wiederbelastung *f* reloading

zyklische Belastung *f* <Syn.: zyklische Beanspruchung *f*> cyclic loading
Belastungs-COD-Diagramm *n* load COD diagram
Belastungsart *f* type of loading
Belastungsablauf *m* loading process
Belastungsanstieg *m* increase of load
Belastungsbedingungen *fpl* <Syn.: Lastbedingungen *fpl*, Beanspruchungsverhältnisse *npl*, Beanspruchungsbedingungen *fpl*> loading conditions *pl*
Belastungseinrichtung *f* <Syn.: Belastungsvorrichtung *f*> loading mechanism
Belastungsfolge *f* <Syn.: Belastungsprogramm *n*> loading program
Belastungsfunktion *f* load function
Belastungsgeschwindigkeit *f* <Syn.: Beanspruchungsgeschwindigkeit *f*> loading rate, rate of loading
lokale Belastungsgeschwindigkeit *f* local load rate
Prüfmaschine *f* mit konstanter Belastungsgeschwindigkeit constant-rate-of-loading instrument
Belastungsgrenze *f* <Syn.: Lastgrenze *f*> load limit
lokale Belastungsgrenze *f* local load limit
Belastungshergang *m* loading history
Belastungskennlinien *fpl* loading characteristics *pl*
Belastungskonfiguration *f* load configuration
Belastungskontrolle *f* load control
Belastungsprogramm *n* loading program
Belastungsrichtung *f* loading direction
Belastungsstufe *f* loading stage
Belastungssystem *n* load system

Belastungsvektor *m* load vector
Belastungsverfahren *n* method of loading
Belastungsversuch *m* loading test
Belastungsvorgang *m* load[ing]
Belastungsvorgeschichte *f* prehistory of loading
Belastungsvorrichtung *f* <Syn.: **Belastungseinrichtung** *f*> loading mechanism
Belastungszeit *f* loading time
Berandung *f* {der plastischen Zone} interface {of plastic zone}
berechnen calculate/to
berechnet <Syn.: theoretisch> calculated
Berechnung *f* calculation; computation
Bereich *m* <Syn.: Zone *f*, Gebiet *n*> {in Werkstoffen} zone {in materials}
Bereich *m* <Syn.: Intervall *n*> {Temperatur, Druck-} range {temperature, pressure...}
Bereich *m* <Syn.: Umfeld *n*> area
innerer Bereich {Rißspitze} inner zone {crack tip}
äußerer Bereich {Rißspitze} outer zone {crack tip}
Berstdruck *m* bursting pressure
bersten burst/to
Bersten *n* bursting
Berstversuch *m* burst test
Beryllium *n*, Be beryllium, Be
Beschichten *n* {Vorgang} coating {process}
Beschichtung *f* {Ergebnis} coating, {result}
beschleunigen accelerate/to
beschleunigt accelerated
beschleunigte Alterungsprüfung *f* accelerated ag[e]ing test
beschleunigte Rißausbreitung *f* accelerated crack propagation
Beschleunigung *f* acceleration
beständig resistant

beständig gegenüber Flammenausbreitung *f* resistant to flame propagation
Beständigkeit *f* resistance
bestimmen determine/to
Bestimmen *n* determining
Bestimmung *f* determination
automatisches Prüfgerät *n* **zur Bestimmung der Vicat-Erweichungstemperatur** automatic Vicat softening point apparatus
Bestimmung *f* **des Erweichungspunktes** soft point determination
experimentelle Bestimmung *f* experimental determination
Gerät *n* **zur Bestimmung der linearen Ausdehnung** linear expansion apparatus
Gerät *n* **zur Bestimmung der Vicat-Erweichungstemperatur** *f* Vicat softening point apparatus
Hochgeschwindigkeits-Prüfmaschine *f* **zur Bestimmung der Schlagzugfestigkeit** high-speed tensile impact machine
Bestimmungsverfahren *n* method of determination
instationäres Bestimmungsverfahren *n* non-steady state method of determining
Beton *m* concrete
Betrieb *m* operation
Betriebs- operating
Betriebsbedingungen *fpl* service conditions *pl*
Betriebsbelastung *f* service loading
Betriebsdauer *f* time of operation
Betriebslast *f* service load
Betriebslebensdauer *f* service life
Betriebsschaden *m* service failure
Betriebsschadensanalyse *f* service failure analysis
Betriebsspannungsniveau *n* working stress level

Betriebstemperatur *f* operating temperature
minimale Betriebstemperatur *f* minimum service temperature
Betriebsversagen *n* {von Konstruktionen} service failure {of structures}
Betriebszugspannung *f* service tensile stress
Beule *f* balge
beurteilen assess/to
Beurteilung *f* assessment
bruchmechanische Beurteilung *f* fracture-mechanical assessment
bevorzugte Spaltebene *f* preferred cleavage plane
Bewegen *n* <Syn.: **Verfahren** *n*> {einer Probe} movement {of the specimen}
Bewegung *f* movement
bewerten valuate/to
Bewertung *f* valuation
zerstörungsfreie Bewertung *f* nondestructive evaluation <abb.: NDE>
Bezugs- <Syn.: **Vergleichs-, Referenz-**> reference
Bezugsebene *f* reference plane
Bezugstemperatur *f* <Syn.: **Referenztemperatur** *f*> reference temperature
Bi → **Bismut**
Biegebeanspruchung *f* <Syn.: **Biegelast** *f*> bending; bending load
Bruchmodul *m* **bei Biegebeanspruchung** rupture modulus in bending
Eigenschaften *fpl* **bei Biegebeanspruchung** bending properties
Messung *f* **unter Biegebeanspruchung** bending measurement
Biegebruch *m* fracture by bending
Biegedorn *m* mandrel
Biegeeigenschaften *fpl* <Syn.: **Eigenschaften** *fpl* **bei Biegebeanspruchung**> bending properties

Biegefestigkeit *f* bending strength, flexural strength, transverse strength
Biegefestigkeit[sbeiwert] *f* [*m*] coefficient of bending strength
Biegelänge *f* {Biegeprüfung} bending length {bending test}
Biegelast *f* <Syn.: **Biegebeanspruchung** *f*> bending load
Biegemodul *m* bending modulus, modulus of bending, flexural modulus, modulus in flexure
Biegemoment *n* bending moment
biegen {eine Probe} flex/to, bend/to {the specimen}
Biegeprobe *f* bend specimen
gekerbte Biegeprobe *f* notched bend test specimen
Biegeprüfgerät *n* flexing tester
Biegeprüfung *f* bending test
Biegespannung *f* bending stress
Biegespannungsintensitätsfaktor *m* bending stress-intensity factor
Biegespannungsverteilung *f* bending stress distribution
Biegeversuch *m* bending test
Elastizitätsmodul *m* **aus dem Biegeversuch** elastic modulus in bend
Spannvorrichtung *f* **für den Biegeversuch** bend test fixture
biegsam <Syn.: **flexibel**> flexible
biegsamer Kunststoff *m* flexible plastic
Biegsamkeit *f* <Syn.: **Flexibilität** *f*> flexibility
Biegung *f* <Syn.: **Biegebeanspruchung** *f*> bending
Anzahl *f* (**Zahl** *f*) **der Biegungen** number of flexings
einseitige Biegung *f* unidirectional bending
reine Biegung *f* pure bending
Bild *n* <Syn.: **Muster** *n*> pattern

Bildung

Bildung f <Syn.: Herausbildung f, Formierung f, Entstehung f, Ausbildung f> formation
Bismut n, Bi bismuth, Bi Wismut n
Blase f {Fehler} blister {defect}
Blausprödigkeit f {Stahl} blue brittleness {steel}
Blech n <Syn.: Scheibe f> plate
gekerbtes Blech n <Syn.: gekerbte Platte f> notched plate
Blechdicke f <Syn.: Plattendicke f; Scheibendicke f> plate thickness
Blei n, Pb lead, Pb
bleibend <Syn.: dauerhaft> permanent
bleibende Dehnung f permanent strain
bleibende (dauerhafte) Schädigung f permanent damage
bleibende Verformung f permanent deformation
Bleilegierung f lead alloy
Blindversuch m blank experiment
blockierte Versetzung f locked dislocation
Bogen m <geometrisch> arc
Bohrung f {z.B. in Proben} <Syn.: Loch n> hole {e.g. in specimens}
elliptische Bohrung f elliptical hole
kreisrunde Bohrung f circular hole
Bor n, B boron, B
Br → Brom
Brandausbreitung f fire propagation test
Prüfung f der Brandausbreitung f fire propagation test
Brandriß m {Metalle} fire-crack {metals}
Brandverhalten n burning characteristics pl
Brandverhalten n der Oberfläche surface burning characteristics pl
brechen break/to

Brechen n <Syn.: Bruch m> breaking
Brechung f refraction
Breite f width
Breitenwachstum n <Syn.: Erweiterung f, Aufweitung f> {Risse} extension {cracks}
brennbar combustible
unbrennbar non-combustible
Brennbarkeit f combustability
Brennbarkeitsprüfung f burning test, fire test
Brenndauer f burning time {the period in seconds that the specimen burns after removal of the ignition source}
brennen burn/to
Brennen n <Syn.: Verbrennen n> burning
Brennlänge f {bei der Flammenausbreitung} spread of flame
Brinellhärte f Brinell hardness number <abb.: HB>
Brinellhärteprüfung f {Eindringprüfung} Brinell hardness test {indentation test}
Brom n, Br bromine, Br
Bronze f bronze
Bruch m fracture, rupture
Bruch m durch Stauchung crushing failure
Bruch m durch Zugbelastung <Syn.: Zugbruch> tensile fracture
Bruch m an Zwillingsbildungen twinning fracture
duktiler Bruch m ductile fracture
dynamischer Bruch m dynamic fracture
ebener Bruch m flat fracture, square fracture
elastisch-plastischer Bruch m elastic-plastic fracture
elastischer Bruch m elastic fracture
energiearmer Bruch m low energy fracture

energiereicher Bruch *m* high-energy fracture
fas[e]riger Bruch *m* <Syn.: Faserbruch *m*> fibrous fracture
instabiler Bruch *m* unstable fracture
intergranularer Bruch *m* <Syn.: Korngrenzbruch *m*> intergranular fracture
interkristalliner Bruch *m* intercrystalline fracture
isolierter Bruch *m* non-cumulative rupture
isotroper Bruch *m* isotropic fracture
katastrophenartiger Bruch *m* catastrophic failure
körniger Bruch *m* granular fracture
kristalliner Bruch *m* <Syn.: Trennbruch *m*> crystalline fracture
mikroduktiler Bruch *m* microductile fracture
nichtkumulativer Bruch *m* non-cumulative fracture
schräg verlaufender Bruch *m* slant fracture
schräger Bruch *m* oblique fracture
seidenartiger Bruch *m* silky fracture
spontan einsetzender Bruch *m* spontaneous fracture
transkristalliner Bruch *m* transcrystalline fracture, transgranular fracture
verzögerter Bruch *m* delayed fracture
Zähbruch *m* <Syn.: duktiler Bruch *m*> ductile fracture
zäher Bruch *m* ductile fracture
zeitabhängiger Bruch *m* time-dependent fracture
Zerrüttungsbruch *m* cumulative fracture
zufälliger Bruch *m* random fracture

Bruchablauf *m* <Syn.: Bruchprozeß *m*, Bruchvorgang *m*> fracture process
Bruchanalyse *f* fracture analysis
elastisch-plastische Bruchanalyse *f* elastic-plastic analysis of fracture
Bruchanalysendiagramm *n* fracture analysis diagram FAD
Bruchanteil *m* percentage of fracture
Brucharbeit *f* fracture work
Bruchart *f* <Syn.: Bruchform *f*> type of fracture, fracture type
Bruchausbildung *f* formation of fracture
Bruchausbreitung *f* propagation of fracture
instabile Bruchausbreitung *f* unstabel propagation of fracture
Bruchausbreitungskriterium *n* criterion for fracture propagation
Bruchausbreitungsrichtung *f* direction of fracture propagation
makroskopische Bruchausbreitungsrichtung *f* macroscopic direction of fracture propagation
Bruchausgangspunkt *m* fracture nucleus
Bruchaussehen *n* fracture appearance
Bruchbahn *f* fracture path
Bruchbedingung *f* condition of breaking
Bruchbeurteilung *f* assessment of fracture
Bruchbild *n* fracture appearance
makroskopisches Bruchbild *n* macroscopic fracture appearance
Bruchdehnung *f* fracture strain
lokale Bruchdehnung *f* local fracture strain
wahre Bruchdehung *f* true fracture strain
Bruchdurchgang *m* <Syn.: Bruchübergang *m*> fracture transition

Bruchebene

Bruchebene *f* der Probe specimen fracture plane
Brucheigenschaften *fpl* fracture properties *pl*
Brucheigenschaften *fpl* in Längsrichtung longitudinal fracture properties *pl*
Brucheigenschaften *fpl* in Querrichtung transverse fracture properties *pl*
Brucheinleitung *f* initiation of fracture
interkristalline Brucheinleitung *f* intercrystalline fracture initiation
Brucheinschnürung *f* necking in tension
Brucheintritt *m* start of fracture
Bruchenergie *f* energy of fracture
kritische spezifische Bruchenergie *f* critical specific fracture energy
spezifische Bruchenergie *f* specific fracture energy, specific energy of fracture
Bruchentstehung *f* formation of fracture
Brucherscheinung *f* fracture appearance
makroskopische Brucherscheinung *f* macroscopic fracture appearance
Brucherscheinungsform *f* type of fracture appearance
Brucherscheinungsübergangstemperatur *f* <Abk.: FATT> fracture appearance transition temperature <abb.: FATT>
Bruchfestigkeit *f* fracture strength
theoretische Bruchfestigkeit *f* theoretical fracture strength
Bruchfläche *f* <Syn.: gebrochene Oberfläche *f*> fractured surface
glatte Bruchfläche *f* smooth fracture surface
schräge Bruchfläche *f* slant fracture surface

Bruchflächen-Analyse *f* <Syn.: Analyse *f* von Bruchflächen> fracture surface analysis
Bruchflächenbewertung *f* valuation of fracture surface
makroskopische Bruchflächenbewertung *f* macroscopic evaluation of fracture surface
Bruchflächenrauhigkeit *f* fracture surface roughness
Bruchform *f* <Syn.: Bruchart *f*> type of fracture
mikroskopische Bruchform *f* microscopic type of fracture
Bruchforschung *f* fracture research
Bruchgeschwindigkeit *f* fracture velocity
Bruchgeschwindigkeitsmessung *f* measurement of fracture velocity
Bruchhöchstgeschwindigkeit *f* maximum fracture speed
Brüchigkeit *f* brittleness
Brüchigkeit *f* bei tiefen Temperaturen <Syn.: Kältebrüchigkeit> low-temperature brittleness
Bruchkennwert *m* parameter of fracture
Bruchkonzept *n* concept of fracture
Bruchkriterium *n* criterion for fracture
elastisch-plastisches Bruchkriterium *n* elastic-plastic fracture criterion
linear-elastisches Bruchkriterium *n* linear elastic fracture criterion
makroskopisches Bruchkriterium *n* macroscopic fracture criterion
mikroskopisches Bruchkriterium *n* microscopic fracture criterion
Bruchlastspielzahl *f* load cycles at fracture
Bruchmechanik *f* mechanics of fracture, fracture mechanism
elastische Bruchmechanik *f* elastic fracture mechanics

elastisch-plastische Bruchmechanik f <Abk.: EPBM> elastic-plastic fracture mechanics, EPFM
linear-elastische Bruchmechanik f <Abk.: LEBM> linear-elastic fracture mechanics, LEFM
nichtlinear-elastische Bruchmechanik f nonlinear elastic fracture mechanics
nicht-lineare Bruchmechanik f nonlinear fracture mechanics
probabilistische Bruchmechanik f probabilistic fracture mechanics
subkritische Bruchmechanik f subcritical fracture mechanics, SCFM
Bruchmechanik-Konzept n concept of fracture mechanics
Energie-Konzept n {Konzept der Bruchmechanik} energy concept {concept of fracture mechanics}
LEBM-Konzept n <Syn.: Konzept n der linear-elastischen Bruchmechanik> linear-elastic fracture mechanics concept, LEFM concept
bruchmechanisch fracture-mechanical
bruchmechanische Beurteilung f fracture-mechanical assessment
bruchmechanische Methode f method of fracture mechanics
bruchmechanischer Kennwert m parameter of fracture mechanics
bruchmechanisches Kriterium n criterion for fracture mechanics
bruchmechanisches Verhalten n fracture-mechanical behavio[u]r
Bruchmechanismus m mechanism of fracture
Bruchmerkmal n characteristic of fracture
makroskopisches Bruchmerkmal n macroscopic characteristic of fracture
mikroskopisches Bruchmerkmal n microscopic characteristic of fracture
Bruchmodenübergang m <Syn.: Bruchmoduswechsel m> fracture mode transition
Bruchmodul m modulus of rupture, rupture modulus
Bruchmodul m **bei Biegebeanspruchung** rupture modulus in bending
Bruchmodul m **bei Torsionsbeanspruchung** modulus of rupture in torsion
Bruchmodus m <Syn.: Bruchtyp m> fracture mode
Bruchmoduswechsel m <Syn.: Bruchmodenübergang m> fracture mode transition
Bruchphänomen n fracture phenomenon
Bruchprozeß m <Syn.: Bruchvorgang m, Bruchablauf m> fracture process
Bruchprozeßzone f fracture process zone
Bruchprüfung f fracture testing
dynamische Bruchprüfung f dynamic fracture testing
Bruchrichtung f direction of fracture
bruchsicher fracture-safe
Bruchsicherheitskriterium n criterion for fracture safety
Bruchspannung f rupture stress
gemessene Bruchspannung f measured fracture stress
kritische Bruchspannung f critical stress of fracture
mikroskopische Bruchspannung f microscopic fracture stress
theoretische Bruchspannung f calculated fracture stress
vorhergesagte Bruchspannung f predicted fracture stress
Bruchstadium n phase of fracture
Bruchtyp m <Syn.: Bruchmodus m> fracture mode

Bruchübergang

Bruchübergang *m* < Syn.: Bruchdurchgang *m* > fracture transition
Bruchuntersuchung *f* fracture research
Bruchuntersuchungsergebnisse *npl* fracture research results *pl*
Bruchursache *f* cause of fracture
Bruchverhalten *n* fracture behavio[u]r, behavio[u]r at fracture
 elasto-plastisches Bruchverhalten *n* elasto-plastic fracture behavio[u]r
 linear-elastisches Bruchverhalten *n* linear-elastic fracture behavio[u]r
 mikroskopisches Bruchverhalten *n* microscopic fracture behavio[u]r
 Sprödbruchverhalten *n* < Syn.: sprödes Bruchverhalten *n* > brittle fracture behavio[u]r
 zähes Bruchverhalten *n* ductile fracture behavio[u]r
 zeitabhängiges Bruchverhalten *n* time-dependent fracture behavio[u]r
Bruchverlauf *m* path of rupture
Bruchvorgang *m* < Syn.: Bruchablauf *m*, Bruchprozeß *m* > fracture process
Bruchwahrscheinlichkeit *f* fracture probability, probability of fracture
Bruchwiderstand *m* fracture resistance, resistance of fracture
 absoluter Bruchwiderstand *m* absolute resistance to fracture
Bruchwinkel *m* angle of failure
Bruchzähigkeit *f* fracture toughness
 dynamische Bruchzähigkeit *f* dynamic fracture toughness
 fiktive Bruchzähigkeit *f* fictitious fracture toughness
 geschwindigkeitsabhängige Bruchzähigkeit *f* rate-dependent fracture toughness
 minimale Bruchzähigkeit *f* minimum fracture toughness
 quasistatische Bruchzähigkeit *f* quasi-static fracture toughness
 statische Bruchzähigkeit *f* static fracture toughness
Bruchzähigkeitseigenschaften *fpl* fracture toughness properties *pl*
Bruchzähigkeitsprobe *f* fracture toughness specimen
Bruchzähigkeitsprüfung *f* fracture toughness testing
Bruchzähigkeits-Prüfverfahren *n* fracture toughness testing method
Bruchzähigkeitswert *m* fracture toughness value
 dynamischer Bruchzähigkeitswert *m* dynamic fracture toughness value
Bruchzone *f* fracture area

C

C-Probe *f* < Syn.: Kompaktprobe *f* > C specimen *f*
C-Probe *f* compact specimen, CS Kompakt-Probe *f*
Ca → Calcium
Cadmium *n*, Cd cadmium, Cd Kadmium n,
Calcium *n*, Ca calcium, Ca Kalzium n,
Cäsium *n*, Cs cesium, Cs
CCT-Probe *f* < Syn.: Mittelrißprobe *f* > {Zugprobe} center-cracked tension specimen
Cd → Cadmium
Charakterisierung *f* characterization
Charakteristik *f* characteristic
charakteristisch characteristic
Charpy-Pendelschlagversuch *m* < Syn.: Pendelschlagversuch *m* nach Charpy > Charpy (impact) test
Charpy-Probe *f* {mit Kerb} Charpy specimen {with notch}

Charpy-Prüfmaschine f Charpy machine
Charpy-Schlagfestigkeit f <Syn.: Schlagfestigkeit f nach Charpy> Charpy impact resistance
Charpy-Versuch m {Kerbempfindlichkeit} Charpy test {notch sensitivity}
instrumentierter Charpy-Versuch m instrumented Charpy test
chemikalienbeständig chemical resistant
chemikalienbeständiger Stahl m chemical resistant steel
chemisch chemical
chemische Analyse chemical analysis
Elektronenspektroskopie f **für die chemische Analyse** electron spectroscopy for chemical analysis ESCA
Chevron-Kerbe f {Kerbe in Proben} Chevron notch
Probe f **mit Chevron-Kerbe** Chevron notch specimen
Chevron-Rißstarterkerbe f Chevron crack starter notch
Chlor m, **Cl** chlorine, Cl
Chrom n, **Cr** chromium, Cr
Chrom-Nickel-Molybdän-Stahl m chromium-nickel-molybdenum steel
Cl → Chlor
CLWL-Probe f crack-line-wedge-loaded <abb.: CLWL> specimen
Co → Cobalt
Cobalt n, **Co** cobalt, Co Kobalt n,
Cobalt-Chrom-Legierung f cobalt-chromium alloy
Cobalt-Chrom-Molybdän-Legierung f cobalt-chromium-molybdenum alloy
Cobalt-Legierung f cobalt alloy
COD. Rißöffnungsverschiebung f COD. crack opening displacement
COD-Auslegungskurve f COD design curve
COD-Konstruktionskurve f COD design curve
COD-Konzept n {Fließbruchmechanik} COD concept {linear-elastic fracture mechanics}
COD-Kriterium n <Syn.: Rißöffnungsverschiebungskriterium n> crack opening displacement <abb.: COD> criterion
Compliance-Methode f {Rißlängenmeßmethode} compliance method {method of crack length measurement}
Computer m <Syn.: Rechner m> computer
Computer-Modellierung f computer simulation
Cr → Chrom
Cs → Cäsium
CT-Probe f <Syn.: Kompakt-Zug-Probe f> <abb.: CT> specimen compact tension
CTOD Rißspitzenöffnungsverschiebung f CTOD crack tip opening displacement
Cu copper, Cu Kupfer n

D

Daten pl <Syn.: Angaben fpl> data
Dauer- <Syn.: Langzeit-> permanent
Dauerbiegebeanspruchung f bending fatigue
Dauerbiegeprüfung f bending fatigue test
Dauerbiegeversuch m fatigue bending test
Dauerbruch m <Syn.: Ermüdungsbruch m, Schwing[ungs]bruch m> fatigue fracture
Dauerbruchanriß m <Syn.: Ermüdungsanriß m, Dauerschwinganriß m> fatigue pre-crack

Dauerbruchfläche

Dauerbruchfläche f <Syn.: **Schwingungsbruchfläche** f> fatigue fracture surface
Dauerfestigkeit f <Syn.: **Dauerschwingfestigkeit** f, **Ermüdungsfestigkeit** f> fatigue strength
thermische Dauerfestigkeit f thermal fatigue strength
Dauerfestigkeitskurve f <Syn.: **Wöhler-Kurve** f> S-N curve, S-N diagram {S = stress, N = number of cycles to failure}, Wöhler curve
dauerhaft <Syn.: **bleibend**> permanent
dauerhafte <Syn.: **bleibende**> **Schädigung** f permanent damage
Dauerhaftigkeit f endurance
Dauerriß m fatigue crack
Dauerschwinganriß m <Syn.: **Dauerbruchanriß** m, **Ermüdungsanriß** m> fatigue pre-crack
Dauerschwingfestigkeit f <Syn.: **Ermüdungsfestigkeit** f, **Dauerfestigkeit** f> fatigue strength
Dauerschwingriß m <Syn.: **Ermüdungsriß** m, **Schwingungsriß**> fatigue crack
Dauerschwingungsbruch m <Syn.: **Versagen** n **durch Ermüdung**> fatigue failure
Dauerversuch m endurance test
Dauerwärmebeständigkeit f thermal endurance
Dauerwärmeeinwirkung f <Syn.: **Langzeitwärmeeinwirkung** f> permanent effect of heat {on plastics}
Daumennagel-Riß m {Biegeprobe} thumbnail crack {bend specimen}
DCB-Probe f <Syn.: **Doppelbalken-[biege]probe** f> double-cantilever beam <abb.: DCB> specimen
DCT-Probe f <Syn.:**scheibenförmige Kompaktzugprobe** f >diskshaped compact [tensile] specimen, DCT specimen

Deformation f <Syn.: **Formänderung** f, **Verformung** f> deformation
Deformation f **infolge Druckbeanspruchung** compressive deformation
inkompressible Deformation f incompressible deformation
plastische Deformation f plastic deformation
Deformationsband n deformation band
Deformationsbehinderung f <Syn.: **Verformungsbehinderung** f> deformation constraint
Deformationsgeschwindigkeit f <Syn.: **Verformungsgeschwindigkeit** f> deformation rate
Deformationskriterium n criterion for deformation
Deformationstheorie f theory of deformation
deformieren <Syn.: **verformen**> deform/to
dehnbar extensible
Dehnbarkeit f extensibility; stretchability
Dehnbarkeit f **nach Wärmealterung** extensibility after heat ag[e]ing
dehnen strain/to
Dehnen n <Syn.: **Dehnung** f> straining
Dehnung f <Syn.: **Verzerrung** f> strain
axiale Dehnung f axial strain
bleibende Dehnung f permanent strain
ebene Dehnung f plane strain
ebene Dehnung f **an der Rißspitze** crack-tip plane strain
elastische Dehnung f elastic strain
inhomogene Dehnung f inhomogeneous strain
kritische Dehnung f critical strain

plastische Dehnung f plastic strain
Dehnung f in axialer Richtung axial strain
Dehnungsanalyse f analysis of strain
Dehnungsbehinderung f strain constraint
plastische Dehnungsbehinderung f plastic strain constraint
Dehnungsenergie f strain energy
elastische Dehnungsenergie f elastic strain energy
Dehnungsenergiedichte f strain-energy density
Dehnungsenergiefunktion f strain-energy function
Dehnungsfeld n strain field f
Dehn[ungs]geschwindigkeit f rate of extension
Dehnungsgeschwindigkeit f <Syn.: Verzerrungsgeschwindigkeit f> strain rate
elastische Dehnungsgeschwindigkeit f <Syn.: Geschwindigkeit f der elastischen Dehnung> rate of elastic straining
plastische Dehnungsgeschwindigkeit f <Syn.: Geschwindigkeit f der plastischen Dehnung> rate of plastic straining
Dehnungsgeschwindigkeitsenergie f strain rate energy
dehnungsinduziert strain-induced
dehnungsinduzierte Anisotropie f strain-induced anisotropy
Dehnungsinkrement n strain increment
Dehnungsintensitätsfaktor m strain intensity factor
Dehnungskomponente f strain component
Dehnungskonzentration f <Syn.: Verzerrungskonzentration f> strain concentration
Dehnungskonzentrationsfaktor m strain concentration factor

plastischer Dehnungskonzentrationsfaktor m plastic strain concentration factor
Dehnungskriterium n criterion for strain
Dehnungsmeßgerät n extensometer
Dehnungsmeßstreifen m strain ga[u]ge
Dehnungsmeßstreifen m für die Rißgeschwindigkeitsmessung f crack-velocity ga[u]ge
Dehnungsmessung f strain measurement
Dehnungstensor m <Syn.: Verzerrungstensor m> strain tensor
Dehnungsverfestigung f <Syn.: Kaltverfestigung f> strain hardening
Dehnungsverteilung f strain distribution
lineare Dehnungsverteilung f linear strain distribution
Dehnungszustand m <Syn.: Verzerrungszustand m> state of strain
ebener Dehnungszustand m <Abk.: EDZ> <Syn.: ebener Verzerrungszustand m, EVZ> state of plane strain
Dehnzone f <Syn.: Stretch-Zone f> {vor der Rißfront} stretch zone
Dekohäsion f <Syn.: Trennung f> decohesion
Delamination f <Syn.: Ablösung f> delamination
Delaminationsbruch m delamination fracture
Diagramm n <Syn.: Schaubild n> diagram
Dichte f density
Dicke f thickness
Dickeneinfluß m {Proben} thickness effect {specimens}
dickwandig thick-walled
dickwandiger Zylinder m thick-walled cylinder

Dienst

Dienst *m* <Syn.: **Wartung** *f*> service
Differentialkalorimetrie *f* differential calorimetry
Differentialthermoanalyse *f* <Abk.: DTA> differential thermal analysis <abb.: DTA>
diffundieren diffuse/to
Diffusion *f* diffusion
Diffusionsgeschwindigkeit *f* diffusion rate, diffusion velocity
Dilatometer *n* {zur Bestimmung der thermischen Ausdehnung} dilatometer {for determination of thermal expansion}
Dilatometrie *f* {Bestimmung der thermischen Ausdehnung} dilatometry {determination of thermal expansion}
Dimension *f* dimension
dimensionieren dimension/to
Dimensionierung *f* dimensioning
dimensionslos dimensionless
  dimensionslose plastische Zone *f* dimensionless plastic zone
  dimensionslose Spannung *f* dimensionless stress
  dimensionsloser Spannungsintensitätsfaktor *m* dimensionless stress intensity factor
direkt direct
direkte Messung *f* direct measurement
diskontinuierlich <Syn.: **unterbrochen**> discontinuous
Diskontinuität *f* <Syn.: **Unstetigkeit** *f*> discontinuity
dog-bone-Modell *n* <Syn.: **Hundeknochen-Modell**> {der plastischen Zone} dog-bone model {of the plastic zone}
Doppelbalken[biege]probe *f* <Syn.: DCB-Probe *f*> double-cantilever beam <abb.: DCB> specimen

konische (keilförmige) Doppelbalkenbiegeprobe *f* <Syn.: TDCB-Probe *f*> tapered double-cantilever beam <abb.: TDCB> specimen
Doppelkerbe *f* double-edge notches *pl*
Doppelkerbprobe *f* double-edge-notched specimen
Doppeltorsions- <Abk.: DT-> double torsion <abb.: DT>
Doppeltorsions-Probe *f* <Syn.: DT-Probe *f*> double torsion <abb.: DT> specimen
Drehmoment *n* <Syn.: **Verdrehmoment** *n*> torsional moment, torque
Drehscheibe *f* {für Drehversuche} torque pulley {for torsion tests}
dreiachsig triaxial
  dreiachsige Fließspannung *f* triaxial yield stress
  dreiachsige Zugspannung *f* triaxial tensile stress
  dreiachsiger Spannungszustand *m* triaxial stress state, triaxial state of stress
Dreiachsigkeit *f* {Spannung} triaxiality {stress}
dreidimensional <Syn.: **räumlich**> three-dimensional
  dreidimensionale elastische Spannungsanalyse *f* three-dimensional elastic stress analysis
  dreidimensionale Elastizität *f* three-dimensional elasticity
  dreidimensionale Spannungsanalyse *f* three-dimensional stress analysis
  dreidimensionale Spannungsverteilung *f* three-dimensional stress distribution
  dreidimensionale Verformung *f* three-dimensional deformation
  dreidimensionaler Körper *m* three-dimensional body
  dreidimensionaler Riß *m* three-dimensional crack

dreidimensionaler Spannungszustand *m* three-dimensional state of stress
dreidimensionales Grenzwertproblem *n* three-dimensional boundary-value problem
dreidimensionales Kontinuum *n* three-dimensional continuum
dreidimensionales Rißproblem *n* <Syn.: räumliches Rißproblem *n*> three-dimensional crack problem
dreidimensionales Rißsystem *n* three-dimensional crack system
Dreipunkt-Belastung *f* three-point loading
Dreipunkt-Biegeprobe *f* <Syn.: 3PB-Probe *f*> three-point bend specimen
Dreipunkt-Biegeprüfung *f* three-point bending test
Dreipunkt-Biegetechnik *f* three-point bending technique
Dreipunkt-Biegeversuch *m* three-point bend[ing] test
Dreipunkt-Biegevorrichtung *f* three-point bending test apparatus
Dreipunkt-Biegung *f* three-point bending
Druck *m* pressure
hydrostatischer Druck *m* hydrostatic pressure
spezifische Wärme *f* bei konstantem Druck *m* specific heat at constant pressure
Druck- {Kraft, Belastung} compressive {force, loading}
druckabhängig pressure-dependent
Druckabhängigkeit *f* pressure dependence
Druckbeanspruchung *f* compression
ebene (zweiachsige) Druckbeanspruchung *f* plain strain compression
einachsige Druckbeanspruchung *f* uniaxial compression
hydrostatische Druckbeanspruchung *f* hydrostatic compression
positive Druckbeanspruchung *f* positive compression
zweiachsige Druckbeanspruchung *f* biaxial compression
Druckbehälter *m* pressure vessel
Druckbelastung *f* compressive (compression) loading
äußere Druckbelastung *f* external compressive loading
einachsige Druckbelastung *f* uniaxial compression loading
innere Druckbelastung *f* internal compressive loading
Druckeigenspannung *f* compressive residual stress
Druckeigenspannungsfeld *n* compressive residual stress field
Druckeigenspannungsverlauf *m* compressive residual stress curve
Druckfestigkeit *f* compressive strength
maximale Druckfestigkeit *f* maximum compressive strength
Druckfestigkeitsprüfung *f* compression test
ebene (zweidimensionale) Druckfestigkeitsprüfung *f* plain strain compression test
Drucklast *f* compressive load
Druckprüfmaschine *f* compression testing machine
Druckprüfung *f* compressive testing
Druckspannung *f* compressive stress
Druckverformung *f* <Syn.: Deformation *f* infolge Druckbeanspruchung> compressive deformation
Druckversuch *m* compression test
Probe *f* für den Druckversuch *m* compression specimen
DT- → Doppeltorsions-
DT-Probe *f* <Syn.: Doppeltorsionsprobe *f*> double torsion <abb.: DT> specimen

Dugdale 178

DT-Prüfung f <Syn.: Reißprüfung f> dynamic tear <abb.: DT> test
DTA → Differentialthermoanalyse f
DTT-Probe f <Syn.: dynamische Reißprobe f> dynamic tear test <abb.: DTT> specimen
Dugdale-Barenblatt-Modell n {elastisches Rißproblem} Dugdale-Barenblatt model {elastic crack problem}
Dugdale-Modell n {Rißbildung} Dugdale model {crack + formation}
Dugdale-Riß m Dugdale crack
Dugdale-Rißmodell n Dugdale crack model
duktil <Syn.: zäh> ductile
duktile Matrix f ductile matrix
duktile Rißausbreitung f ductile crack propagation
duktiler Bruch m <Syn.: zäher Bruch m, Zähbruch m> ductile fracture
duktiler Gewaltbruch m ductile overload fracture
duktiler Schwingbruch m ductile fatigue fracture
duktiler Zugbruch m ductile tensile fracture
duktiler Zustand m ductile state
duktiles Eisen n ductile iron
perlitisches duktiles Eisen n pearlitic ductile iron
duktiles (zähes) Verhalten n {von Werkstoffen} ductile behavio[u]r {of materials}
anisotroper duktiler Werkstoff m anisotropic ductile material
geschwindigkeitsempfindlicher duktiler Werkstoff m rate-sensitive ductile material
isotroper duktiler Werkstoff m isotropic ductile material
Duktil-Spröd[e]-Übergang m ductile-to-brittle-transition

Duktilität <Syn.: Dehnbarkeit f, Verformbarkeit f> ductility
Duktilitätsmessung f measurement of ductility
dünn <Syn.: schmal> thin
dünne Probe f thin specimen
Duplex-Probe f duplex specimen {bimaterial interface}
Durchbiegung f deflection
Durchbrechen n breaking through, complete fracture
Durchgang m <Syn.:Übergang m> transition
durchgehend <Syn.: vollständig, völlig> {Bruch} complete
durchgehender Oberfächenriß m through-the-thickness surface crack
durchgehender Randriß m through-the-thickness edge crack, transitional edge crack
durchgehender Riß m <Syn.: Durchriß m> through-the-thickness crack
gerade (geradlinig) durchgehender Riß m straight-through crack
teilweise durchgehender Riß m <Syn.: Teildurchriß m> part-through crack
Durchlässigkeit f <Syn.: Transparenz f> transparency
Durchmesser m diameter
Durchriß m <Syn.: durchgehender Riß m> transitional crack
Durchschnitt m <Syn.: Mittel n, Mittelwert m> {Mathematik} average {mathematics}
durchschnittlich average
Durchschnitts- average...
Durchstoßbelastung f <Syn.: Durchstoßlast f> penetrative load
Durchstoßlast f <Syn.: Durchstoßbelastung f> penetrative load
Durchstrahlungsprüfung f {Werkstoffe} radiographic testing {of materials}

DWT-Versuch m <Syn.: **Fallgewichtsversuch** m> drop-weight test <abb.: DWT>
Probe f für den Fallgewichtsversuch (DWT-Versuch) drop-weight test <abb.: DWT> specimen
Prüfeinrichtung f für den Fallgewichtsversuch (DWT-Versuch) drop-weight test apparatus
Standardprobe f für den Fallgewichtsversuch (DWT-Versuch) standard drop-weight test <abb.: DWT> specimen
DWTT-Versuch m <Syn.: **Fallgewichtsscherversuch** m> drop-weight tear test <abb.: DWTT>
Probe f für den Fallgewichtsscherversuch (DWTT-Versuch) drop-weight tear test <abb.: DWTT> specimen
Dy → Dysprosium
dynamisch dynamic
dynamische Beanspruchung f dynamic loading
dynamische Belastung f dynamic loading
dynamische Bruchprüfung f dynamic fracture testing
dynamische Bruchzähigkeit f dynamic fracture toughness
dynamische Elastizitätstheorie f dynamic theory of elasticity
dynamische Energiefreisetzung f dynamic energy release
dynamische Energiefreisetzungsrate f dynamic energy release rate
dynamische Konstante f dynamic constant
dynamische Prüfmethode f <Syn.: **Prüfmethode** f mit dynamischer Beanspruchung> dynamic test method
dynamische Reißprobe f <Syn.: **DT-Probe** f> dynamic tear <abb.: test> specimen
dynamische Reißprobe f <Syn.: **DT-Prüfung** f> dynamic tear <abb.: DT> test
dynamische Reißprüfung f <Syn.: **DT-Prüfung** f> dynamic tear <abb.: DT> test
dynamische Rißausbreitung f dynamic crack propagation
dynamische Rißeinleitung f dynamic crack initiation
dynamische Rißwiderstandskurve f dynamic crack resistance curve
dynamische Singularität f dynamic singularity
dynamische Spannungsanalyse f dynamic stress analysis
dynamische Spannungsintensität f dynamic stress intensity
dynamische Spannungsoptik f dynamic photoelasticity
dynamische Spannungsverteilung f dynamic stress distribution
dynamischer Bruch m dynamic fracture
dynamischer Bruchzähigkeitswert m dynamic fracture toughness value
dynamischer Spannungsintensitätsfaktor m dynamic stress-intensity factor
dynamisches Rißarrest-Konzept n concept of dynamic crack arrest
dynamisches Rißproblem n dynamic crack problem
dynamisches Rißverhalten n dynamic crack behavio[u]r
dynamisches Rißwachstum n dynamic crack growth
Theorie f **der dynamischen Rißausbreitung** dynamic crack-propagation theory
Dynstat-Prüfmaschine f Dynstat equipment
Dysprosium, Dy dysprosium, Dy

E

E-Modul *m* >Syn.: **Elastizitätsmodul** *m*> modulus of elasticity
E.S. → ebene Spannung
eben <Syn.: **zweidimensional**> two-dimensional
eben <Syn.: **Ebene** *f*> plane
ebene (zweiachsige) Druckbeanspruchung *f* plain strain compression
ebene (zweidimensionale) Druckfestigkeitsprüfung *f* plain strain compression test
ebene Dehnung *f* (**Verzerrung** *f*) plane strain
ebene Dehnung *f* **an der Rißspitze** crack-tip plane strain
ebene dynamische Spannungsoptik *f* two-dimensional dynamic photoelasticity
ebene Spannung *f* <Abk.: E.S.> plane stress
ebene statische Spannungsoptik *f* plane static photoelasticity
ebene Verformung *f* two-dimensional deformation zweidimensionale Verformung *f*
ebene Verzerrung *f* (**Dehnung** *f*) plane strain
ebener Bruch *m* flat fracture, square fracture
ebener Dehnungszustand *m* <Abk.: EDZ> state of plane strain
ebener Schub *m* plane shear
ebener Spannungszustand *m* <Abk.: ESZ> plane stress state, state of plane stress
ebener Verformungszustand *m* plane deformation state, state of plane deformation
ebener Verzerrungszustand *m* <Abk.: EVZ> state of plane strain
ebenes elastisches Rißproblem *n* plane elastic crack problem
ebenes Rißproblem *n* plane crack problem, plane problem of crack
Ebene *f* <Syn.: **eben**>plane
Eckriß *m* corner crack
EDZ → ebener Dehnungszustand
Effekt *m* <Syn.: **Einfluß** *m*> effect
effektiv <Syn.: **wirksam**> effective
effektive Oberflächenenergie *f* effective surface energy
effektive plastische Zone *f* effective plastic zone
effektive Rißerweiterung *f* effective crack extension
effektive Rißerweiterungskraft *f* effective crack extension force
effektive Rißgröße *f* effective crack size
effektive Rißlänge *f* effective crack length
effektive Rißtiefe *f* effective depth of crack
effektive Spannung *f* effective stress
effektive Spannungsintensität *f* effective crack-intensity
effektive zyklische Spannungsintensität *f* effective cyclic stress-intensity
effektiver Riß *m* effective crack
effektiver Spannungsintensitätsfaktor *m* effective stress-intensity factor
Eichen *n* <Syn.: **Eichung** *f*> calibration
eichen calibrate/to
Eichkurve *f* calibration curve
Eichung *f* <Syn.: **Eichen** *n*> calibration
Eigen-Bruchzähigkeit *f* inherent fracture toughness
Eigenschaften *fpl* properties
Biegeeigenschaften *fpl* <Syn.: **Eigenschaften** *fpl* **bei Biegebeanspruchung**> bending properties *pl*

Eigenschaften *fpl* bei hohen Prüfgeschwindigkeiten high-speed properties *pl*
Eigenschaften *fpl* bei Scherbeanspruchung shear properties *pl*
Kurzzeitprüfung *f* der mechanischen Eigenschaften *fpl* short time mechanical testing
mechanische Eigenschaften *fpl* mechanical properties *pl*
physikalische Eigenschaften *fpl* physical properties *pl*
thermische Eigenschaften *fpl* thermal properties *pl*
thermodynamische Eigenschaften *fpl* thermodynamic properties *pl*
Tieftemperatur-Prüfung *f* der mechanischen Eigenschaften *fpl* low-temperature mechanical testing
Eigenspannung *f* residual stress
Eigenspannungsfeld *n* residual stress field
Eigenspannungsmessung *f* residual stress measurement
Eigenspannungsverlauf *m* residual stress curve
Eigenspannungsverteilung *f* residual stress distribution
Eigenspannungszustand *m* residual stress state
einachsig uniaxial
 einachsige Belastung *f* uniaxial loading
 einachsige Druckbeanspruchung *f* uniaxial compression
 einachsige Druckbelastung *f* uniaxial compression loading
 einachsige Fließspannung *f* uniaxial yield stress
 einachsige Spannung *f* uniaxial stress
 einachsige Zugbeanspruchung *f* <Syn.: einachsige Zugbelastung *f*> uniaxial tensile loading
 einachsige Zugbelastung *f* <Syn.: einachsige Zugbeanspruchung *f*> uniaxial tensile loading
 einachsiger Spannungszustand *m* uniaxial stress state
 einachsiger Zug *m* uniaxial tension
 einachsiger Zugversuch *m* uniaxial tensile test
eindimensional <Syn.: linear> linear
eindringen penetrate/to
Eindringprüfung *f* {Rißnachweis} penetrant inspection {detection of cracks}
Eindringtechnik *f* penetrometer technique
Eindringverfahren *n* penetrometer method
Einfachkantenriß-Biegeprobe *f* <Syn.: SENB-Probe *f*> single-edge notched bend <abb.: SENB> specimen
Einfachkantenrißprobe *f* <Syn.: SEN-Probe *f*> {Kerb + Riß} single-edge notched <abb.: SEN> specimen {notch + crack}
einfetten {eine Probe} lubricate/to {the specimen to prevent sticking}
Einfluß *m* influence, effect
Einfrieren *n* freezing
Einfrierverfahren *n* {Spannungsoptik} stress freezing {photoelasticity}
eingebrachter Riß *m* initiated crack
eingefrorene Spannung *f* frozen stress
eingeschlossener Riß *m* embedded crack
eingespannt <Syn.: festgespannt> {Probe} clamped {specimen}
eingespannte Probe *f* clamped specimen
 freie Länge *f* {der eingespannten Probe} free length {of the clamped specimen}

Einkerben

Einkerben n <Syn.: Kerben n, Einkerbung f> {von Proben} notching {of the specimen}
einkerben <Syn.: kerben> notch/to
Einkerbung f <Syn.: Einkerben n, Kerben n> {von Proben} notching {of the specimen}
Einkristall m single crystal
Einlagerung f inclusion {in materials} Einschluß m
einlassen {z.B. ein Stahlplättchen in eine Probe} cement/to {thin steel plates to each end of a specimen}
Einleitung f <Syn.: Auslösung f, Initiierung f> initiation
einschätzen estimate/to
Einschätzung f estimation
einschließen include/to
Einschluß m <Syn.: Einlagerung f> inclusion {in materials}
  nichtmetallischer Einschluß m nonmetallic inclusion
  spröder Einschluß m brittle inclusion
  zeilenartiger Einschluß m stringer
Einschnüren n <Syn.: Verengung f, Einschnürung f> necking
Einschnürung f <Syn.: Einschnüren n, Verengung f> necking
einschränken <Syn.: begrenzen> limit/to
Einschränkung f <Syn.: Begrenzung f> limitation
einseitig {in eine Richtung} unidirectional
  einseitig angerissene Zugprobe f <Syn.: Zugprobe f mit Einzelrandriß m> single-edge cracked tensile specimen
  einseitig angerissener Augenstab m {Probenform} single-edge cracked eyebar {type of specimen}
  einseitig gekerbte Flachzugprobe f single-edge notched flat tensile specimen

  einseitig gekerbte Zugprobe f single-edge notch tensile specimen
  einseitige Biegung f unidirectional bending
Einspannbedingungen fpl {Probe} grip conditions pl {specimen}
Einspanndruck m <Syn.: Spanndruck m> {Proben} clamping pressure {for a specimen}
Einspannen n <Syn.: Festspannen n, Festklemmen n> {Probe} clamping {specimen}
einspannen <Syn.: festspannen, festklemmen> {eine Probe} clamp/to {a specimen}
Einspannvorrichtung f clamping device
Einspannweite f {von Proben} distance between the clamps
Einstufenbeanspruchung f single-stage loading
Einstufenbelastung f single-stage loading
Einstufenversuch m single-stage test
Eintauchen n immersion
  vollständiges Eintauchen n {einer Probe} total immersion {of the specimen}
Einzel- point...; single...
Einzelfehler m isolated defect, single defect
Einzelkraft f point force
Einzellast f point load
Einzelprobe f single specimen
Einzelrandriß m single edge crack
  einseitig angerissene Zugprobe f <Syn.: Zugprobe f mit Einzelrandriß m> single-edge cracked tensile specimen
Einzelriß m isolated crack
Einzelversuch m single test
Eisen n, Fe iron, Fe
  duktiles Eisen n ductile iron
  perlitisches duktiles Eisen n pearlitic ductile iron

Eisen-Aluminium-Legierung *f* iron-alumin[i]um alloy
ferritische Eisen-Aluminium-Legierung *f* ferritic iron-alumin[i]um alloy
Eisen-Chrom-Aluminium-Legierung *f* iron-chromium-alumin[i]um alloy
Eisen-Chrom-Legierung *f* iron-chromium alloy
Eisenguß *m* iron casting
Eisenlegierung *f* iron alloy
Eisenmetalle *npl* ferrous metals *pl*
elastisch elastic
elastisch-plastische Analyse *f* elastic-plastic analysis
elastisch-plastische Bruchanalyse *f* elastic-plastic analysis of fracture
elastisch-plastische Bruchmechanik *f* <Abk.: EPBM> elastic-plastic fracture mechanics <abb.: EPFM>
elastisch-plastische Inkompressibilität *f* elastic-plastic fracture instability
elastisch-plastische Spannungsverteilung *f* elastic-plastic stress distribution
elastisch-plastische Verformung *f* elastic-plastic deformation
elastisch-plastischer Bruch *m* elastic-plastic fracture
elastisch-plastischer Körper *m* elastic-plastic body
elastisch-plastischer Werkstoff *m* elastic-plastic material
elastisch-plastischer Zustand *m* elastic-plastic state
elastisch-plastisches Bruchkriterium *n* elastic-plastic fracture criterion
elastisch-plastisches Randwertproblem *n* elastic-plastic boundary value problem
elastisch-plastisches Rißproblem *n* elastic-plastic crack problem
elastisch-plastisches Spannungs-Dehnungs-Verhalten *n* elastic-plastic stress-strain behavio[u]r
elastisch-plastisches Verhalten *n* elastic-plastic behavio[u]r
elastisch-plastisches Werkstoffverhalten *n* elastic-plastic material behavio[u]r
elastisch verformt elastically-deformed
elastisch verformter Stahl *m* elastically-deformed steel
elastische Behinderung *f* elastic constraint
elastische Belastung *f* elastic loading
elastische Bruchmechanik *f* elastic fracture mechanics
elastische Dehnung *f* elastic strain
elastische Dehnungsenergie *f* elastic strain energy
elastische Dehnungsgeschwindigkeit *f* <Syn.: Geschwindigkeit *f* der elastischen Dehnung> rate of elastic straining
elastische Energie *f* elastic energy
elastische Formänderungsenergie *f* elastic energy of deformation
elastische Grenzlast *f* elastic limit load
elastische Instabilität *f* elastic instability
elastische Nachgiebigkeit *f* elastic compliance
elastische Rißausbeitung *f* elastic crack propagation
elastische Rißspitzenaufweitung *f* elastic crack-tip extension
elastische Singularität *f* elastic singularity
elastische Spannung *f* elastic stress
elastische Spannungsanalyse *f* elastic stress analysis
elastische Spannungskonzentration *f* elastic stress concentration

Elastizität

elastische Verformung f elastic deformation
elastische Verformungsenergie f elastic deformation energy
elastische Zone f elastic zone
elastischer Bruch m elastic fracture
elastischer Körper m elastic body
elastischer Riß m elastic crack
elastischer Spannungskonzentrationsfaktor m elastic stress-concentration factor
elastischer Sprödbruch m elastic brittle fracture
elastischer Werkstoff m elastic material
elastisches Grenzwertproblem n elastic boundary-value problem
elastisches Rißproblem n elastic crack problem
elastisches Spannungsfeld n elastic stress field
elastisches Versagen n elastic failure
elastisches Werkstoffverhalten n elastic material behavio[u]r
äquivalenter elastischer Riß m equivalent elastic crack
anisotroper elastischer Körper m anisotropic elastic body
dreidimensionale elastische Spannungsanalyse f three-dimensional elastic stress analysis
ebenes elastisches Rißproblem n plane elastic crack problem
isotroper elastischer Werkstoff m isotropic elastic material
Elastizität f elasticity
  anisotrope Elastizität f anisotropic elasticity
  dreidimensionale Elastizität f three-dimensional elasticity
  isotrope Elastizität f isotropic elasticity
  lineare Elastizität f linear elasticity
  nichtlineare Elastizität f nonlinear elasticity
Elastizitätsgrenze f elastic limit, limit of elasticity
Elastizitätskonstanten fpl elastic constants pl
Elastizitätsmodul m < Syn.: E-Modul > Young's modulus (of elasticity)
  Elastizitätsmodul m **aus dem Biegeversuch** elastic modulus in bend
Elastizitätstheorie f theory of elasticity
  dynamische Elastizitätstheorie f dynamic theory of elasticity
elasto-dynamisches Problem n elasto-dynamic problem
elasto-plastische Spannung f elasto-plastic stress
elasto-plastischer Kennwert m elasto-plastic parameter
elasto-plastisches Bruchverhalten n elasto-plastic fracture behavio[u]r
elasto-plastisches Rißproblem n elasto-plastic crack problem
elektrische Prüfmethode f electrical test method
elektrolytische Korrosion f electrolytic corrosion
Elektronenfraktographie f electron fractography
Elektronenmikroskopie f electron microscopy
Elektronenspektroskopie f **für die chemische Analyse** electron spectroscopy for chemical analysis < abb.: ESCA >
Element n < Syn.: Bauteil n > element
Ellipse f ellipse
ellipsenförmig < Syn.: elliptisch > elliptical
ellipsenförmiger Fehler m elliptical flaw, elliptical defect

ellipsenförmiger (elliptischer) Innenriß m elliptical internal crack
ellipsoidförmig <Syn.: ellipsoidisch> ellipsoidal
ellipsoidförmiger Hohlraum m ellipsoidal void
ellipsoidisch <Syn.: ellipsoidförmig> ellipsoidal
elliptisch <Syn.: ellipsenförmig> elliptical
elliptische Bohrung f elliptical hole
elliptische Kerbe f elliptical notch
elliptischer Fehler m elliptical flaw, elliptical defect
elliptischer Innenriß m elliptical internal crack
elliptischer Oberflächenriß m elliptical surface crack
Emission f emission
Empfindlichkeit f sensitivity
empirisch empirical
Enddicke f {der Probe nach Beendigung der Prüfung} final thickness {of specimen}
Ende n end
Endgeschwindigkeit f des Risses terminal crack velocity
endlich finite
  endliche Spannung f {an der Rißspitze} finite stress {at crack tip}
  endliche Verformung f finite deformation
  endlicher Riß m finite crack
  Riß m mit endlicher Länge finite crack
Endrißlänge f final crack length
Energie f energy
  elastische Energie f elastic energy
  innere Energie f internal energy
  kinetische Energie f kinetic energy
  potentielle Energie f potential energy
  Energie f des Rißschließens crack-closure energy
Energie-Konzept n {Konzept der Bruchmechanik} energy concept {concept of fracture mechanics}
Energieanlieferungsrate f energy release rate
energiearmer Bruch m low energy fracture
energiearmer Sprödbruch m low-energy brittle fracture
Energieaufnahme f energy absorption
energiedispersive Röntgenspektrometrie f energy-dispersive x-ray spectrometry <abb.: EDX>
Energieerzeugung f {z.B. an der Rißspitze} energy generation {e.g. at crack tip}
Energiefreisetzung f energy release
  dynamische Energiefreisetzung f dynamic energy release
Energiefreisetzungsrate f energy release rate
  dynamische Energiefreisetzungsrate f dynamic energy release rate
  kritische Energiefreisetzungsrate f critical energy release rate
Energiegleichgewicht n {bei der Rißausbreitung} energy balance {crack propagation}
Energiekriterium n energy criterion
energiereicher Bruch m high-energy fracture
Energieverbrauch m energy consumption
Energieverlust m energy dissipation
entfernen {eine Probe} replace/to {a specimen}
Entfestigung f <Syn.: Erweichung f, Erweichen n> softening
Entflammbarkeit f flammability
Entflammbarkeit f der Oberfläche surface flammability {of materials}
Entflammbarkeits-Prüfgerät n flammability apparatus
Entflammbarkeitsgrad m degree of flammability

Entflammbarkeitsprüfung

Entflammbarkeitsprüfung f flammability test
Enthalpie f enthalpy
entlasten unload/to
Entlastung f < Syn.: **Entlastungsvorgang** > unloading
partielle Entlastung f partial unloading
Entlastungsgerade f unloading line
Entlastungslinie f unloading line
Entlastungsphase f unloading phase
Entlastungsvorgang m < Syn.: **Entlastung** f > unloading
Entnickelung f {Korrosion} denickelification {corrosion}
Entropie f entropy
Entstehung f formation
entwerfen < Syn.: **auslegen** > {Konstruktion} design/to {structure}
Entwurf m < Syn.: **Konstruktion** f > design
Entwurfskriterien npl < Syn.: **Konstruktionskriterien** npl > design criteria pl
Entzinkung f {Korrosion} dezincification {corrosion}
EPBM → elastisch-plastische Bruchmechanik
Er → Erbium
Erbium n, **Er** erbium, Er
Ergebnisse npl results pl
erhöhen < Syn.: **steigern** > raise/to; elevate/to
erhöhte Temperatur f elevated temperature
Ausfall m **bei erhöhten Temperaturen** elevated-temperature failure
Kurzzeitbeständigkeit f **bei erhöhter Temperatur** short-time stability at elevated temperatures pl
Erhöhung f < Syn.: **Anstieg** m, **Zunahme** f > increase
Ermüdung f fatigue
Ermüdung f **durch Reibungsverschleiß** fretting fatigue

Ermüdung f **durch Wärmebeanspruchung** thermal fatigue
niederzyklische Ermüdung f low-cyclic fatigue
statische Ermüdung f static fatigue
thermische Ermüdung f thermal fatigue
Versagen n **durch Ermüdung** fatigue failure
zweiachsige Ermüdung f biaxial fatigue
Ermüdungsanriß m < Syn.: **Dauerschwinganriß** m, **Dauerbruchanriß** m > fatigue pre-crack
Ermüdungsanrißlänge f fatigue pre-crack length
Ermüdungsbeanspruchung f fatigue loading
Ermüdungsbedingung f fatigue condition
Ermüdungsbelastung f fatigue load
Ermüdungsbruch m < Syn.: **Schwing[ungs]bruch** m, **Dauerbruch** m > fatigue fracture
intergranularer Ermüdungsriß m intergranular fatigue fracture
interkristalliner-transkristalliner Ermüdungsbruch m intercrystalline-transcrystalline fatigue fracture
symmetrischer Ermüdungsriß m symmetrical fatigue fracture
Ermüdungsbruchfläche f fatigue-fracture surface
Ermüdungsbruchzone f fatigue-fracture zone
Ermüdungsfestigkeit f < Syn.: **Dauerfestigkeit** f, **Dauerschwingfestigkeit** f > fatigue strength
Ermüdungsgrenze f fatigue limit
Ermüdungskurve f fatigue curve
Ermüdungsmechanismus m fatigue mechanism, mechanism of fatigue
Ermüdungsriß m < Syn.: **Schwingungsriß** m, **Dauerschwingriß** m > fatigue crack

kurzer Ermüdungsriß m short fatigue crack
peripherer Ermüdungsriß m {Korrosion} circumferential corrosion-fatigue crack
Schließen n des Ermüdungsrisses fatigue crack closure
Ermüdungsrißausbreitung f fatigue crack propagation <abb.: FCP>
Ermüdungsrißausbreitungsgeschwindigkeit f rate of fatigue crack propagation
Ermüdungsrißausbreitungsversuch m fatigue crack propagation test
Ermüdungsrißbeschleunigung f fatigue crack acceleration
Ermüdungsrißbildung f fatigue cracking
Ermüdungsrißerzeugung f fatigue crack production
Ermüdungsrißfläche f fatigue crack surface
Ermüdungsrißgeschwindigkeit f fatigue crack growth rate
Ermüdungsrißlänge f fatigue crack length
Ermüdungsrißschwellwert m fatigue crack threshold
Ermüdungsrißübergang m fatigue crack transition
Ermüdungsrißversuch m fatigue crack test
Ermüdungsrißverzögerung f fatigue crack delay
Ermüdungsrißvorhersage f fatique crack prediction
Ermüdungsrißwachstum n fatigue crack growth
Ermüdungsverhalten n fatigue behavio[u]r
Ermüdungsversuch m fatigue test
erneutes Belasten n <Syn.: Wiederbelastung f, wiederholte Belastung f> reloading

Erosion f {Werkstoffzerstörung} erosion {destruction of materials}
Erosionskorrosion f erosion-corrosion
erreichen reach/to
Ersatz- <Syn.: Äquivalent> equivalent
Ersatzriß m {bei theoretischen Betrachtungen} equivalent crack
kreisrunder Ersatzriß m circular equivalent crack
Ersatzspannung f <Syn.: äquivalente Spannung f> equivalent stress
Erscheinung f <Syn.: Phänomen n> phenomenon
Erscheinungsbild n <Oberflächen> appearance Aussehen n;
Erstarren n solidification
Erstarrung f solidification
Erstarrungsschrumpfung f solidification shrinkage
erwärmen heat/to
Erwärmung heating
Erweichen n <Syn.: Entfestigung f> softening
Erweichung f <Syn.: Entfestigung f> softening
Erweichungspunkt m <Syn.: Erweichungstemperatur f> softening point
Erweichungspunktbestimmung f soft point determination
Erweichungstemperatur f <Syn.: Erweichungspunkt m> softening point
erweitern extend/to
sich erweiternder Riß m extending crack
Erweiterung f <Syn.: Aufweitung f, Breitenwachstum n> {Risse} extension {cracks}
erzeugen {einen Riß} produce/to {a crack}

Erzeugung 188

Erzeugung *f* <Syn.: **Herstellung** *f*> {**von Rissen**} generation, production {of cracks}
ESZ → ebener Spannungszustand *m*
ESZ-Bruch *m* plane stress fracture
ESZ-Bruchzähigkeit *f* plane stress fracture toughness
ESZ-Prüfung *f* plane stress testing
Eu → Europium *n*
Europium *n*, **Eu** europium, Eu
EVZ → ebener Verzerrungszustand *m*
EVZ-Bruch *m* plane strain fracture
EVZ-Bruchzähigkeit *f* plane strain fracture toughness
EVZ-Bruchzähigkeit *f* strain tougness
EVZ-Prüfung *f* plane strain testing
Experiment *n* <Syn.: **Versuch** *m*> experiment
experimentell experimental
experimentelle Bestimmung *f* experimental determination
experimentelles Meßverfahren *n* experimental method of measurement
Exponent *m* exponent
Extrapolation *f* extrapolation
extrapolieren extrapolate/to

F

F → Fluor
Facette *f* facet
  interkristalline Facette *f* intercrystalline facet
  transkristalline Facette *f* transcrystalline facet
FAD → Fehler-Abschätzungs-Diagramm *n*
Faktor *m* <Syn.: **Beiwert** *m*> factor
Fall *m* {Beanspruchung} case {loading}
Fallgewicht *n* drop weight
Fallgewichtsenergie *f* drop-weight energy

Fallgewichtsprüfung *f* drop-weight test <abb.: DWT>
Fallgewichtsscherversuch *m* <Syn.: **DWTT-Versuch**> drop-weight tear test <abb.: DWTT>
Probe *f* **für den Fallgewichtsscherversuch** drop-weight tear test <abb.: DWTT> specimen
Fallgewichtsversuch *m* <Syn.: **DWT-Versuch** *m*> drop-weight test <abb.: DWT>
Probe *f* **für den Fallgewichtsversuch** drop-weight test <abb.: DWT> specimen
Prüfeinrichtung *f* **Fallgewichtsversuch (DWT-Versuch)** drop-weight test apparatus
Standardprobe *f* **für den Fallgewichtsversuch (DWT-Versuch)** standard drop-weight test <abb.: DWT> specimen
Fallversuch *m* drop test
Falte *f* {Metallfehler} fold {defect in metal}
fas(e)rig fibrous
Faserbruch *m* <Syn.: **fas[e]riger Bruch** *m*> fibrous fracture
Fasern *fpl* fibers *pl*
Faserspannung *f* fiber stress
Faserstruktur *f* {Schmiedeeisen} fibrous structure {wrought iron}
faserverstärkter Werkstoff *m* fiber-reinforced composite
fas[e]riger Bruch *m* <Syn.: **Faserbruch** *m*> fibrous fracture
FATT → Brucherscheinungsübertragungstemperatur *f*
Fe → Eisen
Federstahl *m* spring steel
Fehler *m* {Berechnung} error {computation}
Fehler *m* {in Werkstoffen} defect, flaw, imperfection {in materials}
  elliptischer Fehler *m* elliptical flaw

ellipsenförmiger Fehler *m* elliptical defect
Fehler-Abschätzungs-Diagramm *n* <Abk.: FAD> failure-assessment-diagram <abb.: FAD>
Fehleranalyse *f* <Syn.: Schadens-[fall]analyse *f*> failure analysis
fehlerfrei defect-free, flaw-free
Fehlergröße *f* {Fehler in Werkstoffen} flaw (defect) size {flaw in materials}
kritische Fehlergröße *f* critical defect size
fehlerhafte Oberfläche *f* defect surface
Fehlerquelle *f* {in Werkstoffen} flaw source {in materials}
Fehlerstelle *f* {in Werkstoffen} flaw position {in materials}
Fehlguß *m* {Metalle, Legierungen} misrun {metals, alloys}
Feinbearbeitung *f* <Syn.: Fertigbearbeitung *f*> {Metalle} finishing {metals}
Feinstruktur *f* microstructure
Feld *n* array; field
FEM → Finite-Element-Methode *f*
Ferrit *m* ferrite
ferritisch ferritic
ferritische Eisen-Aluminium-Legierung *f* ferritic iron-alumin[i]um alloy
ferritischer nichtrostender Stahl *m* ferritic stainless steel
ferritischer Stahl *m* ferritic steel
Fertigbearbeitung *f* <Syn.: Feinbearbeitung *f*> {Metalle} finishing {metals}
fester Körper *m* solid body
Festfressen *n* {Werkstoff} galling {materials}
festgespannt <Syn.: eingespannt> {Probe} clamped {specimen}
Festigkeit *f* strength

theoretische Festigkeit *f* theoretical strength
Festigkeitseigenschaften *fpl* strength properties *pl*
Festigkeitshypothese *f* strength hypothesis
Festigkeitsprüfung *f* strength test
Festigkeitsverhalten *n* strength behavio(u)r
Festigkeitswert *m* strength value
Festklemmen *n* <Syn: Einspannen *n*, Festspannen *n*> {Probe} clamping {specimen}
festklemmen <Syn.: einspannen, festspannen> {eine Probe} clamp/to {a specimen}
Festspannen *n* <Syn.: Festklemmen *n*, Einspannen *n*> {Probe} clamping {specimen}
festspannen <Syn.: festklemmen, einspannen> {eine Probe} clamp/to {a specimen}
Festwerden *n* <Syn.: Erstarrung *f*, Erstarren *n*> solidification
Fiberglas *n* <Syn.: Glasfaser *f*> glass fiber
fiktiv fictitious
fiktive Bruchzähigkeit *f* fictitious fracture toughness
fiktive Rißlänge *f* fictitious crack length
fiktive Rißspitze *f* fictitious crack tip
fiktiver Riß *m* <Syn.: Fiktivriß *m*> fictitious crack
fiktiver Spannungsintensitätsfaktor *m* fictitious stress-intensity factor
Fiktivriß *m* <Syn.: fiktiver Riß *m*> fictitious crack
Finite-Element-Methode *f* <Abk.: FEM> finite element method <abb.: FEM>
Fischauge *n* {Fehler auf Bruchflächen} fisheye {defect on fracture surface}

fixieren <Syn.: sichern> {ein Ende eines Probenkörpers} secure/to {one end of the specimen}
flach flat, shallow
Fläche *f* face
Flächenkorrosion *f* general corrosion
Flächentemperatur *f* face temperature
flache Kerbe *f* shallow notch
flacher Oberflächenriß *m* shallow surface crack
flacher Riß *m* shallow crack
Flachprobe *f* flat specimen
Flachprobe *f* mit einseitigem Randriß single-edge-cracked flat specimen
Flachprobe *f* mit Mittelriß center-cracked flat specimen
Flachzugprobe *f* mit einseitigem Randriß single-edge cracked flat tensile specimen
Flachzugprobe *f* mit Mittelriß center-cracked flat tensile specimen
einseitig gekerbte Flachzugprobe *f* single-edge notched flat tensile specimen
Flammbehandlung *f* <Syn.: Beflammen *n*> flaming
Flamme *f* flame
Flammenausbreitung *f* flame spread distance
beständig gegenüber Flammenausbreitung *f* resistant to flame propagation
Flammenausbreitungswiderstand *m* resistance to flame propagation
Flammfestigkeit *f* flame resistance
Flammfestigkeitsprüfung *f* test for flame resistance
Flammprobe *f* flame test
Flammprüfung *f* flame test
Flammtest *m* flame test
Flammversuch *m* flame test
Flanke *f* flank

flexibel <Syn.: biegsam> flexible
Flexibilität *f* <Syn.: Biegsamkeit *f*> flexibility
Fließ- yield
Fließ- {Werkstoffe} yielding... {materials}
Fließband *n* craze
Fließbedingungen *fpl* yield conditions *pl*
Fließbeginn *m* initial yielding
Fließbehinderung *f* yield constraint
Fließbereich *m* yielding range
Fließbruchmechanik-Konzept *n* concept of elastic-plastic fracture mechanics
fließen flow/to
Fließen *n* {Werkstoffelement} flow {element of material}
Fließen *n* yielding
anisotropes Fließen *n* anisotropic yield
inhomogenes Fließen *n* inhomogeneous yielding
lokales Fließen *n* local yielding
örtliches Fließen *n* local yielding
plastisches Fließen *n* plastic flow plastic yielding
fließen {Werkstoffe} yield/to {materials}
Fließfestigkeit *f* yield strength
Fließfunktion *f* yield function
Fließgrenze *f* yield point
obere Fließgrenze *f* upper yield point
untere Fließgrenze *f* lower yield point
Fließkriterien *npl* yield criteria *pl*
Fließkriterium *n* nach Tresca Tresca's yield criterion
Tresca-Fließkriterium *n* Tresca's yield criterion
Fließkriterium *n* nach von Mises von Mises' yield criterion
Fließlast *f* yield load

Fließlinien *fpl* < Syn.: Lüderssche Linien *fpl*, Lüders-Streifen *mpl* > {inhomogenes Fließen} Piobert lines *pl*, Hartmann lines *pl*
Fließlinien *fpl* {Werkstoffe} flow lines {materials} *pl*
Fließlinientheorie *f* yield line theory
Fließspannung *f* yield stress
  dreiachsige Fließspannung *f* triaxial yield stress
Fließspannungskurve *f* yield stress curve
Fließzone *f* yielding zone
Fließzustand *m* yield state
Fluor *n*, F fluorine,F
Flußmuster *n* river pattern
flüssig liquid
Flüssigkeit *f* liquid
Flüssigkeitsschlag *m* {Korrosion + turbulente Flüssigkeitsströmungen} impingement attack {corrosion + turbulent flow of liquid}
Flüssigkeitsschwindung *f* liquid shrinkage
Form *f* < Syn.: Art *f*, Typ *m* > type
Form *f* der plastischen Zone plastic zone form
Form *f* der Rißspitze shape of crack tip
Rißspitzenform *f* crack-tip shape
Formänderung *f* < Syn.: Deformation *f*, Verformung *f*> deformation
Formänderungsenergie *f* energy of deformation
  elastische Formänderungsenergie *f* elastic energy of deformation
Formbeständigkeit *f* in der Wärme heat distortion point, heat distortion temperature, heat deflection temperature; deformation under heat
Prüfung *f* der Formbeständigkeit in der Wärme plastic yield test
Martens-Prüfung *f* {Prüfung der Formbeständigkeit in der Wärme} Marten's test

Martens-Zahl {zur Kennzeichnung der Formbeständigkeit in der Wärme} Marten's temperature
formen shape/to
Formfaktor *m* shape factor
Formierung *f* < Syn.: Entstehung *f*, Ausbildung *f*, Bildung *f*, Herausbildung *f*> formation
Formstabilität dimensional stability test
Formstabilitätsprüfung *f* dimensional stability test
Forschung *f* research
Fortpflanzung *f* < Syn.: Ausbreitung *f*> {von Rissen} propagation {of cracks}
fortschreitender Riß *m* propagating crack
Fr → Francium
Fraktographie *f* {Bruchflächen} fractography {fracture surface}
fraktographisch fractographic
fraktographische Analyse *f* fractographic analysis
fraktographische Betrachtung *f* fractographic observation
fraktographische Untersuchung *f* fractographic investigation
Francium *n*, Fr francium, Fr
freie Länge *f* {der eingespannten Probe} free length {of the clamped specimen}
freie Oberfläche *f* free surface
Freisetzung *f* {z.B. Energie} dissipation {e.g. of energy}
Frequenz *f* frequency
Front *f* front
Funktion *f* function

G

Ga → Gallium
Gadolinium, *n* Gd gadolinium, Gd
Gallium *n*, Ga gallium, Ga

galvanisch

galvanische Korrosion f <Syn.: **Kontaktkorrosion** f> galvanic corrosion
Galvanometer m galvanometer
Gaseinschluß m {Metalle} gas hole {metals}
Gasporosität f {Metalle} gas porosity {metals}
Gd → Gadolinium
Ge → Germanium
Gebiet n <Syn.: **Bereich** m, **Zone** f> {in Werkstoffen} zone {in materials}
Gebiet n <Syn.: **Bereich** m, **Umfeld** n> area
gebrochen {Probe} broken {specimen}
nicht gebrochen {Probe} unbroken {specimen}
gebrochene Oberfläche f <Syn.: **Bruchfläche** f> fractured surface
Gefüge f {Werkstoffe} structure {materials}
  globulares Gefüge f <Syn.: **Globulargefüge** f> globular structure
  lamellares Gefüge f lamellare structure
  makroskopisches Gefüge f <Syn.: **Makrogefüge** f> {Metall} macrostructure {metal}
  stengeliges Gefüge f columnar structure
Gefügeanisotropie f structure anisotropy
gefüllt filled
gehärteter Stahl m hardened steel
gekerbt {Proben} notched {specimens}
  gekerbte Aufreißprobe f notched tear test specimen
  gekerbte Biegeprobe f notched bend test specimen
  gekerbte Flachzugprobe f notched flat tensile specimen
  gekerbte Oberfläche f {von Proben} notched surface {of the specimen}
  gekerbte Platte f notched plate
  gekerbte Probe f notched specimen
  gekerbte Probe f <Syn.: **gekerbter Probekörper** m> notched {test} specimen
  gekerbte Zugprobe f notched tension test specimen
  gekerbter Körper m notched body
  gekerbter Probekörper m <Syn.: **gekerbte Probe** f> notched {test} specimen
  gekerbter Stab m <Syn.: **Kerbstab** m> notched bar
  gekerbter Zugstab m notched round tension specimen
  gekerbtes Blech n <Syn.: **gekerbte Platte** f> notched plate
  einseitig gekerbte Zugprobe f single-edge notch tensile specimen
  in der Mitte gekerbte Zugprobe f center-notched tensile specimen
  scharf gekerbter Zugstab m sharp-notched round tension specimen
gekrümmt curved
gekrümmte Rißfront f curved crack front
gekrümmter Riß m curved crack
gemessene Bruchspannung f measured fracture stress
gemindert <Syn.: **verkleinert, reduziert, verringert**> reduced
gemischte Beanspruchungsart f mixed-mode loading
gemischter Spannungszustand m mixed-mode stress state
genau exact
Genauigkeit f {z.B. Schadensanalyse} accuracy {e.g. failure analysis}
genormte Probe f <Syn.: **Normprobe** f> standard [test] specimen
genormte Prüfmethode f standard testing method
genormter Versuch m <Syn.: **Normversuch** m> standard test

genormtes Prüfverfahren *n* < Syn.: **Normprüfverfahren** *n* > standard test
Geometrie *f* geometry
geometrieabhängig geometry-dependent
geometrieabhängige Konstante *f* geometry-dependent constant
Geometrieänderung *f* geometry change
Geometrieeinfluß *m* effect of geometry
Gerade *f* line
gerade < Syn.: **geradlinig** > straight
  gerade durchgehender Riß *m* straight-through crack
  gerade Rißfront *f* straight crack front
gerader Riß *m* straight crack
geradlinig < Syn.: **gerade** > straight
geradlinig rectilinear
  geradliniger Riß *m* rectilinear crack
Geradlinigkeit *f* rectilinearity
Gerät *n* **zur Bestimmung der linearen Ausdehnung** linear expansion apparatus
Gerät *n* **zur Bestimmung der Vicat-Erweichungstemperatur** *f* Vicat softening point apparatus
Gerät *n* {i.e.s. **Prüfgerät** *n*, **Prüfvorrichtung** *f*} apparatus, device
gering < Syn.: **niedrig** > low
gerissen < Syn.: **angerissen, rißbehaftet** > cracked
  gerissene Platte *f* cracked plate
Germanium *n*, **Ge** germanium, Ge
gesägter Riß *m* saw cut
Gesamtdicke *f* {**der Probe**} total thickness {of the specimen}
Gesamtlebensdauer *f* {**von Konstruktionen**} total service life {of structures}
Gesamtrißgeschwindigkeit *f* overall crack rate
Gesamtrißlänge *f* total crack length

Gesamtsteifigkeit *f* total stiffness
geschweißte Platte *f* welded plate
Geschwindigkeit *f* velocity, speed
  kritische Geschwindigkeit *f* critical velocity
  Geschwindigkeit *f* **der elastischen Dehnung** < Syn.: **elastische Dehnungsgeschwindigkeit** *f* > rate of elastic straining
  Geschwindigkeit *f* **der plastischen Dehnung** < Syn.: **plastische Dehnungsgeschwindigkeit** *f* > rate of plastic straining
geschwindigkeitsabhängig rate-dependent
geschwindigkeitsabhängige Bruchzähigkeit *f* rate-dependent fracture toughness
geschwindigkeitsempfindlich rate-sensitive
geschwindigkeitsempfindlicher duktiler Werkstoff *m* rate-sensitive ductile material
geschwindigkeitsunabhängig rate-independent
Gesetz *n* law
  Hookesches Gesetz *n* Hooke's law
Gestalt *f* < Syn.: **Form** *f* > shape
  Gestalt *f* **der Grübchen** < Syn.: **Grübchenform** *f* > {**Grübchenbruch**} shape of dimples {dimple rupture}
gestoppt < Syn.: **aufgefangen** {**Riß**} > stopped {crack}
Gewaltbruch *m* overload fracture, rupture
  duktiler Gewaltbruch *m* ductile overload fracture
  spröder Gewaltbruch *m* brittle overload fracture
Gewaltbruchfläche *f* overload fracture surface
Gewicht *n* weight
gewölbt < Syn.: **konvex** > convex
Gießen *n* casting

Glas

Glas *n* glass
Glasfaser *f* glass fiber
glatt {Oberfläche} smooth {surface}
  glatte Bruchfläche *f* smooth acture surface
  glatte Kerbe *f* smooth-ended notch
  glatte Probe *f* {ungekerbt} smooth specimen {unnotched}
  glatte Zugprobe *f* {ungekerbt} smooth tensile specimen {unnotched}
  glatter Zugstab *m* smooth tensile bar
gleichartig < Syn.: homogen > homogeneous
Gleichartigkeit *f* < Syn.: Homogenität *f*> homogeneity
gleichbleibend < Syn.: konstant> constant
Gleichgewicht *n* equilibrium
  statisches Gleichgewicht *n* state equilibrium
Gleichgewichtsriß *m* {freigesetzte Energie = Oberflächenenergie des Risses} equilibrium crack
gleichmäßig angeordnete Risse *mpl* equally spaced cracks *pl*
Gleichung *f* equation
gleichzeitige Messung *f* < Syn.: Parallelmessung *f*> simultaneous measurement
Gleitband *n* slip band
Gleitbandmodell *n* slip-band model
Gleitbandriß *m* slip-band crack
Gleitbandrißausbreitung *f* slip-band crack propagation
Gleitdeformation *f* slip deformation
Gleitebene *f* slip plane
Gleitebenenbruch *m* slip-plane fracture
gleiten slide/to; slip/to
Gleiten *n* slip {sometimes called: slide}
Gleitgeometrie *f* slip geometry
Gleitlinienbildung *f* slip-line formation
Gleitlinienfeld *n* slip-line field
Gleitlinientheorie *f* slip-line theory
Gleitoberfläche *f* sliding surface
Gleitreibung *f* sliding friction
Gleitstufe *f* slip step
Gleitsystem *n* slip system
Gleitung *f* sliding
Gleitverteilung *f* slip distribution
  inhomogene Gleitverteilung *f* inhomogeneous slip distribution
globular {Gefüge} globular {structure}
  globulares Gefüge *f* globular structure
Globulargefüge *f* globular structure
Glühzwilling *m* {Metalle} annealing twin {metals}
Gold *n*, Au gold, Au
Gold-Palladium-Legierung *f* gold palladium alloy
Grad *m* degree
Gradient *m* gradient
graphitische Korrosion *f* graphitic corrosion
Grauguß *m* gray cast iron
  hypereutektischer Grauguß *m* hypereutectic gray cast iron
Grenzbedingungen *fpl* < Syn.: Randbedingungen *fpl*> boundary conditions
Grenze *f* boundary; limit
Grenzfläche *f* {Matrix/Teilchen} interface {matrix/particle}
Grenz[flächen]belastung *f* < Syn.: Randbelastung *f*> boundary loading
Grenzflächenriß *m* {Werkstoff A/Werkstoff B} interface crack {material A/material B}
Grenzgeschwindigkeit *f* {Rißausbreitung} limiting velocity {crack propagation}
Grenzlast *f* limit load
  elastische Grenzlast *f* elastic limit load
  plastische Grenzlast *f* plastic limit load

Grenztemperatur f limiting temperature
Grenztemperatur-Konzept n {Zähigkeitsnachweis} concept of limiting temperature {determination of toughness}
Grenzwertproblem n < Syn.: **Randwertproblem** n > boundary-value problem
  elastisches Grenzwertproblem n elastic boundary-value problem
  dreidimensionales Grenzwertproblem n three-dimensional boundary-value problem
Grenzwertprüfung f {größtmögliche Kerbschärfe und Belastungsgeschwindigkeit} boundary value test {maximum notch sharpness and loading rate}
Grenzwertverfahren n {Fallgewichtsprüfung} boundary value method {drop-weight test}
Griffith-Modell n Griffith model
Griffith-Orowan-Irwin-Kriterium n {Rißausbreitung} Griffith-Orowan-Irwin criterion {crack propagation}
Griffith-Riß m Griffith crack
Griffithsche Theorie f {Sprödbruch} Griffith theory {brittle fracture}
Größe f size
  Größe f **der plastischen Zone** plastic zone size
  Größe f **der Rißspitze** end-region size of crack
  kritische Größe f {eines Risses} critical size {of a crack}
großflächige Probe f large-area specimen
Großplattenversuch m wide-plate test
Grübchen n {Bruchfläche} dimple {fracture surface}
  ovales Grübchen n {Grübchenbruch} oval dimple {dimple rupture}
Grübchen npl dimples pl
  muldenförmige Grübchen npl {Bruchfläche} shallow dimples pl {fracture surface}
  langgestrecktes Grübchen npl {Grübchenbruch} elongated dimples pl {dimple fracture}
  längliche Grübchen npl {Grübchenbruch} elongated dimples pl {dimple fracture}
Grübchenbruch m dimple fracture, dimple rupture **intergranularer Grübchenbruch** m intergranular dimple fracture
Grübchendurchmesser m diameter of dimples
Grübchenform f < Syn.: **Gestalt** f **der Grübchen** > {Grübchenbruch} shape of dimples pl {dimple rupture}
Grübchengröße f dimple size
Grundgerät n basic apparatus
Grundgleichung f basic equation
Grundlage f basis
Grundmetall n base-metal
Grundwerkstoff m basis material
Guß m < Syn.: **Gießen** n > casting
Gußeisen n cast iron
  hochfestes Gußeisen n high-duty cast iron
  hochnickelhaltiges Gußeisen n high-nickel cast iron
  hochsiliciumhaltiges Gußeisen n high-silicon cast iron
  hypereutektisches Gußeisen n hypereutectic cast iron
Gußfehler m casting defect

H

H → Wasserstoff
Haarkristall m whisker
Haarriß m {Eisenmetalle} hairline crack, shatter crack, flake {ferrous metals}
Hafnium n, **Hf** hafnium, Hf
halbelliptisch semi-elliptical

halbempirisch

halbelliptischer Oberflächenfehler m semi-elliptical surface flaw
halbelliptischer Oberflächenriß m semi-elliptical surface crack
halbelliptischer Riß m semi-elliptical crack
halbempirisch semi-empirical
halbkreisförmiger Riß m semi-circular crack
halbunendlich semi-infinite
halbunendliche Zugprobe f semi-infinite tensile specimen
halbunendlicher Kerb m semi-infinite notch
halbunendlicher Riß m semi-infinite crack
härtbar hardenable
härtbarer Kohlenstoffstahl m hardenable carbon steel
lichtbogengeschweißter härtbarer Kohlenstoffstahl m arc-welded hardenable carbon steel
harte (starre) Probe f rigid specimen
Härte f hardness
Härten n <Syn.: **Härtung** f> quenching
Härteprüfung f hardness test
harter Kunststoff m rigid plastic
Härteriß m quenching crack, hardening crack
  intergranularer Härteriß m intergranular quenching crack
Härterißanfälligkeit f quench-cracking susceptibility
Härtung f <Syn.: **Härten** n> quenching
Hauptachse f {Ellipse} major axis {ellipse}
Hauptbelastungsrichtung f principal loading direction
Hauptgleitebene f principal slip plane
Hauptnormalspannung f principal normal stress
Hauptnormalspannungskriterium n principal normal stress criterion
Hauptnormalzugspannung f principal normal tensile stress
Hauptrichtung f <Syn.: **Vorzugsrichtung** f> {Kristall} preferred orientation {crystal}
Hauptriß m dominant crack, main crack
Hauptrißfront f dominant crack front
Hauptschubspannung f principal shear stress
Hauptspannung f principal stress
Hauptspannungsebene f principal-stress plane
He → Helium
Helium n, **He** helium, He
Herausbildung f <Syn.: **Formierung** f, **Entstehung** f, **Ausbildung** f, **Bildung** f> formation
Herauslösen n leaching
  selektives Herauslösen n {Korrosion} selective leaching {corrosion}
Herauspressung f {Ermüdungsbruch} extrusion {fatigue fracture}
Herstellung f <Syn.: **Erzeugung** f> {von Rissen} production {of cracks}
heterogen <Syn.: **ungleichartig**> heterogeneous
heterogener Werkstoff m heterogeneous material
Heterogenität f <Syn.: **Ungleichartigkeit** f> heterogeneity
Hf → Hafnium
Hg → Quecksilber
Hill-Probe f {eine flache Zugprobe} Hill specimen {a flat tensile specimen}
hitzebeständig heat-resistant
hitzebeständige Legierung f heat-resistant alloy
  lichtbogengeschweißte hitzebeständige Legierung f arc-welded heat-resistant alloy
Ho → Holmium

hoch high
Eigenschaften *fpl* **bei hohen Prüfgeschwindigkeiten** high-speed properties *pl*
Prüfung *f* **bei hohen Temperaturen** high-temperature test
hochfeste Aluminiumlegierung *f* high-strength alumin[i]um alloy
hochfester Stahl *m* high-strength steel
hochfester Werkstoff *m* high-strength material
hochfestes Gußeisen *n* high-duty cast iron
Hochgeschwindigkeits-Belastung *f* high-speed loading
Hochgeschwindigkeits-Prüfmaschine *f* **zur Bestimmung der Schlagzugfestigkeit** high-speed tensile impact machine
Hochgeschwindigkeits-Zugprüfmaschine *f* high-speed tension testing machine
Hochgeschwindigkeitsprüfung *f* high-speed test
Hochgeschwindigkeitsversuch *m* high-speed test
hochlegierter Stahl *m* high-alloy steel
hochnickelhaltiges Gußeisen *n* high-nickel cast iron
hochreine Metalle *npl* high-purity metals *pl*
hochreines Kupfer *n* high-purity copper
hochsiliciumhaltiges Gußeisen *n* high-silicon cast iron
Höchstlast *f* <Syn.: **Lastmaximum** *n*, **Maximalbeanspruchung** *f*> maximum load
hochtemperaturbeständiger Werkstoff *m* high-temperature material
hochwarmfeste Legierung *f* high-temperature alloy
hohl <Syn.: **konkav**> concave

Hohlraum *m* <Syn.: **Pore** *f*> {in Werkstoffen} void {in materials}; cavity
ellipsenförmiger Hohlraum *m* ellipsoidal void
Hohlraum *m* **an Korngrenzen** <Syn.: **Korngrenzenhohlraum** *m*> {Kristall} grain-boundary cavity {crystal} Korngrenzenhohlraum *m*
röhrenförmiger Hohlraum *m* {Bruchfläche} tubular void {fracture surface}
Hohlraumbildung *f* void formation
Hohlraumvereinigung *f* <Syn.: **Hohlraumzusammenschluß** *m*> void coalescence
Hohlraumwachstum *n* void growth
Hohlraumzusammenschluß *m* <Syn.: **Hohlraumvereinigung** *f*> void coalescence
Hohlwölbung *f* <Syn.: **Konkavität** *f*> {Bruchstelle} concavity {of failure locus}
Holmium *n*, **Ho** holmium, Ho
homogen <Syn.: **gleichartig**> homogeneous
homogene Belastung *f* homogeneous loading
homogene Spannungsverteilung *f* homogeneous distribution of stress[es]
homogene Verformung *f* homogeneous deformation
homogener Körper *m* homogeneous body
homogener Spannungszustand *m* homogeneous state of stress
homogenes Spannungsfeld *n* homogeneous field of stress
Homogenität *f* <Syn.: **Gleichartigkeit** *f*> homogeneity
Homogenitätsgrad *m* degree of homogeneity
Hookesches Gesetz *n* Hooke's law

Hundeknochen-Modell *n* < Syn.: **dog-bone-Modell** *n* > {der plastischen Zone} dog-bone model {of the plastic zone}
hydrostatisch hydrostatic
hydrostatische Druckbeanspruchung *f* hydrostatic compression
hydrostatische Spannung *f* hydrostatic stress
hydrostatischer Druck *m* hydrostatic pressure
hypereutektisch hypereutectic
hypereutektischer Grauguß *m* hypereutectic gray cast iron
hypereutektisches Gußeisen *n* hypereutectic cast iron
Hypothese *f* hypothesis

I

ideal < Syn.: **vollkommen** > ideal, perfect
ideale Plastizität *f* ideal plasticity
ideal-spröder Werkstoff *m* ideal brittle material
ideale Plastizität *f* ideal plasticity
In → Indium
Indium *n*, **In** indium, In
Industrieatmosphäre *f* {Korrosion} industrial atmosphere {corrosion}
induzieren {einen Bruch} induce/to {a fracture}
induzierte Anisotropie *f* induced anisotropy
infinitesimale Verformung *f* infinitesimal deformation
Ingenieur-Bruchmechanik *f* engineering fracture mechanics
inhomogen < Syn.: **ungleichartig** > inhomogeneous
inhomogene Dehnung *f* inhomogeneous strain
inhomogene Gleitverteilung *f* inhomogeneous slip distribution
inhomogene Spannungsverteilung *f* inhomogeneous stress distribution
inhomogene Verformung *f* inhomogeneous deformation
inhomogener Verfestigungszustand *m* inhomogeneous state of hardening
inhomogener Werkstoff *m* inhomogeneous material
inhomogenes Fließen *n* inhomogeneous yielding
inhomogenes Spannungsfeld *n* inhomogeneous stress field
Inhomogenität *f* < Syn.: **Ungleichartigkeit** *f* > inhomogeneity
Initiation *f* < Syn.: **Initiierung** *f*, **Auslösung** *f* > {von Rissen} initiation {of cracks}
initiieren < Syn.: **auslösen** > {Risse} initiate/to {cracks}
Initiierung *f* < Syn.: **Auslösung** *f*, **Initiation** *f* > {von Rissen} initiation {of cracks}
Initiierung *f* < Syn.: **Einleitung** *f*, **Auslösung** *f* > initiation
inkompressibel incompressible
Inkompressibilität *f* incompressibility
elastisch-plastische Inkompressibilität *f* elastic-plastic fracture instability
inkompressible Deformation *f* incompressible deformation
Inkrement *n* increment
inkremental incremental
Inkubationszeit *f* {Rißleitung} incubation time {crack initiation}
innen internal
Innen- inner, internal
Innendurchmesser *m* {von Proben} inside diameter {of the specimen}
Innenfläche *f* inner surface
Riß *m* **auf der Innenfläche** crack at the inner surface

Innenkerb *m* internal notch
scharfer Innenkerb *m* sharp internal notch
Innenriß *m* internal crack
ellipsenförmiger Innenriß *m* elliptical internal crack
elliptischer Innenriß *m* elliptical internal crack
kreisförmiger Innenriß *m* circular internal crack
innere inner, internal
innere Druckbelastung *f* internal compressive load
innere Energie *f* internal energy
innere Kraft *f* internal force
innere Oxidation *f* {Korrosionsprodukte} internal oxidation, subsurface corrosion {corrosion products}
innere Reibung *f* internal friction
innerer Bereich *m* {Rißspitze} inner zone {crack tip}
innerer Wärmeriß *m* internal hot tear
Inspektion *f* <Syn.: Kontrolle *f*> inspection
Inspektionsintervall *n* inspection interval
Inspektionsverfahren *n* inspection technique
instabil unstable
instabile Bruchausbreitung *f* unstable propagation of fracture
instabile Rißausbreitung *f* unstable crack propagation
instabile Rißauslösung *f* unstable crack initiation
instabile Rißerweiterung *f* unstable crack extension
instabiler Bruch *m* unstable fracture
instabiler Mikroriß *m* unstable microcrack
instabiler Riß *m* unstable crack

instabiles Rißwachstum *n* unstable crack growth
Instabilität *f* instability
elastische Instabilität *f* elastic instability
mechanische Instabilität *f* {z.B. Knicken oder Einschnüren} mechanical instability
plastische Instabilität *f* plastic instability
Instabilitäts-Kennwert *m* instability parameter
Instabilitätsanalyse *f* instability analysis
instationär <Syn.: Übergangs-> transient
instationäre Belastung *f* transient loading
instationäre Rißausbreitung *f* non-steady crack propagation
instationäres Bestimmungsverfahren *n* non-steady state method of determining
instrumentiert {Versuch} instrumented {test}
instrumentierter Charpy-Versuch *m* instrumented Charpy test
instrumentierter Kerbschlagbiegeversuch *m* instrumented notched-bar impact test
Integral *n* integral
Intensität *f* intensity
interdendritischer Riß *m* interdendritic crack
intergranular <Syn.: interkristallin> {zwischen Kristalliten, Körnern, entlang der Korngrenzen} intercrystalline, intergranular {between crystals, grains, along the grain boundaries}
intergranularer Bruch *m* <Syn.: Korngrenzbruch *m*> intergranular fracture

interkristallin

intergranularer Ermüdungsbruch *m* intergranular fatigue fracture
intergranularer Grübchenbruch *m* intergranular dimple fracture
intergranularer Härteriß *m* intergranular quenching crack
intergranularer Kriechbruch *m* intergranular creep rupture
interkristallin <Syn.: **intergranular**> {zwischen Kristallen, Körnern, entlang der Korngrenzen} intercrystalline, intergranular {between crystals, grains, along the grain boundaries}
interkristalline Brucheinleitung *f* intercrystalline fracture initiation
interkristalline Facette *f* intercrystalline facet
interkristalline Korrosion *f* <Syn.: **Korngrenzenkorrosion** *f*> intercrystalline corrosion, intergranular corrosion, grain-boundary corrosion
interkristalline Rißausbreitung *f* intercrystalline crack propagation
interkristalline Rißbildung *f* intercrystalline cracking
interkristalline Rißbildung *f* intergranular cracking
interkristalline Spannungsrißkorrosion *f* intergranular stress-corrosion cracking
interkristalliner Bruch *m* intercrystalline fracture
interkristalliner Mikroriß *m* intercrystalline microcrack
interkristalliner Spaltbruch *m* intercrystalline cleavage fracture
interkristalliner Sprödbruch *m* intercrystalline brittle fracture
interkristalliner-transkristalliner Ermüdungsbruch *m* intercrystalline-transcrystalline fatigue fracture

intermetallische Verbindung *f* intermetallic compound
Intervall *n* <Syn.: **Bereich** *m*> {Temperatur, Druck-} range {temperature, pressure...}
intrakristallin intracrystalline
intrakristallin <Syn.: **transgranular, transkristallin**> {durch Kristallkörner hindurch} transcrystalline, intracrystalline, transgranular {through the grains}
Ir → Iridium
Iridium *n*, **Ir** iridium, Ir
irreversibel <Syn.: **nicht umkehrbar**> irreversible
ISO-Spitzkerb *m* <Syn.: **ISO-V-Kerb** *m*> ISO-V-notch
ISO-V-Kerb *m* <Syn.: **ISO-Spitzkerb** *m*> ISO-V-notch
ISO-V-Probe *f* {gekerbt} ISO-V-specimen {notched}
Isochromate *f* {Spannungsoptik} isochromatic line {photoelasticity}
Isokline *f* {Spannungsoptik} isocline {photoelasticity}
isoliert isolated
isolierter Bruch *m* non-cumulative rupture
isothermisch isothermal
isotrop <Syn.: **richtungsunabhängig**> isotropic
isotrope Elastizität *f* isotropic elasticity
isotrope Verfestigung *f* isotropic hardening
isotroper Bruch *m* isotropic fracture
isotroper duktiler Werkstoff *m* isotropic ductile material
isotroper elastischer Werkstoff *m* isotropic elastic material
isotroper Spannungszustand *m* isotropic state of stress
isotroper Streifen *m* isotropic strip
isotroper Werkstoff *m* isotropic material

isotroper Zylinder *m* isotropic cylinder
isotropes Spannungsfeld *n* isotropic stress field
Isotropie *f* isotropy
Izod-Probe *f* {zur Bestimmung der Schlagfestigkeit} Izod impact strength specimen
Izod-Prüfung *f* {Bestimmung der Schlagfestigkeit} Izod-test {determination of impact strength}
Izod-Schlagprüfgerät *n* < Syn.: Schlagprüfgerät *n* nach Izod > Izod impact testing machine

J

J-Integral *n* {mathematischer Ausdruck: Bruchzähigkeit} J-integral {mathematical expression: fracture toughness}
  kritisches J-Integral *n* critical J-integral
  zyklisches J-Integral *n* cyclic J-integral
J-Integral-Auslegungskurve *f* J-integral design curve
J-Integral-Konzept *n* {Fließbruchmechanik} J-integral concept {linear-elastic fracture mechanics}
J-Prüfung *f* J-testing

K

K → Kalium
Kadmium *n*, **Cadmium** *n*, **Cd** cadmium, Cd
kalibrieren calibrate/to
Kalibrieren *n* calibration
Kalibrierung *f* calibration
Kalium *n*, **K** potassium, K
Kalotten-Tassen-Bruch *m*, **Teller-Tassen-Bruch** *m* cup-cone fracture
Kaltbiegeversuch *m* < Syn.: Kältebiegeversuch *m* > cold bend test
kaltbrüchiger Stahl *m* < Syn.: kaltspröder Stahl *m* > cold-brittle steel
Kältebeständigkeit *f* cold resistance
Kältebiegefestigkeit *f* cold bend strength
Kältebiegetemperatur *f* cold bend temperature
Kältebiegeversuch *m* < Syn.: Kaltbiegeversuch *m* > cold bend test
Kältebrüchigkeit *f* < Syn.: Brüchigkeit *f* bei tiefen Temperaturen > low-temperature brittleness
Kältebruchtemperatur *f* brittleness temperature
Kältebruchtemperatur *f* bei Schlagbeanspruchung impact brittleness temperature, brittleness temperature by impact
Kältebruchtemperaturprüfung *f* brittleness temperature test
Kältekammer *f* cold chamber
Kaltguß *m* cold shot
Kaltriß *m* cold crack, mechanical crack
Kaltschweißstelle *f* {Gußfehler} cold shut {casting defect}
kaltspröder Stahl *m* < Syn.: kaltbrüchiger Stahl *m* > cold-brittle steel
Kaltverfestigung *f* < Syn.: Dehnungsverfestigung *f* > strain hardening
Kaltverformung *f* cold deformation
Kalzium *n*, **Calcium** *n*, **Ca** calcium, Ca
Kammer *f* chamber
Kammertemperatur *f* chamber temperature
Kante *f* < Syn.: Rand *m* {von Proben} edge
Kantenfehler *m* edge defect
Kantenriß *m* < Syn.: Randriß *m* > edge crack
  radialer Kantenriß *m* radial crack
  symmetrischer Kantenriß *m* double-edge crack

kartesische Koordinaten *fpl* Cartesian coordinates *pl*
kartesisches Koordinatensystem *n* Cartesian coordinate system
katastrophenartig catastrophic
katastrophenartige Rißerweiterung *f* catastrophic crack extension
katastrophenartiger Bruch *m* catastrophic failure
katastrophenartiger Verschleiß *m* catastrophic wear
Kat[h]ode *f* cathode
Kaustik-Methode *f* method of caustics
Kavitation *f* {Bildung von Hohlräumen an Korngrenzen} cavitation
Kavitationserosion *f* cavitation erosion
Kavitationsschädigung *f* < Syn.: Schädigung *f* durch Kavitation > cavitation damage
kegelförmig < Syn.: konisch > conical
Keil *m* wedge
keilbelastet wedge-loaded
keilbelastete Kompakt-Probe *f* wedge-loaded compact test specimen
Keilbelastung *f* wedge loading
keilförmig {Proben} tapered {specimens}
keilförmige Doppelbalkenbiegeprobe *f* < Syn.: TDCB-Probe *f* > tapered double-cantilever beam < abb.: TDCB > specimen
keilförmige Verformung *f* wedge-type deformation
Keimbildung *f* nucleation
Keim *m* < Syn.: Keimstelle *f* > nucleus
Keimstelle *f* < Syn.: Keim *m* > {Risse, Bruch} nucleus {cracks, fracture}
Kenngröße *f* < Syn.: Parameter *m*, Kennwert *m* > parameter
Kennlinien *fpl* characteristics
Kennwert *m* < Syn.: Kenngröße *f*, Parameter *m* > parameter

bruchmechanischer Kennwert *m* parameter of fracture mechanics
elasto-plastischer Kennwert *m* elasto-plastic parameter
Kennzeichen *n* < Syn.: Charakteristik *f* > characteristic
kennzeichnend characteristic
Kennzeichnung *f* < Syn.: Charakterisierung *f* > characterization
Kennzeichnung *f* < Syn.: Markierung *f* > {auf der Probe} mark {on the specimen}
keramisch ceramic
keramischer Werkstoff *m* ceramic material
Kerb *m* < Syn.: Kerbe *f* > notch
halbunendlicher Kerb *n* semi-infinite notch
makroskopischer Kerb *n* macroscopic notch
mikroskopischer Kerb *n* microscopic notch
Probe *f* mit einseitigem Kerb *n* single-edge notch specimen
runder Kerb *n* circular notch
scharfer Kerb *n* < Syn.: Spitzkerbe *f* > sharp notch
Kerbabmessungen *fpl* notch dimensions *pl*
Kerbaufweitung *f* < Syn.: Kerböffnung *f* > notch extension
Kerbbiegeprobe *f* notch bend test specimen
Kerbbiegeversuch *m* notch bend test
Kerbdicke *f* notch thickness
Kerbe *f* < Syn.: Kerb *m* > notch
elliptische Kerbe *f* elliptical notch
flache Kerbe *f* shallow notch
glatte Kerbe *f* smooth-ended notch
Kerbeinfluß *m* < Syn.: Kerbwirkung *f* > effect of notch
Kerbeinfräsung *f* machined notch
kerbempfindlich {Werkstoffe} notch sensitive {materials}

Kerbempfindlichkeit f notch sensitivity
Kerbempfindlichkeitszahl f notch sensitivity ratio <abb.: NSR>
kerben <Syn.: einkerben> notch/to
Kerben n <Syn.: Einkerbung f, Einkerben n> {von Proben} notching {of the specimen}
Kerbende n end of the notch
Kerbenebene f notch plane
Kerbfestigkeitsverhältnis n notch-unnotch ratio
Kerbform f type of notch
Kerbgeometrie f notch geometry
Kerbgrund m notch root
Kerbgrund-Krümmungsradius m notch root radius of curvature
Kerbgrundradius m notch root radius
Kerbkonfiguration f notch configuration
Kerblage f location of the notch
Kerblänge f notch length
Kerblinie f notch line
Kerb[ober]fläche f notch surface
Kerböffnung f notch extension
Kerbproblem n notch problem
Kerbradius m notch radius
Kerbschärfe f notch acuity, notch sharpness
Kerbschlagbiegeprobe f notched-bar impact test specimen
Kerbschlagbiegeprüfung f notched-bar impact testing
Kerbschlagbiegeversuch f notched-bar impact test
instrumentierter Kerbschlagbiegeversuch m instrumented notched-bar impact test
Kerbschlagfestigkeit f impact strength
Kerbschlagprobe f notch impact test specimen
Kerbschlagzähigkeit f notch impact toughness

Kerbschlagzähigkeits-Temperatur-Kurve f <Syn.: Kerbschlagzähigkeits-Temperaturverlauf m> notch impact toughness-temperature curve
Kerbschlagzähigkeits-Temperaturverlauf m <Syn.: Kerbschlagzähigkeits-Temperatur-Kurve f> notch impact toughness-temperature curve
Kerbschlagzähigkeitswert m notch impact toughness value
Kerbspannung f notch stress
Kerbspannungslehre f <Syn.: Kerbtheorie f> theory of notch stresses
Kerbspitze f notch tip
Kerbsprödigkeit f notch brittleness
Kerbstab m <Syn.: gekerbter Stab m> notched bar
Kerbtheorie f <Syn.: Kerbspannungslehre f> theory of notch stresses
Kerbtiefe f notch depth
Kerbwirkung f <Syn.: Kerbeinfluß m> effect of notch
Kerbwirkung f notch effect
Kerbwirkungszahl f {ungekerbte Probe/gekerbte Probe} fatigue notch factor {unnotched specimen/notched specimen}
Kerbzugfestigkeit f notch tensile strength, notched-bar tensile strength
Kerbzugprobe f notched-bar tensile test specimen
Kerbzugversuch m notch tension test, notched tensile test, notched-bar tensile test
Kessel m boiler
Kesselstahl m boiler steel
kfz → kubisch-flächenzentriert
kinetisch kinetic
kinetische Energie f kinetic energy
Kippgrenze f {Kristall} tilt boundary {crystal}
klein {crack} small {crack}

Kleinbereichsfließen

Kleinbereichsfließen *n* small-scale yielding
kleiner Riß *m* small crack
Kleinwinkelkorngrenze *f* small-angle grain boundary
Klima- climatic
  Klimaprüfung *f* climatic testing
Knetlegierung *f* wrought alloy
  warmfeste Knetlegierung *f* heat-resistant wrought alloy
Knickfestigkeit *f* cross-breaking strength, buckling strength
Knickfestigkeitsprüfung *f* cross-breaking (strength) test
Knickkriterium *n* criterion for buckling
Knollenbildung *f* {Korrosion} tuberculation {corrosion}
Knoop-Härte *f* {Eindringhärte} Knoop hardness number <abb.: HK> {indentation hardness}
Knoten *m* {Methode der finiten Elemente} node {finite-element method}
Knoten *m* {Versetzung} node
Kobalt *n*, **Cobalt** *n*, **Co** cobalt, Co
Koeffizient *m* <Syn.: Beiwert *m*> coefficient
Kohäsion *f* cohesion
Kohäsions- cohesive
  Kohäsionsfestigkeit *f* cohesion strength
  Kohäsionskraft *f* cohesive force
  Kohäsionsmodul *m* modulus of cohesion
  Kohäsionszone *f* cohesion zone
kohäsiv cohesive
Kohlenstoff *m*, **C** carbon, C
Kohlenstoff-Molybdän-Stahl *m* carbon-molybdenum steel
kohlenstoffarmer Stahl *m* low-carbon steel
  lichtbogengeschweißter kohlenstoffarmer Stahl *m* arc-welded low-carbon steel

kohlenstoffreicher Stahl *m* high-carbon steel
Kohlenstoffstahl *m* carbon steel
  lichtbogengeschweißter härtbarer Kohlenstoffstahl *m* arc-welded hardenable carbon steel
  unlegierter Kohlenstoffstahl *m* plain carbon steel
Kollaps *m* collaps
  plastischer Kollaps *m* <Syn.: plastisches Versagen *n*> plastic collaps
kollinear collinear
  kollinearer Riß *m* collinear crack
Kollokation *f* collocation
kompakt compact <abb.: C>
Kompakt-Probe *f* <Syn.: C-Probe *f*, CS> compact specimen
  keilbelastete Kompakt-Probe *f* wedge-loaded compact test specimen
Kompakt-Zug-Probe *f* <Syn.: CT-Probe *f*> compact tension <abb.: CT> specimen
  scheibenförmige Kompaktzugprobe *f* <Syn.: DCT-Probe *f*> disk-shaped compact [tensile] specimen <abb.: DCT> specimen
kompatibel compatible
Kompatibilität *f* compatibility
Kompatibilitätsbedingungen *fpl* compatibility conditions *pl*
komplex complex
  komplexe Spannung *f* complex stress
  komplexe Spannungsfunktion *f* complex stress function
Komponente *f* {Mathematik} component {mathematics}
Kompressionsmodul *m* compression modulus, bulk modulus {of elasticity}, volumetric modulus of elasticity, hydrostatic modulus
Konfiguration *f* configuration
konisch <Syn.: kegelförmig> conical

konische <Syn.: keilförmige> Doppelbalken[biege]probe *f* <Syn.: TDCB-Probe *f*> tapered double-cantilever beam <abb.: TDCB> specimen
konkav <Syn.: hohl> concave
Konkavität *f* <Syn.: Hohlwölbung *f*> {Bruchstelle} concavity {of failure locus}
konstant <Syn.: gleichbleibend> constant
  konstante Amplitude *f* constant amplitude
  konstante Kraft *f* constant force
  konstante Last *f* constant load
  konstante Lastamplitude *f* constant load amplitude
  konstante Spannung *f* constant stress
  konstante Verformung *f* constant deformation
konstantes Spannungsniveau *n* constant stress level
Konstante *f* constant
  dynamische Konstante *f* dynamic constant
  geometrieabhängige Konstante *f* geometry-dependent constant
  Poissonsche Konstante *f* Poisson's ratio
konstruieren <Syn.: entwerfen> construct/to
Konstruktion *f* <Syn.: Entwurf *m*> design
Konstruktion *f* <Syn.: Bauwerk *n*> construction
  Betriebsversagen *n* {von Konstruktionen} service failure {of structures}
  Gesamtlebensdauer *f* { von Konstruktionen} total service life {of structures}
Konstruktions- constructional

Konstruktionswerkstoff *m* constructional material material of construction
Konstruktionskriterien *npl* <Syn.: Entwurfskriterien *npl*> design criteria *pl*
Kontakt *m* contact
  Versprödung *f* **bei Kontakt mit schmelzflüssigen Metallen** liquid-metal embrittlement, LME
Kontaktkorrosion *f* <Syn.: galvanische Korrosion *f*> galvanic corrosion
kontinuierlich <Syn.: ununterbrochen> continuous
Kontinuum *n* continuum
  linear-elastisches Kontinuum *n* linear-elastic continuum
  dreidimensionales Kontinuum *n* three-dimensional continuum
Kontinuummechanik *f* continuum mechanics
Kontinuumstheorie *f* continuum theory
Kontraktion *f* <Syn.: Schrumpfung *f*> {Rißspitze} contraction {crack tip}
Kontrolle *f* <Syn.: Inspektion *f*> inspection
Kontrolle *f* <Syn.: Überwachung *f*> control
kontrollieren <Syn.: überwachen; steuern> control/to
Kontrolltest *m* <Syn.: Kontrollversuch *m*> control test
Kontrollversuch *m* <Syn.: Kontrolltest *m*> control test
Kontur *f* <Syn.: Profil *n*> {Riß} contour {crack}
konvex <Syn.: gewölbt> convex
Konvexität *f* <Syn.: Wölbung *f*> {Bruchstelle} convexity {of failure locus}
Konzentration *f* concentration

konzentriert concentrated
konzentriert <Syn.: **in einem Punkt angreifend** {Kraft} concentrated
konzentrisch <Syn.: **mittig**> concentric
konzentrischer Rundstab *m* concentric round bar
Rundstab *m* **mit konzentrischem Außenriß** circumferentially cracked round bar specimen
Konzept *n* concept
Konzept *n* **der Bruchmechanik** <Syn.: **Bruchmechanik-Konzept** *n*> concept of fracture mechanics
Konzept *n* **der linear-elastischen Bruchmechanik** concept of linear-elastic fracture mechanics
Konzept *n* **der linear-elastischen Bruchmechanik** <Syn.: **LEBM-Konzept** *n*> linear-elastic fracture mechanics <abb.: LEFM> concept
Konzept *n* **der Sprödbruchtheorie** concept of brittle fracture theory
Koordinaten *fpl* coordinates *pl*
kartesische Koordinaten *fpl* Cartesian coordinates *pl*
Koordinatensystem *n* coordinate system
kartesisches Koordinatensystem *n* Cartesian coordinate system
Korn *n* grain
Korngrenzbruch *m* <Syn.: **intergranularer Bruch** *m*> intergranular fracture
Korngrenze *f* grain boundary
Anreicherung *f* **an den Korngrenzen** grain-boundary enrichment
Bildung *f* **von Hohlräumen an Korngrenzen** cavitation
Korngrenzenanreicherung *f* <Syn.: **Anreicherung** *f* **an den Korngrenzen**> grain-boundary enrichment

Korngrenzenausscheidung *f* segregation in grain boundary
Korngrenzengleiten *n* grain-boundary sliding
Korngrenzenhohlraum *m* <Syn.: **Hohlraum** *m* **an Korngrenzen**> {Kristall} grain-boundary cavity {crystal}
Korngrenzenkorrosion *f* <Syn.: **interkristalline Korrosion** *f*> grain-boundary corrosion, intercrystalline corrosion, intergranular corrosion
Korngrenzenriß *m* grain-boundary crack
Korngrenzenseigerung *f* grain-boundary segregation
Korngröße *f* grain size
körnig granular
körniger Bruch *m* granular fracture
Körper *m* body
anisotroper elastischer Körper *m* anisotropic elastic body
beanspruchter <Syn.: **belasteter**> **Körper** *m* loaded body
belasteter <Syn.: **beanspruchter**> **Körper** *m* loaded body
dreidimensionaler Körper *m* three-dimensional body
elastisch-plastischer Körper *m* elastic-plastic body
elastischer Körper *m* elastic body
fester Körper *m* solid body
gekerbter Körper *m* notched body
homogener Körper *m* homogeneous body
linear-elastischer Körper *m* linear-elastic body
nicht beanspruchter <Syn.: **unbelasteter**> **Körper** *m* unloaded body
starrer Körper *m* rigid body
unbelasteter <Syn.: **nicht beanspruchter**> **Körper** *m* unloaded body
unendlicher Körper *m* infinite body

Körper *m* <Syn.: Prüfkörper *m*> piece
Korrektur *f* <Syn.:Ausgleich *m*> correction
Korrekturfaktor *m* corrective factor
Korrekturfunktion *f* correction function
normierte Korrekturfunktion *f* normalized correction function
Korrelation *f* <Syn.: Wechselbeziehung *f*> correlation
Korrelationsparameter *m* correlation parameter
korrelieren <Syn.: in Wechselbeziehung stehen> correlate/to
korrigieren <Syn.: ausgleichen> correct/to
korrodieren corrode/to
korrodiert corroded
korrodierte Oberfläche *f* corroded surface
Korrosion *f* corrosion
Ausfall *m* **durch Korrosion** corrosion failure
Spannungsrißkorrosion *f* {Messing: Korrosion + innere Spannung} seasoning cracking {brass: corrosion + internal stress}
elektrolytische Korrosion *f* electrolytic corrosion
graphitische Korrosion *f* graphitic corrosion
intergranulare Korrosion *f* intergranular corrosion
interkristalline Korrosion *f* grain-boundary corrosion
Korngrenzenkorrosion *f* intercrystalline corrosion
Korrosion *f* **unter Ablagerungen** {z.B. Karosserieteile von Kraftfahrzeugen} deposit corrosion, deposit attack
Korrosion *f* **zwischen Dendriten** {Gußlegierungen} interdendritic corrosion {alloy castings}

selektive Korrosion *f* selective corrosion
korrosionsbeständige Legierung *f* corrosionresistant alloy
korrosionsbeständiger Stahl *m* corrosion-resistant steel
Korrosionsbeständigkeit *f* corrosion resistance
Korrosionsermüdung *f* <Syn.: Schwingrißkorrosion *f*> corrosion fatigue <abb.: CF>
Ausfall *m* **durch Korrosionsermüdung** corrosion-fatigue failure
Korrosionsermüdungsriß *m* corrosion fatigue crack
Korrosionsermüdungsrißwachstum *n* corrosion fatigue crack growth
Korrosionsprodukt *n* corrosion product
korrosiv corrosive
korrosiver Verschleiß *m* corrosive wear
Kr → **Krypton**
Kraft *f* force
äußere Kraft *f* external force
innere Kraft *f* internal force
konstante Kraft *f* constant force
punktförmig angreifende Kraft *f* concentrated force
Kraftverlängerungskurve *f* load-extension curve
Kratzerbildung *f* <Syn.: Riefenbildung *f*> {Metalloberfläche} scoring {metal surface}
Kreis- circular
Kreisabschnittriß *m* part-circular crack
Kreisriß *m* <Syn.: kreisförmiger Riß> circular crack
Kreisrißbildung *f* circular-crack initiation
kreisbogenförmiger Riß *m* circular arc crack
kreisförmig <Syn.: kreisrund> circular

kreisförmiger Außenriß m circular external crack
kreisförmiger Innenriß m circular internal crack
kreisförmiger Riß m <Syn.: Kreisriß m> circular crack
kreisrund <Syn.: kreisförmig> circular
kreisrunde Bohrung f circular hole
kreisrunder Ersatzriß m circular equivalent crack
Kriechbedingungen fpl creep conditions pl
Kriechbereich m <Syn.: Kriechzone f> creep zone
Kriechbruch m <Syn.: Zeitstandbruch m> creep rupture, creep fracture
intergranularer Kriechbruch m intergranular creep rupture
Kriechbruchfestigkeit f creep-rupture strength
Kriechdehnung f creep strain
Kriechen n <Syn.: Fließen n> {Werkstoffe} creep {materials}
primäres Kriechen n primary creep
stationäres Kriechen n steady-state creep
kriechen <Syn.: fließen> {Werkstoffe} creep/to {materials}
Kriechfestigkeit f creep strength
Kriechgeschwindigkeit f creep rate
Kriechgrenze f creep limit
Kriechkurve f creep curve
Kriechriß m creep crack
Kriechrißausbreitung f creep crack propagation
Kriechrißbildung f creep cracking
Kriechrißwachstum n creep crack growth
Kriechtemperatur f creep temperature
Kriechverhalten n creep behavio[u]r
Kriechversuch m creep test

Kriechzone f <Syn.: Kriechbereich m> creep zone
Kristall m crystal
Kristallbaufehler m imperfection of crystal
Kristallebene f crystallographic plane
Kristallgitter n crystal lattice
kristallin crystalline
kristalliner Bruch m <Syn.: Trennbruch m> crystalline fracture
Kristallinität f crystallinity
kristallographisch crystallographic
kristallographisches Rißausbreitungsmodell n crystallographic crack-propagation model
Kristallstruktur f crystal structure
Kriterium n, Kriterien npl criterion, criteria pl
bruchmechanisches Kriterium n criterion for fracture mechanics
Kriterium n für die Rißbildung criterion of cracking
makroskopisches Kriterium n macroscopic criterion
mikroskopisches Kriterium n microscopic criterion
kritisch critical
kritische Anrißgröße f critical pre-crack size
kritische Bruchspannung f critical stress of fracture
kritische Dehnung f critical strain
kritische Energiefreisetzungsrate f critical energy release rate
kritische Fehlergröße f critical defect size
kritische Geschwindigkeit f critical velocity
kritische Größe f {eines Risses} critical size {of a crack}
kritische Last f critical load
kritische Rißabmessungen fpl critical crack dimensions pl
kritische Rißgröße f critical crack size

kritische Rißlänge *f* critical crack length
kritische Rißöffnungsverschiebung *f* critical crack opening displacement <abb: COD>
kritische Rißspitzenöffnung *f* critical crack tip opening
kritische Rißtiefe *f* critical crack depth
kritische Spannung *f* critical stress
kritische spezifische Bruchenergie *f* critical specific fracture energy
kritische Temperatur *f* critical temperatur
kritische Zugspannung *f* critical tensile stress
kritischer Spannungsintensitätsfaktor *m* critical stress-intensity factor
kritisches J-Integral *n* critical J-integral
Krümmung *f* <Syn.: Wölbung *f*> curvature
Krümmungsradius *m* {Rißende} radius of curvature {at the end of a crack}
Krypton *n*, Kr krypton, Kr
kubisch <Syn.: räumlich> cubic[al]
kubischer Ausdehnungskoeffizient *m* coefficient of cubic[al] expansion
kubischer Wärmeausdehnungskoeffizient *m* coefficient of cubical thermal expansion
kubisch-flächenzentriert <Abk.: kfz> {Metall} face-centered cubic <abb.: fcc> {metal}
kubisch-raumzentriert {Metall} body-centered cubic
Kugel- spherical
Kugelfallprobe *f* falling-weight test
Kugelfallprüfmaschine *f* {zur Bestimmung der Schlagzähigkeit} falling weight impact strength apparatus

kugelförmig spherical
kugelförmige Pore *f* spherical pore
Kühlbad *n* cooling bath
Kühlen *n* <Syn.: Abkühlen *n*> {Proben} cooling {specimens}
kühlen <Syn.: abkühlen> {Proben} cool/to {specimens}
Kühlereinheit *f* cooler unit
kumulativer Bruch *m* <Syn.: Zerrüttungsbruch *m*> cumulative fracture
künstlicher Riß *m* artificial crack
Kunststoff *m* plastic
biegsamer Kunststoff *m* flexible plastic
harter Kunststoff *m* rigid plastic
nicht gefüllter Kunststoff *m* unfilled plastic
weicher Kunststoff *m* non-rigid plastic
Kunststoffprobe *f* polymeric sample
Kupfer *n*, Cu copper, Cu
hochreines Kupfer *n* high-purity copper
Kupferlegierung *f* copper alloy
Kupfer-Nickel-Legierung *f* copper-nickel alloy
Kupfer-Wismut-Legierung *f* copper-bismuth alloy
Kupfer-Zink-Legierung *f* copper-zinc alloy
Kurve *f* <Syn.: Verlauf *m*> {Diagramme, Kennlinien} curve
Kurvenschar *f* family of curves
kurzer Ermüdungsriß *m* short fatigue crack
kurzer Riß *m* short crack
Kurzstabprobe *f* short bar specimen
Kurzzeitbeständigkeit *f* bei erhöhter Temperatur short-time stability at elevated temperatures
Kurzzeitprüfung *f* der mechanischen Eigenschaften short term mechanical testing

L

La → Lanthan
Laboratorium n < Syn.: Labor n >
  laboratory
Laborversuch m laboratory test
  Probe f für Laborversuche laboratory specimen
Lage f < Syn.: Ort m, Stelle f > location
lamellar lamellar
lamellares Gefüge n lamellar structure
Lamellierung f < Syn.: Schichtung f > lamination
Landatmosphäre f {Korrosion} rural atmosphere {corrosion}
lang long
Länge f length
  Länge f der plastischen Zone length of plastic zone
  freie Länge f {der eingespannten Probe} free length {of the clamped specimen}
  Riß m mit endlicher Länge, endlicher **Riß** m finite crack
  langer Riß m long crack
langgestreckt < Syn.: oval > oval
langgestreckte Grübchen npl {Grübchenbruch} elongated dimples pl {dimple fracture}
längliche Grübchen npl {Grübchenbruch} elongated dimples pl {dimple fracture}
Längs- longitudinal
Längsrichtung f longitudinal direction
  Brucheigenschaften fpl in Längsrichtung longitudinal fracture properties pl
Längsriß m longitudinal crack
Längsscherung f longitudinal shear, out-of-plane shear
Längsschwindung f linear shrinkage

langsames Rißwachstum n slow crack growth
Langzeit- < Syn.: Dauer- > permanent
Langzeitwärmeeinwirkung f < Syn.: Dauerwärmeeinwirkung f > permanent effect of heat {on plastics}
Lanthan n, **La** lanthanum, La
Last f < Syn.: Beanspruchung f > load
  äußere Last external load
  konstante Last f constant load
  kritische Last f critical load
  unter Last f < Syn.: beansprucht, belastet > loaded
Last-Verformungs-Diagramm n load-deformation diagram
Last-Verformungs-Kurve f load-deformation curve
Lastabfall m decreasing of load
Lastabsenkung f decreasing of load
Lastamplitude f load amplitude
  konstante Lastamplitude f constant load amplitude
Lastangriff m action of load
Lastangriffspunkt m load-application point
Lastaufbringung f load application
Lastbedingungen fpl < Syn.: Beanspruchungsverhältnisse npl, Beanspruchungsbedingungen fpl, Belastungsbedingungen fpl > loading conditions pl
lastfrei < Syn.: unbelastet > unloaded
lastfreier Zentralriß m unloaded central crack
Lastgrenze f < Syn.: Belastungsgrenze f > load limit
Lastkomponente f {z.B. eine Spannung} load component
Lastkonzentration f load concentration

Lastkonzentrationsfaktor *m* load concentration factor
Lastmaximum *n* <Syn.: **Höchstlast** *f*> maximum load
Lastniveau *n* <Syn.: **Laststufe** *f*> load level
Lastrichtung *f* <Syn.: **Beanspruchungsrichtung** *f*> direction of loading
Lastspiel *n* <Syn.: **Lastwechsel** *m*, **Lastzyklus** *m*> load cycle
Lastspielfrequenz *f* <Syn.: **Lastspielzahl** *f*> number of stress cycles
Lastspielzahl *f* <Syn.: **Lastspielfrequenz** *f*> number of stress cycles
Lastspitze *f* load peak
Laststufe *f* load increment
Lastüberhöhung *f* <Syn.: **Überlast** *f*, **Überlastung** *f*, **Überbeanspruchung** *f*> overload
Lastverschiebungskurve *f* load-displacement curve
nichtlineare Lastverschiebungskurve *f* non-linear load-displacement curve
Lastverteilung *f* <Syn.: **Verteilung** *f* **der Belastung**> load distribution
lineare Lastverteilung *f* linear load distribution
Lastwechsel *m* <Syn.: **Lastzyklus** *m*, **Lastspiel** *n*> load cycle
Lastwechselfrequenz *f* number of load cycles
Lastzyklus *m* <Syn.: **Lastspiel** *n*, **Lastwechsel** *m*> load cycle
laufen {Risse} run/to {cracks}
laufend <Syn.: **aktuell**> current
laufender Riß *m* <Syn.: **in Bewegung befindlicher Riß** *m*> moving crack, running crack
laugenrißbeständiger Stahl *m* steel resistant to caustic cracking

Laugenrissigkeit *f* {Spannungsrißkorrosion} caustic cracking, caustic embrittlement {stress-corrosion cracking}
Lebensdauer *f* life
Lebensdauerberechnung *f* calculation of service life
Lebensdauerermittlung *f* determination of service life
LEBM → **linear-elastische Bruchmechanik** *f*
LEBM-Konzept *n* <Syn.: **Konzept** *n* **der linear-elastischen Bruchmechanik**> linear-elastic fracture mechanics concept, LEFM concept
Leck-vor-Bruch-Bedingung *f* leak-before-break condition
Leck-vor-Bruch-Kriterium *n* leak-before-break criterion
Leck-vor-Bruch-Prüfung *f* leak-before-break test
Leck-vor-Bruch-Verhalten *n* leak-before-break behavio[u]r
Legieren *n* <Syn.: **Zulegieren** *n*> alloying
legierter Stahl *m* <Syn.: **Legierungsstahl** *m*> alloy steel
lichtbogengeschweißter legierter Stahl *m* arc-welded alloy steel
Legierung *f* alloy
alterungsfähige Legierung *f* age-hardenable alloy
austenitische Legierung *f* austenitic alloy
hochwarmfeste Legierung *f* high-temperature alloy
korrosionsbeständige Legierung *f* corrosion-resistant alloy
lichtbogengeschweißte hitzebeständige Legierung *f* arc-welded heat-resistant alloy
niedrigschmelzende Legierung *f* low-melting alloy
schweißbare Legierung *f* weldable alloy

Legierungselement

Legierungselement n alloying element
Legierungsstahl m < Syn.: legierter Stahl m > alloy steel
Legierungszusatz m alloying addition
Leichtmetallegierung f light alloy
Leitfähigkeit f conductivity
  Material n **mit geringer Leitfähigkeit** low-conductivity material
Leitfähigkeitsmessung f conductivity measurement
Li → Lithium
lichtbogengeschweißt arc-welded
lichtbogengeschweißter härtbarer Kohlenstoffstahl m arc-welded hardenable carbon steel
lichtbogengeschweißter kohlenstoffarmer Stahl m arc-welded low-carbon steel
lichtbogengeschweißte Aluminiumlegierung f arc-welded alumin[i]um alloy
lichtbogengeschweißte hitzebeständige Legierung f arc-welded heat-resistant alloy
lichtbogengeschweißte Titanlegierung f arc-welded titanium alloy
lichtbogengeschweißter legierter Stahl m arc-welded alloy steel
lichtbogengeschweißter nichtrostender Stahl m arc-welded stainless steel
lichtbogengeschweißtes Titan n arc-welded titanium
lichtdurchlässig < Syn.: transparent > transparent
Ligament n ligament
  rißfreies Ligament n uncracked ligament
Ligamentbreite f ligament width
Ligamentgröße f ligament size
ligamentunabhängig ligament-independent
linear linear

lineare Ausdehnung f linear expansion
Gerät n **zur Bestimmung der linearen Ausdehnung** linear expansion apparatus linear expansion measurement
Messung der f **linearen Ausdehnung** f linear expansion measurement
lineare Dehnungsverteilung f linear strain distribution
lineare Elastizität f linear elasticity
lineare Lastverteilung f linear load distribution
linearer Ausdehnungskoeffizient m coefficient of linear expansion
linearer Wärmeausdehnungskoeffizient m coefficient of linear thermal expansion
mittlerer linearer Wärmeausdehnungskoeffizient m average coefficient of linear thermal expansion
linear-elastisch linear-elastic
linear-elastische Bruchmechanik f < Abk.: LEBM > linear-elastic fracture mechanics < abb.: LEFM >
linear-elastische Lösung f linear-elastic solution
linear-elastische Spannungsintensität f linear-elastic stress intensity
linear-elastische Verfestigung f linear elastic hardening
linear-elastische Verformung f linear-elastic deformation
linear-elastischer Körper m linear-elastic body
linear-elastischer Werkstoff m linear-elastic material
linear-elastisches Bruchkriterium n linear elastic fracture criterion
linear-elastisches Bruchverhalten n linear-elastic fracture behavio[u]r
linear-elastisches Kontinuum n linear-elastic continuum

linear-elastisches Spannungsfeld *n* linear elastic stress field
linear-elastisches Verformungsfeld *n* linear elastic deformation field
zweidimensionales linear-elastisches Verformungsfeld *n* two-dimensional linear-elastic deformation field
linear-elastisches Verhalten *n* linear-elastic behavio[u]r
Linie *f* line
Linien *fpl* lines *pl*
Lüderssche Linien *fpl* < Syn.: Lüders-Streifen *mpl*, Fließlinien *fpl*> {inhomogenes Fließen} Hartmann lines *pl*, Piobert lines *pl*
Linien *fpl* < Syn.: Streifen *mpl*> marks *pl*
Lippen *fpl* lips *pl*
Lithium *n*, Li lithium, Li
Loch *n* < Syn.: Bohrung *f* >hole {e.g. in specimens}
Lochfraß *m* {Korrosion} pitting {corrosion}
lokal < Syn.: örtlich > local
lokale Belastungsgeschwindigkeit *f* local load rate
lokale Belastungsgrenze *f* local load limit
lokale Bruchdehung *f* local fracture strain
lokale Rißausbreitung *f* local crack propagation
lokale Spannungskomponente *f* local stress component
lokale Verschiebung *f* local displacement
lokaler Rißwiderstand *m* < Syn.: örtlicher Rißwiderstand *m*> local crack resistance
lokales Fließen *n* < Syn.: örtliches Fließen *n*> local yielding
lokales Spannungsfeld *n* local stress field
longitudinal longitudinal

Longitudinalwelle *f* longitudinal wave
Lösung *f* solution
linear-elastische Lösung *f* linear-elastic solution
Lüders-Streifen *mpl* < Syn.: Lüdersche Linien *fpl*, Fließlinien *fpl*> {inhomogenes Fließen} Piobert lines *pl*, Hartmann lines *pl* {inhomogeneous yielding}
Luft *f* air
Lufttemperatur *f* air temperature
Lunker *m* {Fehler} shrinkage cavity {defect}

M

Magnesium *n*, Mg magnesium, Mg
Magnesiumlegierung *f* magnesium alloy
Magnetpulverprüfung *f* magnetic powder testing {detection of cracks}
Makrobruch *m* macrofailure
Makrofehler *m* macrodefect, macroflaw
Makrofraktographie *f* macrofractography
Makrogefüge *f* < Syn.: makroskopisches Gefüge *n*> {Metall} macrostructure {metal}
Makrolunker *m* macroshrinkage
Makromorphologie *f* {Bruchfläche} macromorphology {fracture surface}
Makroriß *m* {Anrisse, Kerbe, Risse} macrocrack {pre-cracks, notches, cracks}
makroskopisch macroscopic
makroskopische Bruchausbreitungsrichtung *f* macroscopic direction of fracture propagation
makroskopische Brucherscheinung *f* < Syn.: makroskopisches Bruchbild *n*> macroscopic fracture appearance

Makroverformung

makroskopische Bruchflächenbewertung f macroscopic evaluation of fracture surface
makroskopische Rißausbreitungsrichtung f macroscopic direction of crack propagation
makroskopischer Kerb m macroscopic notch
makroskopischer Riß m macroscopic crack
makroskopischer Spannungsintensitätsfaktor m macroscopic stress-intensity factor
makroskopischer Spannungszustand m macroscopic state of stress
makroskopisches Bruchbild n <Syn.: makroskopische Brucherscheinung f > macroscopic fracture appearance
makroskopisches Bruchkriterium n macroscopic fracture criterion
makroskopisches Bruchmerkmal n macroscopic characteristic of fracture
makroskopisches Gefüge n <Makrogefüge f> {Metall} macrostructure {metal}
makroskopisches Kriterium n macroscopic criterion
makroskopisches Rißwachstum n macroscopic crack growth
Makroverformung f {Verformung im Makrobereich} macrodeformation
Mangan n, Mn manganese, Mn
Manganstahl m manganese steel
austenitischer Manganstahl m austenitic manganese steel
Marke f mark
Markierung f <Syn.: Kennzeichnung f> {auf der Probe} mark {on the specimen}
Martens-Prüfung f {Prüfung der Formbeständigkeit in der Wärme} Marten's test

Martens-Zahl {zur Kennzeichnung der Formbeständigkeit in der Wärme} Marten's temperature
Martensit m {Stahl} martensite {steel}
martensitischer nichtrostender Stahl m martensitic stainless steel
Maß n {für Eigenschaften} measure {of properties}
Maßänderung f dimensional change
Maschine f (i.e.s.) Prüfmaschine f machine
Maschine f zur Prüfung der Verformung <Syn.: Verformungs-Prüfmaschine f> deformation testing machine
Masse f <Syn.: Gewicht n> mass; weight
Masseänderung f weight change
Masseverlust m bei Erwärmung {in Prozent} loss in weight on heating {in percent}
Masseverlustprüfung f weight loss test
Material n material
Material n mit geringer Leitfähigkeit low-conductivity material
Stoßfestigkeit f {von Materialien} shock resistance {of materials}
Materialprüfung f <Syn.: Werkstoffprüfung f> materials testing, testing of materials
Matrix f matrix
duktile Matrix f ductile matrix
maximal maximum
maximale Druckfestigkeit f maximum compressive strength
maximale Rißgeschwindigkeit f maximum crack velocity
maximaler Rißwiderstand m maximum crack resistance
Maximalbeanspruchung f <Syn.: Höchstlast f, Lastmaximum n> maximum load
Maximalspannung f maximum stress
Maximum n maximum

Mechanik f mechanics
mechanisch mechanical
mechanische Eigenschaften fpl mechanical properties pl
mechanische Instabilität f {z.B. Knicken oder Einschnüren} mechanical instability
mechanische Prüfmethode f mechanical test method
mechanische Prüfung f mechanical test
mechanische Spannung f mechanical stress
mechanische Überlastung f mechanical overload
mechanischer Abbau m mechanical degradation
mechanisches Verhalten n mechanical behavio[u]r
Mechanismus m **der Rißbildung** cracking mechanism
Mechanismus m {Vorgang} <Syn.: Vorrichtung f> mechanism
Medium n, **Medien** npl medium
anisotropes Medium n anisotropic medium
Meeresatmosphäre f <Syn.: Seeatmosphäre f> {Korrosion} marine atmosphere {corrosion}
mehrachsig multiaxial
mehrachsige Spannung f multiaxial stress
mehrachsige Zugbeanspruchung f multiaxial tensile load
mehrachsiger Spannungszustand m multiaxial stress state, multiaxial state of stress
Mehrachsigkeit f multiaxiality
mehrfach <Syn.: vielfach> multiple
Mehrfach- multiple
Mehrfachgleitung f multiple slip
Mehrfachlastweg m multiple load path

Mehrfachriß m <Syn.: verzweigter Riß m> branched crack
Mehrstufenversuch m multistage test
Meißelstahl m chisel steel
Merkmal n <Syn.: Kennzeichen n, Charakteristik f> characteristic
Meßgenauigkeit f {eines Gerätes} precision, accuracy {of the apparatus}
Meßmarke f {an Proben} ga[u]ge mark {on specimens}
messen measure/to
Messen n measuring
Messing n brass
Messung f measurement
direkte Messung f direct measurement
gleichzeitige Messung f <Syn.: Parallelmessung f> simultaneous measurement
Messung f **der linearen Ausdehnung** linear expansion measurement
Messung f **der Schlagbiegefestigkeit** flexural impact strength measurement
Messung f **der Schlagfestigkeit** impact resistance measurement
Messung f **der Tragfähigkeit** bearing measurement
Messung f **für Schlagzugfestigkeit** tensile impact strength measurement
Messung f **unter Biegebeanspruchung** bending measurement
Messung f **unter Scherbeanspruchung** shear measurement
stationäre Messung f {Leitfähigkeit} steady state measurement {of conductivity}
Meßverfahren n measurement technique
experimentelles Meßverfahren n experimental method of measurement
Metall n metal
Metall- metallic
Metallbeschichtung f metal coating

Metalle

Metalle *npl* metals *pl*
  hochreine Metalle *npl* high-purity metals *pl*
metallisch metallic
  metallischer Werkstoff *m* metallic material
Metallographie *f* metallography
Methode *f* method
  bruchmechanische Methode *f* method of fracture mechanics
  photoelastische < Syn.: **spannungsoptische**> **Methode** *f* photoelastic method
Mg → Magnesium
Mikro-Dilatometer *n* microdilatometer
Mikroanalyse *f* microanalysis
Mikrobereich *m* microscale
  Mikroverformung *f* {Verformung im Mikrobereich} microdeformation
Mikrobruch *m* microfracture
Mikrobruchfläche *f* microfracture surface
Mikrodehnung *f* microstrain
mikroduktil microductile
  mikroduktile Rißausbreitung *f* microductile crack propagation
  mikroduktiler Bruch *m* microductile fracture
Mikrofehler *m* microdefect, microflaw
Mikrofraktographie *f* microfractography
Mikrogefüge *n* < Syn.: **Feinstruktur** *f*, **Mikrostruktur** *f*> microstructure
Mikrohohlraum *m* microvoid
Mikrolunker *m* microshrinkage
Mikropore *f* micropore
Mikroriß *m* microcrack
  aufgefangener Mikroriß *m* arrested microcrack, stopped microcrack
  instabiler Mikroriß *m* unstable microcrack
  interkristalliner Mikroriß *m* intercrystalline microcrack
  stabiler Mikroriß *m* stable microcrack
  transkristalliner Mikroriß *m* transcrystalline microcrack
Mikrorißbildung *f* microcrack formation, formation of microcracks
Mikroskop *n* microscope
Mikroskopie *f* microscopy
mikroskopisch microscopic
  mikroskopische Bruchform *f* microscopic type of fracture
  mikroskopische Bruchspannung *f* microscopic fracture stress
  mikroskopische Rißverzweigung *f* microscopic crack branching
  mikroskopische Spaltbruchfestigkeit *f* microscopic cleavage-fracture strength
  mikroskopischer Kerb *m* microscopic notch
  mikroskopischer Riß *m* microscopic crack
  mikroskopisches Bruchkriterium *n* microscopic fracture criterion
  mikroskopisches Bruchmerkmal *n* microscopic characteristic of fracture
  mikroskopisches Bruchverhalten *n* microscopic fracture behavio[u]r
  mikroskopisches Kriterium *n* microscopic criterion
Mikrosondenanalyse *f* electron probe microanalysis < abb.: EPMA>
Mikrospaltriß *m* micro-cleavage crack
Mikrostruktur *f* < Syn.: **Feinstruktur** *f*, **Mikrogefüge** *n*> microstructure
Mikroverformung *f* {Verformung im Mikrobereich} microdeformation
Mikroverformungstensor *m* microdeformation tensor
Mindest- minimum
  Mindestabmessungen *fpl* {Proben} minimum dimensions *pl* {specimens}

Mindestbreite f {Proben} minimum width {specimens}
Mindestbruchlast minimum load for fracture
Mindestdicke f {Proben} minimum thickness {specimens}
Mindestprobenbreite f minimum specimen width
Mindestprobendicke f minimum specimen thickness
Mindestrißgeschwindigkeit f{für die Verzweigung} minimum crack speed {for branching}
minimal minimal
  minimale Betriebstemperatur f minimum service temperature
  minimale Bruchzähigkeit f minimum fracture toughness
Minimal- minimal
Minimalbruchzähigkeit f minimum fracture toughness
Minimalspannung f minimum stress
Minimum n minimum
Mischbruch m mixed-mode fracture
Mitte f < Syn.: Mittelpunkt m > center {US}, centre {GB}
  in der Mitte gekerbte Zugprobe f center-notched tensile specimen
Mittel n < Syn.: Mittelwert m, Durchschnitt m > {Mathematik} average {mathematics}
Mittel- average...
Mittellast f average load
Mittel- mean
Mitteldehnung f mean strain
mittelgekohlter Stahl m medium-carbon steel
Mittellinienlunkerung f center line shrinkage
Mittelpunkt m center {US}, centre {GB}
Mittelriß m center crack
  Flachprobe f **mit Mittelriß** center-cracked flat specimen
  Flachzugprobe f **mit Mittelriß** center-cracked flat tensile specimen
  Probe f **mit Mittelriß** {Zugprobe} center-cracked specimen {tensile specimen}
  Zugprobe f **mit Mittelriß** < Syn.: **mittig angerissene Zugprobe** f> center-cracked tensile <abb.: CCT> specimen
Mittelrißprobe f < Syn.: CCT-Probe f> {Zugprobe} center-cracked tension <abb.: CCT>
Mittelspannung f mean stress
Mittelwert m < Syn.: Mittel n, Durchschnitt m > {Mathematik} average {mathematics}
Mittenriß m center crack
mittig < Syn.: konzentrisch > concentric
  mittig angerissene Zugprobe f < Syn.: Zugprobe f mit Mittelriß > center-cracked tensile <abb.: CCT> specimen
mittig < Syn.: in der Mitte > central
  mittlere Probe f {von mehreren nebeneinander angeordneten Proben} central specimen
  mittlere Rißlänge f average crack length
  mittlere Spannungsintensität average stress intensity
  mittlere Verbrennungsgeschwindigkeit f average burning rate
mittlerer mean
  mittlerer linearer Wärmeausdehnungskoeffizient m average coefficient of linear thermal expansion
Mn → Mangan
Mo → Molybdän
Modell n model
  nichtlineares Modell n nonlinear model
modellieren simulate/to
Modellierung f simulation
Modellversuch m model test

Modifikation

Modifikation f <Syn.: Abänderung f> modification
modifizieren <Syn.: abändern> modify/to
Modul m, Moduln mpl modulus, moduli pl
Modus m {z.B. Art und Weise der Beanspruchung} mode
Moiré-Linienmuster n {Spannungsoptik} moiré fringes
Moiré-Muster n {Spannungsoptik} moiré pattern
Moiré-Verfahren n {Spannungsoptik} moiré technique
Molybdän n, Mo molybdenum, Mo
Moment n {Mechanik} moment {mechanics}
monoton monotonic
monotone Beanspruchung f monotonic loading
monotone Belastung f monotonic loading
Montage f <Syn.: Aufbau m, Anordnung f> assembly
muldenförmige Grübchen npl {Bruchfläche} shallow dimples pl {fracture surface}
münzförmiger Riß m <Syn.: pfennigförmiger Riß m> penny-shaped crack
Muschelbruch m conchoidal fracture
Muster n <Syn.: Bild n, Anordnung f> pattern

N

Na → Natrium
Nachgiebigkeit f compliance
  elastische Nachgiebigkeit f elastic compliance
  normierte Nachgiebigkeit f normalized compliance
  theoretische Nachgiebigkeit f theoretical compliance
Nachgiebigkeitsmessung f compliance measurement
Nachschwindung f after-shrinkage
Nachweis m {z.B. von Rissen in Werkstoffen} detection {e.g. of cracks in materials}
nachweisbar detectable
  nachweisbare Rißtiefe f detectable crack depth
  nachweisbarer Riß m detectable crack
Nachweisbarkeit f detectability
nachweisen {z.B. Risse in Werkstoffen} detect/to {e.g. cracks in materials}
Nadelstichpore f {Metalloberfläche} pinhole {metal surface}
nahe near
Nähe f <Syn.: Umfeld n> vicinity, neighbo[u]rhood
  in der Nähe der Rißspitze near crack tip
nähern {Mathematik} approximate/to {mathematics}
Näherung f {Mathematik} approximation {mathematics}
Näherungslösung f approximation solution
Natrium n, Na sodium, Na
natürliche Anisotropie f inherent anisotropy
Nb → Niob
Nd → Neodym
NDT-Temperatur f {Grenztemperatur, bei der ein Riß nicht mehr aufgehalten werden kann} nil ductility temperature <abb.: NDT>
Ne → Neon
NE-Metalle npl <Syn.: Nichteisenmetalle npl> nonferrous metals pl
Neben- secondary
  Nebenachse f {Ellipse} minor axis {ellipse}
  Nebenriß m <Syn.: Sekundärriß m> secondary crack

Nebenrißlänge f secondary-crack length, branching-crack length
Nenn- <Syn.: Nominal-> nominal
Nenndehnung f nominal strain
Nennfestigkeit f nominal strength
Nennscherspannung f nominal shear stress
Nennspannung f <Syn.: Nominalspannung f> nominal stress
Nennzugfestigkeit f nominal tensile strength
Neodym n, Nd neodymium, Nd
Neon n, Ne neon, Ne
Ni → Nickel
Niblink-Versuch m {Rißeinleitungstemperatur} Niblink test {crack-initiation temperature}
nichtaustenitischer Stahl m non-austenitic steel
Nichtbrennbarkeit f non-combustibility
Prüfung f der Nichtbrennbarkeit (Unbrennbarkeit) non-combustibility test
Nichteisenmetalle npl <Syn.: NE-Metalle npl> nonferrous metals pl
Nichteisenmetallegierungen fpl nonferrous alloys pl
nichtkristallin non-crystalline
nichtkumulativer Bruch m non-cumulative fracture
nichtlinear non-linear
nichtlineare Bruchmechanik f nonlinear fracture
nichtlineare Elastizität f nonlinear elasticity
nichtlineare Lastverschiebungskurve f non-linear load-displacement curve
nichtlineares Modell n nonlinear model
nichtlineares Rißproblem n non-linear crack problem

nichtlinear-elastische Bruchmechanik f nonlinear elastic fracture mechanics
Nichtlinearität f non-linearity
nichtmetallisch nonmetallic
nichtmetallischer Einschluß m nonmetallic inclusion
nichtmetallischer Werkstoff m nonmetallic material
nichtrostend <Syn.: rostfrei> stainless
nichtrostender Stahl m stainless steel
ausscheidungshärtender nichtrostender Stahl m precipitation-hardening stainless steel
austenitischer nichtrostender Stahl m austenitic stainless steel
ferritischer nichtrostender Stahl m ferritic stainless steel
lichtbogengeschweißter nichtrostender Stahl m arc-welded stainless steel
martensitischer nichtrostender Stahl m martensitic stainless steel
superplastischer nichtrostender Stahl m superplastic stainless steel
nichtsingulare Spannung f nonsingular stress
Nickel n, Ni nickel, Ni
Nickel-Chrom-Molybdän-Vanadium-Stahl m nickel-chromium-molybdenum-vanadium steel
Nickel-Kupfer-Legierung f nickel-copper alloy
Nickel-Molybdän-Vanadium-Legierung f nickel-molybdenum-vanadium alloy
Nickellegierung f nickel alloy
Niederdruck-Verformungsprüfgerät n low-pressure deformation tester
niederzyklisch low-cycle
niederzyklische Ermüdung f low-cycle fatigue
niedrig <Syn.: gering> low

niedriglegiert

niedriglegierter Stahl *m* low-alloy steel
niedrigschmelzende Legierung *f* low-melting alloy
Niedrigspannungsbruch *m* low-stress fracture
Niob *n*, **Nb** niobium, Nb, columbium, Cb
Niob[ium]legierung *f* niobium alloy
nitriergehärteter Stahl *m* nitrided steel
nitrierter Stahl *m* nitrided steel
Niveau *n* <Syn.: **Stufe** *f*> level
Nominal- <Syn.: **Nenn-**> nominal
Nominalspannung *f* <Syn.: **Nennspannung** *f*> nominal stress
nominell nominal
Norm *f* <Syn.: **Standard** *m*> standard
Norm-Probe *f* <Syn.: **genormte Probe** *f*> standard |test| specimen
Norm-Prüfverfahren *n* standard test
Norm-Versuch *m* <Syn.: **genormter Versuch** *m*> standard test
normal <Syn.: **senkrecht**> normal
Normaldehnung *f* normal strain
Normale *f* <Syn.: **Senkrechte** *f*> normal
Normalkraft *f* normal force
Normalspannung *f* normal stress
Normalspannungshypothese *f* hypothesis of normal stresses
Normalspannungskomponente *f* normal stress component, normal component of stress
Normalspannungskriterium *n* criterion of normal stresses
Normalspannungsverteilung *f* normal stress distribution
Normaltemperatur *f* normal temperature
normieren {Mathematik} normalize/to {mathematics}
normiert normalized

normierte Korrekturfunktion *f* normalized correction function
normierte Nachgiebigkeit *f* normalized compliance
normierte Rißöffnung *f* normalized crack extension
normierte Spannung *f* generalized stress
normierte Umfangsspannung *f* normalized circumferential stress
Normierung *f* {Mathematik} normalization {mathematics}
Normprüfverfahren *n* <Syn.: **genormtes Prüfverfahren** *n*> standard test
Normtemperatur *f* standard temperature
Normung *f* standardization
Null *f* zero
Nullage *f* <Syn.: **Nullstellung** *f*> zero position
Nullpunkt *m* zero point
Nullstellung *f* <Syn.: **Nullage** *f*> zero position

O

O → Sauerstoff
obere upper
 obere Fließgrenze *f* upper yield point
Oberfläche *f* surface
 Brandverhalten *n* **der Oberfläche** surface burning characteristics *pl*
 Entflammbarkeit *f* **der Oberfläche** surface flammability {of materials}
 fehlerhafte Oberfläche *f* defect surface
 freie Oberfläche *f* free surface
 gebrochene Oberfläche *f* <Syn.: **Bruchfläche** *f*> fractured surface
 gekerbte Oberfläche *f* {von Proben} notched surface {of the specimen}
 korrodierte Oberfläche *f* corroded surface

Rißbildung f auf der Oberfläche {von Proben} surface cracking {of the specimen}
Oberflächen-Rißöffnungs-Verschiebung f surface crack opening displacement <abb.: SCOD>
Oberflächenbehandlung f surface treatment
Oberflächenbeschichtung f surface coating
Oberflächendefekt m surface defect
Oberflächenenergie f surface energy
  effektive Oberflächenenergie f effective surface energy
  spezifische Oberflächenenergie f specific surface energy
  wahre Oberflächenenergie f true surface energy
Oberflächenfehler m surface flaw
  halbelliptischer Oberflächenfehler m semi-elliptical surface flaw
  Probe f mit Oberflächenfehler m surface flaw specimen
Oberflächenhärte f surface hardness
Oberflächenkerb m surface notch
Oberflächenkraft f surface force
Oberflächenmikroriß m surface microcrack
Oberflächenrauheit f surface roughness
Oberflächenriß m surface crack
  elliptischer Oberflächenriß m elliptical surface crack
  flacher Oberflächenriß m shallow surface crack
  halbelliptischer Oberflächenriß m semi-elliptical surface crack
  rechteckiger Oberflächenriß m rectangular surface crack
  schubbeanspruchter Oberflächenriß m <Syn.: scherbeanspruchter> shear-loaded surface crack
  zugbeanspruchte Probe f mit Oberflächenriß <Syn.: SCT-Probe f> surface-crack tensile <abb.: SCT-specimen>
  zugbelasteter Oberflächenriß m tensile-loaded surface crack
Oberflächenrißlänge f surface-crack length
Oberflächenrißverhalten n surface-crack behavio[u]r
Oberflächenspannung f surface tension
Oberflächentemperatur f surface temperature
Oberflächenverfestigung f hardening
Oberflächenwelle f surface wave
Oberspannung f {Dauerbiegeversuch} maximum stress {fatigue test}
offen open
  offener Riß m open crack
Öffnung f opening
optisch optical
  optische Prüfmethode f optical test method
  optische Rißlängenmessung f optical measurement of crack length
Orientierung f orientation
  Orientierung f der Rißebene crack plane orientation
Ort m <Syn.: Stelle f, Anordnung f, Lage f> location
orthotrop orthotropic
  orthotrope Platte f orthotropic plate
  orthotropes Rißsystem n orthotropic crack system
Orthotropie f orthotropy
örtlich <Syn.: lokal> local
  örtliche Spannungsrelaxation f local stress relaxation
  örtlicher Rißwiderstand m <Syn.: lokaler Rißwiderstand m> local crack resistance
  örtlicher Spannungsfaktor m local stress factor

örtliches Fließen *n* < Syn.: lokales Fließen *n* > local yielding
Os → Osmium
Osmium *n*, Os osmium, Os
oval < Syn.: langgestreckt > oval
ovaler Riß *m* oval crack
ovales Grübchen *n* {Grübchenbruch} oval dimple {dimple rupture}
Oxidation *f* oxidation
innere Oxidation *f* {Korrosionsprodukte} internal oxidation, subsurface corrosion {corrosion products}
oxidativ oxidative
oxidativer Verschleiß *m* {Oxidfilm} oxidative wear {oxide film}

P

P → Phosphor
Palladium *n*, Pd palladium, Pa
Parabel- parabolic
Parabelkerbe *f* parabolic notch
parabelförmig < Syn.: parabolisch > parabolic
parabolisch < Syn.: parabelförmig > parabolic
parallel parallel
paralleler Riß *m* parallel crack
Parallelmessung *f* < Syn.: gleichzeitige Messung *f* > simultaneous measurement
Parameter *m* < Syn.: Kennwert *m*, Kenngröße *f* > parameter
partiell < Syn.: teilweise > partial
partielle Entlastung *f* partial unloading
Pb → Blei
Pd → Palladium
Peak *n* < Syn.: Spitze *f* > peak
Pendel *n* < Syn.: Schlagpendel *n* > {Pendelschlagwerk} striker {pendulum impact tester}
Pendelhammer *m* impact pendulum

Pendelschlagversuch *m* nach Charpy < Syn.: Charpy-Pendelschlagversuch *m* > Charpy (impact) test
Pendelschlagwerk *n* pendulum impact tester, pendulum machine
peripher circumferential
peripherer Ermüdungsriß *m* {Korrosion} circumferential corrosion-fatigue crack
Peripherie *f* circumference
Perlit *m* pearlite
perlitisch pearlitic
perlitischer Stahl *m* pearlitic steel
perlitisches duktiles Eisen *n* pearlitic ductile iron
Pfad *m* < Syn.: Bahn *f*, Weg *m* > path
pfennigförmiger Riß *m* < Syn.: münzförmiger Riß *m* > penny-shaped crack
Phänomen *n* < Syn.: Erscheinung *f* > phenomenon
Phänomenologie *f* phenomenology
Phase *f* < Syn.: Stadium *n* > phase
Phasengrenze *f* phase boundary
Phosphor *m*, P phosphorus, P
photoelastisch < Syn.: spannungsoptisch > photoelastic
photoelastische Methode *f* photoelastic method
Photoelastizität *f* < Syn.: Spannungsoptik *f* > photoelasticity
physikalisch physical
physikalische Bedingungen *fpl* {einer Prüfung} physical conditions *pl* {of the test}
physikalische Eigenschaften *fpl* physical properties *pl*
physikalische Rißlänge *f* physical crack length
physikalischer Riß *m* physical crack
Planimetrie *f* {Flächenmessung} planimetry
plastisch {Werkstoff} plastic {material}

plastische Deformation f (**Verformung** f) plastic deformation
plastische Dehnung f plastic strain
plastische Dehnungsbehinderung f plastic strain constraint
plastische Dehnungsgeschwindigkeit f < Syn.: **Geschwindigkeit** f **der plastischen Dehnung** > rate of plastic straining
plastische Grenzlast f plastic limit load
plastische Instabilität f plastic instability
plastische Rißausbreitung f plastic crack propagation
plastische Rißspitzenaufweitung f plastic crack-tip extension
plastische Singularität f plastic singularity
plastische Spannung f plastic stress
plastische Verformung f plastic deformation
zyklische plastische Verformung f cyclic plastic deformation
plastische Verformungsenergie f energy of plastic deformation
plastische Zone f plastic zone
Berandung f {**der plastischen Zone**} interface {of plastic zone}
dimensionslose plastische Zone f dimensionless plastic zone
effektive plastische Zone f effective plastic zone
Form f **der plastischen Zone** plastic zone form
Größe f **der plastischen Zone** plastic zone size
Länge f **der plastischen Zone** length of plastic zone
Radius m **der plastischen Zone** radius of the plastic zone
Verlängerung f **der plastischen Zone** plastic zone elongation
plastischer Bereich m plastic region

Plastizität

plastischer Dehnungskonzentrationsfaktor m plastic strain concentration factor
plastischer Kollaps m < Syn.: **plastisches Versagen** n > plastic collaps
plastischer Spannungskonzentrationsfaktor m plastic stress-concentration factor
plastisches Fließen n plastic yielding; plastic flow
plastisches Verhalten n plastic behavio[u]r
plastisches Versagen n < Syn.: **plastischer Kollaps** m > plastic collaps, plastic failure
Plastizität f plasticity
ideale Plastizität f ideal plasticity
Plastizitätskorrektur f {**Rißlänge**} plasticity correction {crack length}
Plastizitätstheorie f plasticity theory
Platin n, Pt platinum, Pt
Platin-Gallium-Legierung f platinum-gallium alloy
Platin-Kohlenstoff-Legierung f platinum-carbon alloy
Platin-Rhodium-Legierung f platinum-rhodium alloy
Platte f < Syn.: **Blech** n, **Scheibe** f > plate
gekerbte Platte f notched plate
gerissene Platte f cracked plate
geschweißte Platte f welded plate
orthotrope Platte f orthotropic plate
Platte f **mit durchgehendem Riß** through-cracked plate
rechteckige Platte f rectangular plate
Plattenbreite f < Syn.: **Scheibenbreite** f > plate width
Plattendicke f < Syn.: **Blechdicke** f, **Scheibendicke** f > plate thickness
plattenförmige Probe f plate specimen
Plattenwerkstoff m sheet material

Plutonium

Plutonium-Gallium-Legierung *f* plutonium-gallium alloy
Poissonsche Konstante *f* < Syn.: **Querkontraktionszahl** *f*> Poisson's ratio
polar {Mathematik} polar {mathematics}
Polar- {Mathematik} polar {mathematics}
Polarkoordinaten *fpl* {Mathematik} polar coordinates *pl* {mathematics}
polieren {eine Probe} polish/to {a specimen}
polykristallin polycrystalline
polykristalliner Werkstoff *m* polycrystalline material
Polymer *n* < Syn.: **Polymeres** *n* > polymer
pop-in {plötzliche Rißinitiation, Rißeinbruch} pop-in {the first discrete crack extension}
Pore *f* {in Werkstoffen} void {in materials} Hohlraum *m*
kugelförmige Pore *f* spherical pore
prismatische Pore *f* prismatic void
zylindrische Pore *f* cylindrical pore
Porenbildung void formation
Porendurchmesser *m* void diameter
Porenwachstum *n* void growth
porig < Syn.: **porös** > porous
Porigkeit *f* < Syn.: **Porosität** *f*> porosity
porös < Syn.: **porig** > porous
Porosität *f* < Syn.: **Porigkeit** *f*> porosity
Position *f* < Syn.: **Lage** *f*, **Stelle** *f*> position
positiv positive
positive Druckbeanspruchung *f* positive compression
positive Spitzenlast *f* positive peak load
Potential- potential...

Potentialsondenverfahren *n* {Rißtiefenbestimmung} electric potential method {determination of crack depth}
potentiell potential
potentielle Energie *f* potential energy
potentieller Riß *m* potential crack
Potentiometer *m* potentiometer
primäres Kriechen *n* primary creep
Prinzip *n* principle
prismatisch prismatic
prismatische Pore *f* prismatic void
probabilistisch {auf der Wahrscheinlichkeitstheorie beruhend} probabilistic
probabilistische Bruchmechanik *f* probabilistic fracture mechanics
Probe *f* < Syn.:**Probekörper** *m*, **Prüfkörper** *m*> specimen; [test] sample
Anfangsdicke *f* {der Probe zu Beginn der Prüfung} initial thickness {of specimen}
angerissene Probe *f* < Syn.: **Probe** *f* **mit Anriß** > {Prüfung} pre-cracked specimen
aus zwei Werkstoffen bestehende Probe *f* bimaterial specimen
befestigte Probe *f* < Syn.: **befestigter Körper** *m*> mounted specimen
Bruchebene *f* **der Probe** specimen fracture plane
dünne Probe *f* thin specimen
Enddicke *f* {der Probe nach Beendigung der Prüfung} final thickness {of specimen}
eingespannte Probe *f* clamped specimen
gekerbte Probe *f* notched specimen
gekerbte Probe *f* < Syn.: **gekerbter Probekörper** *m*> notched {test} specimen
genormte Probe *f* < Syn.: **Norm-Probe** *f*> standard [test] specimen

Probebelastung

glatte Probe *f* {ungekerbt} smooth specimen {unnotched}
großflächige Probe *f* large-area specimen
harte (starre) Probe *f* rigid specimen
"jungfräuliche" Probe *f* new specimen
mittlere Probe *f* {von mehreren nebeneinander angeordneten Proben} central specimen
nicht-versprödete Probe *f* nonembrittled specimen
plattenförmige Probe *f* plate specimen
Probe *f* **für den Druckversuch** compression specimen
Probe *f* **für den Fallgewichtsversuch** < Syn.: **Probe** *f* **für den DWT-Versuch** > drop-weight test < abb.: DWT > specimen
Probe *f* **für den Fallgewichtsscherversuch** < Syn.: **Probe für den DWTT-Versuch** > drop-weight tear test < abb.: DWTT > specimen
Probe *f* **für den Explosions-Beulungsversuch** explosion tear test < abb.: ETT > specimen
Probe *f* **für Laborversuche** laboratory specimen
Probe *f* **mit Anriß** < Syn.: **angerissene Probe** *f* > pre-cracked specimen {testing}
Probe *f* **mit Chevron-Kerbe** Chevron notched specimen
Probe *f* **mit durchgehendem Riß** through-thickness crack specimen
Probe *f* **mit einseitigem Kerb** single-edge notch specimen
Probe *f* **mit Mittelkerb** center-notched specimen, centrally notched specimen
Probe *f* **mit Mittelriß** {Zugprobe} center-cracked specimen {tensile specimen}
Probe *f* **mit Oberflächenfehler** surface flaw specimen
Probe *f* **mit "Schlüsselloch"-Kerb** {Charpy-Versuch} keyhole-notch specimen {Charpy test}
streifenförmige Probe *f* < Syn.: **Streifenprobe** *f* > strip specimen
temperierte Probe *f* < Syn.: **wärmebehandelte Probe** *f* > heat treated specimen
transparente Probe *f* transparent specimen
ungekerbte Probe *f* < Syn.: **ungekerbter Probekörper** *m* > unnotched (test) specimen
versprödete Probe *f* embrittled specimen
vorgewärmte < Syn.: **angewärmte** > **Probe** *f* pre-heated specimen
wärmebehandelte Probe *f* < Syn.: **temperierte Probe** *f* > heat-treated specimen
zellige < Syn.: **porige** > **Probe** *f* cellular specimen
zugbeanspruchte Probe *f* **mit Oberflächenriß** < Syn.: **SCT-Probe** *f* > surface-crack tensile < abb.: SCT > specimen
Probebelastung *f* < Syn.: **probeweise Belastung** *f* > trial loading
Probeinneres *n* inner zone of specimen
Probekörper *m* < Syn.: **Prüfkörper** *n*, **Probe** *f* > specimen
befestigter Probekörper *m* < Syn.: **befestigte Probe** *f* > mounted specimen
gekerbter Probekörper *m* < Syn.: **gekerbte Probe** *f* > notched {test} specimen
(mechanisch) bearbeiteter Probekörper *m* machined specimen
ungekerbter Probekörper *m* < Syn.: **ungekerbte Probe** *f* > unnotched {test} specimen

Probenabmessungen 226

Probenabmessungen *fpl* specimen dimensions *pl*
Probenart *f* <Syn.: Probentyp *m*> type of specimen
Probenbelastung *f* loading of specimen
Probenberandung *f* <Syn.: Probenrand *m*> edge of the specimen
Probenbereich *m* specimen area
Probenbreite *f* specimen width, width of specimen
Probendicke *f* specimen thickness, thickness of specimen, sample thickness
Probenende *n* end of the specimen
Probenfläche *f* specimen area
Probenform *f* specimen design, form of specimen
Probengeometrie *f* specimen geometry
Probengröße *f* specimen size
Probenhalter *m* sample holder
Probenhalterung *f* sample holder
Probenkonfiguration *f* specimen configuration
Probenlage *f* location of specimen
Probenmitte *f* <Syn.: Probenmittelpunkt *m*> center of specimen
Probenmittelebene *f* middle plane of specimen
Probenmittelpunkt *m* center of specimen
Probenoberfläche *f* specimen surface
Probenorientierung *f* orientation of specimen
Probenquerschnitt *m* specimen cross-section
Probenrand *m* <Syn.: Probenberandung *f*> edge of the specimen
Probenseite *f* side surface of the specimen
Probenstirnseite *f* end face of the specimen
Probentemperatur *f* temperature of specimen, temperature of the sample

Probentiefe *f* specimen depth
Probentyp *m* <Syn.: Probenart *f*> type of specimen
Probenverformung *f* deformation of specimen
Probenvorbereitung *f* specimen preparation
Probestab *m* <Syn.: Prüfstab *m*> test bar
Probestabform *f* type of test bar
Probestück *n* specimen
probeweise Belastung *f* <Syn.: Probebelastung *f*> trial loading
Problem *n* problem
elasto-dynamisches Problem *n* elastodynamic problem
Problemlösung *f* problem solution
Produktion *f* <Syn.: Erzeugung *f*, Herstellung *f*> {von Rissen} production {of cracks}
Produktionskontrolle *f* <Syn.: Produktionsüberwachung *f*> production control
Produktionsüberwachung *f* <Syn.: Produktionskontrolle *f*> production control
Profil *n* <Syn.: Kontur *f*> {Riß} contour {crack}
Profil *n* <Syn.:Verlauf *m*> profile
Programme *n* program
proportional proportional
Proportional- porportional
Proportionalprobe *f* {alle Maße stehen in festen Verhältnissen zueinander} proportional (test) specimen
Proportionalität *f* proportionality
Proportionalitätsgrenze *f* proportional limit
Prozeß *m* <Syn.: Vorgang *m*> process
Prozeßzone *f* process zone
Prüf- testing
Prüfanordnung *f* test assembly
Prüfaufbau *m* test assembly

Prüfbedingungen *fpl* {z.B Temperatur, Druck, Belastungsgeschwindigkeit} test conditions *pl* {e.g. temperature, pressure, loading rate}
Prüfeinrichtung *f* <Syn.: **Prüfgerät** *n*> test apparatus
Prüfeinrichtung *f* für den Fallgewichtsversuch (DWT-Versuch) drop-weight test <abb.: DWT> apparatus
Prüfen *n* testing
prüfen <Syn.: **testen**> test/to
Prüfergebnisse *npl* test data *pl*
Prüfgerät *n* <Syn.: **Prüfeinrichtung** *f*, **Prüfvorrichtung** *f*> test apparatus
automatisches Prüfgerät *n* zur Bestimmung der Vicat-Erweichungstemperatur automatic Vicat softening point apparatus
Prüfgeschwindigkeit *f* testing speed
Eigenschaften *fpl* bei hohen Prüfgeschwindigkeiten high-speed properties *pl*
Prüfkörper *m* test piece, test specimen
Prüfkörper *m* für den Schlagzugversuch <Syn.: **Schlagzugprobe** *f*> tensile impact specimen
Prüfkörper *m* für den Zugversuch <Syn.: **Zugprobe** *f*> tensile test piece
Prüfkörperanordnung *f* test specimen assembly
Prüfkörperdicke *f* test piece thickness
Prüfkörperform *f* shape of test piece
Prüflast *f* test load
Prüfmaschine *f* testing machine
weiche Prüfmaschine *f* soft testing machine
Prüfmaschine *f* mit konstanter Belastungsgeschwindigkeit constant-rate-of-loading instrument
Prüfmaschine *f* für die Bestimmung der Schlagzugfestigkeit <Syn.: **Schlagzugfestigkeits-Prüfmaschine** *f*> tensile impact testing machine
Maschine *f* zur Prüfung der Verformung <Syn.: **Verformungs-Prüfmaschine** *f*> deformation testing machine
Prüfmaterial *n* test material
Prüfmethode *f* testing method
dynamische Prüfmethode *f* <Syn.: **Prüfmethode** *f* mit dynamischer Beanspruchung** dynamic test method
elektrische Prüfmethode electrical test method
mechanische Prüfmethode *f* mechanical test method
nicht genormte Prüfmethode *f* nonstandard method
optische Prüfmethode *f* optical test method
Prüfmethode *f* mit dynamischer Beanspruchung <Syn.: **dynamische Prüfmethode** *f*> dynamic test method
Prüfmethode *f* mit schlagartiger Beanspruchung <Syn.: **Prüfmethode** *f* mit Schlagbeanspruchung> impact test method
Prüfmethode *f* mit Schlagbeanspruchung <Syn.: **Prüfmethode** *f* mit schlagartiger Beanspruchung> impact test method
Prüfmethode *f* mit statischer Beanspruchung <Syn.: **statische Prüfmethode** *f*> static test method
quasi-stationäre Prüfmethode *f* quasi-steady state method
statische Prüfmethode *f* <Syn.: **Prüfmethode** *f* mit statischer Beanspruchung> static test method
Prüfplatte *f* test plate

Prüfstab

Prüfstab *m* < Syn.: Probestab *m* >
 test bar
Prüftechnik *f* test technique
Prüftemperatur *f* testing temperature
Prüfung *f* < Syn.: Prüfen *n* > testing
 absolute Prüfung *f* absolute test
 mechanische Prüfung *f* mechanical test
 Prüfung *f* bei außergewöhnlichen Temperaturen {abweichend von der Raumtemperatur} non-ambient temperature test
 Prüfung *f* bei hohen Temperaturen high-temperature test
 Prüfung *f* der Biegsamkeit flexibility test
 Prüfung *f* der Brandausbreitung fire propagation test
 Prüfung *f* der Formbeständigkeit in der Wärme plastic yield test
 Prüfung *f* der Formstabilität < Syn.: Formstabilitätsprüfung *f* > dimensional stability test
 Prüfung *f* der Nichtbrennbarkeit < Syn.: Unbrennbarkeit > non-combustibility test
 Prüfung *f* der Sprödigkeit < Syn.: Sprödigkeitsprüfung *f* > brittleness test
 Prüfung *f* der Steifigkeit < Syn.: Steifigkeitsprüfung *f* > stiffening test
 Prüfung *f* der Zündbarkeit ignitability test
 Prüfung *f* mit Schlagbeanspruchung < Syn.: Schlagprüfung *f* > impact testing
 zerstörungsfreie Prüfung *f* < Abk.: ZfP > non-destructive testing < abb.: NDT >
Prüfverfahren *n* test(ing) method
 genormtes Prüfverfahren *n* < Syn.: Normprüfverfahren *n* > standard < Syn.: standardized > test

quasi-dynamisches Prüfverfahren *n* quasi-dynamic method {for determining conductivity}
thermisches Prüfverfahren *n* thermal method
thermisches Prüfverfahren *n* thermal test method
Prüfvorrichtung *f* < Syn.: Apparat *m*, Gerät *n* > {i.e.s. Prüfgerät *n*} apparatus
Prüfvorrichtung *f* < Syn.:Prüfgerät *n* > tester
Pt → Platin
Punkt *m* point
 in einem Punkt angreifend {Kraft} concentrated
punktförmig angreifende Kraft *f* concentrated force

Q

quadratisch square
Qualität *f* quality
qualitativ qualitative
Qualitätskontrolle *f* quality control
Qualitätsprüfung *f* quality control test
Qualitätsüberwachung *f* quality control
quantifizieren {Bruchflächen} quantify/to {fracture surfaces}
Quantifizierung *f* quantification
quantitativ quantitative
quasi-dynamisches Prüfverfahren *n* quasi-dynamic method {for determining conductivity}
Quasi-Spaltbruch-Facette *f* {Bruchfläche} quasi-cleavage facet {fracture surface}
Quasispaltbruch *m* quasi-cleavage fracture
Quasispródbruch *m* quasi-brittle fracture
quasistationäre Prüfmethode *f* quasi-steady state method

quasistatische Bruchzähigkeit *f* quasi-static fracture toughness
quasistatische Rißeinleitung *f* quasi-static crack initiation
quasistatische Rißerweiterung *f* quasi-static crack extension
quasistatische Rißgeschwindigkeit *f* quasi-static crack velocity
Quecksilber *n*, **Hg** mercury, Hg
Quelle *f* source
quer transversal, transverse
Quer- <Syn.: in Querrichtung> transversal, transverse
Querdehnung *f* transverse strain
Quergleitung *f* {Kristall} cross slip {crystal}
Querkontraktionszahl *f* <Syn.: Poissonsche Konstante *f*> Poisson's ratio
Querrichtung *f* cross direction
  Brucheigenschaften *fpl* **in Querrichtung** transverse fracture properties *pl*
  Verschiebung *f* **in Querrichtung, transversale Verschiebung** *f* transverse displacement
Querschnitt *m* cross-section, section
  rechteckiger Querschnitt *m* rectangular cross section
Querschnittsabnahme *f* reduction in area
Querschnittsfläche *f* cross-sectional area
Querschnittsreduzierung *f* reduction in cross section
Querschnittsverringerung *f* reduction in cross section
querverlaufender Warmriß *m* transverse heating crack

R

R → Rißwiderstand

R-Kurve *f* <Syn.: **Rißwiderstandskurve** *f*> crack resistance curve, R-curve
R-Kurve *f* <Syn.: **Rißwiderstandskurve** *f*> R curve, crack resistance curve
R-Kurven-Konzept *n* {R = Rißwiderstand} R curve concept {R = crack resistance}
R-Kurvenbestimmung *f* determination of crack resistance curve
Ra → Radium
radial radial
  radialer Kantenriß *m* radial edge crack
Radialspannung *f* radial stress
Radium *n*, **Ra** radium, Ra
Radius *m* radius
  wirksamer Radius *m* effective radius
  Radius *m* **der plastischen Zone** radius of the plastic zone
Randbedingungen *fpl* <Syn.: **Grenzbedingungen** *fpl*> boundary conditions *pl*
Randbelastung *f* <Syn.: **Grenz[flächen]belastung** *f*> boundary loading
Randfaser-Nennspannung *f* nominal stress of outer fibers
Randfaserspannung *f* stress of outer fibers
Randgebiet *n* **des Risses** <Syn.: **Rißumgebung** *f*> crack periphery
Randkerbe *f* edge notch
Randriß *m* <Syn.: **Kantenriß** *m*> edge crack
  durchgehender Randriß *m* through-the-thickness edge crack
  Flachprobe *f* **mit einseitigem Randriß** single-edge-cracked flat specimen
  Flachzugprobe *f* **mit einseitigem Randriß** single-edge cracked flat tensile specimen

Randspannung 230

Streifen *m* mit einseitigem Randriß single-edge cracked strip
Randspannung *f* boundary stress
Randwert *m* boundary value
Randwertproblem *n* <Syn.: Grenzwertproblem *n*> boundary-value problem
elastisch-plastisches **Randwertproblem** *n* elastic-plastic boundary value problem
RAR → Rißausbreitungsrichtung *f*
Rasterelektronenmikroskop *n* <Abk.: REM> scanning electron microscope
Rasterelektronenmikroskopie *f* <Abk.: REM> scanning electron microscopy
Rastlinien *fpl* {Bruchfläche} clamshell marks *pl*, beach marks *pl*, arrest lines *pl*, tide marks *pl* {fracture surface}
Rate *f* <Syn.: Geschwindigkeit *f*> {Vorgang} rate {process}
Rauheit *f* roughness
Rauhigkeit *f* roughness
Raum *m* space
räumlich <Syn.: kubisch> cubical
räumlich <Syn.: dreidimensional> three-dimensional
räumliche **Spannungsoptik** *f* three-dimensional photoelasticity
räumliches **Rißproblem** *n* <Syn.: dreidimensionales **Rißproblem** *n*> three-dimensional crack problem
Raumtemperatur *f* room temperature; ambient temperature
Prüfung *f* bei außergewöhnlichen **Temperaturen** {abweichend von der **Raumtemperatur**} non-ambient temperature test
Rayleighwellengeschwindigkeit *f* Rayleigh wave velocity
Rb → Rubidium

RCT-Probe *f* <Syn.: Rund-Kompakt-Zugprobe *f*> round compact tension <abb.: RCT> specimen
Re → Rhenium
realer **Riß** *m* natural crack
Rechner *m* <Syn.: Computer *m*> computer
rechteckig rectangular
rechteckige **Platte** *f* rectangular plate
rechteckiger **Oberflächenriß** *m* rectangular surface crack
rechteckiger **Querschnitt** *m* rectangular cross section
Reduktion *f* {chemisch} reduction {chemical}
reduziert <Syn.: verringert, gemindert, verkleinert> reduced
reduzierte **Spannung** *f* reduced stress
Reduzierung *f* <Syn.: Verminderung *f*, Verkleinerung *f*, Verringerung *f*> reduction
Referenz- <Syn.: Bezugs-, Vergleichs-> reference
Referenzbruchzähigkeit *f* reference fracture toughness
Referenzkurve *f* reference curve
Referenzspannungsintensitätsfaktor *m* reference stress-intensity factor
Referenztemperatur *f* <Syn.: Bezugstemperatur *f*> reference temperature
Reflexion *f* reflexion, reflection
Region *f* <Syn.: Bereich> region
Regressionskurve *f* regression curve
Reibkorrosion *f* fretting corrosion
Reibung *f* friction
 innere **Reibung** *f* internal friction
Reibungsspannung *f* friction stress
Reibverschleiß *m* {Werkstoffe} fretting {materials}
 Ermüdung *f* durch **Reibverschleiß** fretting fatigue

rein {Belastung: Werkstoff} pure
{loading: Material}
reine Biegung *f* pure bending
reine Schubbeanspruchung *f* pure
shear loading
reiner Schub *m* pure shear
Reinsteisen *n* high-purity iron
Reißen *n* < Syn.: **Zerreißen** *n* >
tearing
reißen < Syn.: **rissig werden** >
crack/to
Reißfestigkeit *f* < Syn.: **Zerreißfestigkeit** *f* > tearing strength
Reißmodul *m* tearing modulus
Reißprobe *f* tear test
  dynamische Reißprobe *f* < Syn.:
  DT-Probe *f* > dynamic tear test
  specimen
Reißprüfung *f* tear test
  dynamische Reißprüfung *f* < Syn.:
  DT-Prüfung *f* > dynamic tear
  < abb.: DT > test
relativ relative
  relative Rißabmessungen *fpl*
  relative crack size
  relative Rißgröße *f* relative crack
  size
  relative Rißlänge *f* relative crack
  length
  relative Rißtiefe *f* relative crack
  depth
Relaxation *f* relaxation
Relaxationsriß *m* stress-relief crack
REM → **Rasterelektronenmikroskopie** *f*
REM → **Rasterelektronenmikroskop** *n*
reversibel < Syn.: **umkehrbar** >
reversible
Reversibilität *f* reversibility
Rh → **Rhodium**
Rhenium *n*, **Re** rhenium, Re
Rhodium *n*, **Rh** rhodium, Rh
Richtung *f* direction
richtungsunabhängig < Syn.:
  isotrop > isotropic

Riefen *fpl* < Syn.: **Rillen** *fpl* >
{Metalloberfläche} flutes *pl* {metal
surface}
Riefen *fpl* < Syn.: **Schwingungsstreifen** *mpl* > {Schwingungsbruch} striations *pl* {fatigue fracture}
Riefenbildung *f* striation formation
Riefenbildung *f* < Syn.: **Rillenbildung** *f* > {Metalloberfläche} fluting
{metal surface}
Riefenbildung *f* < Syn.: **Kratzerbildung** *f* > {Metalloberfläche} scoring
{metal surface}
Riefenbreite *f* striation spacing
Riefenmechanismus *m* mechanisms
of striation formation
Rillen *fpl* < Syn.: **Riefen** *fpl* > {Metalloberfläche} flutes *pl* {metal
surface}
Rillenbildung *f* < Syn.: **Riefenbildung** *f* > {Metalloberfläche} fluting
{metal surface}
Riß *m* crack; fissure, check
  abgestumpfter Riß *m* < Syn.:
  stumpfer Riß *m* > blunt crack
  arretierender Riß *m* arresting crack
  arretierter Riß *m* arrest crack
  aufgefangener Riß *m* arrested
  crack, stopped crack
  äquivalenter elastischer Riß *m*
  equivalent elastic crack
  äquivalenter ruhender Riß *m*
  equivalent stationary crack
  äußerer Riß *m* external crack
  beidseitiger Riß *m* double-edge
  crack {specimens}
  dreidimensionaler Riß *m* three-
  dimensional crack
  durchgehender Riß *m* < Syn.:
  Durchriß *m* > transitional crack,
  through-the thickness crack
  effektiver Riß *m* effective crack
  eingebrachter Riß *m* initiated crack
  eingeschlossener Riß *m* embedded
  crack

Riß

elastischer Riß *m* elastic crack
endlicher Riß *m* <Syn.: Riß *m* mit endlicher Länge> finite crack
fiktiver Riß *m* <Syn.: Fiktivriß *m*> fictitious crack
flacher Riß *m* shallow crack
fortschreitender Riß *m* propagating crack
gekrümmter Riß *m* curved crack
gerade <Syn.: geradlinig> durchgehender Riß *m* straight-through crack
gerader Riß *m* straight crack
geradliniger Riß *m* rectilinear crack
gesägter Riß *m* saw cut
halbelliptischer Riß *m* semielliptical crack
halbkreisförmiger Riß *m* semicircular crack
halbunendlicher Riß *m* semiinfinite crack
in Bewegung befindlicher Riß *m* <Syn.: laufender Riß *m*> moving crack
instabiler Riß *m* unstable crack
interdendritischer Riß *m* interdendritic crack
kleiner Riß *m* small crack
kollinearer Riß *m* collinear crack
kreisbogenförmiger Riß *m* circular arc crack
kreisförmiger Riß *m* <Syn.: Kreisriß *m*> circular crack
kurzer Riß *m* short crack
künstlicher Riß *m* artificial crack
langer Riß *m* long crack
laufender Riß *m* <Syn.: in Bewegung befindlicher Riß *m*> moving crack, running crack
makroskopischer Riß *m* macroscopic crack
mikroskopischer Riß *m* microscopic crack

münzförmiger Riß *m* <Syn.: pfennigförmiger Riß *m*> penny-shaped crack
nachweisbarer Riß *m* detectable crack
offener Riß *m* open crack
ovaler Riß *m* oval crack
paralleler Riß *m* parallel crack
pfennigförmiger Riß *m* <Syn.: münzenförmiger Riß *m*> penny-shaped crack
physikalischer Riß *m* physical crack
Platte *f* mit durchgehendem Riß through-cracked plate
potentieller Riß *m* potential crack
Probe *f* mit durchgehendem Riß through-thickness crack specimen
realer Riß *m* natural crack
Riß *m* auf der Außenfläche crack at the outer surface
Riß *m* auf der Innenfläche crack at the inner surface
Riß *m* mit endlicher Länge <Syn.: endlicher Riß *m*> finite crack
ruhender Riß *m* <Syn.: stehender Riß *m*> non-propagating crack
scharfer Riß *m* sharp crack
scherbeanspruchter Riß *m* <Syn.: schubbeanspruchter Riß *m*> shear-loaded crack
schräg[liegend]er Riß *m* inclined crack
schubbeanspruchter Riß *m* <Syn.: scherbeanspruchter Riß *m*> shear-loaded crack
sich ausbreitender Riß *m* propagating crack
sichelförmiger Riß *m* half-moon crack
sich erweiternder Riß *m* extending crack
sich langsam ausbreitender Riß *m* slowly propagating crack
stehender Riß *m* nonextending crack

stehender Riß m < Syn.: ruhender Riß m > non-propagating crack
Streifen m mit Riß cracked strip
stumpfer Riß m < Syn.: abgestumpfter Riß m > blunt crack
subkritischer Riß m subcritical crack
teilweise durchgehender Riß m < Syn.: Teildurchriß m > part-through crack
tiefer Riß m < Syn.: Tiefenriß m > deep crack
trapezförmiger Riß m trapezoidal crack
unbegrenzt schmaler Riß m indefinitely crack
unbelasteter Riß m unloaded crack
verzweigter Riß m < Syn.: Mehrfachriß m > branched crack
viertelelliptischer Riß m quarter-elliptical crack
zweidimensionaler Riß m two-dimensional crack
Riß-Initiierung f < Syn.: Rißauslösung f, Rißeinleitung f > crack initiation
Rißabmessungen fpl crack size, crack dimensions pl
kritische Rißabmessungen fpl critical crack dimensions pl
relative Rißabmessungen fpl < Syn.: relative Rißgröße f > relative crack size
Rißabstumpfungsgerade f < Syn.: Wölbungsgerade f > {Risse} blunting line {cracks}
rißähnlich < Syn.: rißartig > crack-like
Rißarrest m < Syn.: Rißauffang m, Rißarretierung f > crack arrest
Rißarrestexperiment n crack-arrest experiment
Rißarrestkonzept n crack arrest concept

dynamisches Rißarrest-Konzept n concept of dynamic crack arrest
statisches Rißarrestkonzept n concept of static crack arrest
Rißarrestparameter m crack-arrest parameter
Rißarrestprobe f crack-arrest specimen
Rißarrestprozeß m < Syn.: Rißarrestvorgang m > crack-arrest process
Rißarrestsicherheitsanalyse f crack-arrest safety analysis
Rißarreststreifen mpl crack-arrest marks pl
Rißarrestvorgang m < Syn.: Rißarrestprozeß m > crack-arrest process
Rißarrestzähigkeit f < Syn.: Rißauffangzähigkeit f > crack-arrest toughness
Rißarrestzone f crack-arrest zone
Rißarretierung f < Syn.: Rißauffang m, Rißarrest m > crack arrest
Rißart f crack type, type of crack
rißartig < Syn.: rißähnlich > crack-like
Rißauffang m < Syn.: Rißarrest m, Rißarretierung f > crack arrest
Rißauffangbedingungen fpl crack-arrest conditions
Rißauffangkraft f crack-arrest force
Rißauffangtemperatur f crack-arrest temperature
Rißauffangtemperatur-Kurve f crack-arrest temperature curve
Rißauffangversuch m crack-arrest test
Rißauffangzähigkeit f < Syn.: Rißarrestzähigkeit f > crack-arrest toughness
Rißaufweitung f < Syn.: Rißerweiterung f > crack extension
stationäre Rißaufweitung f < Syn.: stationäre Rißerweiterung f > steady-state crack extension

Rißausbreitung *f* <Syn.: **Rißentwicklung** *f*, **Rißfortschritt** *m*> crack propagation
beschleunigte Rißausbreitung *f* accelerated crack propagation
duktile Rißausbreitung *f* ductile crack propagation
dynamische Rißausbreitung *f* dynamic crack propagation
elastische Rißausbreitung *f* elastic crack propagation
interkristalline Rißausbreitung *f* intercrystalline crack propagation
lokale Rißausbreitung *f* local crack propagation
mikroduktile Rißausbreitung *f* microductile crack propagation
instabile Rißausbreitung *f* unstable crack propagation
instationäre Rißausbreitung *f* nonsteady crack propagation
plastische Rißausbreitung *f* plastic crack propagation
schnelle Rißausbreitung *f* rapid crack propagation
spröde Rißausbreitung *f* brittle crack propagation
stabile Rißausbreitung *f* stable crack propagation
stationäre Rißausbreitung *f* steady-state crack propagation
transkristalline Rißausbreitung *f* transcrystalline crack propagation
Theorie *f* **der dynamischen Rißausbreitung** dynamic crack-propagation theory
unterkritische Rißausbreitung *f* <Syn.: **vorkritische Rißausbreitung** *f*> subcritical crack propagation
vorkritische Rißausbreitung *f* <Syn.: **unterkritische Rißausbreitung** *f*> subcritical crack propagation

Rißausbreitungsart *f* crack-propagation mode
Rißausbreitungsbedingungen *fpl* crack-propagation conditions *pl*
Rißausbreitungsberechnung *f* crack-propagation calculation
Rißausbreitungsbereich *m* region of crack propagation
Rißausbreitungscharakteristik *f* crack-propagation characteristic
Rißausbreitungsdaten *pl* crack-propagation data
Rißausbreitungsenergie *f* crack-propagation energy
Rißausbreitungsgeschwindigkeit *f* velocity of crack propagation
Rißausbreitungsgrenze *f* border of crack propagation
Rißausbreitungskonstante *f* crack-propagation constant
Rißausbreitungskraft *f* crack-driving force
Rißausbreitungskraft-Kriterium *n* criterion for crack extension force, criterion for crack-driving force
Rißausbreitungskurve *f* crack-propagation curve
Rißausbreitungsmechanismus *m* crack-propagation mechanism
Rißausbreitungsmessung *f* measurement of crack propagation
Rißausbreitungsmodell *n* crack-propagation model
kristallographisches Rißausbreitungsmodell *n* crystallographic crack-propagation model
Rißausbreitungsproblem *n* crack-propagation problem
Rißausbreitungsrichtung *f* <Abk.: RAR> crack-propagation direction
makroskopische Rißausbreitungsrichtung *f* macroscopic direction of crack propagation
Rißausbreitungsschema *n* crack-propagation pattern

Rißausbreitungsstadium n stage of crack propagation
Rißausbreitungstheorie f crack-propagation theory
Rißausbreitungsuntersuchung f crack-propagation study
Rißausbreitungsverhalten n crack-propagation behavio[u]r
Rißausbreitungsversuch m crack-propagation test
Rißausbreitungsvorgang m crack-propagation process
Rißausbreitungswiderstand m crack propagation resistance
Rißausbreitungswinkel m angle of crack extension
theoretischer Rißausbreitungswinkel m theoretical angle of crack extension, theoretical crack angle
Rißausbreitungszeit f crack-propagation time
Rißauslösung f <Syn.: **Rißeinleitung** f, **Riß-Initiierung** f> crack initiation
instabile Rißauslösung f unstable crack initiation
Rißbeanspruchung f <Syn.: **Rißbelastung** f> loading of crack
Rißbeanspruchungsart f mode of crack loading
rißbehaftet <Syn.: angerissen, gerissen> cracked
rißbehafteter Bereich m cracked area
Rißbelastung f <Syn.: **Rißbeanspruchung** f> loading of crack
Rißbereich m crack region
Rißbiegeprüfung f flex cracking method
Rißbildung f <Syn.: **Rißverlauf** m> cracking
intergranulare Rißbildung f intergranular cracking
interkristalline Rißbildung f intercrystalline cracking

Kriterium n für die **Rißbildung** criterion of cracking
Mechanismus m der **Rißbildung** cracking mechanism
Rißbildung f auf der **Oberfläche** {von Proben} surface cracking {of specimen}
Rißbildung f durch **Umgebungseinflüsse** environmental cracking
stufenweise Rißbildung f stepwise cracking
transkristalline Rißbildung f <Syn.: **transkristalline Rißbildung** f> transcrystalline cracking
verzögerte Rißbildung f delayed cracking
wasserstoffinduzierte Rißbildung f hydrogen-induced cracking <abb.: HIC>
wasserstoffinduzierte verzögerte Rißbildung f hydrogen-induced delayed cracking
Rißbildungsenergie f formation energy of crack
Rißbildungsneigung f tendency to cracking
Rißbreite f crack width
Rißebene f crack plane, plane of crack
Orientierung f der **Rißebene** crack plane orientation
Rißeigenfunktion f eigenfunction of crack
Rißeinbringung f <Syn.: **Rißerzeugung** f> {in Proben} production of cracks {in specimens}
Rißeinleitung f <Syn.: **Rißauslösung** f, **Rißinitiierung** f> crack initiation
dynamische Rißeinleitung f dynamic crack initiation
quasistatische Rißeinleitung f quasistatic crack initiation
Rißeinleitungsort m location of crack initiation

Rißeinleitungstemperatur

Rißeinleitungstemperatur f crack-initiation temperature
Rißeinleitungszähigkeit f crack-initiation toughness
Rißende n end of the crack
Rißentwicklung f <Syn.: Rißfortschritt m, Rißausbreitung f> crack propagation
Rißerweiterung f crack extension
 aktuelle Rißerweiterung f current crack extension
 effektive Rißerweiterung f effective crack extension
 instabile Rißerweiterung f unstable crack extension
 katastrophenartige Rißerweiterung f catastrophic crack extension
 quasistatische Rißerweiterung f quasi-static crack extension
 scheinbare Rißerweiterung f virtual crack extension <abb.: VCE>
 spontane Rißerweiterung f spontaneous crack extension
 stabile Rißerweiterung f stable crack extension
 stationäre Rißerweiterung f <Syn.: stationäre Rißaufweitung f> steady-state crack extension
Rißerweiterungsenergie f energy of crack extension
Rißerweiterungskraft f crack extension force
 effektive Rißerweiterungskraft f effective crack extension force
Rißerweiterungskriterium n criterion of crack extension
Rißerweiterungsvorgang m process of crack extension
Rißerzeugung f <Syn.: Rißeinbringung> {in Proben} production of cracks {in specimens}
Rißflächenoxidation f oxidation of the crack surface
Rißflächenverschiebung f crack surface displacement
Rißflanke f crack flank
 spannungsfreie Rißflanke f stress-free crack flank
Rißflankendrehung f rotation of crack flank
Rißform f crack shape
Rißformanalyse f analysis of crack shape
Rißfortschreiten n crack propagating
Rißfortschritt m <Syn.: Rißausbreitung f, Rißentwicklung f> crack propagation
Rißfortschrittsrate f crack-propagation rate
Rißfortschrittsverschiebung f crack-propagation displacement
rißfrei crack-free
rißfreies Ligament n uncracked ligament
Rißfront f crack front
 gekrümmte Rißfront f curved crack front
 gerade Rißfront f straight crack front
Rißfrontbereich f area of crack front
Rißfrontkrümmung f crack-front curvature
 vertikale Rißfrontkrümmung f vertical crack-front curvature
Rißgeschwindigkeit f crack speed, crack velocity
 maximale Rißgeschwindigkeit f maximum crack velocity
 quasistatische Rißgeschwindigkeit f quasi-static crack velocity
Rißgeschwindigkeitsmessung f measurement of crack speed
 Dehnungsstreifen m für die Rißgeschwindigkeitsmessung f crack-velocity ga[u]ge
Rißgröße f <Syn.: Rißabmessungen fpl> crack size

absolute Rißgröße f absolute crack size
effektive Rißgröße f effective crack size
kritische Rißgröße f critical crack size
relative Rißgröße f <Syn.: relative **Rißabmessungen** fpl> relative crack size
Rißgrund m root of the crack
Rißgruppe f <Syn.: **Rißsystem** n> crack system
Rißinitiation f crack initiation
plötzliche Rißinitiation f< Syn.: **Rißeinbruch** m> pop-in {the first discrete crack extension}
Rißinitiierungs-Spannungsintensitätsfaktor m crack initiation stress-intensity factor
Rißinitiierungsbedingung f crack initiation condition
Rißinitiierungskonzept n crack initiation concept
Rißinitiierungsprozeß m crack initiation process
Rißinitiierungszähigkeit f crack initiation toughness
Rißinkrement n crack increment
Rißinstabilität f crack instability
Rißkeim m crack nucleus
Rißkeimbildung f crack nucleation, nucleation of cracks
Rißlage f location of the crack
Rißlänge f crack length
 aktuelle Rißlänge f current crack length
 äquivalente Rißlänge f equivalent crack length
 Belastung f quer zur **Rißlänge** crack line loading
 effektive Rißlänge f <Syn.: wirksame **Rißlänge** f> effective crack length
 fiktive Rißlänge f fictitious crack length
 kritische Rißlänge f critical crack length
 mittlere Rißlänge f average crack length
 physikalische Rißlänge f physical crack length
 relative Rißlänge f relative crack length
 wirksame Rißlänge f <Syn.: effektive **Rißlänge** f> effective crack length
Rißlängenabhängigkeit f dependence from the crack length
Rißlängenänderung f <Syn.: **Rißzuwachs** m> change in crack length
Rißlängenbereich m range of crack length
Rißlängenbestimmung f determination of the crack length
Rißlängenmessung f measurement of crack length
 optische Rißlängenmessung f optical measurement of crack length
Rißlaufweg m <Syn.: **Rißpfad** m> crack path
Rißligament f crack ligament
Rißlinie f crack line
Rißmodell n crack model
Rißmuster n crack pattern
Rißnachweis m detection of cracks
Rißneigung f tendency for cracking
Rißnennquerschnitt m nominal cross-section of the crack
Riß[ober]fläche f crack surface
 spannungsfreie Riß[ober]fläche f stress-free crack surface
Rißöffnung f crack opening
 normierte Rißöffnung f normalized crack extension
Rißöffnungsart f <Syn.: **Rißöffnungsmodus** m> crack opening modus
Rißöffnungsfaktor m crack opening factor

Rißöffnungsmessung *f* crack opening measurement
Rißöffnungsmodus *m* <Syn.: **Rißöffnungsart** *f*> crack opening modus
Rißöffnungsverschiebung *f* <Abk.: COD> crack opening displacement <abb.: COD>
kritische Rißöffnungsverschiebung *f* critical crack opening displacement <abb.: COD>
Rißöffnungsverschiebungskriterium *n* <Syn.: **COD-Kriterium** *n*> crack opening displacement <abb.: COD> criterion
Rißorientierung *f* crack orientation
Rißpfad *m* <Syn.: **Rißlaufweg** *m*> crack path
Rißproblem *n* crack problem
dreidimensionales Rißproblem *n* <Syn.: **räumliches Rißproblem** *n*> three-dimensional crack problem
dynamisches Rißproblem *n* dynamic crack problem
ebenes Rißproblem *n* plane crack problem, plane problem of crack
ebenes elastisches Rißproblem *n* plane elastic crack problem
elastisches Rißproblem *n* elastic crack problem
elastisch-plastisches Rißproblem *n* elastic-plastic crack problem
elasto-plastisches Rißproblem *n* elasto-plastic crack problem
nichtlineares Rißproblem *n* nonlinear crack problem
räumliches Rißproblem *n* <Syn.: **dreidimensionales Rißproblem** *n*> three-dimensional crack problem
zweidimensionales Rißproblem *n* two-dimensional crack problem
Rißprofil *n* crack profile
Rißquerschnitt *m* crack section
Rißquerschnitt *m* cross-section of the crack
Rißschließen *n* crack-closure
Energie *f* **des Rißschließens** crack-closure energy
Risse *mpl* cracks *pl*
gleichmäßig angeordnete Risse *mpl* equally spaced cracks *pl*
nachweisen {z.B. **Risse in Werkstoffen**} detect/to {e.g. cracks in materials}
Stillstand *m* **von Rissen** <Syn.: **Arretierung** *f*> arresting of cracks
Rißserie *f* collinear cracks *pl*
rissig werden <Syn.: **reißen**> crack/to
Rißspalt *m* crack fissure, crack slit
Rißspitze *f* crack tip
Abstand *m* **von der Rißspitze** distance from crack tip
Abstumpfung *f* <Syn.: **Abstumpfen** *n*> **der Rißspitze** crack tip blunting
ebene Dehnung *f* **an der Rißspitze** crack-tip plane strain
fiktive Rißspitze *f* fictitious crack tip
Form *f* **der Rißspitze** <Syn.: **Rißspitzenform** *f*> crack-tip shape, shape of crack tip
Größe *f* **der Rißspitze** endregion size of crack
in der Nähe der Rißspitze near crack tip
ruhende Rißspitze *f* non-propagating crack tip
Spannung *f* **an der Rißspitze** crack-tip stress
Spannungsintensitätsfaktor *m* **an der Rißspitze** crack-tip stress intensity factor
Spannungsverteilung *f* **an der Rißspitze** crack-tip stress distribution

Versetzungsstruktur f {z.B. an der Rißspitze} dislocation structure {e.g. at crack tip}
Rißspitzenaufweitung f crack-tip extension
  elastische Rißspitzenaufweitung f elastic crack-tip extension
  plastische Rißspitzenaufweitung f plastic crack-tip extension
Rißspitzenbereich m crack-tip region
Rißspitzenelement n crack-tip element
Rißspitzenfeld n crack-tip field
Rißspitzenform f < Syn.: Form f der Rißspitze > crack-tip shape
Rißspitzengeometrie f crack-tip geometry
Rißspitzengeschwindigkeit f crack-tip velocity
Rißspitzenkonfiguration f crack-tip configuration
Rißspitzenkontur f crack-tip contour
Rißspitzenöffnung f crack-tip opening
  kritische Rißspitzenöffnung f critical crack tip opening
Rißspitzenöffnungsverschiebung f < Abk.: CTOD > crack tip opening displacement < abb.: CTOD >
Rißspitzenprofil n crack-tip profile
Rißspitzenradius m radius of the crack tip
Rißspitzensingularität f crack-tip singularity
Rißspitzentemperatur f crack-tip temperature
Rißspitzenumfeld n area around the crack tip
Rißspitzenumgebung f neighbo[u]rhood of crack tip, crack tip vicinity
Rißspitzenverformung f crack-tip deformation
Rißspitzenverhalten n crack-tip behavio[u]r

Rißspitzenverschiebung f crack-tip displacement
Rißspitzenzone f crack-tip zone
Rißstabilität f crack stability
Rißstart m crack start
Rißstarter m {Ausgangsstelle des Bruch[e]s} crack starter
Rißstarterkerbe f crack starter notch
Rißstoppstreifen m arrest strip
Rißsystem n < Syn.: Rißgruppe f > crack system
  dreidimensionales Rißsystem n three-dimensional crack system
  orthotropes Rißsystem n orthotropic crack system
  symmetrisch belastetes Rißsystem n symmetrically loaded crack system
  zweidimensionales Rißsystem n two-dimensional crack system
Rißtiefe f crack depth
  effektive Rißtiefe effective depth of crack
  kritische Rißtiefe f critical crack depth
  nachweisbare Rißtiefe f detectable crack depth
  relative Rißtiefe f relative crack depth
Rißtiefenbestimmung f determination of crack depth
Rißtiefenmessung f measurement of crack depth
Rißumgebung f < Syn.: Randgebiet n des Risses > crack periphery
Rißursprung m crack origin
Rißverhalten n crack behavio[u]r
  dynamisches Rißverhalten n dynamic crack behavio[u]r
Rißverlauf m < Syn.: Rißbildung f > cracking
Rißverzweigung f crack branching
  mikroskopische Rißverzweigung f microscopic crack branching

Rißverzweigungsproblem *n*
branched crack problem
Rißwachstum *n* crack growth
allmähliches Rißwachstum *n* slow crack growth
dynamisches Rißwachstum *n* dynamic crack growth
instabiles Rißwachstum *n* unstable crack growth
langsames Rißwachstum *n* slow crack growth
makroskopisches Rißwachstum *n* macroscopic crack growth
stabiles Rißwachstum *n* stable crack growth
statisches Rißwachstum *n* static crack growth
subkritisches Rißwachstum *n* subcritical crack growth
unterkritisches Rißwachstum *n* subcritical crack growth < abb.:SCC >
Rißwachstumsbedingung *f* condition of crack growth
Rißwachstumsgeschwindigkeit *f* crack growth velocity, crack growth rate
Rißwachstumskriterium *n* crack-growth criterion
Rißwachstumsrate *f* crack growth rate
Rißwachstumsrichtung *f* direction of crack growth
Rißwachstumsstadium *n* crack growth stage
Rißwachstumsumfeld *n* < Syn.: RW-Feld *n* > area of crack growth
Rißwachstumswinkel *m* angle of crack growth
Rißwiderstand *m* < Abk.: R > crack resistance
lokaler Rißwiderstand *m* < Syn.: örtlicher Rißwiderstand *m* > local crack resistance
maximaler Rißwiderstand *m* maximum crack resistance
örtlicher Rißwiderstand *m* < Syn.: lokaler Rißwiderstand *m* > local crack resistance
Rißwiderstandskurve *f* < Syn.: R-Kurve *f* > crack resistance curve, R-curve
dynamische Rißwiderstandskurve *f* dynamic crack resistance curve
Rißzähigkeit *f* crack toughness
Rißzähigkeitsmessung *f* crack toughness measurement
Rißzähigkeitsverhalten *n* crack toughness behavio[u]r
Rißzähigkeitsversuch *m* crack toughness test
Rißzähigkeitswert *m* crack toughness value
Rißzuwachs *m* < Syn.: Rißlängenänderung *f* > change in crack length
Robertson-Probe *f* {Zugprobe} Robertson specimen {tensile test specimen}
Robertson-Versuch *m* {Rißstopp} Robertson test {crack arrest}
Rockwellhärte *f* Rockwell hardness number
Rockwellhärteprüfung *f* Rockwell hardness test
röhrenförmiger Hohlraum *m* {**Bruchfläche**} tubular void {fracture surface}
Röntgen-Photoelektronen-Spektroskopie *f* X-ray photoelectron spectroscopy < abb.: XPS >
röntgenographisch roentgenographic
röntgenographische Spannungsmessung *f* roentgenographic measurement of stresses
Röntgenspektrometer *m* X-ray spectrometer
Röntgenspektrometrie *f* X-ray spectrometry
energiedispersive Röntgenspektrometrie *f* energy-dispersive x-ray spectrometry < abb.: EDX >

Röntgenstrahlenbeugung f X-ray diffraction
Rosettenbruch m rosette fracture
Rost m {Korrosionsprodukt} rust {corrosion product}
rostfrei <Syn.: nichtrostend> stainless
Ru → Ruthenium
Rubidium n, Rb rubidium, Rb
Rücksprunghärte f Scleroscope hardness number
Rücksprunghärteprüfung f Scleroscope hardness testing
Rückverformung f {nach der Entlastung} recovery {after removal of the load}
ruhend <Syn.: statisch> static
ruhende Belastung f <Syn.: statische Belastung f> static loading
ruhende Rißspitze f non-propagating crack tip
ruhender Riß m <Syn.: stehender Riß m> non-propagating crack
äquivalenter ruhender Riß m equivalent stationary crack
rund round
  runde Zugprobe <Syn.: Zugstab m> tensile bar
  runder Kerb m circular notch
Rund- round
Rund-Kompakt-Zugprobe f <Syn.: RCT-Probe f> round compact tension <abb.: RCT> specimen
Rundprobe f round specimen
Rundprobe f mit Umdrehungskerbe circumferentially notched round bar specimen
Rundscheiben-Zugprobe f disk-shaped tensile specimen
Rundstab m round bar
  konzentrischer Rundstab m concentric round bar
  Rundstab m mit konzentrischem Außenriß circumferentially cracked round bar specimen

Rundstab m mit Umlaufkerbe circumferential-notched bar
Ruthenium n, Ru ruthenium, Ru
RW-Feld n → Rißwachstumsumfeld n

S

S → Schwefel
S.I. → Spannungsintensität f
Samarium n, Sm samarium, Sm
Sauerstoff m, O oxygen, O
säurebeständiger Stahl m acid-proof steel
säurefester Stahl m acid-proof steel
Sb → Antimon
Sc → Scandium
Scandium n, Sc scandium, Sc
Schaden m damage
Schadenforschung f failure research
Schaden[sfall] m {im Sinne von Schaden} failure
Schadens(fall)analyse f <Syn.: Fehleranalyse f; Bruch m> failure analysis
Schadensforschung f failure research
Schadensursache f cause of failure
schädigen damage/to
Schädigung f damaging
  bleibende Schädigung f <Syn.: dauerhafte Schädigung f> permanent damage
  dauerhafte Schädigung f <Syn.: bleibende Schädigung f> permanent damage
  Schädigung f durch Kavitation <Syn.: Kavitationsschädigung f> cavitation damage
  Schädigung f durch Wasserstoff <Syn.: Wasserstoffschädigung f> {Versprödung, Rißbildung, Blasenbildung} hydrogen damage {embrittlement, cracking, blistering}
Schädigungsarbeit f damaging energy

Schädigungskraft 242

Schädigungskraft *f* damaging force
Schädigungskriterium *n* criterion for damage
Schädigungsprozeß *m* damage process
Schale *f* shell
Schall- acoustic
  Schallemission *f* acoustic emission
  Schallemissionsanalyse *f* < Abk.: SEA > acoustic emission analysis
  Schallemissionsprüfung *f* acoustic emission inspection
scharf gekerbter Zugstab *m* sharp-notched round tension specimen
scharfer Außenkerb *m* sharp external notch
scharfer Innenkerb *m* sharp internal notch
scharfer Kerb *m* < Syn.: Spitzkerbe *f* > sharp notch
scharfer Riß *m* sharp crack
scharnierförmige Verformung *f* hinge-type deformation
Schaubild *n* < Syn.: Diagramm *n* > diagram
Schaumkunststoff *m* cellular plastics
Scheibe *f* disk {US}, disc {GB}
  unendliche Scheibe *f* < Syn.: unendlich ausgedehnte Scheibe *f* > infinite plate
  Scheibenbreite *f* < Syn.: Plattenbreite *f* > plate width
  Scheibendicke *f* < Syn.: Plattendicke *f* > plate thickness
scheibenförmige Kompaktzugprobe *f* < Syn.: DCT-Probe *f* > disk-shaped compact [tensile] < abb.: DCT > specimen
scheinbar < Syn.: virtuell > virtual
  scheinbare Rißerweiterung *f* virtual crack extension < abb.: VCE >
Scherband *n* shear band

scherbeanspruchter Oberflächenriß *m* < Syn.: schubbeanspruchter Oberflächenriß *m* > shear-loaded surface crack
scherbeanspruchter Riß *m* < Syn.: schubbeanspruchter Riß *m* > shear-loaded crack
Scherbeanspruchung *f* < Syn.: Schubbeanspruchung *f* > shear load
  Eigenschaften *fpl* **bei Scherbeanspruchung** shear properties *pl*
  Messung *f* **unter Scherbeanspruchung** shear measurement
Scherbruch *m* < Syn.: Schubbruch *m* > shear fracture
Scherbruchanteil *m* < Syn.: Schubbruchanteil *m* > percentage shear fracture
Scherdehnung *f* < Syn.: Schubverzerrung *f* > shear strain
Scherebene *f* shear plane
Schereigenschaften *fpl* < Syn.: Eigenschaften *fpl* bei Scherbeanspruchung > shear properties *pl*
Scherfestigkeit *f* < Syn.: Schubfestigkeit *f* > shear strength
  theoretische Scherfestigkeit *f* < Syn.: theoretische Schubfestigkeit *f* > theoretical shear strength
Schergeschwindigkeit *f* shear rate
Schergrenze *f* shear limit
Scherkraft *f* < Syn.: Schubkraft > shear force
Scherlippen *fpl* shear lips *pl*
Scherlippenanteil *m* percentage shear lips
Scherlippenbildung *f* shear lip formation, formation of shear lips
Scherlippenzone *f* shear-lip zone
Schermodus *m* shearing mode
Scherspannung *f* < Syn.: Schubspannung *f* > shear stress

Scherspannungskomponente f
<Syn.: Schubspannungskomponente f> shear stress component
Scherspannungskonzentration f
<Syn.: Schubspannungskonzentration f> shear stress concentration
Scherspannungsverteilung f <Syn.: Schubspannungsverteilung f> shear stress distribution
Scherung f <Abscherung f> shearing
Scherungsinstabilität f shear instability
Scherungsmodul m <Syn.: Schubmodul m, Schub[elastizitäts]modul m> rigidity modulus, modulus of rigidity
Scherungswellengeschwindigkeit f shear-wave velocity, shear-wave speed
Scherversuch m <Syn.: Schubversuch m> shear test
Schubmodul m shear modulus
Schichtung f <Syn.: Lamellierung f> lamination
Schienenstahl m rail steel
Schlag m <Syn.: Aufprall m, Stoß m, Aufschlag m> impact
schlagartige Beanspruchung f
<Syn.: Schlagbeanspruchung f, Schlagbelastung f, Stoßbelastung f> impact loading
Prüfmethode f mit schlagartiger Beanspruchung <Syn.: Schlagbeanspruchung> impact test method
Prüfmethode f mit Kältebruchtemperatur f bei Schlagbeanspruchung impact brittleness temperature
Prüfung f mit Schlagbeanspruchung <Syn.: Schlagprüfung f> impact testing
Zugfestigkeit bei Schlagbeanspruchung <Syn.: Schlagzugfestigkeit f> tensile impact strength

Schlagbeanspruchung f brittleness temperature by impact
Kältebruchtemperatur f bei Schlagbeanspruchung f brittleness temperature by impact
Schlagbeanspruchung f <Syn.: schlagartige Beanspruchung f, Schlagbelastung f, Stoßbelastung f impact loading
Prüfmethode f mit Schlagbeanspruchung <Syn.: Prüfmethode f mit schlagartiger Beanspruchung> impact test method
Schlagbelastung f < Syn.: Stoßbelastung f, schlagartige Beanspruchung f, Schlagbeanspruchung f> impact loading
Schlagbiegefestigkeit f flexural impact strength
Messung f der Schlagbiegefestigkeit flexural impact strength measurement
Schlagbiegeprüfung f impact flexural test
Schlagbiegeversuch m impact flexural test
Schlagenergie f {Izod-Versuch, Charpy-Versuch} impact energy {Izod test, Charpy test}
Schlagfestigkeit f impact resistance
Messung f der Schlagfestigkeit impact resistance measurement
Schlagfestigkeit f nach Charpy <Syn.: Charpy-Schlagfestigkeit f> Charpy impact resistance
Schlagfestigkeitsangaben fpl impact strength data pl
Schlagfestigkeitsmessung f impact resistance measurement
Schlagfläche f striking surface
Schlaggeschwindigkeit f impact velocity
Schlagpendel n <Syn.: Pendel n> striker

Schlagprüfgerät

Schlagprüfgerät n < Syn.: Pendelschlagwerk n, Schlagprüfmaschine f> impact testing machine
Schlagprüfgerät n nach Izod < Syn.: Izod-Schlagprüfgerät n> Izod impact testing machine
Schlagprüfmaschine f < Syn.: Schlagprüfgerät n, Pendelschlagwerk n> impact testing machine
Schlagprüfung f < Syn.: Schlagversuch m> impact test
Schlagprüfung f < Syn.: Prüfung f mit Schlagbeanspruchung> impact testing
Schlagverdrehversuch m impact torsion test
Schlagversuch m < Syn.: Schlagprüfung f> impact test
Schlagvorrichtung f impact mechanism
Schlagzähigkeit f impact strength
Kugelfallprüfmaschine f {zur Bestimmung der Schlagzähigkeit} falling weight impact strength apparatus
Schlagzugfestigkeit f < Syn.: Zugfestigkeit bei Schlagbeanspruchung> tensile impact strength
Hochgeschwindigkeits-Prüfmaschine f zur Bestimmung der Schlagzugfestigkeit high-speed tensile impact machine
Messung f der Schlagzugfestigkeit tensile impact strength measurement
Prüfmaschine f für die Bestimmung der Schlagzugfestigkeit f tensile impact testing machine
Schlagzugfestigkeits-Prüfmaschine f < Syn.: Prüfmaschine f für die Bestimmung der Schlagzugfestigkeit> tensile impact testing machine
Schlagzugprobe f < Syn.: Prüfkörper m für den Schlagzugversuch> tensile impact specimen
Schlagzugversuch m impact tensile test
Schlankheitsgrad m {Probestab} slenderness ratio {test bar}
Schleifriß m grinding crack
Schließen n < Syn.: Schließung f> closure
Schließen n des Ermüdungsrisses fatigue crack closure
Schließung f < Syn.: Schließen n> {Riß} closure
schmal < Syn.: dünn> thin
schmaler Riß m thin crack
unbegrenzt schmaler Riß m indefinitely thin crack
schmelzen melt/to
Schmelztemperatur f melting temperature
Schmiederiß m forging crack
schnell rapid
schnelle Rißausbreitung f rapid crack propagation
Schnellarbeitsstahl m high-speed steel
Schnittpunkt m intersection point
Schock m shock
schräg inclined, slanting, oblique
schräg (liegend) < Syn.: schräg verlaufend> oblique
schräg verlaufend < Syn.: schräg (liegend)> oblique
schräg verlaufender Bruch m oblique fracture, slant fracture
schräge Bruchfläche f slant fracture surface
schräger Bruch m oblique failure
schräg[liegend]er Riß m inclined crack
Schrägriß m oblique crack
Schraubenversetzung f screw dislocation
Schritt m < Syn.: Stufe f > step
schrittweise < Syn.: stufenweise> gradual

schrittweise Belastung f <Syn.: stufenweise Belastung f> gradual loading
Schrumpfen n <Syn.: Schrumpfung f, Schwindung f, Schwinden n> shrinkage
schrumpfen <Syn.: sich zusammenziehen> {Rißspitze} contract/to {crack tip}
Schrumpfriß m <Syn.: Schwindungsriß m> shrinkage crack
Schrumpfung f {Metalle} solid shrinkage {metals}
Schrumpfung f <Syn.: Kontraktion f> {Rißspitze} contraction {crack tip}
Schrumpfung f <Syn.: Schrumpfen n, Schwindung f, Schwinden n> shrinkage
Schub m <Syn.: Scherung f> shear
ebener Schub m plane shear
reiner Schub m pure shear
Schub-Komponente f shear component
schubbeanspruchter Oberflächenriß m <Syn.: scherbeanspruchter Oberflächenriß m> shear-loaded surface crack
schubbeanspruchter Riß m <Syn.: scherbeanspruchter Riß m> shear-loaded crack
Schubbeanspruchung f <Syn.: Scherbeanspruchung f> shear loading
reine Schubbeanspruchung f pure shear loading
Schubbruch m <Syn.: Scherbruch m> shear failure, shear fracture
Schubbruchanteil m <Syn.: Scherbruchanteil m> percentage shear fracture
Schubdifferenzmethode f shear-difference method

Schubfestigkeit f <Syn.: Scherfestigkeit f> shear strength
theoretische Schubfestigkeit f <Syn.: theoretische Scherfestigkeit f> theoretical shear strength
Schubkraft <Syn.: Scherkraft f> shear force
Schubmodul m <Syn.: Scher[ungs]modul m> shear modulus, modulus of rigidity
Schubspannung f <Syn.: Scherspannung f> shear stress
Schubspannungskomponente f <Syn.: Scherspannungskomponente f> shear stress component
Schubspannungskonzentration f <Syn.: Scherspannungskonzentration f> shear stress concentration
Schubspannungsvektor m shear stress vektor
Schubspannungsverteilung f <Syn.: Scherspannungsverteilung f> shear stress distribution
Schubversuch m <Syn.: Scherversuch m> shear test
Schubverzerrung f <Syn.: Scherdehnung f> shear strain
Schub[elastizitäts]modul m <Syn.: Scherungsmodul m > rigidity modulus
Schülpe f {Gußfehler} buckle {casting defect}
Schwefel m, S S sulphur (GB), sulfur (US), S
schweißbar {Werkstoffe} weldable {materials}
schweißbare Legierung f weldable alloy
Schweißbarkeit f {Werkstoffe} weldability {materials}
schweißen weld/to
Schweißprüfung f {von geschweißten Bauteilen} weldment testing

Schweißrißbeständigkeit

Schweißrißbeständigkeit *f* weldcrack resistance
Schwelle *f* threshold
Schwellenwert *n* threshold value
Schwellspannungsintensität *f* threshold stress intensity
Schwellwert *m* threshold
Schwinden *n* < Syn.: Schwindung *f*, Schrumpfung *f*, Schrumpfen *n* > shrinkage
   axiale Schwindung *f* axial shrinkage
Schwindung *f* < Syn.: Schwinden *n*, Schrumpfen *n*, Schrumpfung *f* > shrinkage
Schwindungsriß *m* < Syn.: Schrumpfriß *m* > shrinkage crack
Schwingbeanspruchung *f* < Syn.: schwingende Beanspruchung *f* vibration loading
Schwingbelastung *f* < Syn.: schwingende Belastung *f* > vibration loading
Schwingbruch *m* fatigue fracture
   duktiler Schwingbruch *m* ductile fatigue fracture
schwingen vibrate/to
schwingende Beanspruchung *f* < Syn.: Schwingbeanspruchung *f* > vibration loading
schwingende Belastung *f* < Syn.: Schwingbelastung *f* > vibration loading
Schwingrißkorrosion *f* < Syn.: Korrosionsermüdung *f* > corrosion fatigue < abb.: CF >
Schwingung *f* vibration
Schwing[ungs]bruch *m* < Syn.: Dauerbruch *m*, Ermüdungsbruch *m* > fatigue fracture
   spröder Schwingungsbruch *m* brittle fatigue fracture
Schwingungsbruchfläche *f* < Syn.: Dauerbruchfläche *f* > fatigue fracture surface
Schwingungsriß *m* < Syn.: Dauerschwingriß *m*, Ermüdungsriß *m* > fatigue crack
Schwingungsrißkorrosion *f* corrosion fatigue cracking
Schwingungsstreifen *mpl* < Syn.: Riefen *fpl* > {Schwingungsbruch} striations *pl* {fatigue fracture}
SCT-Probe *f* < zugbeanspruchte Probe *f* mit Oberflächenriß > surface-crack tensile < abb.: SCT > specimen
Se → Selen
SEA → Schallemissionsanalyse
Seeatmosphäre *f* < Syn.: Meeresatmosphäre *f* > {Korrosion} marine atmosphere {corrosion}
Segregation *f* < Syn.: Ausscheidung *f* > segregation
seidenartiger Bruch *m* silky fracture
seigern {Metallographie} segregate/to {metallography}
Seigerungszone *f* segregation zone
Seite *f* {von Proben} side {specimen}
Seitenfläche *f* {von Proben} side {specimen}
Seitenkerbe *f* {Proben} side groove {specimen}
Sekantenmodul *m* secant modulus
Sekantenmodulus *m* secant modulus
sekundär < Syn.: untergeordnet > secondary
Sekundär- < Syn.: Neben- > secondary
Sekundärgleitebene *f* secondary slip plane
Sekundärriß *m* < Syn.: Nebenriß *m* > secondary crack
Selbstentzündungstemperatur *f* flash ignition temperature
selbsttätig < Syn.: automatisch > automatic
selbst[ver]löschend {Eigenschaft eines Materials} self-extinguishing

selektive Korrosion *f* selective corrosion
selektives Herauslösen *n* {Korrosion} selective leaching {corrosion}
Selen *n*, **Se** selenium, Se
SEN-Probe *f* < Syn.: **Einfachkantenrißprobe** *f*> {Kerb + Riß} single-edge notched <abb.:SEN> specimen
SENB-Probe *f* < Syn.: **Einfachkantenriß-Biegeprobe** *f*> single-edge notched bend <abb.: SENB> specimen
senkrecht normal
Senkrechte *f* vertical
Sensibilisierung *f* {Stahl: Korrosion} sensitization {steel: corrosion}
Si → **Silizium**
sicher safe
Sicherheit *f* safety
Sicherheitsabschätzung *f* < Syn.: **Sicherheitsbewertung** *f*> evaluation of safety
Sicherheitsanalyse *f* safety analysis
Sicherheitsbeiwert *m* < Syn.: **Sicherheitsfaktor** *m* > safety factor, factor of safety
Sicherheitsbewertung *f* < Syn.: **Sicherheitsabschätzung** *f*> evaluation of safety
Sicherheitsfaktor *m* < Syn.: **Sicherheitsbeiwert** *m* > safety factor
Sicherheitskonzept *n* safety concept
sichern < Syn.: **fixieren** > {ein Ende eines Probenkörpers} secure/to {one end of the specimen}
Sichtprüfung *f* visual control
Silber *n*, **Ag** silver, Ag
Silicium *n* → **Silizium**
Silizium *n*, **Silicium** *n*, **Si** silicon, Si
Singularität *f* singularity
  dynamische Singularität *f* dynamic singularity
  elastische Singularität *f* elastic singularity
  plastische Singularität *f* plastic singularity
Singularitätselement *n* element of singularity
Sm → **Samarium**
Sn → **Zinn**
Sonderbronze *f* bronze alloy
Sonderstahl *m* special steel
Spalt *m* crevice {defect}
Spaltanriß *m* cleavage pre-crack
spaltbar < Syn.: **spaltfähig** > cleavable
Spaltbarkeit *f* cleavability
Spaltbruch *m* cleavage fracture, fracture by cleavage
  interkristalliner Spaltbruch *m* intercrystalline cleavage fracture
  spröder Spaltbruch *m* brittle cleavage fracture
  transkristalliner Spaltbruch *m* transcrystalline cleavage fracture
Spaltbruchbedingung *f* cleavage fracture condition
Spaltbruchbereich *m* cleavage fracture zone
Spaltbruchbildung *f* cleavage fracture formation
Spaltbruchfacetten *fpl* cleavage facets
Spaltbruchfestigkeit *f* cleavage fracture strength
  mikroskopische Spaltbruchfestigkeit *f* microscopic cleavage-fracture strength
Spaltbruchfläche *f* cleavage fracture surface
Spaltbruchkriterium *n* cleavage fracture criterion
Spaltbruchspannung *f* cleavage fracture stress
Spaltebene *f* cleavage plane
  bevorzugte Spaltebene *f* preferred cleavage plane
Spalten *n* < Syn.: **Spaltung** *f*> cleavage

spalten

spalten <Syn.: aufspalten> cleave/to
spaltfähig <Syn.: spaltbar> cleavable
Spaltkeilprobe f <Syn.: WOL-Probe f> wedge-opening loading <abb.: WOL> specimen
Spaltkorrosion f crevice corrosion
Spaltkraft f split force
Spaltriß m cleavage crack
Spaltspannung f cleavage stress
Spaltstufe f {Spaltbruch} cleavage step {cleavage fracture}
Spaltung f <Syn.: Spalten n> cleavage
Spalt[bruch]ebene f cleavage plane
Spannbacken mpl {Zugprüfmaschine} compression chucks {for tensile machine}
Spanndruck m <Syn.: Einspanndruck m> {Proben} clamping pressure {for a specimen}
Spannung f {Mechanik, Elektronik} stress {mechanics}; voltage {electrical engineering}
  äquivalente Spannung f <Syn.: Ersatzspannung f> equivalent stress
  dimensionslose Spannung f dimensionless stress
  ebene Spannung f <Abk.: E.S.> plane stress
  effektive Spannung f effective stress
  einachsige Spannung f uniaxial stress
  eingefrorene Spannung f frozen stress
  elastische Spannung f elastic stress
  elasto-plastische Spannung f elasto-plastic stress
  endliche Spannung f {an der Rißspitze} finite stress {at crack tip}
  hydrostatische Spannung f hydrostatic stress
  komplexe Spannung f complex stress
  konstante Spannung f constant stress
  kritische Spannung f critical stress
  mechanische Spannung f mechanical stress
  mehrachsige Spannung f multiaxial stress
  nichtsinguläre Spannung f nonsingular stress
  normierte Spannung f generalized stress
  plastische Spannung f plastic stress
  reduzierte Spannung f reduced stress
  Spannung f **an der Rißspitze** crack-tip stress
  thermische Spannung f <Syn.: Wärmespannung f> thermal stress
  zweiachsige Spannung f biaxial stress
Spannungs-Dehnungs-Beziehung f stress-strain relation
Spannungs-Dehnungs-Diagramm n stress-strain diagram
Spannungs-Dehnungs-Eigenschaften fpl stress-strain properties pl
Spannungs-Dehnungs-Kurve f stress-strain curve
Spannungs-Dehnungs-Verhalten n stress-strain behavio[u]r
  elastisch-plastisches Spannungs-Dehnungs-Verhalten n elastic-plastic stress-strain behavio[u]r
  zyklisches Spannungs-Dehnungs-Verhalten n cyclic stress-strain behavio[u]r
Spannungs-Verschiebungsfeld n stress-displacement field
Spannungsabbau m stress reduction
Spannungsamplitude f stress amplitude
Spannungsanalyse f stress analysis, analysis of stress[es]

248

dreidimensionale elastische Spannungsanalyse f three-dimensional elastic stress analysis
dreidimensionale Spannungsanalyse f three-dimensional stress analysis
dynamische Spannungsanalyse f dynamic stress analysis
elastische Spannungsanalyse f elastic stress analysis
statische Spannungsanalyse f static stress analysis
Spannungsanstieg m increase of stress
Spannungsbedingung f stress condition
Spannungsbegrenzung f stress limitation
Spannungserhöhung f stress elevation, stress intensification
Spannungsfaktor m stress-intensity factor
  örtlicher Spannungsfaktor m local stress factor
Spannungsfaktorverteilung f stress-intensity factor distribution
Spannungsfeld n stress field
  elastisches Spannungsfeld n elastic stress field
  homogenes Spannungsfeld n homogeneous field of stress
  inhomogenes Spannungsfeld n inhomogeneous stress field
  isotropes Spannungsfeld n isotropic stress field
  linear-elastisches Spannungsfeld n linear elastic stress field
  lokales Spannungsfeld n local stress field
  statisches Spannungsfeld n static stress field
  ungleichförmiges Spannungsfeld n non-uniform stress field
  zweidimensionales Spannungsfeld n two-dimensional stress field
spannungsfrei stressfree
spannungsfreie Rißflanke f stressfree crack flank
spannungsfreie Riß[ober]fläche f stress-free crack surface
Spannungsfunktion f stress function
  komplexe Spannungsfunktion f complex stress function
Spannungsgeschichte f {von Werkstoffen} stress history {of materials}
Spannungsgradient m stress gradient
Spannungsinkrement n stress increment
Spannungsintensität f, S.I. stress intensity
  dynamische Spannungsintensität f dynamic stress intensity
  effektive Spannungsintensität f effective stress intensity
  effektive zyklische Spannungsintensität f effective cyclic stress-intensity
  linear-elastische Spannungsintensität f linear-elastic stress intensity
  mittlere Spannungsintensität f average stress intensity
  zyklische Spannungsintensität f cyclic stress intensity
Spannungsintensitätsbereich m stress intensity range
Spannungsintensitätsfaktor m stress-intensity factor
  dimensionsloser Spannungsintensitätsfaktor m dimensionless stress intensity factor
  dynamischer Spannungsintensitätsfaktor m dynamic stress-intensity factor
  effektiver Spannungsintensitätsfaktor m effective stress-intensity factor

fiktiver Spannungsintensitätsfaktor *m* fictitious stress-intensity factor
kritischer Spannungsintensitätsfaktor *m* critical stress-intensity factor
makroskopischer Spannungsintensitätsfaktor *m* macroscopic stress-intensity factor
Spannungsintensitätsfaktor *m* **an der Rißspitze** crack-tip stress-intensity factor
statischer Spannungsintensitätsfaktor *m* static stress-intensity factor
zyklischer Spannungsintensitätsfaktor *m* {Rißwachstum bei schwingender Beanspruchung} cyclic stress-intensity factor
Spannungsintensitätsfaktorkurve *f* stress-intensity factor curve
Spannungsintensitätsfaktorwert *m* stress-intensity factor value
Spannungsintensitätskonzept *n* concept of stress intensity
Spannungsintensitätsparameter *m* stress-intensity parameter
Spannungsintensitätsverteilung *f* stress-intensity distribution
Spannungskomponente *f* stress component
  lokale Spannungskomponente *f* local stress component
Spannungskonzentration *f* stress concentration
  elastische Spannungskonzentration *f* elastic stress concentration
Spannungskonzentrationsfaktor *f* stress concentration factor
  elastischer Spannungskonzentrationsfaktor *m* elastic stress-concentration factor
  plastischer Spannungskonzentrationsfaktor *m* plastic stress-concentration factor

theoretischer Spannungskonzentrationsfaktor *m* theoretical stress concentration factor
Spannungskorrosionsbruch *m* stress-corrosion fracture
Spannungskorrosionsriß *m* stress-corrosion crack
Spannungskorrosionsrißbildung *f* <Syn.: Spannungsrißkorrosion *f*> <Abk.: SRK> stress corrosion cracking <abb.: SCC>
Spannungskorrosionsschwellwert *m* stress corrosion threshold
Spannungskriterium *n* stress criterion
Spannungslinie *f* stress line
Spannungsmessung *f* stress measurement
  röntgenographische Spannungsmessung *f* roentgenographic measurement of stresses
Spannungsnachweis *m* stress detection
Spannungsniveau *n* stress level
  konstantes Spannungsniveau *n* constant stress level
Spannungsoptik *f* <Syn.: Photoelastizität *f*> photoelasticity
  dynamische Spannungsoptik *f* dynamic photoelasticity
  ebene statische Spannungsoptik *f* plane static photoelasticity
  ebene dynamische Spannungsoptik *f* two-dimensional dynamic photoelasticity
  räumliche Spannungsoptik *f* three-dimensional photoelasticity
spannungsoptisch <Syn.: photoelastisch> photoelastic
Spannungspunkt *m* stress point
Spannungsrelaxation *f* stress relaxation
  örtliche Spannungsrelaxation *f* local stress relaxation

Spannungsrißaufweitungsdiagramm *n* stress-crack extension diagram
Spannungsrißaufweitungskurve *f* stress-crack extension diagram
Spannungsrißkorrosion *f* {Messing: Korrosion + innere Spannung} seasoning cracking {brass: corrosion + internal stress}
Spannungsrißkorrosion *f* < Abk.: SRK > < Syn.: Spannungskorrosionsrißbildung *f* > stress corrosion cracking < abb.: SCC >
interkristalline Spannungsrißkorrosion *f* intergranular stress-corrosion cracking
Spannungssingularität *f* stress singularity
Spannungsspitze *f* stress peak
Spannungssymmetrie *f* stress symmetry
Spannungssystem *n* stress system
Spannungstensor *m* stress tensor
Spannungstrajektorie *f* stress trajectory
Spannungsumlagerung *f* stress deviation
Spannungsvektor *m* stress vector
Spannungsverformungsfeld *n* stress deformation field
Spannungsverhältnis *n* {Wechselspannungsamplitude/Mittelspannung oder Minimalspannung/Maximalspannung} stress ratio {alternating stress amplitude/mean stress or minimum stress/maximum stress}
Spannungsverlauf *m* < Syn.: Spannungsverteilung *f* > {z.B. vor der Rißspitze} stress distribution {e.g. at crack tip}
Spannungsverteilung *f* < Syn.: Spannungsverlauf *m* > {z.B. vor der Rißspitze} stress distribution {e.g. at crack tip}
dreidimensionale Spannungsverteilung *f* three-dimensional stress distribution
dynamische Spannungsverteilung *f* dynamic stress distribution
elastisch-plastische Spannungsverteilung *f* elastic-plastic stress distribution
homogene Spannungsverteilung *f* homogeneous distribution of stress[es]
inhomogene Spannungsverteilung *f* inhomogeneous stress distribution
Spannungsverteilung *f* **an der Rißspitze** crack-tip stress distribution
Spannungswellenemission *f* stress wave emission
Spannungszustand *m* stress state, state of stress
aktueller Spannungszustand *m* current stress state
dreiachsiger Spannungszustand *m* triaxial stress state, triaxial state of stress
dreidimensionaler Spannungszustand *m* three-dimensional state of stress
ebener Spannungszustand *m* < Abk.: ESZ > plane stress state
einachsiger Spannungszustand *m* uniaxial stress state
gemischter Spannungszustand *m* mixed-mode stress state
homogener Spannungszustand *m* homogeneous state of stress
isotroper Spannungszustand *m* isotropic state of stress
makroskopischer Spannungszustand *m* macroscopic state of stress
mehrachsiger Spannungszustand *m* multiaxial state of stress
zweiachsiger Spannungszustand *m* biaxial stress state
Spannvorrichtung *f* **für den Biegeversuch** bend test fixture

Spektroskopie *f* spectroscopy
Spezial- special
  Spezialfall *m* special case
speziell <Syn.: besonders> special
spezifisch <Syn.: kennzeichnend> specific
  spezifische Bruchenergie *f* specific fracture energy, specific energy of fracture
  kritische spezifische Bruchenergie *f* critical specific fracture energy
  spezifische Oberflächenenergie *f* specific surface energy
  spezifische Wärme *f* specific heat
  spezifische Wärme *f* **bei konstantem Volumen** specific heat at constant volume
  spezifische Wärme *f* **bei konstantem Druck** specific heat at constant pressure
  spezifische Wärmekapazität *f* specific heat
Spitze *f* {Rißspitze; Belastung} tip {of a crack}; peak {load}
Spitzenlast *f* peak load
  positive Spitzenlast *f* positive peak load
Spitzkerbe *f* < Syn.: scharfer Kerb *m* > sharp notch
spontan spontaneous
  spontan einsetzender Bruch *m* spontaneous fracture
  spontane Belastung *f* spontaneous loading
  spontane Rißerweiterung *f* spontaneous crack extension
Sprödbruch *m* brittle fracture
  elastischer Sprödbruch *m* elastic brittle fracture
  energiearmer Sprödbruch *m* low-energy brittle fracture
  interkristalliner Sprödbruch *m* intercrystalline brittle fracture
Sprödbruchanalyse *f* analysis of brittle fracture

Sprödbruchbereich *m* zone of brittle fracture
Sprödbruchfläche *f* brittle fracture surface
Sprödbruchkonzept *n* concept of brittle fracture
Sprödbruchkriterium *n* criterion of brittle fracture
Sprödbruchneigung *f* tendency to brittle fracture
Sprödbruchprüfung *f* brittle fracture test
Sprödbruchsicherung *f* brittle fracture safety
Sprödbruchtheorie *f* brittle fracture theory, theory of brittle fracture
  Konzept *n* **der Sprödbruchtheorie** concept of brittle fracture theory
Sprödbruchverhalten *n* < Syn.: sprödes Bruchverhalten *n* > brittle fracture behavio[u]r
Sprödbruchwiderstand *m* resistance to brittle fracture
spröd[e] brittle
  spröde Rißausbreitung *f* brittle crack propagation
  spröder Einschluß *m* brittle inclusion
  spröder Gewaltbruch *m* brittle overload fracture
  spröder Schwingungsbruch *m* brittle fatigue fracture
  spröder Spaltbruch *m* brittle cleavage fracture
  spröder Werkstoff *m* brittle material
  spröder Zustand *m* brittle state
  sprödes Bruchverhalten *n* < Syn.: Sprödbruchverhalten *n* > brittle fracture behavio[u]r
  sprödes Erosionsverhalten *n* brittle erosion behavio[u]r
  sprödes Verhalten *n* {von Werkstoffen} brittle behavio[u]r {of materials}

spröd[e] werden <Syn.: **versprö-den**> embrittle/to
Spröd[e]-Zäh-Übergang m <Syn.: **Übergang** m "spröd[e]-zäh"> brittle-ductile transition
Sprödigkeit f {Werkstoffe} brittleness {materials}
Sprödigkeitsprüfung f <Syn.: **Prüfung** f **der Sprödigkeit**> brittleness test
Sprödigkeitstemperatur f <Syn.: **Versprödungstemperatur** f> brittle point
Sprödigkeitstemperatur f <Syn.: **Versprödungstemperatur** f; **Kältebruchtemperatur** f> brittleness temperature
Sr → Strontium
SRK → Spannungsrißkorrosion f
Stab m {Probe} bar, rod {specimen}
gekerbter Stab m <Syn.: **Kerbstab** m> notched bar
stabil stable
stabile Rißausbreitung f stable crack propagation
stabile Rißerweiterung f stable crack extension
stabiler Mikroriß m stable microcrack
stabiles Rißwachstum n stable crack growth
Stabilität f stability
Stabilitätskriterium n {Griffith-Riß} stability criterion {Griffith crack}
Stadium n stage
Stahl m steel
alterungsbeständiger Stahl m non-ag[e]ing steel
augenrißbeständiger Stahl m steel resistant to caustic cracking
ausscheidungshärtender nichtstender Stahl m precipitation-hardening stainless steel
austenitischer nichtstender Stahl m austenitic stainless steel
austenitischer Stahl m austenitic steel
beizspröder Stahl m acid brittle steel
chemikalienbeständiger Stahl m chemical resistant steel
elastisch verformter Stahl m elastically deformed steel
ferritischer nichtstender Stahl m ferritic stainless steel
ferritischer Stahl m ferritic steel
gehärteter Stahl m hardened steel
hochfester Stahl m high-strength steel
hochlegierter Stahl m high-alloy steel
kaltbrüchiger Stahl m <Syn.: **kaltspröder Stahl** m> cold-brittle steel
kaltspröder Stahl m <Syn.: **kaltbrüchiger Stahl** m> cold-brittle steel
kohlenstoffarmer Stahl m low-carbon steel
kohlenstoffreicher Stahl m high-carbon steel
korrosionsbeständiger Stahl m corrosion-resistant steel
legierter Stahl m <Syn.: **Legierungsstahl** m> alloy steel
lichtbogengeschweißter legierter Stahl m arc-welded alloy steel
lichtbogengeschweißter kohlenstoffarmer Stahl m arc-welded low-carbon steel
lichtbogengeschweißter nichtstender Stahl m arc-welded stainless steel
martensitischer nichtstender Stahl m martensitic stainless steel
mittelgekohlter Stahl m medium-carbon steel
nichtaustenitischer Stahl m non-austenitic steel
nichtstender Stahl m stainless steel

Stahlguß

niedriglegierter Stahl *m* low-alloy steel
nitriergehärteter Stahl *m* <Syn.: nitrierter Stahl *m*> nitrided steel
nitrierter Stahl *m* <Syn.: nitriergehärteter Stahl *m*> nitrided steel
perlitischer Stahl *m* pearlitic steel
säurebeständiger Stahl *m* <Syn.: säurefester Stahl *m*> acid-proof steel
säurefester Stahl *m* <Syn.: säurebeständiger Stahl *m*> acid-proof steel
superplastischer nichtrostender Stahl *m* superplastic stainless steel
ultrahochfester Stahl *m* ultrahigh-strength steel
versprödeter Stahl *m* embrittled steel
zäher Stahl *m* tough steel
Stahlguß *m* steel casting
Stahlplättchen *n* {in eine Probe} thin steel plate {in specimens}
Standard *m* <Syn.: Norm *f*> standard
Standard-Biegeprobe *f* standard bend specimen
Standard-Bruchmechanik-Probe *f* standard fracture specimen
Standard-C-Form-Zugprobe *f* standard arc-shaped (tension) specimen
Standard-Kompakt-Zugprobe *f* standard compact tension <abb.: CT> specimen
Standard-Rundscheiben-Zugprobe *f* standard disk-shaped compact (tension) specimen
Standard-Stahl *m* standard steel
Standardabweichung *f* standard deviation
Standardprobe *f* {für Prüfungen} standard specimen {for testing}
Standardprobe *f* für den Fallgewichtsversuch (DWT-Versuch) standard drop-weight test <abb.: DWT> specimen
Stapelfehler *m* {Kristall} stacking fault {crystal}
Stapelfehlerenergie *f* {Kristall} stacking fault energy {crystal}
starr <Syn.: steif> rigid
starrer Körper *m* rigid body
Starrheit *f* <Syn.: Steifheit *f*> rigidity
Starrkörperverformung *f* rigid-body deformation
Starrkörperverschiebung *f* rigid-body displacement
Statik *f* {Mechanik ruhender Körper} statics
stationär <Syn.: ruhend> stationary
stationäre Bedingungen *f pl* steady state conditions *pl*
stationäre Messung *f* {Leitfähigkeit} steady state measurement {of conductivity}
stationäre Rißaufweitung *f* <Syn.: stationäre Rißerweiterung *f*> steady-state crack extension
stationäre Rißausbreitung *f* steady-state crack propagation
stationäre Rißerweiterung *f* <Syn.: stationäre Rißaufweitung *f*> steady-state crack extension
stationäres Kriechen *n* steady-state creep
statisch <Syn.: ruhend> static
statische Belastung *f* <Syn.: ruhende Belastung *f*> static loading
statische Bruchzähigkeit *f* static fracture toughness
statische Ermüdung *f* static fatigue
statische Prüfmethode *f* <Syn.: Prüfmethode *f* mit statischer Beanspruchung> static test method

statische Spannungsanalyse f static stress analysis
statische Spannungsoptik f static photoelasticity
ebene statische Spannungsoptik f plane static photoelasticity
statische Verformung f static deformation
statische Zugfestigkeit f static tensile strength
statischer Spannungsintensitätsfaktor m static stress-intensity factor
statisches Gleichgewicht n state equilibrium
statisches Rißarrestkonzept n concept of static crack arrest
statisches Rißwachstum n static crack growth
statisches Spannungsfeld n static stress field
Stauchen n < Syn.: Stauchung f > crushing
stauchen < Syn.: zerdrücken, zerquetschen; zerkleinern > crush/to
Stauchprobe f crush test
Stauchung f < Syn.: Stauchen n > crushing
Bruch m durch Stauchung crushing failure
Stegbildung f {in Werkstoffen} formation of bridges {in materials}
stehender Riß m < Syn.: ruhender Riß m > non-propagating crack, non-extending crack
steif < Syn.: starr > rigid
Steifheit f < Syn.: Starrheit f > rigidity
Steifigkeit f stiffness
Steifigkeitsprüfung f < Syn.: Prüfung f der Steifigkeit > stiffening test
steigern < Syn.: erhöhen > raise/to
Stelle f < Syn.: Position f, Lage f > position

stengeliges Gefüge n columnar structure
Stereographie stereography
steuern control/to
Stickstoff m, N nitrogen, N
Stillstand m < Syn.: Arretierung f von Rissen > arresting of cracks
stochastisch stochastic
Stoppen n < Syn.: Anhalten n, Arrest m > {Risse} arrest {cracks}
Stoppen n < Syn.: Anhalten n, Arretieren n > {Risse} arresting {cracks}
stoppen {einen Riß} arrest/to {a crack}
Stoß m < Syn.: Aufprall m, Aufschlag m, Schlag m > impact
Stoßbelastung f < Syn.: Schlagbelastung f, Schlagbeanspruchung f, schlagartige Beanspruchung f > impact loading
Stoßbruch m impact fracture
Stoßfestigkeit f {von Materialien} impact resistance, shock resistance {of materials}
strahlen < Syn.: Strahlung aussenden > radiate/to
Strahlenschaden m {Werkstoffe} radiation damage {materials}
Strahlung aussenden < Syn.: strahlen > radiate/to
Strahlung f radiation
Strahlungsversprödung f radiation-induced embrittlement
Streckgrenze f tensile yield strength, tensile yield point
Streckgrenzenverhältnis n yield point-to-tensile strength ratio
Streifen m strip
isotroper Streifen m isotropic strip
ungerissener Streifen m uncracked strip
Streifen m mit einseitigem Randriß single-edge cracked strip
Streifen m mit Riß cracked strip

Streifen

Streifen *mpl* <Syn.: **Linien** *fpl*> marks *pl*
streifenförmige Probe *f* strip specimen
Streifenprobe *f* strip specimen
Stretch-Zone *f* <Syn.: **Dehnzone** *f*> {vor der Rißfront} stretch zone
Streuband *n* scatterband
streuen scatter/to
Streuen *n* <Syn.: **Streuung** *f*> scattering
Streulichtverfahren *n* {Spannungsoptik} scattered light photoelasticity
Streustromkorrosion *f* stray-current corrosion
Streuung *f* <Syn.: **Streuen** *n*> scattering
Strontium *n*, **Sr** strontium, Sr
Struktur *f* structure
Stufe *f* level; step
Stufenversetzung *f* edge dislocation
  stufenweise Belastung *f* <Syn.: **schrittweise Belastung** *f*> gradual loading, stepwise loading
  stufenweise Rißbildung *f* stepwise cracking
stufenweise <Syn.: **schrittweise**> gradual, stepwise
stumpf {Riß} blunt {crack}
  stumpfer Riß *m* <Syn.: **abgestumpfter Riß** *m*> blunt crack
Subkorn *n* subgrain
Subkorngrenze *f* subgrain boundary
Subkornstruktur *f* subgrain structure, sub-boundary structure
subkritisch <Syn.: **unterkritisch, vorkritisch**> subcritical
  subkritische Bruchmechanik *f* subcritical fracture mechanics <abb.: SCFM>
  subkritischer Riß *m* subcritical crack
  subkritisches Rißwachstum *n* subcritical crack growth

Sulfid-Spannungsrißkorrosion *f* sulfide stress-cracking <abb.: SSC>
Superlegierung *f* superalloy
superplastisch {Werkstoffe} superplastic {materials}
  superplastischer nichtrostender Stahl *m* superplastic stainless steel
Superposition *f* superposition
Superpositionsprinzip *n* superposition principle
Superpositionsmethode *f* method of superposition
Symmetrie *f* symmetry
Symmetrieachse *f* axis of symmetry
symmetrisch belastetes Rißsystem *n* symmetrically loaded crack system
symmetrische Belastung *f* symmetric loading
symmetrischer Ermüdungsbruch *m* symmetrical fatigue fracture
symmetrischer Kantenriß *m* double-edge crack
System *n* system

T

Ta → Tantal
Tafel *f* sheet
tangential tangential
Tangential- tangential
  Tangentialkraft *f* tangential force
  Tangentialspannung *f* tangential stress, hoop stress
  Tangentialspannungskomponente *f* tangential stress component
Tantal *n*, **Ta** tantalum, Ta
Tb → Terbium
Tc → Technetium
TDCB-Probe *f* <Syn.: **konische (keilförmige) Doppelbalken[biege]probe** *f* tapered double-cantilever beam <abb.: TDCB> specimen
Te → Tellur
Technetium *n*, **Tc** technetium, Tc

Technik f technique
Teil n, **Teil** m part
Teilchen n particle
Teilchenbruch m {das Brechen von z.B. harten Teilchen} particles failure
Teildurchriß m <Syn.: teilweise durchgehender Riß m> part-through crack
Teillast f partial load
teilweise <Syn.: partiell> partial
teilweise durchgehender Riß m <Syn.: Teildurchriß m> part-through crack
Teller-Tassen-Bruch m <Syn.: Kalotten-Tassen-Bruch m> cup-cone fracture
Tellur n, **Te** tellurium, Te
TEM → Transmissions-Elektronenmikroskopie f
TEM → Transmissions-Elektronenmikroskop n
Temperatur f temperature
  erhöhte Temperatur f elevated temperature
  kritische Temperatur f critical temperature
  Kurzzeitbeständigkeit f **bei erhöhter Temperatur** short-time stability at elevated temperatures
  Temperaturen fpl **im Bereich der Temperatur des flüssigen Stickstoffs** cryogenic temperatures pl
Temperatur-Einwirkungszeitgrenzen fpl temperature-time limits pl
temperaturabhängig temperature-dependent
Temperaturabhängigkeit f {von Eigenschaften} temperature dependence {of properties}
Temperaturbereich m temperature range
Temperaturbeständigkeit f temperature stability

Temperaturdifferenz f <Syn.: Temperaturunterschied m> temperature difference
Temperatureinfluß m influence of temperature, temperature effect
Temperaturerhöhung f {bei der Prüfung} temperature increase {during testing}
Temperaturgradient m temperature gradient
Temperaturgrenze f temperature limit
Temperaturunterschied m <Syn.: **Temperaturdifferenz** f> temperature difference
Temperaturverhalten n {z.B. von Kunststoffen} temperature behavio[u]r {e.g. of plastisc}
Temperaturverlauf m temperature profile
Temperaturverschiebung f temperature shift
Temperaturverteilung f temperature distribution
Temperguß m malleable iron
Temperierbad n temperature bath
temperierte Probe f <Syn.: wärmebehandelte Probe f> heat-treated specimen
Tensor m tensor
Terbium n, **Tb** terbium, Tb
Test m <Syn.: Prüfung f, Versuch m> test
testen <Syn.: prüfen> test/to
Textur f texture
TGA → thermogravimetrische Analyse f
Th → Thorium
Thallium n, **Tl** thallium n, Tl
theoretisch theoretical; calculated
theoretische Bruchfestigkeit f theoretical fracture strength
theoretische Bruchspannung f calculated fracture stress

thermisch

theoretische Festigkeit f theoretical strength
theoretische Nachgiebigkeit f theoretical compliance
theoretische Scherfestigkeit f theoretical shear strength
theoretische Schubfestigkeit f theoretical shear strength
theoretische Zugfestigkeit f theoretical tensile strength
theoretischer Rißausbreitungswinkel m theoretical angle of crack extension, theoretical crack angle
theoretischer Spannungskonzentrationsfaktor m theoretical stress concentration factor
thermisch thermal
  thermische Alterung f <Syn.: Wärmealterung f> heat ag[e]ing
  thermische Analyse f thermal analysis
  thermische Ausdehnung f <Syn.: Wärmeausdehnung f> thermal expansion
  thermische Beständigkeit f <Syn.: Wärmebeständigkeit f> thermal stability
  thermische Dauerfestigkeit f thermal fatigue strength
  thermische Eigenschaften fpl thermal properties pl
  thermische Ermüdung f <Syn.: Ermüdung f durch Wärmebeanspruchung> thermal fatigue
  thermische Spannung f <Syn.: Wärmespannung f> thermal stress
  thermisches Prüfverfahren n thermal [test] method
  thermodynamische Eigenschaften fpl thermodynamic properties pl
Thermoelement n thermocouple
Thermogravimetrie f thermogravimetry

thermogravimetrische Analyse f <Abk.: TGA> thermogravimetric analysis <abb..: TGA>
Thermoschock m <Syn.: Wärmeschock m> thermal shock
Thermoschockriß m thermal-shock crack
Thorium n, Th thorium, Th
Thulium n, Tm thulium, Tm
Ti → Titan
tief <Syn.: tiefliegend> deep
tiefer Riß m <Syn.: Tiefenriß f> deep crack
Tiefe depth
Tiefenriß f <Syn.: tiefer Riß m> deep crack
Tiefenrißwachstum n deep crack growth
tiefliegend <Syn.: tief> deep
Tieftemperaturbeständigkeit f resistance to low temperature
Tieftemperaturmessung f low-temperature measurement
Tieftemperaturprüfgerät n low-temperature apparatus
Tieftemperaturprüfraum m low-temperature working chamber
Tieftemperaturprüfung f low-temperature testing
Tieftemperatur-Prüfung f der mechanischen Eigenschaften low-temperature mechanical testing
Tieftemperaturrißausbreitungsversuch m cryogenic crack propagation test
Tieftemperaturversuch m cryogenic test
Tiefziehen n {Metalle} deep-drawing {metals}
tiefziehen {Metalle} deep-draw/to {metals}
Titan n, Ti titanium, Ti
  lichtbogengeschweißtes Titan n arc-welded titanium

Titanlegierung f titanium alloy
lichtbogengeschweißte Titanlegierung f arc-welded titanium alloy
Titanstahl m titanium steel
Tl → Thallium
Tm → Thulium
Topographie f topography
Torsion f <Syn.: Verdrehung f> twist, torsion
Torsions- <Syn.: Verdrehungs-Verdreh-> torsional...
Torsionsbruch m torsion fracture
Torsionsfestigkeit f torsion strength
Torsionsgewaltbruch m torsion overload fracture
Torsionsmodul m torsion modulus
Torsionsschwingbruch m torsion fatigue fracture
Torsionsspannung <Syn.: Verdreh-spannung f> torsion stress
Torsionssteifheits-Prüfmethode f torsional stiffening test method
Torsionswiderstand <Syn.: Verdrehwiderstand m> torsion resistance
tragen {eine Probe} carry/to {a specimen}
Tragfähigkeit f bearing strength
Messung f **der Tragfähigkeit** bearing measurement
transgranular <Syn.: transkristallin, interkristallin> {durch Kristallkörner hindurch} transcrystalline, intracrystalline, transgranular {through the grains}
transkristallin <Syn.: intrakristallin, transgranular> {durch Kristallkörner hindurch} transcrystalline, intracrystalline, transgranular {through the grains}
transkristalline Facette f transcrystalline facet
transkristalline Rißausbreitung f transcrystalline crack propagation
transkristalline Rißbildung f <Syn.: transgranulare Rißbildung f> transcrystalline cracking, transgranular cracking
transkristalliner Bruch m transcrystalline fracture, transgranular fracture
transkristalliner Mikroriß m transcrystalline microcrack
transkristalliner Spaltbruch m transcrystalline cleavage fracture
Transmissions-Elektronenmikroskopie f <Abk.: TEM> transmission electron microscopy <abb.: TEM>
Transmissions-Elektronenmikroskop n <Abk.: TEM> transmission electron microscope <abb.: TEM>
transparent <Syn.: lichtdurchlässig> transparent
transparente Probe f transparent specimen
Transparenz f <Syn.: Durchlässigkeit f> transparency
transversal <Syn.: quer, Quer-, in Querrichtung> transversal, transverse
transversale Verschiebung f <Syn.: Verschiebung f in Querrichtung> transverse displacement
Transversalwelle f transversal wave
Transversalwellengeschwindigkeit f transversal wave velocity
trapezförmig trapezoidal
trapezförmiger Riß m trapezoidal crack
Trennbruch m <Syn.: kristalliner Bruch m> crystalline fracture
Trennbruchebene f plane of crystalline fracture
Trennebene f plane of separation
trennen separate/to
Trennfestigkeit f rupture strength
Trennmechanismus m mechanism of separation

Trennung

Trennung *f* separation
Tribologie *f* tribology
Tunnelriß *m* tunnel crack
turbulent turbulent
Typ *m* <Syn.: Art *f*, Form *f*> type

U

U → Uran
überbeanspruchen <Syn.: überlasten> overload/to
Überbeanspruchung *f* <Syn.: Überlastung *f*, Lastüberhöhung *f*> overload
Übergang *m* "spröd[e]-zäh" <Syn.: Spröd[e]-Zäh-Übergang *m*> brittle-ductile transition
Übergang *m* <Syn.: Durchgang *m*> transition
Übergangs- transient
 Übergangsbereich *m* transition range
 Übergangskriechen *n* transient creep
 Übergangstemperatur *f* <Syn.: Umwandlungstemperatur *f*> transition temperature
 Übergangstemperaturbereich *m* transition temperature range
 Übergangstemperaturgrenzbereich *m* limiting transition temperature range
 Übergangstemperaturkonzept *n* {Sprödbruchverhalten} concept of transition temperature {brittle-fracture behavio[u]r}
 Übergangstemperaturverhalten *n* transition-temperature behavio[u]r
 Übergangsverhalten *n* transition behavio[u]r
Übergangszone *f* transition zone
Überlast *f* <Syn.: Überlastung *f*, Überbeanspruchung *f*, Lastüberhöhung *f*> overload

überlasten <Syn.: überbeanspruchen> overload/to
Überlastspannung *f* overload stress
Überlastung *f* <Syn.: Überbeanspruchung *f*, Lastüberhöhung *f*> overload
 mechanische Überlastung *f* mechanical overload
Überlastwirkung *f* overload effect
Überprüfung *f* <Syn.: Inspektion *f*> inspection
übertragbar <Syn.: anwendbar> applicable
Übertragbarkeit *f* <Syn.: Anwendbarkeit *f*> {z.B. von Ergebnissen} applicability {e.g. of results}
überwachen <Syn.: steuern> control/to
Überwachung *f* <Syn.: Kontrolle *f*> control
ultrahochfester Stahl *m* ultrahigh-strength steel
Ultraschall- ultrasonic
 Ultraschallmessung *f* {Rißgeschwindigkeit} ultrasonic measurement {crack velocity}
 Ultraschallprüfung *f* ultrasonic testing
Umdrehungskerbe *f* circumferential notch
 Rundprobe *f* mit Umdrehungskerbe circumferentially notched round bar specimen
Umfang *m* <Syn.: Peripherie *f*> circumference
Umfangs- circumferential
 Umfangskerb *m* circumferential notch
 Umfangsriß *m* circumferential crack
 Umfangsspannung *f* circumferential stress
 normierte Umfangsspannung *f* normalized circumferential stress

Umfeld *n* <Syn.: **Umgebung** *f*, **Nähe** *f*> vicinity, neighbo[u]rhood; environment
Umfeld *n* {z.B. von Rissen} periphery {e.g. of cracks}
Umformbarkeit <Syn.: **Verformbarkeit** *f* unter Druckbelastung> malleability
Umformverfestigung *f* {Metalle} work-hardening, hardening {metals}
Umgebung *f* <Syn.: **Nähe** *f*, **Umfeld** *n*> vicinity, neighbo[u]rhood; environment
Umgebungs- environmental
Umgebungs- {Temperatur} ambient…{temperature}
Umgebungseinflüsse *mpl* environmental effects *pl*
Rißbildung *f* durch **Umgebungseinflüsse** environmental cracking
Umgebungstemperatur *f* ambient temperature, environmental temperature
umgebungsbegünstigte Versprödung *f* environmentally assisted embrittlement
umkehrbar <Syn.: **reversibel**> reversible
Umlaufkerbe *f* {einer Rundprobe} circumferential notch {of a round test specimen}
Rundstab *m* mit **Umlaufkerbe** circumferential-notched bar
Umwandlungstemperatur *f* <Syn.: **Übergangstemperatur** *f*> transition temperature
Umwandlungswärme *f* latent heat
unbegrenzt schmaler Riß *m* indefinitely thin crack
unbelastet <Syn.: **lastfrei**> unloaded
  unbelasteter Körper *m* <Syn.: **nicht beanspruchter Körper** *m*> unloaded body
  unbelasteter Riß *m* unloaded crack

unbrennbar <Syn.: **nicht brennbar**> non-combustible
unelastisch inelastic
  unelastische Verformung *f* inelastic deformation
  unelastisches Verhalten *n* inelastic behavio[u]r
Unelastizität *f* inelasticity
unendlich infinite
  unendlich ausgedehnte Scheibe *f* <Syn.: **unendliche Scheibe** *f*> infinite plate
  unendliche Belastung *f* infinite loading
  unendliche Scheibe *f* <Syn.: **unendlich ausgedehnte Scheibe** *f*> infinite plate
  unendlicher Körper *m* infinite body
ungefüllt <Syn.: **nicht gefüllt**> unfilled
ungekerbt unnotched
  ungekerbte Probe *f* <Syn.: **ungekerbter Probekörper** *m*> unnotched (test) specimen
  ungekerbte Zugprobe *f* unnotched tensile specimen
  ungekerbter Probekörper *m* <Syn.: **ungekerbte Probe** *f*> unnotched (test) specimen
ungerissen <Syn.: **rißfrei**> uncracked
  ungerissener Streifen *m* uncracked strip
ungleichartig <Syn.: **heterogen**> heterogeneous
ungleichartig <Syn.: **inhomogen**> inhomogeneous
Ungleichartigkeit *f* <Syn.: **Heterogenität** *f*> heterogeneity
Ungleichartigkeit *f* <Syn.: **Inhomogenität** *f*> inhomogeneity
ungleichförmiges Spannungsfeld *n* non-uniform stress field
unlegierter Kohlenstoffstahl *m* plain carbon steel

Unstetigkeit

Unstetigkeit f <Syn.: **Diskontinuität** f> discontinuity
Unsymmetrie f <Syn.: **Asymmetrie** f> asymmetry,
unsymmetrisch <Syn.: **asymmetrisch**> asymmetric
unterbrochen <Syn.: **diskontinuierlich**> discontinuous
untere Fließgrenze f lower yield point
untergeordnet secondary
unterkritisch <Syn.: **vorkritisch, subkritisch**> subcritical
unterkritische Rißausbreitung f <Syn.: **vorkritische Rißausbreitung** f> subcritical crack propagation
unterkritisches Rißwachstum n subcritical crack growth <abb.: SCC>
Unterspannung f {Dauerbiegeversuch} minimum stress {fatigue test}
untersuchen study/to
Untersuchung f study; investigation
fraktographische Untersuchung f fractographic investigation
ununterbrochen <Syn.: **kontinuierlich**> continuous
Uran n, U uranium, U
Ursache f {z.B. eines Bruch[e]s} cause {e.g. of fracture}

V

VAD → **Versagensanalyse-Diagramm** n
Vanadium n, V vanadium, V
Vanadium-Niob-Legierung f vanadium-niobium alloy
Vanadiumstahl m vanadium steel
Vektor m vector
Veränderung f <Syn.: **Änderung** f> change
Verarmung f {Legierung} depletion {alloy}

Verbindung f {Werkstoffe} joint {materials}
Verbindung f {Metall} compound {metal}
intermetallische Verbindung f intermetallic compound
Verbrennen n <Syn.: **Verbrennung** f> burning
Verbrennung f <Syn.: **Verbrennen** n> burning
Verbrennungsgeschwindigkeit f burning rate, rate of burning
mittlere Verbrennungsgeschwindigkeit f average burning rate
Verbundwerkstoff m composite, composite material
Verdreh- <Syn.: **Verdrehungs-**> torsional...
verdrehen <Syn.: **auf Verdrehung** f **beanspruchen**> twist/to
Verdrehmoment n <Syn.: **Drehmoment** n> torsional moment
Verdrehspannung f <Syn.: **Torsionsspannung**> torsion stress
Verdrehung f <Syn.: **Torsion** f> torsion
Verdrehungs- <Syn.: **Verdreh-**> torsional...
Verdrehungsbeanspruchung f torsional load
Verdrehungsbelastung f torsional load
Verdrehungsbruch m torsion fracture
Verdrehversuch m torsion[al] test
Verdrehwiderstand m <Syn.: **Torsionswiderstand**> torsion resistance
Verdreh[ungs]festigkeit f torsional strength
Verdunstungsgeschwindigkeit f rate of evaporation
Vereinigung f <Syn.: **Zusammenwachsen** n> {von Hohlräumen, Rissen} coalescence {of voids, cracks}

Verengung f < Syn.: Einschnürung f, Einschnüren n > necking
Verfahren n process; method
Verfahren n < Syn.: Bewegen n > {einer Probe} movement {of the specimen}
verfestigen {Metalle} work-harden/to {metals}
Verfestigen < Syn.: Umformverfestigung f > {Metalle} work-hardening, hardening {metals}
Verfestigung f < Syn.: Härtung f > hardening
isotrope Verfestigung f isotropic hardening
linear-elastische Verfestigung f linear elastic hardening
Verfestigungseffekt m effect of hardening
Verfestigungsexponent m hardening exponent
verfestigungsfähig {Metalle} work-hardenable {metals}
verfestigungsfähiger Werkstoff m work-hardenable material
Verfestigungskurve f hardening curve
Verfestigungsverhalten n hardening behavio[u]r
Verfestigungszustand m state of hardening
inhomogener Verfestigungszustand m inhomogeneous state of hardening
verformbar < Syn.: duktil, dehnbar > deformable
Verformbarkeit f < Syn.: Duktilität, Dehnbarkeit f > ductility
Verformbarkeit f < Syn.: Verformungsfähigkeit f > deformability
Verformbarkeit f unter Druckbelastung < Syn.: Umformbarkeit > malleability
verformen < Syn.: deformieren > deform/to

verformt deformed
elastisch verformt elastically-deformed
elastisch verformter Stahl m elastically-deformed steel
Verformung f < Syn.: Deformation, Formänderung f > deformation
bleibende Verformung f permanent deformation
dreidimensionale Verformung f three-dimensional deformation
ebene Verformung f < Syn.: zweidimensionale Verformung f > two-dimensional deformation
elastische Verformung f elastic deformation
elastisch-plastische Verformung f elastic-plastic deformation
endliche Verformung f finite deformation
homogene Verformung f homogeneous deformation
infinitesimale Verformung f infinitesimal deformation
inhomogene Verformung f inhomogeneous deformation
linear-elastische Verformung f linear-elastic deformation
keilförmige Verformung f wedge-type deformation
konstante Verformung f constant deformation
plastische Verformung f < Syn.: plastische Deformation f > plastic deformation
scharnierförmige Verformung f hinge-type deformation
statische Verformung f static deformation
unelastische Verformung f inelastic deformation
zeitabhängige Verformung f time-dependent deformation

Verformungs-

zweidimensionale Verformung f
<Syn.: **ebene Verformung f**> two-dimensional deformation
zyklische plastische Verformung f cyclic plastic deformation
Verformungs-Prüfmaschine f
<Syn.: **Maschine f zur Prüfung der Verformung**> deformation testing machine
Verformungsanalyse f analysis of deformation
Verformungsbehinderung f <Syn.: **Deformationsbehinderung f**> deformation constraint
Verformungsbruch m plastic fracture
Verformungseigenschaften fpl deformation properties pl
Verformungsenergie f energy of deformation
  elastische Verformungsenergie f elastic energy of deformation
  plastische Verformungsenergie f energy of plastic deformation
Verformungsenergiedichtefaktor m {Bruchkriterium} factor of deformation energy density {fracture criterion}
Verformungsfähigkeit f <Syn.: **Verformbarkeit f**> deformability
Verformungsfeld n deformation field
  linear-elastisches Verformungsfeld n linear elastic deformation field
  zweidimensionales linear-elastisches Verformungsfeld n two-dimensional linear-elastic deformation field
  zweidimensionales Verformungsfeld n two-dimensional deformation field
Verformungsgebiet n {Riß} deformation zone {crack}
Verformungsgeschwindigkeit f
<Syn.: **Deformationsgeschwindigkeit f**> deformation rate

Verformungsgrad m degree of deformation
Verformungsgradient m deformation gradient
Verformungskraft f deformation force
Verformungsrichtung f direction of deformation
Verformungstensor m deformation tensor
Verformungsverhalten n deformation behavio[u]r
Verformungswiderstand m resistance to deformation, deformation resistance
Verformungszustand m deformation state
  ebener Verformungszustand m plane deformation state, state of plane deformation
Vergleich m comparison
Vergleichbarkeit f {von Prüfergebnissen} comparability {of test results}
vergleichen compare/to
vergleichend <Syn.: **Vergleichs-**> comparative
Vergleichs- <Syn.: **vergleichend**> comparative
Vergleichs- <Syn.: **Referenz-, Bezugs-**> reference
Vergleichsmaterial n {für Prüfungen} reference material {for testing}
Vergleichsmessung f comparison measurement
Vergleichsmethode f comparison method
Vergleichsprobe f reference specimen
Vergleichsprüfung f comparison test, comparative test
Vergrößerung f magnification
Verhalten n {Werkstoffe} behavio[u]r {materials}
  bruchmechanisches Verhalten n fracture-mechanical behavio[u]r

duktiles Verhalten *n* ductile behavio[u]r
duktiles Verhalten *n* <Syn.: **zähes Verhalten** *n*> {von Werkstoffen} ductile behavio[u]r {of materials}
elastisch-plastisches Verhalten *n* elastic-plastic behavio[u]r
linear-elastisches Verhalten *n* linear-elastic behavio[u]r
mechanisches Verhalten *n* mechanical behavio[u]r
plastisches Verhalten *n* plastic behavio[u]r
sprödes Verhalten *n* {von Werkstoffen} brittle behavio[u]r {of materials}
unelastisches Verhalten *n* inelastic behavio[u]r
vollplastisches Verhalten *n* perfectly plastic behavio[u]r
zähes Verhalten *n* ductile behavio[u]r
zähes Verhalten *n* <Syn.: **duktiles Verhalten** *n*> {von Werkstoffen} ductile behavio[u]r {of materials}
Verhältnis *n* ratio
Verhältnisse *npl* <Syn.: **Bedingungen** *fpl*> conditions *pl*
verkleinert <Syn.: **reduziert, verringert, gemindert**> reduced
Verkleinerung *f* <Syn.: **Verringerung** *f*, **Reduzierung** *f*, **Verminderung** *f*> reduction
Verlängerung *f* elongation
  Verlängerung *f* **der plastischen Zone** plastic zone elongation
Verlauf *m* <Syn.: **Profil** *n*> profile
Verlauf *m* {Diagramme, Kennlinien} curve
Verlust *m* {Energie, Masse} loss {energy, weight}
vermindern <Syn.: **absenken, verringern**> {Belastung, Last} decrease/to

Verminderung *f* <Syn.: **Verkleinerung** *f*, **Verringerung** *f*, **Reduzierung** *f*> reduction
verringern <Syn.: **vermindern, absenken**> {Belastung, Last} decrease/to
verringert <Syn.: **gemindert, verkleinert, reduziert**> reduced
Verringerung *f* <Syn.: **Verminderung** *f*, **Verkleinerung** *f*, **Reduzierung** *f*> reduction
Versagen *n* <Syn.: **Schaden[sfall]** *m*, **Bruch** *m*> failure
  elastisches Versagen *n* elastic failure
  plastisches Versagen *n* plastic failure
  plastisches Versagen *n* <Syn.: **plastischer Kollaps** *m*> plastic collaps
  Versagen *n* **durch Ermüdung** <Syn.: **Dauerschwingungsbruch** *m*> fatigue failure
versagen <Syn.: **ausfallen**> fail/to
Versagensanalyse-Diagramm *n* <Abk.: VAD> failure-analysis diagram <abb.: FAD>
Versagensbedingungen *fpl* failure conditions *pl*
Versagensbeurteilung *f* failure assessment
Versagenseinleitung *f* initiation of failure
Versagenshypothese *f* failure hypothesis
Versagenskriterium *n* failure criterion
Versagenslast *f* failure load
Versagenssicherheit *f* fail-safety
Versagenswahrscheinlichkeit *f* <Syn.: **Ausfallwahrscheinlichkeit** *f*> failure probability
Verschiebung *f* displacement

Verschiebungsfeld

lokale Verschiebung *f* local displacement
transversale Verschiebung *f* transverse displacement
Verschiebung *f* in Querrichtung transverse displacement
Verschiebungsfeld *n* displacement field
Verschiebungsfunktion *f* displacement function
Verschiebungsgradient *m* displacement gradient
Verschiebungskomponente *f* component of displacement
Verschiebungskriterium *n* displacement criterion
Verschiebungsmessung *f* displacement measurement
Verschiebungsvektor *m* displacement vector
Verschleiß *m* wear
  abrasiver Verschleiß *m* abrasive wear
  adhäsiver Verschleiß *m* adhesive wear
  katastrophaler Verschleiß *m* catastrophic wear
  korrosiver Verschleiß *m* corrosive wear
  oxidativer Verschleiß *m* {Oxidfilm} oxidative wear {oxide film}
  Verschleiß *m* durch Werkstoffermüdung fatigue wear
Verschleißgeschwindigkeit *f* wear rate
Verschränkungs[korn]grenze *f* {Kristall} twist boundary {crystal}
Versetzung *f* dislocation
  blockierte Versetzung *f* locked dislocation
Versetzungsanordnung *f* patterns *pl* of dislocation
Versetzungsaufstauung *f* pile-up of dislocations
Versetzungsbewegung *f* movement of dislocations
Versetzungsdichte *f* dislocation density
Versetzungsgeschwindigkeit *f* dislocation velocity
Versetzungshindernis *n* dislocation barrier
Versetzungsknoten *m* dislocation node
Versetzungskonfiguration *f* dislocation array
Versetzungslinie *f* dislocation line
Versetzungsmodell *n* dislocation model
Versetzungsreihe *f* dislocation row
Versetzungsring *m* dislocation loop
Versetzungsstruktur *f* {z.B. an der Rißspitze} dislocation structure {e.g. at crack tip}
Versetzungstheorie *f* dislocation theory
Versetzungsverteilung *f* dislocation distribution
Versetzungsvervielfältigung *f* multiplication of dislocations
verspröden < Syn.: spröd[e] werden > embrittle/to
versprödet durch Wasserstoff *m* < Syn.: wasserstoffversprödet > hydrogen-embrittled
versprödete Probe *f* embrittled specimen
  nicht versprödete Probe *f* nonembrittled specimen
versprödeter Stahl *m* embrittled steel
Versprödung *f* embrittlement
  adsorptionsinduzierte Versprödung *f* adsorption-induced embrittlement
  umgebungsbegünstigte Versprödung *f* environmentally assisted embrittlement

Versprödung f bei Kontakt mit schmelzflüssigen Metallen liquid-metal embrittlement <abb.: LME>
Versprödung f durch Neutronenstrahlung neutron embrittlement
Versprödung f mit festen (nichtschmelzflüssigen) Metallen solid-metal embrittlement <abb.: SME>
Versprödungstemperatur f <Syn.: Sprödigkeitstemperatur f> brittle point
versteifen stiffen/to
Versteifung f stiffening
Versteifungsblech n stiffening sheet
Versteifungselement n stiffening element
Versuch m <Syn.: Experiment n> experiment
Versuch m <Syn.: Prüfung f, Test m> test
  genormter Versuch m standard test
Versuchsanordnung f test arrangement, experimental arrangement
Versuchsdauer f test duration
Versuchsdurchführung f test procedure
Versuchsergebnisse f test results *pl*
Versuchsfrequenz f test frequency
Versuchsparameter m test parameter
Versuchsprogramm n test program
Versuchsprotokoll n test report
Versuchspunkt m test point
Versuchstemperatur f test temperature
Verteilung f distribution
  Verteilung f der Belastung <Syn.: Lastverteilung f> load distribution
vertikal <Syn.: senkrecht> vertical
Vertikale f <Syn.: Senkrechte f> vertical
vertikale Rißfrontkrümmung f vertical crack-front curvature
Verunreinigung f {Metalle} impurity {metals}

Verunreinigung f {Oberfläche} contamination {surface}
verursachen {z.B. einen Bruch} cause/to {e.g. a fracture or failure}
Verwerfung f warping
Verzerrung f distortion
Verzerrung f <Syn.: Dehnung f> strain
  ebene Verzerrung f <Syn.: ebene Dehnung f> plane strain
Verzerrungsalterung f strain ag[e]ing
Verzerrungsenergie-Freisetzungsrate f strain energy release rate
Verzerrungsenergiedichte f strain energy density
Verzerrungsenergiekriterium n distortion energy criterion
Verzerrungsgeschwindigkeit f <Syn.: Dehnungsgeschwindigkeit f> strain rate
Verzerrungskonzentration f <Syn.: Dehnungskonzentration> strain concentration
Verzerrungstensor m <Syn.: Dehnungstensor m> strain tensor
Verzerrungszustand m <Syn.: Dehnungszustand m> state of strain
  ebener Verzerrungszustand m <Abk.: EVZ> <Syn.: ebener Dehnungszustand m> <Abk.: EDZ> state of plane strain
verzögern {Rißausbreitung} delay/to {crack propagation}
verzögerte Rißbildung f delayed cracking
  wasserstoffinduzierte verzögerte Rißbildung f hydrogen-induced delayed cracking
verzögerter Bruch m delayed fracture
Verzögerung {Rißausbreitung} delay {crack propagation}
Verzögerungsfaktor m retention factor

Verzweigen *n* <Syn.: **Verzweigung** *f*> {Risse} bifurcation, branching {cracks}
verzweigt {Risse} branched {cracks}
verzweigter Riß *m* <Syn.: **Mehrfachriß** *m*> branched crack
Verzweigung *f* <Syn.: **Verzweigen** *n*> {Risse} bifurcation, branching {cracks}
Verzweigungsgeschwindigkeit *f* branching velocity
Vicat-Erweichungstemperatur *f* Vicat softening point
  automatisches Prüfgerät *n* **zur Bestimmung der Vicat-Erweichungstemperatur** automatic Vicat softening point apparatus
  Gerät *n* **zur Bestimmung der Vicat-Erweichungstemperatur** *f* Vicat softening point apparatus
  Vicat-Prüfgerät *n* {zur Bestimmung der Vicat-Erweichungstemperatur} Vicat apparatus {determination of softening point}
Vicat-Nadel *f* Vicat needle
Vicat-Prüfgerät *n* {zur Bestimmung der Vicat-Erweichungstemperatur} Vicat apparatus {determination of softening point}
Vickershärte *f* Vickers hardness number <abb.: VH>
Vickershärteprüfung *f* {Eindringhärte} Vickers hardness test {indentation hardness}
vielfach <Syn.: **mehrfach**> multiple
Vier-Punkt-Biegung *f* four-point bending
Vierpunkt-Biegeprobe *f* four-point bend test specimen
Vierpunkt-Biegeprüfung *f* four-point bending test
Vierpunkt-Biegetechnik *f* four-point bending technique

Vierpunkt-Biegeversuch *m* four-point bend test
Vierpunkt-Biegeversuch *m* four-point bending test
Vierpunkt-Biegevorrichtung *f* four-point bending test apparatus
Viertelellipsenfehler *m* quarter-elliptical flaw
viertelelliptischer Riß *m* quarter-elliptical crack
virtuell <Syn.: **scheinbar**> virtual
viskoelastisch viscoelastic
Viskoelastizität *f* viscoeleaticity
viskoplastisch viscoplastic
Viskoplastizität *f* viscoplasticity
visuell visual
vollkommen <Syn.: **vollständig, ideal**> ideal, perfect
vollplastischer Zustand *m* perfectly plastic state
vollplastisches Verhalten *n* perfectly plastic behavio[u]r
vollständig <Syn.: **vollkommen, ideal**> ideal, perfect
vollständiges Eintauchen *n* {einer Probe} total immersion {of the specimen}
Volumen *n* volume
  spezifische Wärme *f* **bei konstantem Volumen** specific heat at constant volume
Volumenänderung *f* volume change
Volumenelement *n* volume element
volumetrisch volumetric
Vorausbestimmung *f* predetermination
Voraussage *f* <Syn.: **Vorhersage** *f*> {Bruch, Ausfall} prediction {fracture, failure}
voraussagen <Syn.: **vorhersagen**> {Bruch, Ausfall} predict/to {fracture, failure}
Vorbeanspruchung *f* preload
Vorgang *m* **Prozeß** *m*, process

vorgewärmte (angewärmte) Probe *f* pre-heated specimen
vorherbestimmen <Syn.: im voraus bestimmen> predetermine/to
vorhergesagte Bruchspannung *f* predicted fracture stress
Vorhersage *f* <Syn.: Voraussage *f*> {Bruch, Ausfall} prediction {fracture, failure}
vorhersagen <Syn.: voraussagen> {Bruch, Ausfall} predict/to {fracture, failure}
vorkritisch <Syn.: subkritisch, unterkritisch> subcritical
vorkritische Rißausbreitung *f* <Syn.: unterkritische Rißausbreitung *f*> subcritical crack propagation
Vorrichtung *f* <Syn.: Gerät *n*> device
Vorspannung *f* initial stress
Vorzugsrichtung *f* <Syn.: Hauptrichtung *f*> {Kristall} preferred orientation {crystal}

W

W → Wolfram
wachsen {Risse} grow/to {cracks}
Wachstum *n* growth
Wachstumscharakteristik *f* growth characteristic
Wachstumsgeschwindigkeit *f* growth rate
Wachstumsparameter *m* growth parameter
wahr <Syn.: wirklich> true
  wahre Bruchdehnung *f* true fracture strain
  wahre Oberflächenenergie *f* true surface energy
Wahrscheinlichkeit *f* probability
Wahrscheinlichkeitstheorie *f* theory of probability

Wallner-Linien *fpl* {Bruchfläche} Wallner lines *pl* {fracture surface}
Walzgrat *m* lap
Walzriß *m* rolling crack
Wand *f* wall
Warmbrüchigkeit *f* hot brittleness
Wärme *f* heat
  Formbeständigkeit *f* **in der Wärme** deformation under heat
  Formbeständigkeit *f* **in der Wärme** heat deflection temperature, heat distortion point, heat distortion temperature
  Prüfung *f* **der Formbeständigkeit in der Wärme** plastic yield test
  spezifische Wärme *f* **bei konstantem Druck** specific heat at constant pressure
  spezifische Wärme *f* **bei konstantem Volumen** specific heat at constant volume
Wärme- <Syn.: thermisch> thermal
Wärmealterung *f* <Syn.: thermische Alterung *f*> heat ag[e]ing
  Dehnbarkeit *f* **nach Wärmealterung** extensibility after heat ag[e]ing
Wärmeausdehnung *f*, **thermische Ausdehnung** *f* thermal expansion
Wärmeausdehnungskoeffizient *m* coefficient of thermal expansion
  kubischer Wärmeausdehnungskoeffizient *m* coefficient of cubical thermal expansion
  linearer Wärmeausdehnungskoeffizient *m* coefficient of linear thermal expansion
  mittlerer Wärmeausdehnungskoeffizient *m* average coefficient of linear thermal expansion
wärmebehandelte Probe *f* <Syn.: temperierte Probe *f*> heat-treated specimen

Wärmebehandlung

Wärmebehandlung f {Stahl} heat treatment {steel}
Wärmebeständigkeit f heat resistance
Wärmebeständigkeit f < Syn.: **Formbeständigkeit** f in der Wärme > plastic yield
Wärmebeständigkeit f < Syn.: **thermische Beständigkeit** f > thermal stability
Wärmedämmung f < Syn.: **Wärmeisolierung** f > thermal insulation
Wärmeeinflußzone f < Abk.: WEZ > heat-affected zone < abb.: HAZ >
Wärmeisolierung f < Syn.: **Wärmedämmung** f > thermal insulation
Wärmekammer f heating chamber
Wärmekapazität f specific heat
Wärmeleitfähigkeit f < Syn.: **Wärmeleitvermögen** n > thermal conductivity
Wärmeleitfähigkeits-Prüfgerät n thermal conductivity test apparatus
Wärmeleitfähigkeitsmessung f thermal conductivity measurement
Wärmeleitvermögen n < Syn.: **Wärmeleitfähigkeit** f > thermal conductivity
Wärmeriß m hot tear
innerer Wärmeriß m internal hot tear
Wärmeschock m < Syn.: **Thermoschock** m > thermal shock
Wärmeschrank m **mit zwängsläufiger Durchlüftung** oven with fan circulation of the air
Wärmespannung f < Syn.: **thermische Spannung** f > thermal stress
Wärmestreckgrenze f thermal yield strength
Wärmeströmung f heat flow
Wärmeströmungsmeßgerät n heat flow meter
warmfeste Knetlegierung f heat-resistant wrought alloy

Warmriß m hot crack
querverlaufender Warmriß m transverse heating crack
Wartung f service
Wasser n water
Wasserstoff m, H hydrogen, H
versprödet durch Wasserstoff m < Syn.: **wasserstoffversprödet** > hydrogen-embrittled
Schädigung f **durch Wasserstoff** < Syn.: **Wasserstoffschädigung** f > {Versprödung, Rißbildung, Blasenbildung} hydrogen damage {embrittlement, cracking, blistering}
Wasserstoffblasenbildung f {Metalloberfläche} hydrogen blistering {metal surface}
wasserstoffinduzierte Rißbildung f hydrogen-induced cracking < abb.: HIC >, hydrogen cracking
wasserstoffinduzierte verzögerte Rißbildung f hydrogen-induced delayed cracking
Wasserstoffschädigung f < Syn.: **Schädigung** f **durch Wasserstoff** > {Versprödung, Rißbildung, Blasenbildung} hydrogen damage {embrittlement, cracking, blistering}
Wasserstoffsprödigkeit f hydrogen embrittleness
wasserstoffversprödet < Syn.: **versprödet durch Wasserstoff** m > hydrogen-embrittled
Wasserstoffversprödung f hydrogen embrittlement
Wechselbeanspruchung f alternating loading cycling loading
Wechselbeziehung f < Syn.: **Korrelation** f > correlation
Wechselbiegebeanspruchung f alternating bending
Wechsellast f alternating load, cyclic load
Weg m < Syn.: **Pfad** m, **Bahn** f > path
weich soft

weiche Prüfmaschine soft testing machine
weicher Kunststoff m non-rigid plastic
Weißmetal n white metal
Welle f wave
Wellenfront f wave front
Wellengeschwindigkeit f wave velocity
Wellengleichung f wave equation
Wellenlänge f wave length
wellig {Blech} buckle {sheet}
Werkstoff m <Syn.: Material n> material
 anisotroper duktiler Werkstoff m anisotropic ductile material
 anisotroper Werkstoff m anisotropic material
 anrißfreier Werkstoff m material without pre-crack
 duktiler Werkstoff m, **zäher Werkstoff** m ductile material
 elastischer Werkstoff m elastic material
 elastisch-plastischer Werkstoff m elastic-plastic material
 faserverstärkter Werkstoff m fiber-reinforced material
 geschwindigkeitsempfindlicher duktiler Werkstoff m rate-sesitive ductile material
 heterogener Werkstoff m heterogeneous material
 hochfester Werkstoff m high-strength material
 hochtemperaturbeständiger Werkstoff m high-temperature material
 ideal-spröder Werkstoff m ideal brittle material
 inhomogener Werkstoff m inhomogeneous material
 isotroper duktiler Werkstoff m isotropic ductile material
 isotroper elastischer Werkstoff m isotropic elastic material
 isotroper Werkstoff m isotropic material
 keramischer Werkstoff m ceramic material
 linear-elastischer Werkstoff m linear-elastic material
 metallischer Werkstoff m metallic material
 nichtmetallischer Werkstoff m nonmetallic material
 polykristalliner Werkstoff m polycrystalline material
 spröder Werkstoff m brittle material
 verfestigungsfähiger Werkstoff m work-hardenable material
 zäher Werkstoff m <Syn.: duktiler Werkstoff m> ductile material
werkstoffabhängig material-dependent
Werkstoffanisotropie f anisotropy of materials
Werkstoffauswahl f material selection
Werkstoffbeschaffenheit f <Syn.: Werkstoffzustand f> material condition
Werkstoffdaten fpl materials data
Werkstoffehler m material defect
Werkstoffeigenschaften fpl material properties pl
Werkstoffermüdung g fatigue of materials
 Verschleiß m durch Werkstoffermüdung fatigue wear
Werkstofffehler m material flaw
Werkstoffkonstante f material constant
Werkstoffkunde f <Syn.: Werkstoffwissenschaft f> materials science
Werkstoffmatrix f matrix of material

Werkstoffprüfung *f* <Syn.: **Materialprüfung** *f*> materials testing, testing of materials
Werkstoffschädigung *f* damage of materials
Werkstoffstruktur *f* material structure
Werkstofftrennung *f* separation of material
werkstoffunabhängig material-independent
Werkstoffverhalten *n* material behavio[u]r
   elastisches Werkstoffverhalten *n* elastic material behavio[u]r
   elastisch-plastisches Werkstoffverhalten *n* elastic-plastic material behavio[u]r
Werkstoffversprödung *f* material embrittlement
Werkstoffwissenschaft *f* <Syn.: **Werkstoffkunde** *f*> materials science
Werkstoffzähigkeit *f* material toughness
Werkstoffzustand *m* <Syn.: **Werkstoffbeschaffenheit** *f*> material condition
Werkzeug *n* tool
Werkzeugstahl *m* tool steel
Wert *m* value
WEZ → **Wärmeeinflußzone** *f*
Wickelkörper *m* {zum Aufwickeln der Probe} winder
Widerstand *m* resistance
Widerstand-Temperatur-Kennlinien *fpl* resistance-temperature characteristics *pl*
Wiederbelastung *f* <Syn.: **wiederholte Belastung** *f*, **erneutes Belasten** *n*> reloading
Wiedereinleitung *f* {von Rissen} reinitiation {of cracks}
wiederholen {eine Prüfung} repeat /to {a test}
wiederholte Belastung *f* <Syn.: **erneutes Belasten** *n*, **Wiederbelastung** *f*> reloading
Wiederholungsprüfung *f* repeat test
Winkel *m* angle
Winkel- angular
Winkelabhängigkeit *f* angular dependence
winkelförmig <Syn.: **wink[e]lig**> angular
Winkelfunktion *f* angular function
wink[e]lig <Syn.: **winkelförmig**> angular
Wirbelstromverfahren *n* {Nachweis von Rissen} eddy-current method {detection of cracks}
wirklich <Syn.: **wahr**> true
wirksam <Syn.: **effektiv**> effective
wirksame Rißlänge *f* <Syn.: **effektive Rißlänge** *f*> effective crack length
wirksamer Radius *m* effective radius
Wismut *n*, **Bismut** *n*, **Bi** bismuth, Bi
Wissenschaft *f* science
Wöhler-Kurve *f* <Syn.: **Dauerfestigkeitskurve** *f*> S-N curve, S-N diagram {S = stress, N = number of cycles to failure}, Wöhler curve
WOL-Probe *f* <Syn.: **Spaltkeilprobe** *f*> wedge-opening loading <abb.: WOL specimen>
Wölbung *f* <Syn.: **Krümmung** *f*> curvature
Wölbung *f* <Syn.: **Konvexität** *f*> {Bruchstelle} convexity {of failure locus}
Wolfram *n*, **W** tungsten, W
Wolframlegierung *f* tungsten alloy

X

Xe → **Xenon**
Xenon *n*, **Xe** xenon, Xe

Y

Y → Yttrium
Yb → Ytterbium
Ytterbium *n*, Yb ytterbium, Yb
Yttrium *n*, Y yttrium, Y

Z

zäh <Syn.: duktil> tough, ductile
Zäh-Spröd[e]-Übergang *m* ductile-brittle transition
Zäh-Spröd[e]-Übergangstemperatur *f* ductile-to-brittle transition temperature
Zähbruch *m* <Syn.: duktiler Bruch *m*, zäher Bruch *m*> ductile fracture
zäher Bruch *m* <Syn.: duktiler Bruch *m*, Zähbruch *m*> ductile fracture
zäher Stahl *m* tough steel
zäher (duktiler) Werkstoff *m* ductile material
zähes Bruchverhalten *n* ductile fracture behavio[u]r
zähes Verhalten *n* ductile behavio[u]r
zähes Verhalten *n* <Syn.: duktiles Verhalten *n*> {von Werkstoffen} ductile behavio[u]r {of materials}
Zähigkeit *f* toughness
Zähigkeitsparameter *m* toughness parameter
Zähigkeitsverhalten *n* toughness behavio[u]r
Zahl *f* <Syn.: Anzahl *f*> number
zeilenartiger Einschluß *m* stringer
Zeilengefüge *n* {Metalle} banded structure {metals}
Zeit *f* time
  Zeit *f* bis zum Ausfall time-to-failure
  Zeit *f* bis zum Bruch time-to-failure
zeitabhängig time-dependent
zeitabhängige Verformung *f* time-dependent deformation
zeitabhängiger Bruch *m* time-dependent fracture
zeitabhängiges Bruchverhalten *n* time-dependent fracture behavio[u]r
Zeitmessung *f* time measurement
Zeitstand- {Werkstoffe} creep... {materials}
Zeitstandbruch *m* <Syn.: Kriechbruch *m*> creep rupture
Zeitstandfestigkeit *f* creep resistance
Zeitstandversuch *m* creep-rupture test
zeitunabhängig time-independent
zellig <Syn.: porig> cellular
zellige (porige) Probe *f* cellular specimen
zentral <Syn.: mittig, in der Mitte> central
Zentralriß *m* central crack
  lastfreier Zentralriß *m* unloaded central crack
zerkleinern <Syn.: zerquetschen> crush/to
zerlegen <Syn.: abtasten> {elektronisch} scan/to
Zerlegung *f* <Syn.: Abtasten *n*, Abtastung *f*> {elektronisch} scanning
zerquetschen Syn.: stauchen, zerdrücken> crush/to
Zerreißen *n* <Syn.: Reißen *n*> tearing
zerreißen {Werkstoff} tear/to {materials}
Zerreißfestigkeit *f* <Syn.: Reißfestigkeit *f*> tearing strength
Zerreißspannung *f* breaking stress
Zerreißversuch *m* tear
Zerrüttungsbruch *m* <Syn.: kumulativer Bruch *m*> cumulative fracture
Zerrüttungsriß *m* cumulative crack
zersetzen decompose/to

Zersetzung

zersetzen <Syn.: abbauen> {Metalle: Oberflächen} degrade/to {metals: surface}
Zersetzung f decomposition
Zersetzung f <Syn.: Abbau m> {Metalle: Oberflächen} degradation {materials: surface}
Zersetzungstemperatur f decomposition temperature
Zersplittern n <Syn.: Zerspringen n {bei Schlagbeanspruchung}> shattering {under impact shock}
Zerspringen n <Syn.: Zersplittern n> {bei Schlagbeanspruchung} shattering {under impact shock}
zerstören destroy/to
zerstörend destructive
Zerstörung f destruction
zerstörungsfrei non-destructive
zerstörungsfreie Bewertung f non-destructive evaluation <abb.: NDE>
zerstörungsfreie Prüfung f <Abb.: ZfP> non-destructive testing <abb.: NDT>
ZfP → zerstörungsfreie Prüfung f
Zink n, Zn zinc, Zn
Zinklegierung f zinc alloy
Zinn n, Sn tin, Sn
Zinnbronze f tin bronze
Zinnlegierung f tin alloy
Zirconium n, Zr zirconium, Zr Zirkonium n,
Zirkonium n, Zirconium n, Zr zirconium, Zr
Zn → Zink
Zone f, Gebiet n, Bereich m {in Werkstoffen} zone {in materials}
  dimensionslose plastische Zone f dimensionless plastic zone
  effektive plastische Zone f effective plastic zone
  elastische Zone f elastic zone
  Form f der plastischen Zone plastic zone form
  Größe f der plastischen Zone plastic zone size
  Länge f der plastischen Zone length of plastic zone
  plastische Zone f plastic zone
  Radius m der plastischen Zone radius of the plastic zone
  Verlängerung f der plastischen Zone plastic zone elongation
Zr → Zirconium
Zufall m random
zufällig random
  zufälliger Ausfall m random failure
  zufälliger Bruch m random failure
Zufalls- random
Zufallsbelastung f random stress loading
Zug m; Zugspannung f tension
  einachsiger Zug m uniaxial tension
  zweiachsiger Zug m biaxial tension
Zug-Druck-Versuch m tensile-compression test
zugbeanspruchte Probe f <Syn.: Zugprobe f> tensile specimen
zugbeanspruchte Probe f mit Oberflächenriß, SCT-Probe f surface-crack tensile <abb.: SCT> specimen
Zugbeanspruchung f, Zugbelastung f tensile loading
  einachsige Zugbeanspruchung f, einachsige Zugbelastung f uniaxial tensile loading
  mehrachsige Zugbeanspruchung f multiaxial tensile load
zugbelastbar <Syn.: auf Zug(beanspruchung) belastbar, Zug-> tensile
Zugbelastbarkeit f tensibility
zugbelastet loaded in tension
zugbelasteter Oberflächenriß m tensile-loaded surface crack
Zugbelastung f <Syn.: Zugbeanspruchung f> tensile loading

einachsige Zugbelastung f <Syn.: einachsige Zugbeanspruchung f> uniaxial tensile loading
duktiler Zugbruch m ductile tensile fracture
Zugbruch m <Syn.: Bruch m durch Zugbelastung> tensile fracture
Zugbruchfläche f tensile fracture surface
Zugdehnung f tensile strain
Zugeigenspannung f residual tensile stress
Zugfestigkeit bei Schlagbeanspruchung <Syn.: Schlagzugfestigkeit f> tensile impact strength
Zugfestigkeit f tensile strength
  statische Zugfestigkeit f static tensile strength
  theoretische Zugfestigkeit f theoretical tensile strength
Zugfestigkeitswert m tensile strength value
Zugkraft f tensile force
Zuglast f tensile load
Zugprobe f tensile specimen
  einseitig angerissene Zugprobe f, Zugprobe f mit Einzelrandriß m single-edge cracked tensile specimen
  einseitig gekerbte Zugprobe f single-edge notch tensile specimen
  gekerbte Zugprobe f notched tension-test specimen
  glatte Zugprobe f {ungekerbt} smooth tensile specimen {unnotched}
  halbunendliche Zugprobe f semi-infinite tensile specimen
  in der Mitte gekerbte Zugprobe f center-notched tensile specimen
  mittig angerissene Zugprobe f <Syn.: Zugprobe f mit Mittelriß m> center-cracked tensile <abb.: CCT> specimen
  runde Zugprobe f tensile bar
  runde Zugprobe f, Zugstab m tensile bar
  ungekerbte Zugprobe f unnotched tensile specimen
  zweiseitig angerissene Zugprobe f double-edge cracked tensile specimen
  Zugprobe f mit Einzelrandriß m <Syn.: einseitig angerissene Zugprobe f> single-edge cracked tensile specimen
  Zugprobe f mit Mittelriß <Syn.: mittig angerissene Zugprobe f> center-cracked tensile <abb.: CCT> specimen
Zugprüfmaschine f tensile testing machine
Zugschwellbelastung f threshold tensile load
Zugspannung f tensile stress
  dreiachsige Zugspannung f triaxial tensile stress
  kritische Zugspannung f critical tensile stress
Zugspannungsfeld n tensile stress field
  zweiachsiges Zugspannungsfeld n biaxial tensile stress field
Zugspannungskriterium n tensile stess criterion
Zugstab m {Zugversuch} tensile bar {tensile bar}
  glatter Zugstab m smooth tensile bar
  scharf gekerbter Zugstab m sharp-notched round tension specimen
Zugstababmessungen fpl tensile bar dimensions pl
Zugverformung f tensile deformation
Zugversuch m, Zerreißversuch m tensile test
  einachsiger Zugversuch m uniaxial tensile test
Zulegieren n <Syn.: Legieren n> alloying
Zunahme f <Syn.: Erhöhung f, Anstieg m> increase
Zündbarkeit f ignitability

Prüfung *f* der Zündbarkeit ignitability test
Zündeigenschaften *fpl* <Syn.: Zündverhalten *n*> ignition properties *pl* {of plastic}
zünden ignite/to
Zündquelle *f* ignition source
Zündtemperatur *f* ignition temperature
Zündverhalten *n* <Syn.: Zündeigenschaften *fpl*> ignition properties *pl* {of plastic}
Zündversuch *m* ignition test
zunehmen <Syn.: erhöhen, ansteigen> increase/to
zusammenschrumpfen {Rißspitze} shrink/to {crack tip}
Zusammensetzung *f* {Werkstoffe} composition {materials}
Zusammenwachsen *n* <Syn.: Vereinigung *f* {von Hohlräumen, Rissen}> coalescence {of voids, cracks}
zusammenwachsen <Syn.: sich vereinigen {Hohlräume, Risse}> coalesce/to {voids, cracks}
Zusatzmetall *n* filler metal
Zustand *m* state
  duktiler Zustand *m* ductile state
  elastisch-plastischer Zustand *m* elastic-plastic state
  spröder Zustand *m* brittle state
  vollplastischer Zustand *m* perfectly plastic state
zweiachsig biaxial
zweiachsige Druckbeanspruchung *f* biaxial compression
zweiachsige Ermüdung *f* biaxial fatigue
zweiachsige Spannung *f* biaxial stress
zweiachsiger Spannungszustand *m* biaxial stress state
zweiachsiger Zug *m* biaxial tension
zweiachsiges Zugspannungsfeld *n* biaxial tensile stress field

Zweiachsigkeit *f* biaxiality
zweidimensional <Syn.: eben> two-dimensional
zweidimensionale Verformung *f* <Syn.: ebene Verformung *f*> two-dimensional deformation
zweidimensionaler Riß *m* two-dimensional crack
zweidimensionales linear-elastisches Verformungsfeld *n* two-dimensional linear-elastic deformation field
zweidimensionales Rißproblem *n* two-dimensional crack problem
zweidimensionales Spannungsfeld *n* two-dimensional stress field
zweidimensionales Verformungsfeld *n* two-dimensional deformation field
zweiseitig angerissene Zugprobe *f* double-edge cracked tensile specimen
Zwilling *m* twin
Zwillingsband *n* twin band
Zwillingsbildung *f* twinning, twin formation
  Bruch *m* an Zwillingsbildungen twinning fracture
Zyklen *mpl* cycles *pl*
zyklisch cyclic
zyklische Beanspruchung *f* cyclic loading
zyklische Beanspruchung *f* mit konstanter Amplitude constant amplitude cyclic loading
zyklische Belastung cyclic loading
zyklische plastische Verformung *f* cyclic plastic deformation
zyklische Spannungsintensität *f* cyclic stress intensity
  effektive zyklische Spannungsintensität *f* effective cyclic stress-intensity

zyklischer Spannungsintensitätsfaktor *m* {Rißwachstum bei schwingender Beanspruchung} cyclic stress-intensity factor
zyklisches J-Integral *n* cyclic J integral
zyklisches Spannungs-Dehnungs-Verhalten *n* cyclic stress-strain behavio[u]r
Zyklus *m* cycle

Zylinder *m* cylinder
   dickwandiger Zylinder *m* thick-walled cylinder
   isotroper Zylinder *m* isotropic cylinder
Zylinderkoordinaten *fpl* cylindrical coordinates *pl*
zylindrisch cylindrical
zylindrische Pore *f* cylindrical pore

Abkürzungen

DIN Deutsche Industrie-Norm
EN Europische Norm
BSI British Standards Institute
IOS International Organization for Standardization
ASTM American Society for Testing and Materials

ANSI American National Standards Institute
NBS National Bureau of Standards
BAM Bundesanstalt für Materialprüfung
DVS Deutscher Verband für Schweißtechnik
VDI Verein Deutscher Ingenieure